FINANCIAL MANAGEMENT
OF THE
SMALL FIRM

FINANCIAL MANAGEMENT
OF THE
SMALL FIRM

Ernest W. Walker

Professor of Finance
Graduate School of Business
University of Texas

J. William Petty II

Associate Professor of Finance
School of Business
Texas Tech University

PRENTICE-HALL, INC., Englewood Cliffs, New Jersey 07632

Library of Congress Cataloging in Publication Data

WALKER, ERNEST WINFIELD.
   Financial management of the small firm.

   Includes bibliographies and index.
   1. Small business--Finance. I. Petty, J. William
      joint author. II. Title.
HF5550.W19   658.1'5904   78-873
ISBN 0-13-316091-2

© 1978 by Prentice-Hall, Inc., Englewood Cliffs, N.J. 07632

Printed in the United States of America

10 9 8 7 6 5 4 3 2 1

PRENTICE-HALL INTERNATIONAL, INC., *London*
PRENTICE-HALL OF AUSTRALIA PTY. LIMITED, *Sydney*
PRENTICE-HALL OF CANADA, LTD., *Toronto*
PRENTICE-HALL OF INDIA PRIVATE LIMITED, *New Delhi*
PRENTICE-HALL OF JAPAN, INC., *Tokyo*
PRENTICE-HALL OF SOUTHEAST ASIA PTE. LTD., *Singapore*
WHITEHALL BOOKS LIMITED, *Wellington, New Zealand*

TO OUR FAMILIES

Margaret	*Donna*
Marshall	*Krista*
Eledith	*Kate*

CONTENTS

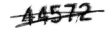

PART II
Planning

PART IV
Financial Leverage

PART V
Valuation

PART VI
Investment Decision Making

PART VII
Working Capital Management

PART VIII
Sources of Financing

PREFACE

Large-sized businesses in the United States have been receptive to the advancements made in financial theory during the past twenty years, and the smaller firms, recognizing the advantages to be gained, are eager to adapt new techniques for their benefit. Unfortunately, most financial writings have pointed out the difficulties encountered by small firms in raising debt and equity capital rather than offering evaluation tools which would improve the decision-making process. The authors of this book are attempting to make available to the managers of small firms the same financial theories utilized by large firms as well as offering suitable techniques and models which may be employed in an analytical framework designed to improve the efficiency of the small firm. For example, we offer managers a model enabling them to evaluate investment decisions with the same degree of expertise as their larger counterparts. In addition, we present theoretical as well as practical material designed to aid the manager in the development of financial strategies and policies. While the book is primarily intended for use by seniors and graduate students in academic institutions, it can be employed effectively in executive development programs and should be a useful resource for businessmen in their financial operations. A sound basis in financial accounting is an essential prerequisite for the use of the material in this book. A basic understanding of statistics and microeconomics is also required; however, the book does not dwell on the mathematical theories underlying the financial concepts presented.

We would like to thank our colleagues in our respective universities for their many constructive comments and criticisms. In addition we are grateful to our friends in the academic and business field for their helpful comments. Since this is the first edition, the authors are acutely aware of the deficiencies that will become apparent in the concepts we have developed for use by the managers of dynamic small firms. We invite the readers to submit their criticisms so that future revisions can amend any weaknesses.

Ernest W. Walker
J. William Petty II

part I

INTRODUCTION
AND
FORMS OF ORGANIZATION

chapter 1

INTRODUCTION

The subject of finance has undergone major changes since the decade of the fifties. That is, major contributors to financial literature have shifted their interest from the institutional to the theoretical and managerial viewpoints. Unfortunately, most of their writings have alluded to large rather than small firms. While only a very few firms account for the large majority of total receipts and assets of all corporations, the importance of small businesses should not be overlooked since most of the 12 million business enterprises in the United States fall into this category. These firms account for approximately two-fifths of all gainfully employed individuals and produce approximately one-third of the business-produced GNP.

In denoting importance, statistics are obviously important, but they do not tell the whole story. For example, a study recently completed by Thomas W. Harrel of the Stanford Graduate School of Business concluded that "five years after the MBA, men in small business had higher compensation, were better satisfied with their jobs in small business, and participated more broadly in management than those in larger companies of 1,000 or more employees."[1] While it is impossible to support, it is nevertheless believed that small business will increase in importance in the future primarily because we are entering a stage in which technology will play an even greater role than it has in the past. That is, if we are to survive and prosper, we must substitute new products for those presently in use. Many of these products will be "found" and "developed" by small businesses. Once developed, the large companies will probably "take over" and exploit their use. To illustrate, the soft-ware industry was actually created by thousands of small companies, but a study of the development of this industry reveals that it took the "majors" to exploit these products. While service-type companies will continue to be

[1]Thomas W. Harrel, "Differences Between Men in Big and Small Business," *The Dynamic Small Firm, Selected Readings*, ed. by Ernest W. Walker (Austin, Texas: Lone Star Publishers, Inc., 1975), p. 3.

dominated by small companies, it is believed that they will enjoy an increasing importance in high-technology areas.

Another important factor that favors the continued importance of small business is the desire of college-trained individuals to seek out small business as a means of aiding them to fulfill their goals of (1) contributing to society and (2) achieving greater pleasure from their "work." While the college-trained individual is not finding a complete "assembly-line" type of work environment, it is becoming so highly specialized that many young men and women are actively seeking work opportunities which permit them to express themselves. It would seem that the small firm could provide this opportunity if some of the risks could be ameliorated. It is toward this end that this book is dedicated.

In summary, in the latter part of the nineteenth century, the business community in the United States consisted of approximately 300,000 businesses. Today there are approximately 12 million businesses, and by far the majority are classified as small. Looking at it another way, approximately 95 percent of all businesses have less than 100 employees, and about 99 percent have less than 500 employees. It is difficult to predict with any degree of accuracy, but it is almost a foregone conclusion that the importance of small businesses will increase during the last quarter of this century.

What Is a Small Business?

The answer to this question is extremely difficult since everyone has an idea of a small business. In the eyes of one person it may be a locally owned and operated store in which the owner is the boss, whereas another person could easily consider a plant with 500 employees as being small. Actually, both may be right; therefore, it is difficult to develop a simple definition.

Of the many definitions that have been offered, the one that was formulated by the Small Business Administration (SBA) is probably the most widely used. They generally define a small business as one that is independently owned and operated and is nondominant in its field of operations. They further specify that the following conditions be met: (1) A manufacturing company is small if its average employment in the preceding four calendar quarters did not exceed 250, including employees of any affiliates. If employment exceeded 250 but was not above 1,500, the SBA bases its determination on a specific size standard for the particular industry. (2) Wholesale firms are small if yearly sales are not over $5 to $15 million, depending on the industry. (3) Retailing and service firms are small if annual sales or receipts are not over $1 to $5 million, depending on the industry.

It should be understood that the SBA uses these definitions for the specific purpose of ascertaining the eligibility of a loan applicant. As a consequence, this agency is forced to use a very specific definition. Since the writers' purposes are to formulate a set of theories, strategies, policies, and procedures that may be used by management of "small" businesses in order to optimize the "wealth" of all interested parties, i.e., workers, suppliers, customers, and owners, it is not necessary to have a restrictive definition. In the light of these goals, it is better to denote the type of firms that will be studied rather than attempting to delineate the study through the use of a definition. It must be stated at the outset that little or no attention will be given to the "Mom and Pop" type of businesses. Let us say quickly that these firms have many problems which are financial in nature, and, certainly, attention should be given to them; however, their needs and problems are highly personal, and their solutions do not, as a general rule, follow any logical pattern. At the other end of the spectrum, it would be natural to expect us to delete from our study all firms exceeding a certain size, say $5 million in assets. It is believed that any arbitrary size would harm the study since many firms in the $20–$50 million asset range are managed in the same way as a $500,000 firm. It is for this reason we do not feel that small businesses should be studied from a dollar point of view. In general, we want to develop a set of theories, strategies, and policies for firms which are *growth oriented* and do not have easy access to the capital and money markets, particularly the former. We do not intend to exclude any particular type of business, but the reader should always remember that theories, strategies, and policies will have different impacts on different types of businesses. An effort will be made to point this out as we proceed.

Structure of the Book

It is believed that all businesses tend to be governed by the same set of theories regardless of size. On the other hand, there is no question that small- and middle-sized firms are subject to greater risks, business and financial, than large firms and are more vulnerable to "bad" decisions than their larger counterparts. The resolution of this problem does not require that small- and middle-size firms follow different theories; rather, they should formulate and promulgate different strategies, policies, and procedures. Accepting this assumption, an effort is made to develop a set of strategies, policies, and procedures that managers can use when formulating decisions relating to the (1) investment of funds in fixed and current assets and (2) the procurement of funds. The accomplishment of this end requires a characterization of small- and middle-size firms as well as a discussion of the techniques that may be used to determine the amount of funds which is needed. Not only is attention given to the amounts of funds that are required, but factors which influence the relative level of debt and equity capital are discussed. Also, there is a discussion of the factors that influence the debt mix, which is extremely important in the management of risk in the smaller firm.

The selection of the type of legal organization is of major importance if the owner of the small business wishes to minimize risk; therefore, a discussion of the general nature and characteristics of proprietorships, partnerships, and corporations is included. Particular attention is given to the prerequisites that must be met when forming subchapter S and 1244 corporations.

It is the writers' opinion that growth-type firms will either acquire other firms as a means of expansion or will be sold to other growth firms. In either event it is imperative that buyers and sellers know how to arrive at a fair value of the firm to be sold or acquired. To accomplish this, the authors have included a chapter that will aid the "buyer" or "seller" when determining these values.

There is no question that financial institutions of all kinds either have undergone or will undergo major changes in their operational practices. It is, therefore, important to include a section on sources of funds (equity as well as debt) which smaller firms can tap. For the sake of convenience, this section will be divided into (1) sources of short-term funds, (2) sources of intermediate funds, (3) sources of long-term funds, and (4) going public.

In addition to the above, there will be included at the end of the chapters a set of questions and problems. The questions are designed to highlight the material contained in the chapters, and the problems are constructed in such a way that will permit the student to employ the concepts which have been presented. At the end of each section will be a comprehensive bibliography of selected references.

chapter 2

LEGAL FORMS
OF BUSINESS ORGANIZATION

Proprietorships, partnerships, and corporations are by far the most important forms of legal organization in the United States today. Major emphasis in this chapter is on a discussion of the characteristics of these three forms of organization and the effects of these characteristics upon the financial activities of the firm. The function of forming the organization belongs to management's legal advisors; however, the responsibility for selecting the type of organization the business will assume is vested entirely in the firm's owners. In making this decision, management attempts to choose the type of legal organization with characteristics that will aid the firm in achieving its goals. Although some characteristics do not directly affect the finance function, many do: Therefore, it is mandatory for students of finance to comprehend thoroughly the characteristics of each type of organization as well as the impact of each on the firm's financial activities.

To accomplish this, the following factors are used to portray the characteristics of the three forms of organization mentioned above, and each plays an important role in management's decision: (1) ease of formation, (2) cost of formation, (3) liability of owners, (4) durability and stability of each firm, (5) directness of control and ease of direction, and (6) legal status and sphere of activity.

Proprietorships

While relatively more business firms operate as proprietorships than as corporations and partnerships, they are far less important from the standpoint of the dollar volume of business receipts. To illustrate, in 1972, 78 percent of these three classes of business firms were proprietorships, yet they accounted for only 10.8 percent of all business receipts; see Table 2-1. It is interesting to note that while the number of proprietorships grew from 5,689,000 in 1945 to 10,173,000 in 1972, an increase of 78.8 percent, their relative importance actually declined from 84.4 percent to 78.3 percent. The same trend prevailed regarding business receipts and net profits. To illustrate, proprietorships accounted for 20.7 percent of all business receipts in 1945 but only 10.8 percent in 1972. In 1945 they received 30.0 percent of all profits, but by 1972 their share had declined to 26.9 percent of the total. It should be noted, however, that the total volume of net profit not only increased in each year depicted but was considerably less volatile than the net profit of corporations.

The proprietorship type of business was the earliest and by far the most simple of all legal forms or organizations. It is a common-law form of

TABLE 2-1

Proprietorships, Partnerships, and Corporations—
Number, Business Receipts, and Net Profit

1945–1972

(number in thousands, money figures in billions)

	1945	*1950*	*1955*	*1960*	*1965*	*1970*	*1971*	*1972*
Proprietorships, number[1]	5,689	6,865	8,239	9,090	9,078	9,400	9,745	10,173
Business receipts[2]	$ 79	NA	$139	$171	$ 199	$ 238	$ 255	$ 276
Net profit (less loss)[3]	$ 12	$ 15	$ 18	$ 21	$ 28	$ 33	$ 34	$ 39
Partnerships, number	627	NA	NA	941	914	936	959	992
Total receipts[4]	$ 47	NA	NA	$ 74	$ 75	$ 93	$ 100	$ 104
Net profit (less loss)[3]	$ 7	NA	NA	$ 8	$ 10	$ 10	$ 9	$ 9
Corporations, number	421	629	807	1,141	1,424	1,665	1,733	1,813
Total receipts[4]	$255	$458	$642	$849	$1,195	$1,751	$1,906	$2,171
Net profit (less loss)[3]	$ 21	$ 43	$ 47	$ 44	$ 74	$ 66	$ 80	$ 97

[1]Individually owned businesses and farms.
[2]Receipts from sales and services less allowances, rebates, and returns; excludes capital gains or losses and investment income not associated with the tax payer's business.
[3]Net profit (or income) is defined differently by legal forms of organization, basically as follows: (a) proprietorships: total taxable receipts less total deductions, including cost of sales and operations; investment and other income are not included; (b) partnerships: total taxable receipts less total deductions, including cost of sales and operations; investments and other income, except capital gains, are included; (c) corporations: total taxable receipts less total deductions, including capital gains and constructive income from foreign corporations.
[4]Total taxable receipts before deductions of cost of goods sold, cost of operations, and net loss from sales of property other than capital assets; includes nontaxable interest, and excludes all other nontaxable income.
SOURCE: United States Bureau of the Census, *Statistical Abstract of the United States,* 1969 and 1975 (90th & 96th ed.), Washington, D.C., 1969 and 1975, pp. 472 and 624.

organization and requires no formally drawn documents. Moreover, the state does not require the owners to pay any organizational fees or taxes before the firm starts doing business. Since the proprietorship has no legal status, it ceases to exist at the will of the proprietor or upon his death. It is true that the assets of the firm can be bequeathed upon the death of the owner and the firm can continue to operate, but the resultant business is not the same as the original proprietorship.

The owners of individual proprietorships, unlike owners of corporate enterprises, are personally liable for the debts of the business firm. This characteristic has certain advantages from a capital-raising viewpoint, since creditors may look to the owner's personal assets as security. This may also serve as a deterrent, however, since it jeopardizes the personal assets the proprietor may have accumulated from other sources. It is for this reason that proprietors turn to the corporate form of organization as quickly as is feasible.

The low cost and ease of forming the proprietorship are chief advantages when compared to other forms of organization. Although the owner must pay certain license fees in order to do business, they are usually nominal. From the viewpoint of creating the proprietorship, no agreements are necessary since the proprietor is the sole owner of the assets, and as long as the business engages in lawful endeavors, no permission is required of state officials.

In most instances, the owner is also the manager and does not share control with anyone. Moreover, this form of business is relatively free from legal restrictions. As long as the owner adheres to the basic laws regarding contracts, negotiable instruments, deeds, and mortgages, he is free to move in any direction that he chooses.

The profits of the proprietorship are taxed at the owner's tax rate whether they are retained in the business, paid out in the form of salaries, or withdrawn as profits. Furthermore, they are taxed only one time, whereas in the corporate organizations income is taxed when earned and then again when distributed to the shareholders as cash dividends. Finally, a proprietorship may operate in any state the owner chooses without incurring abnormal expenditures.

Partnerships

A general partnership is a voluntary organization of two or more individuals who combine their capital, skills, and efforts in order to increase their profit. Although the partnership is a common-law organization, several states have passed statutes governing its formation and operation. In states where no statutes exist, the partnership agreement may be implied, oral, or written. In any event, agreements usually cover these points: names of the partners, name and nature of the business, amount and type of capital invested, duration of the partnership, agency powers of the various partners, and method of dividing profits and losses. (The last point is most important because in the absence of an agreement, the law holds that each partner will share profits and losses equally.)

The general partnership has many of the same characteristics as the proprietorship; for example, it is relatively easy to form, from the standpoint of both cost—organizational fees, taxes, and miscellaneous expenses—and effort required to bring it into existence.

As a general rule, it is better to have an attorney draw up the articles of copartnership since this tends to reduce misunderstandings concerning the sharing of profits and losses and the powers of each partner. For this service the attorney's fees are small compared to those charged for securing a charter for a corporation. The agreement does not need to be filed with any state official; once drawn, the partnership is in effect and ready to begin doing business. The only costs of formation are the attorney's fee and license fees when required.

Larger sums of equity capital can usually be raised by partnerships than by proprietorships, since several individuals may be called upon to supply equity capital. Moreover, it is also possible to obtain larger amounts of debt capital, since each partner has unlimited liability. Although this may be an advantage in some cases, it often serves to limit the amount of equity capital that can be acquired. That is, many individuals are hesitant to enter into a partnership since they are liable for the firm's debts. Although each partner may limit his liability by agreement, he may still be sued by the creditors for the entire amount of the claim. It is true that he in turn can sue the other members of the partnership for their share, but if they do not have sufficient personal assets to satisfy their share, he will be liable for the entire sum. It is easy to see why a person with large personal assets would be hesitant about entering into an agreement with individuals whose personal assets are limited.

The partnership lacks stability; that is, the partnership ceases to exist when any partner (1) dies, (2) is held incompetent, (3) withdraws from the partnership, or (4) goes bankrupt. Although the remaining partners may reform and continue the business, the original business is dissolved, and the assets must be divided according to the agreement, or equally if no valid agreement exists.

Instability is one characteristic of the partnership that creates serious problems. Since the partnership is a voluntary association, it may have difficulty surviving. For example, no partner is required to remain in the business endeavor. A shareholder of a corporation may sever his relationship with the firm by selling his interest, but the firm will continue to function. This is not true with the partnership; if a partner wishes to sell his interest to another individual, the remaining partners can refuse to accept the newcomer. If they accept the new partner, another partnership must be created, and all outstanding contracts must be renegotiated.

The general partnership is a common-law organization, but some states have created what might be referred to as a statutory partnership. The most common form is that of limited partnership. This organization differs from the general partnership in that it is formed under the limited partnership statutes, and one or more of the partners may have limited liability; that is, their liability is limited to the amount they have invested. For these special partners to enjoy limited liability, their names cannot appear in the name of the firm, and they cannot actively engage in the management of the endeavor. If either of these two provisions is violated, the partner or partners lose their claim of limited liability. A serious disadvantage of the limited partnership is that states not having limited partnership statutes may refuse to recognize the firm as a limited partnership and may treat it as a general partnership. One of the principal advantages of the partnership—general or limited—is the ability of each partner to treat all losses that occur as an ordinary loss rather than a capital loss. With the advent of the 1244 corporation, this advantage has largely been negated since the shareholder can claim losses resulting from worthless stock as ordinary losses ($25,000 per year on a single return or $50,000 on a joint return). It is true that operating losses cannot be treated in this way, but if the shareholders choose the subchapter S as well as the 1244 provisions of the Internal Revenue Code, then losses within certain limits may be treated the same as if they had occurred in a partnership. These provisions will be discussed later in this chapter.

Corporations

The corporation is by far the most important type of business organization in existence today from the viewpoint of assets employed and sales made. It is interesting to note that in 1972 corporations accounted for only 4 percent of all business firms yet they enjoyed 85 percent of all business receipts. From the viewpoint of the small businessman the corporation is very important in that 1,614,000 or 89 percent of all corporations have receipts of less than $1 million annually. Incidently, there were more corporations with sales of less than $1 million than there were partnerships, e.g., 1,614,000 compared to 979,000 partnerships. It is undoubtedly true that without the corporation, the United States would not have achieved the economic position that it enjoys today. One authority had this to say about the corporation: "Its position in the Western world is the result of men's effort to create a business unit that will maximize the production of economic goods, minimize capital risk and facilitate managerial control."[1]

[1]W. Bayard Taylor, *Financial Policies of Business Enterprise*, 2nd ed., (New York: Appleton-Century-Crofts, 1956), p. 21.

It can also be said that the corporation is the outgrowth of need. That is, the corporation has corrected many of the weaknesses inherent in proprietorships and partnerships. This has been done in several ways.

First, the corporation is organized under specific statutes. Like a citizen, it can sue; be sued; buy, sell, or own property; commit a crime; and be punished by sentences up to and including death. However, unlike a citizen, it must request and receive permission before doing business in its home state or other states.

Second, individuals who invest equity funds in the corporation have limited liability; however, if shareholders pay less than par or stated value for stock, they are liable for the difference, should it become necessary to satisfy creditors' claims. (Some states provide that stockholders may be assessed an amount up to but not exceeding the par value of their stock for unpaid wages of labor.) This provision makes it possible for corporations to accumulate large sums of capital. Had this not been possible our economy might not have achieved its present importance.

The corporation's life is said to be permanent. In most states incorporators receive a permanent charter, although a few states set a maximum number of years for which a charter may be issued. It should be emphasized that the renewal of the charter in these states is a perfunctory act, and the corporation possesses permanency and stability. This is a very important characteristic, since investors do not have to worry about reinvesting their funds or renegotiating the terms of their agreement every time an "owner" dies, goes insane, or becomes bankrupt.

The corporation possesses certain characteristics that may be considered disadvantageous: cost and difficulty of forming the corporation, taxation, inability to do business in states other than the one in which it is domiciled without paying additional fees, legal restrictions, and the lack of interest of many stockholders.

Each state has enacted legislation setting forth the requirements for the formation of the corporate organization. This in no way implies that the formation of the corporation is prohibitive but only that management should consider these factors when selecting the legal form of organization.

At one time, taxation was a major factor in determining whether a small business should incorporate. However, now that corporations may elect to be taxed as unincorporated businesses, this factor is of considerably less importance.

It was stated earlier that a corporation is regarded as a "citizen" of the state in which it is incorporated. If the firm wishes to do business in any other state, it must qualify. To qualify simply means that the firm is required to pay the necessary fees and taxes and file such documents as articles of incorporation, bylaws, statements of financial condition, and statements revealing the amount of capital and assets to be employed in that state. It should be noted that if the firm performs only functions that are intrastate in nature, it does not need to qualify, but if it performs functions that are considered to be interstate, it must qualify. The following acts are considered doing intrastate business:

1. Sales of goods by salesmen who possess the power to make contracts.
2. Storage of goods in a warehouse.
3. Ownership of real property.
4. Purchase and temporary storage of goods prior to shipment to the home office.
5. Sales of goods requiring installation by an agent.

Business enterprises of kinds are subject to governmental regulations provided that (1) they are big, (2) they affect the public interest, or (3) they possess a corporate structure. The government does not look with favor upon any business that may be large enough to create either a monopoly or a monopsony, and to prevent these conditions, the government requires businesses to subject themselves to certain regulatory provisions. Businesses such as public utilities are subject to legal restrictions because their activities affect public interest. Both state and federal governments require corporations to file statements revealing their financial conditions. Although individual proprietorships and partnerships are subject to a degree of governmental control, the corporation is subject to even more; however, it should be emphasized that corporations do not consider themselves too highly regulated in comparison to other forms of organization. Whether management considers that it should be regulated by the government at all is another question, but a discussion of this matter is not within the scope of this book.

Some managers consider it to their advantage for shareholders to be uninterested in the affairs of the corporate organization, but even if this is the case, management has the problem of informing owners of past accomplishments and future plans. All except a very small number of corporations submit quarterly and annual reports to their shareholders. The finance executive is vitally interested in this requirement, since each report received by shareholders contains financial information; in fact, many reports contain little else. Since owners of proprietorships and partnerships are so close to the affairs of the business, their reports are less formal and require much less effort to prepare.

Formation of the Corporation

Although statutes governing the formation of business corporations vary among states, the procedures for their formation tend to follow a common pattern. In forming a corporation, incorporators are called upon to make decisions concerning the following: (1) the name of the corporation, (2) the location of the principal office, (3) the period of corporate duration, (4) the selection of the incorporators and first board of directors, (5) the state of incorporation, (6) the nature and scope of business activity, and (7) the plan of capitalization, including the method of distributing the securities.

Name of the firm

Those selecting the name of the firm should be mindful that the name will help advertise and exploit the firm's products and services. Since most names do perform this function, state laws protect the names of firms by disallowing a name designed to deceive or cause confusion. Many states require that the name indicate its corporate character. Furthermore, the statutes generally prohibit the use of names in the title which improperly imply (1) that the business is performing a function prohibited by law, (2) that it is some form of public agency, or (3) that it is a part of some other organization when in fact it is not. When selecting a name, it is unwise to indicate a local or regional area. If the name of a state or section of the country is made a part of the corporate name, potential customers in other areas or states may become discouraged from using its products or services.

Location of the principal office

Since all incorporation laws require that the name of the principal office as well as the name of the registered agent be included in the articles of incorporation, these decisions should be made prior to the drafting of the articles of incorporation. In most cases the registered office need not be the same as the corporation's place of business. The registered agent may be an individual resident of the state, whose business office is identical with such registered offices; or a domestic corporation; or a foreign corporation authorized to do business in the state. The principal function of the registered agent is to receive any notice, process, or demand that is served.

Period of duration of the corporate charter

Generally speaking, incorporators want the life of the corporation to be permanent; therefore, in states that provide for perpetual existence, the charter will ordinarily stipulate this. If, however, the statutes limit the period of duration, the articles of incorporation set forth the maximum number of years permitted.

Identity of incorporators and directors

Although statutes vary concerning requirements with respect to the identity of incorporators and directors, most states require that the names and addresses of both incorporators and the board of directors be included in the articles of incorporation.

State of incorporation

The selection of the state in which to incorporate is usually a very simple matter if the firm is small or if the product is distributed locally. On the other hand, for firms that are international, national, or regional in character, the selection of the state of incorporation is far from a simple process. In arriving at the decision of whether to incorporate in one state or another, the following factors must be considered: (1) citizenship requirement of incorporators; (2) statutes pertaining to directors; (3) requirements for capitalization; (4) requirements regarding liability of shareholders; (5) requirements regarding dividends; (6) stockholder rights regarding books and records of corporation, limitations with respect to prosecution of stockholders' suits, dissenters' rights, and preemptive rights; (7) costs, including taxes, required in the formation as well as the operation of the business endeavor; and (8) statutory provisions regarding sale of assets, amendment of charter, and merger.

A brief explanation of these factors will give the student an insight into the problem of selecting the "home" of the business. First, a few states require that at least one of the incorporators be a resident of the state in which it is incorporated. This in itself presents no problem since *dummies* may be used to satisfy the requirement; however, some states may require that the annual shareholder meeting be held in the state of incorporation. This could present a problem, particularly if management wants to hold regional stockholder meetings in order to improve stockholder participation.

Second, citizenship and residence requirements for members of the board of directors are very liberal. For example, the Texas Business Incorporation Act does not require directors to be residents of the state of Texas unless the articles of incorporation or bylaws so require. Most states require that directors be shareholders, but again this presents no problem, since ownership of one share generally satisfies the requirement. Furthermore, this requirement can be modified by the articles of incorporation and bylaws. Classification of the board is permitted in most states and therefore presents no problem. Also, statutory requirements concerning removal and changing the number of the board members are generally lenient.

Third, the statutory provisions concerning capitalization should be examined thoroughly before deciding on the state in which to incorporate. For example, statutes concerning classification of stock—par or no par, voting and nonvoting, and preferred, common, or classified—should be carefully examined, since these characteristics do influence the success or failure of the firm. Moreover, the statutes should be examined to determine whether there is a limitation with respect to the amount and character of debt. (Arizona, for example, limits debt to two-thirds of the capital stock.)

Fourth, a few states require that shareholders be liable beyond their investment for corporate debts resulting from unpaid wages.

Fifth, as a general rule, the corporation can pay dividends out of surplus or profits, but a few states require that dividends be paid out of current profits. This provision may seriously limit a corporation, since there is always the possibility that a firm will not operate at a profit. In this case, the payment of dividends must be curtailed for that period regardless of the state of the surplus and cash account.

Sixth, the operations of a corporation may be influenced by the statutes regarding (1) the rights of shareholders to inspect the books; (2) limitations regarding the prosecution of shareholders suits; (3) the right of the shareholder to dissent, particularly in the case of the sale of assets; and (4) the right of shareholders to purchase their proportionate share of any new stock that is issued. For example, in Texas the preemptive right is guaranteed unless specifically limited by the articles of incorporation and bylaws. Furthermore, this exclusion must also appear on the certificate of ownership. Only two states require preemptive rights; three-fourths of all states specify that the preemptive right is provided unless specifically denied; and five states deny this right unless provided by the charter.

Seventh, the cost of incorporation is probably the most important of the above factors. Careful analysis should be made of organization taxes and fees as well as annual taxes and fees.

Nature and scope of business

With certain exceptions, a natural citizen of a state can enter into and carry on any specific business endeavor that is not otherwise prohibited by the laws of the state without securing prior approval of the state.[2] This is not true with the corporation. To engage legally in business endeavors, the corporation, through approval of its petition to incorporate, is delegated by the state certain "powers" to act. If a corporation engages in transactions that are outside the purposes for which it was created, it may be enjoined by the state, since it is performing *ultra vires* acts.

There often exists in the minds of students of finance a confusion regarding *purpose* and *power* clauses. The purpose clauses are intended to set forth the nature of the business of the corporation, whereas the power clauses set forth the manner and means through which the firm can achieve its goals. Early incorporation acts required that a corporation list each purpose for which the firm was incorporated. These specific purpose provisions have been replaced by a *general-purpose* clause, which allows the corporation to state in more general terms the nature of the business enterprise.

---

[2]In certain instances this is not true; for example, some states require that a person obtain permission to operate a liquor store. Furthermore, some endeavors require that a tax be paid before actual operations can be started, e.g., sale of tobacco, liquor, etc.

The statutes of most states grant corporations the necessary general powers to carry out the firm's objectives. These powers are supplemented by *implied* powers that are "reasonably" necessary for the corporation to carry out its stated purposes. To illustrate, the Business Incorporation Act of Texas sets forth 18 *expressed* powers that a corporation has, plus the following implied power: "Whether included in the foregoing or not, to have and exercise all powers necessary or appropriate to effect any or all of the purposes for which the corporation is organized." Requirements with respect to enumeration of powers in the articles of incorporation vary among states. Therefore, it is wise to follow local precedent, which, of course, conforms to the law of the state involved.

Capitalization

Incorporators, in conjunction with their accountants and attorneys, must determine and set forth in the articles of incorporation (1) the type, kind, and number of shares of stock to be authorized; (2) the par or no-par status of the stock; (3) the voting rights of each type and class of stock; and (4) the preemptive status of the stock. Although amending the charter is relatively easy to accomplish insofar as the state is concerned, it may be difficult as well as expensive to get the shareholders to agree to changes after the firm is in operation.

Also included in the articles of incorporation are the amount of stock to be issued initially and the amount that is to be paid for the stock. Statutes require a minimum consideration to be received before the corporation can begin doing business. This usually amounts to $1,000 or 10 percent of the authorized stock, whichever is smaller.

Incorporation procedure

After the articles of incorporation have been drawn up, the document is filed with the appropriate official, usually the Secretary of State. This official will issue a certificate of incorporation only after confirming that the articles of incorporation adhere to the business incorporation act and that the required fees have been paid. Upon issuance of the certificate, usually called the charter, the corporate existence begins. At this time, the incorporators normally call an organization meeting of the board of directors to adopt the corporate bylaws, to elect officers, and to transact other business.

Corporate bylaws

In addition to the authority granted by the statutes and articles of incorporation, the corporation is also governed by its bylaws. It has been said that the bylaws govern the internal affairs of the corporate firm. Although the statutes differ with respect to the content, most bylaws contain provisions for the regulation and management of the affairs of the corporation and generally include the following:

1. Time and place of annual and special meetings of the shareholders.
2. Voting rights.
3. Board of directors (number, classification, election, term of office, and regular and special meetings).
4. Officers of the corporation.
5. Committees of the board of directors.
6. Bank accounts.
7. Certificate seal.
8. Books and records.
9. Stock certificate (issuance, signature, and transfer procedures).
10. Dividends and reserves.
11. Fiscal year and annual audits.
12. Contracts.
13. Amendment procedures.

Management of the Corporation

The management of corporate organizations, unlike that of proprietorships, is vested in its shareholders, directors, and officers. The shareholders, by virtue of ownership, are the true managers of the enterprise. As a practical matter, except in small firms, shareholders cannot manage the operation; therefore, they elect and delegate the authority to manage to the board of directors. The board, in turn, delegates the details of management to the officers. It should be pointed out that officers have no authority to act unless that authority is properly delegated by the charter, bylaws, the board of directors, or a specified combination of these. Moreover, the authority to act in certain areas cannot be delegated to either the board or the officers; generally these areas include (1) the sale of assets, (2) merger and consolidation, and (3) amending the charter or bylaws.

Shareholders as managers

Shareholders manage the affairs of the corporation by (1) adopting the charter and bylaws, (2) electing the board of directors, and (3) approving or disapproving the board's actions. Each of the acts is accomplished through the voting process. Under common law each stockholder is guaranteed one vote regardless of the number of shares owned. This method of voting has been replaced by statutes that control the incorporation procedures. The statutes provide that each shareholder has one vote per share, which means that a simple majority of stockholders can control every act. To give minority interests a voice in the affairs of the corporation, cumulative voting for directors has been required or allowed in nearly all states. Under cumulative voting, each shareholder has a number of votes equal to the number of voting shares he owns multiplied by the number of directors to be elected, and he can accumulate his votes and cast them for any one or several directors. An example illustrates the process: Assume there are 1,000 shares outstanding and nine members on the board of directors. If all nine are to be elected at one time, a shareholder with 101 shares can elect one director. That is, by casting all 909 (101 × 9) votes for one candidate, the shareholder is assured of the candidate's election. If a majority is desired, 501 shares are required. Staggering the terms of directors tends to offset some of the advantages gained from the cumulative voting technique. For example, if only three directors are elected each year rather than all nine, 251 shares are required to elect one director. It should be noted, however, that the owners of 251 shares would have three members on the board at all times, but if all nine are being elected at one time, it requires 301 shares, or 50 more shares, to elect three directors.[3]

Only shareholders of record are allowed to vote; that is, unless the shareholder's name appears in the corporate records, he is not permitted a vote. To avoid confusion, the bylaws provide for the closing of the stock transfer book for a reasonable period. After this date and until after the shareholders' meeting, the buyers of stock are not allowed to vote on issues presented at that particular meeting. In some states, the law allows the corporation to prepare a list of shareholders as of a particular date—anywhere from 10 to 30 days before the shareholders' meeting—and this list becomes the official authority for whether a shareholder is allowed to vote.

Unlike board members, a shareholder may authorize another person to vote his stock by giving him his power of attorney in writing; this is called a *proxy*. It is revocable, and the holder of the latest-dated proxy possesses the right to these votes. Moreover, even though a stockholder transfers his right to vote to another person or group of people, he may at the very last minute revoke the proxy and cast the vote in person. It has been stated by many authorities that management has been able to perpetuate itself by being able to obtain the proxies of uninterested shareholders. Obviously, since existing management has easy access to stockholder records and since the expense of soliciting proxies is assumed by the corporation, present management has a tremendous advantage over any dissenting group wishing to obtain control.

The shareholders exercise their managerial duties at regular and special meetings. The rules governing these meetings are set forth in the statutes, the

---

[3]The following formula gives a method of determining the smallest number of shares necessary to elect the desired number of directors:

$$\frac{\text{Total number of shares outstanding} \times \text{Number of directors desired}}{\text{Number of directors to be elected} + 1} + 1$$

charter, or the bylaws and cover such things as the time, place, nature, quorum, and order of business. For the regular annual meetings of shareholders, each shareholder must be given adequate notice, for example, not less than 10 or more than 50 days before the date of the meeting. The failure to hold a regular meeting is not sufficient ground to revoke the firm's charter; however, statutes set forth in detail the procedure that any interested shareholder may use to force management to hold annual meetings.

As a general rule, special meetings of the shareholders may be called by the president, the board of directors, the holders of not less than one-tenth of all shares entitled to vote at the meeting in question, or any officer designated by the corporate bylaws. Also, the statutes usually require that the notice of any special meeting of the shareholders set forth the purpose or purposes for which the meeting is to be held.

Directors as managers

It is the law that a corporation can act only through its legally elected board of directors except in instances where the corporation has conferred special authority upon one or more of its officers. However, to carry on the many and varied functions that must be performed, directors delegate to officers and employees the authority to act on certain matters. It should be emphasized that although authority to act is delegated, the responsibility for the actions cannot be delegated. The law requires that directors maintain the highest fidelity to the interest of the corporation and that they use reasonable care in the discharge of their duties. The statutes, charter, and bylaws will, in most instances, set forth in detail the number, qualifications, duties, method of election, term of office, and classification of directors as well as resignation and removal procedures and the method of filling vacancies.

In general, boards of directors are expected to perform the following: (1) select the major officers of the firm, (2) delegate sufficient authority to the officers to operate the business unit, (3) approve the broad objectives of the business operations, and (4) serve as a control unit with respect to predetermined objectives. These powers may be limited or restricted by statutes, articles, and bylaws. As a general rule directors in small businesses perform as officers.

The law holds directors responsible for their acts. Directors may be punished under common law if they (1) make secret profits, (2) waste the firm's assets, (3) lose the firm's assets while committing acts of negligence, (4) allow the corporate entity to act outside its purposes, or (5) make fraudulent statements and acts.

Directors are also governed by statutes and are liable under the statutes for (1) doing business without proper authorization, (2) allowing the corporation to perform an unlawful purpose, (3) issuing improper stock certificates, (4) failing to maintain proper entries in the books of accounts, (5) authorizing illegal dividends, (6) misappropriating corporate funds, or (7) violating the law regarding political contributions. Although this is not a complete list, it is sufficiently comprehensive to show the nature of acts for which directors are responsible by law.

Shareholders also hold directors responsible for their acts. In many instances it is the shareholders who bring legal action against directors. In addition, shareholders may relieve directors of their duties if they have sufficient reason to believe that the directors are not acting in the shareholders' best interest.

Since board members are not permitted to act individually, the statutes, charter, or bylaws set forth the rules and regulations governing the regular and special meetings necessary for boards to act collectively. These rules and regulations cover such items as (1) regular and special meetings, (2) time and place, (3) notice, (4) quorum, (5) order of business, and (6) the presiding officer. Since various state laws differ, it is advisable for the student to study the statutes governing corporations in his state as well as the bylaws of a business firm in order to see the specific regulations covering these items.

It should be emphasized that minutes of both regular and special meetings of directors must be carefully drawn and maintained, since court rulings are often based on this record. Furthermore, any committee designated by the regular board is governed by the same rules used to guide the procedures of the board; therefore, the minutes of meetings held by these committees should also be recorded and maintained.

Officers of the corporation

The statutes will as a general rule set forth the minimum number of officers of a corporation, their titles, a general statement of duties, and provisions for removal. The bylaws usually set forth the officers' qualifications, term of office, duties, and compensation.

Subchapter S Corporations

It was mentioned previously that corporations have certain tax disadvantages when compared to unincorporated firms. The two primary disadvantages are (1) the so-called double taxation problem and (2) the discrepancy between the tax treatment of losses sustained by unincorporated businesses and losses sustained by corporations. Congress attempted to resolve both of these problems by (1) allowing corporations with certain characteristics to be taxed as if they were unincorporated businesses—subchapter S corporations—and (2) allowing original investors of corporations organized under Section 1244 of the Internal Revenue Code to treat a loss on disposition or on total worthlessness of stock as an ordinary loss rather than a capital loss.

A corporation must meet the following conditions if it is to be taxed as an unincorporated business:

1. The corporation must be a domestic corporation.
2. It may not be a member of an affiliated group; i.e., it cannot own 80 percent or more of both voting and nonvoting stock of any domestic corporation.
3. There must be no more than ten shareholders.[4]
4. Shareholders must be individuals or estates, not trusts or partnerships.
5. Shareholders must be U.S. citizens or resident aliens.
6. Stock must be of one class.
7. No more than 80 percent of gross receipts can be derived from royalties, rents, dividends, interest, annuities, or sale and exchange of stock and securities.

In making the election for subchapter S status, the corporation must file a statement of election and a statement of consent by the firm's shareholders. In the latter case, all shareholders must agree. The election is terminated if one of the following occurs:

1. A new shareholder fails to consent.[5]
2. The corporation and shareholders voluntarily consent to revoke the election.
3. The corporation ceases to be a small business corporation.
4. More than 20 percent of income is *passive investment income.*

Such election may be made either in the month preceding or in the first month of the firm's taxable year. The Treasury has recommended that stockholders be allowed to elect subchapter S status during the six-month period prior to the taxable year. They have not, however, recommended that an election be permitted after the first month of the taxable year. This restriction is understandable since a later election would permit tax avoidance. It should be noted that an election cannot be voluntarily revoked during the year in which it is made. The logic behind this provision is clear; however, if revocation is desired, shareholders could create a situation in which the election is nonvoluntarily revoked. This type of action is not recommended since serious repercussions could result if fraud were evident.

The small businessman should also know that the amount of the loss that may be claimed by a stockholder is limited to the extent of his basis in

[4]The Tax Reform Act of 1976 changed this provision so that a corporation will be permitted to have 15 shareholders after the first five years of its existence. Also, if the number of shareholders goes above 10 during the first five years solely because of new shareholders who inherited their stock, the additional shareholders will be permitted, but the number cannot exceed 15.

[5]Under the present law the election continues unless the new shareholder affirmatively acts to terminate it. Prior to the 1976 change the new shareholder had to affirmatively consent to the election.

the corporation's stock and in debt owed to him by the corporation. Furthermore, a shareholder cannot reclaim the losses even though he has "rebuilt" his basis in his stock. This seems to be quite disadvantageous. Accordingly to offset this apparent discrepancy, the Treasury has recommended that a shareholder should be able to claim losses any time the basis in the stock has been rebuilt.

Another disadvantage of existing provisions is the fact that shareholders cannot claim the capital losses of the corporation as their own. A paradox seems to exist since they are permitted to treat their pro rata shares of the corporation's capital gain as their own to the extent of the corporation's taxable income for the year. Again recommendations have been made to correct this disadvantage.

The most serious disadvantage of the subchapter S corporation is the possibility of unintended revocation. For example, if at any time during the taxable year a subchapter S corporation fails to meet any of the prerequisites of being a subchapter S corporation, its election is terminated retroactively to the beginning of the year. It is this disadvantage that prevents many firms from choosing this corporate form. In addition to the above, the following may also be considered disadvantages:

1. Distributions in property other than cash result in shareholders being taxed on the amount in excess of taxable income for the year.
2. Earnings and profits in excess of taxable income result in shareholders being charged with a dividend on distribution of the excess amount.
3. Different taxable years of the corporation and of shareholders may cause a problem regarding the amount of loss or gain.

The effect of subchapter S is to change the tax-paying status of the corporation; that is, it pays no corporate income tax but passes it on to the shareholders. The corporation's taxable income is computed in the same manner as regular corporation income except that the following are not allowed: (1) dividends-received deductions, (2) deductions for partially tax-exempt interest, (3) deductions for net operating loss carry-backs and carry-overs, and (4) deductions for dividends received on certain preferred stock.

The amount of income or loss to be included each year is generally each shareholder's pro rata share of taxable income or net operating loss. Net operating losses, unlike income, are prorated among stockholders based on the number of days each individual held stock in the company during the taxable year.

Section 1244 Stock

It has been stated many times that small businesses are high-risk endeavors and as such are not attractive investments primarily because federal tax rules require that losses on stock (whether by sale, liquidation, or worthlessness) be treated as long-term capital losses for tax purposes and can be used only (1) to offset capital gains or (2) to offset ordinary income to the extent of only $1,000 per year ($2,000 of loss each time if the investment was held more than six months). If the small businessman created a sole proprietorship or partnership, he would be able to deduct the operating losses from his individual tax return. Likewise, any losses resulting from the sale of business assets could be deducted against ordinary income (within limits). If the losses exceed current income, the excess can either be carried back or carried forward to other taxable years. As a consequence, many small businesses avoid the corporate form even though it has certain advantages over an unincorporated business.

In 1958, Section 1244 was added to the Internal Revenue Code primarily to encourage a flow of equity capital into small businesses. It was believed that this could be accomplished if investors could deduct, to a limited extent, a loss on the sale, exchange, or liquidation of corporate stock as an ordinary loss rather than as a capital loss.[6] To prevent abuses of this privilege, the IRS Code set forth specific requirements regarding the (1) stockholders, (2) corporation, and (3) stock.

To qualify the shareholders must be individuals; i.e., corporations, trusts, and estates cannot enjoy the benefits of 1244 stock. Second, the shareholder must be an original investor. Some problems have arisen when underwriters have taken a position in the firm's stock. One solution to this problem is for the underwriter to act as an agent and sell the securities on a best-efforts basis, thus allowing the purchaser to qualify for the benefits provided by Section 1244. A partnership may receive 1244 stock, and any individual who is a partner in the partnership at the time the stock is issued and whose distributive share of partnership income reflects the loss sustained by the partnership is entitled to an ordinary loss rather than a capital loss. Only the original owner of 1244 stock can enjoy the tax advantage; that is, if the stock is sold, it reverts to its regular status of a capital asset. Any exchange of stock will disqualify it from its 1244 status except in the case of "E" and "F" tax-free reorganizations under Section 368, provided the new stock remains in the hands of qualified shareholders who owned the original shares before the reorganization took place.[7]

To qualify the stock must also meet certain requirements. First, it must be common stock issued for cash or property. In other words, the stock cannot be obtained in exchange for services or other equity securities. Second, no part of a prior issue can be outstanding at the time of the issue of the 1244 stock. Third, the stock cannot have any preferences or convertible

---

[6]Joint returns are limited to $50,000, and single returns are limited to $25,000.

[7]In the E-type reorganization the benefits are retained if Section 1244 stock is exchanged for common stock of the same corporation by the original owners. In an F reorganization Section 1244 stock is traded for Section 1244 stock of the successor corporation.

features. Moreover, if warrants are held prior to the issue, then the 1244 benefits are denied. Also, the issue of stock options, rights, or warrants after the 1244 stock has been issued is considered a subsequent issue, thus causing the issue to lose its status.

Finally the stock must be issued under a plan that meets all the requirements of Section 1244. To be acceptable, the plan must (1) be written, (2) set forth clearly the company's intention to issue a specific number of common shares, (3) reveal the maximum amount to be received for the stock, and (4) establish the two-year time limitation. The plan must be adopted by the board and included in the minutes of the corporation.

The stock must be issued by a small corporation; that is, it must be domestic in character and meet the following requirements: (1) The amount of money and the net tax basis of other property to be exchanged for the Section 1244 stock cannot exceed, in the aggregate, $500,000, and (2) total equity of the company, including the 1244 stock to be issued, cannot exceed $1 million at the time of the issue. In addition to being a small corporation, the firm must derive more than 50 percent of its aggregate gross receipts from sources other than royalties, rents, annuities, interest, dividends, or profit from sale of securities during the five years prior to the loss (or its entire corporate life if less than five years). Failure to adhere to this requirement will cause the stock to lose its status. Finally, the corporation must be created under the laws of the United States, state or territory. It should be emphasized that there is no 1244 corporation; rather, the stock is qualified under Section 1244 of the Internal Revenue Code. The majority of small corporations should consider issuing their stock under this section since the shareholders have everything to gain and nothing to lose. Moreover, there are few, if any, disadvantages for the firm that can qualify. A word of caution: It is essential to get the advice of an expert on the subject before issuing 1244 stock.

Summary

Proprietorships, partnerships, and corporations are by far the most important legal forms of organization in the United States. The following factors have been used to compare these three forms of organization: (1) ease and cost of formation, (2) liability of owners, (3) durability and stability, (4) control and ease of direction, and (5) legal status and sphere of activity. It was shown that corporations are by far the most complex, but they do possess a major advantage in that their owners have limited liability. It was pointed out, however, that this advantage could be circumvented by having the owners waive this right by personally securing all debts.

It was also pointed out in this chapter that corporations have certain tax disadvantages when compared to unincorporated firms. These disadvantages are (1) the double taxation problem and (2) the discrepancy between the tax treatment of losses sustained by unincorporated businesses and those sustained by corporations. These problems were particularly disadvantageous for small corporations, and Congress attempted to alleviate them by allowing them to be taxed as unincorporated businesses as well as allowing original investors of corporations that have complied with Section 1244 of the Internal Revenue Code to treat losses on disposition or on total worthlessness of stock as an ordinary loss rather than as a capital loss. The losses are limited to $50,000 for a person filing a joint return and to $25,000 for an individual filing a single tax return. There are specific requirements that must be met if the corporations are to enjoy these tax advantages. A word of warning: If these requirements are not closely adhered to, the managers and owners can suffer serious operational problems; therefore it is essential that these sections of the Internal Revenue Code be carefully evaluated before the final choice is made as to the type of organization.

QUESTIONS

1. Using the following factors, compare the various types of legal organizations: (1) cost of formation, (2) liability, and (3) sphere of activity.

2. Trace the relative importance of unincorporated firms. Explain the changes that have occurred.

3. Draft a charter of a hypothetical corporation.

4. Outline the steps that would be required in setting up the corporation in question 3.

5. What factors should be considered when selecting the home for the corporation in questions 3 and 4?

6. Discuss the various ways in which stockholders are allowed to vote.

7. What do corporate bylaws generally include?

8. Explain the role of the director as a manager.

9. List and discuss the logic behind each of the conditions required if a corporation is to assume subchapter S status.

10. What do you consider to be the greatest disadvantage of the subchapter S corporation? Why?

11. The IRS set forth specific requirements regarding stockholders, corporations, and stock if a firm is to qualify under section 1244 of the Internal Revenue Code. What are these requirements, and why do you believe the IRS required that they be met?

2-1. A group of lawyers has asked your advice in selecting the form of business organization that would be appropriate for them. The following data are for your information:

Mr. Smith: age, 35; current annual income, $16,000; estimated personal net worth, $5,000; and liquid assets, $2,000.

Mr. White: age, 30; current annual income, $14,000; estimated personal net worth, $5,000; and liquid assets, $1,000.

Mr. Black: age, 40; current annual income, $40,000; estimated personal net worth, $150,000; and liquid assets, $10,000.

Mr. Brown: age, 59; current annual income, $30,000; estimated personal net worth, $400,000; and liquid assets, $150,000.

The four men desire to join in forming an office in which they could all practice and whose profits they could share. Mr. Brown owns a building valued at $120,000, which would be suitable for the office. The four believe that they would acquire the necessary equipment for no more than $80,000 and that they would need no more than a $20,000 investment in working capital. Thus a total of $100,000 would suffice to open the law firm.

Each lawyer is willing to contribute all his liquid assets in forming the firm; none of the four, however, desires to go into debt.

Of the four, Mr. Black has the largest practice. Mr. Brown has had a large practice but at the present time is working only three and a half days a week. Over the next six years he hopes to reduce the amount of time he works to a day or less a week, so that he can enjoy his many hobbies and civic activities. Both Mr. Smith and Mr. White have been practicing for only a short period of time, but both had outstanding academic records and are highly regarded by their clients and by the other two lawyers. All four are married and have families.

The lawyers have agreed that their respective shares in the earnings of the firm should be related to their contributions and that such contributions may be made in several forms: reputation, number of clients attracted, and quantity and quality of work performed. They have not yet agreed upon the relative size of their respective shares. Mr. Smith and Mr. White are most interested in improving their current income. Mr. Black would like to maintain his current income but is most concerned with increasing his net worth. Mr. Brown is principally concerned with creating a retirement income for himself and increasing the size of the estate he hopes to leave to his grandchildren. Each hopes that the law firm will grow and that eventually eight or ten lawyers will be needed to handle the clients.

The lawyers have been considering forming either a general or a limited partnership or, alternatively, a corporation which would operate the firm and would pay each of them a salary. (Such corporations are legal in their state.)

They have requested your advice, asking specifically the following:

  a. Which form of business organization you recommend and why.
  b. The reasons you rejected the alternative forms.
  c. The problems or disadvantages they may encounter if they use your recommended form.
  d. The share that each should have in the firm, why he should have it, and how it will meet his requirements.

2-2. Three wealthy individuals, A, B, and C, have agreed to form a new construction business. All are in the 70 percent marginal tax bracket from other investment income. Each plans to invest $50,000 in the business, and the additional capital needed to buy land, office buildings, and equipment will be borrowed. The investment in property, offices, and equipment will be $600,000. Start-up costs are expected to be about $20,000.

The individuals anticipate a rather substantial loss in the first year but expect the business to be profitable by the fourth year. When profits do materialize, they will be reinvested in the business. The anticipated profits and losses for the future years are as follows:

Year	Profit (loss)
1	$(100,000)
2	(50,000)
3	(25,000)
4	250,000
5 & subsequent years	400,000

Because they will be doing considerable business in the city, they expect to invest modest sums in bonds issued by the city.

  Requirements:
  a. Discuss the variables that should be considered in (1) selecting either the subchapter S or regular corporate form of organization and (2) getting the business started. Be sure to include tax as well as nontax considerations.
  b. Assume that the subchapter S form was chosen. When, if ever, would it be advantageous to drop the subchapter S status?

2-3. Following bankruptcy proceedings, the stock of XYZ Corporation was worthless. Two of the major stockholders, Smith and Jones, each purchased stock when it was issued five years earlier. Smith had originally invested $25,000, while Jones and his wife invested $50,000 in the stock. All are in the 70 percent marginal tax bracket.

  Requirements:
  Consider the tax consequences to Smith and Mr. and Mrs. Jones. Also consider the tax treatment if the stock of XYZ had been 1244 stock.

BIGGS, SHERIDAN A., "Survival of the Smallest or How a Small Business Can Reach the Other End of the 1970's," *Price Waterhouse Review*, Price Waterhouse, Inc.

CARTER, ARTHUR L. and NORMAN SHETHAR, "Section 1244 Offers Financing Opportunities as Well as Tax Advantages," *Journal of Taxation*, January 1964.

COHEN, HOWARD R., "Section 1244—A Taxpayer's Delight," *Illinois Bar Journal*, February, 1970.

CORLEY, R. N., and R. L. BLACK, *The Legal Environment of Business*, 2nd ed., New York: McGraw-Hill, 1968.

DAVIES, ROBERT N., KELVYN H. LAWRENCE, and F. HODGE O'NEAL, *Choosing a Form of Business Organization*, Durham, North Carolina: Duke University, 1963.

"Federal Taxation—Failure to Obtain Ordinary Loss Deduction for Section 1244 Stock," *Tulane Law Review*, Vol. XLV, 1971.

GRIM, DOUGLAS P., "Drafting a 1244 Plan," *Law Notes*, American Bar Association, October 1971.

"How to Organize and Capitalize a Corporation," *Tax Planning*, Institute for Business Planning, Inc.

JOHNSON, PAUL, "Small Business Stock," *American Bar Association Journal*, Vol. 54, September, 1968.

KATTEN, MELVIN L., "Tax Court Reviews Purpose for Section 1244," *The National Public Accountant*, February, 1969.

LANDON, JAMES H., Notes: An Approach to Legislative Revision of Subchapter S," *Tax Law Review*, Vol. 26, Crowell, Collier & Macmillan, Inc., 1971.

ROHRLICH, CHESTER, *Organizing Corporate and Other Business Enterprises*, New York: Mathew Bender, 1967.

SCHNEIDER, IRVING, Editor, *Subchapter S: Its Opportunities and Pitfalls*, New York: Panel Publishers, Inc., 1965.

SOLOMON, EZRA, "What Should We Teach in a Business Finance Course?" *Journal of Finance*, Vol. 21, No. 2, pp. 411–415, May, 1966.

STROUD, WILLIAM, "Section 1244 Stock: A No-Cost Insurance Policy Against Failure of a Corporation," *Taxation for Accountants*, August, 1972.

YOUNG, JOHN H., "Income Tax Consequences of Investment Losses of Individuals," *Tax Law Review*, New York University School of Law, Fall, 1971.

part II

PLANNING

chapter 3

PLANNING FUNCTION
IN THE DYNAMIC SMALL FIRM

In the dynamic small business the planning function is given very little consideration, yet it may be the most important function that the manager performs. There are several reasons little or no attention is given to this activity. First, very few small businessmen are planning oriented; that is, the owner-manager is so involved with day-to-day activities that he never "learns" the fundamentals of planning. The authors are acquainted with an owner-manager of a garbage disposal company who is on the job by 5:30 every morning in order to see that the trucks are promptly dispatched. While this is an important function, it certainly doesn't warrant the personal attention of the company's president. This involvement diverts his time and energy from the overall planning that needs his guidance. Incidently, the company has a constant cash flow problem which analysis reveals is the direct result of poor financial planning and may very well cause the firm to fail. When this was pointed out to the president, he said, "I simply don't have time to run my company and plan at the same time." What he meant was that he didn't have time to manage the operational functions and managerial functions at the same time.

Another reason owner-managers don't effectively manage is their lack of interest in this particular type of activity. Many managers of small businesses achieve their position as a direct result of their technical knowledge. This is particularly true of high-technology firms. In many cases the owner-managers have been educated as engineers, chemists, or physicists or in some other technical field. They generally go directly from college into the production or research and development phase of some large firm. After serving effectively for several years, they decide to form their own businesses. Rather than joining with someone with administrative ability, they usually go into business with another technically trained individual, and, as a result, the new firm is overloaded with technical talent and short of management types. Since the managers have been trained and experienced only in the technical areas, they have little or no interest in the planning and control phases of the business. If they are lucky, they will learn the importance of these functions and either direct their attention to them or hire someone who is trained in these areas. Unfortunately, many firms fail before this lesson is learned.

When discussing the planning functions with small businessmen, they generally make the following observations:

1. I don't have time to plan for the future; I'm too busy with day-to-day activities.
2. I don't have enough funds to waste them on nonproductive activities.
3. My company is not very large, and I really don't need to do that kind of planning.
4. I'm not interested in spending my time on abstract theories; they may work in big companies but certainly not in mine.

While it is true that planning may be different for small and large companies, it certainly isn't less important. If anything, it is more important. For example, small businesses have less funds; therefore, they must be used effectively. Second, managers of small businesses usually don't have an adequate staff; therefore, they must make every move count, and the only way this can be done is to have carefully designed goals, strategies, policies, and procedures. Finally, the same theories apply to small and large companies alike; the only difference is in their application. This being true, small businessmen must plan, organize, control, and replan the business functions if they are to use their resources effectively.

Business Functions

The business organization, regardless of size, is created and allowed to exist by the society in which it operates. In our society the ideal organization is one that produces and distributes economic values effectively and efficiently; in fact, if values are not created and distributed, the chances for survival are greatly reduced. This concept holds true for all forms of organizations.

Economic theory tells us that value takes the shape of either form or place utility and is created through the production and distribution functions. That is, all firms that produce value *directly* must perform either the production or distribution function or both. To illustrate, a manufacturing firm performs both production and distribution functions, while a retail firm performs primarily the distribution function. For these functions to be performed effectively and efficiently, the firm must have the correct amount of debt and equity capital. These functions—production, distribution, and finance—may be referred to as value- or utility-creating functions since the first two create value directly and the latter creates value indirectly; more will be said about this later. While these are not the only functions that are performed, they are vital if the firm is to meet its primary goal of creating utility or value.

Managerial Functions

If each of the business functions is to be discharged efficiently and effectively, managers must carry out the following functions: planning, organizing, control, and replanning. Regardless of the size of the firm, each member of the management team must fulfill to some degree all of these functions; however, in the larger companies certain managers will be responsible for performing only one or even a part of one of these functions. In the smaller firm the manager is generally called upon to perform *all* of these functions. Obviously, not only does this mean that he must be more of a generalist than his counterpart in the large firm but also that he must work longer hours if the firm is to operate effectively.

The primary managerial function is planning. Generally authorities have agreed that planning is deciding in advance what will be done in both the short and long term. If this is true, then planning, in our way of thinking, must include the following processes: (1) establishing the objectives of the firm, (2) formulating strategies, (3) determining operating policies, and (4) creating procedures. It should be emphasized that these steps or phases of planning are not done in isolation; rather, each is dependent on the other.

Objectives

In developing the firm's financial objective the manager of the small firm should remember that unless all firms create more goods and services than they employ, society will experience a net loss. If such a condition continues, either the government or the people who make up the society will demand changes designed to correct the situation. The manager should also remember that unless the individual company creates and distributes value there is a high probability that it will lose its competitive position and experience partial or complete loss. To assure that the firm will create and distribute values to the society in which it operates, the manager should establish goals for each business function. The long-run goal of the finance function is to assure management that it has the correct amount of each type of funds so that all other factors of production will produce at their optimum over the long run. This objective not only deals with the amount of capital employed but also the type and maturity of each kind of debt. The following illustrates the importance of this objective. The reader knows that return on investment increases in direct proportion to the number of times capital is turned. However, the degree of risk is increased as turnover is increased; i.e., if the firm doesn't have adequate capital (turnover is excessive), there is a likelihood that it will lose sales, thus causing return to fall below the optimum. On the other hand, if the firm has excessive capital (turnover is too low), the return will be below the optimum return. Finally, if the maturities of the firm do not coincide with the internal generation of funds, the firm will face excessive risk, which may cause it to lose value. Stated differently, the owner-manager has as his goal full employment of funds at all times. In a dynamic economy, this is not possible; occasionally the manager must establish short-term or temporary objectives which on the surface would appear to contradict the firm's long-term objective. For example, the owner-manager may set up reserves in working capital in order to assure solvency. The amount of reserves is determined by the amount of risk that the firm can safely assume at that particular time. Not only does the owner-manager manipulate working capital in order to minimize risk but he may employ "incorrect" types of capital so as to minimize risk. For example, the level of risk may call for a 50 percent equity level, but due to the cost of debt capital, the manager may actually use less debt capital even though the return to equity may suffer. Once the cost of debt has been readjusted downward, he will attempt to decrease equity by increasing debt. It should be noted that secondary financing is much easier to accomplish in the smaller company than in the larger firm.[1]

Strategies

The second phase of planning is the formation of the strategy that serves as the basis for the firm's policies. Strategy as used in this book is the process by which or the way in which the firm's goals are achieved. For example, the financial goal of the firm is to optimize its use of capital both in amount and type. These factors are determined by the level of risk the firm should take. For example, if the level of business risk can be reduced, the firm will be in position to reduce the total amount of capital required and increase the proportion of debt or risk capital.

The characteristics of small firms support the conclusion that they incur more business and financial risk than larger firms and are thus more susceptible to "incorrect" investment decisions. To offset these risks, smaller firms should use different strategies. For example, large firms usually follow the strategy of accepting projects with (1) the highest expected value and (2) the smallest relative dispersion of net operating income. The logic behind this is that the market value of a firm's stock is adversely affected when earnings fluctuate. In other words, the value of a firm whose earnings per share (EPS) fluctuate will be less than for one whose income is stable. On the other hand,

---

[1]Secondary financing is accomplished when one obligation is increased in order to decrease another obligation. Primary financing is performed when an obligation is increased in order to increase an asset.

the strategy of the small firm should be different from that of a larger firm in that the primary criterion of an investment should not be expected value and risk associated with dispersion but rather avoiding risk of insolvency. It should be remembered that the stock of a small firm is not traded in the market place and the price of the stock is usually unaffected by variations in earning. However, a small firm, unlike the larger firm, is extremely sensitive to losses. For example, Ford Motor Company could assume the losses associated with the Edsel due to its diversification of products, but very few small firms could afford the luxury of a relative loss of such magnitude. The writers are of the opinion that at the time of the decision to build Edsel, Ford's management knew there was some probability of loss but they also knew that the expected value of the Edsel far exceeded the harm resulting from the loss that actually occurred. While it is not known for sure, it is presumed that the "numbers' surrounding the decision regarding the Mustang revealed an equal probability of loss, but in this case the losses were not realized.

If the small firm follows the strategy of accepting only a small probability of loss (there can never be a certainty regarding loss), it follows logically that the expected value will be less. This loss in expected value can be more than offset by the firm's reducing the amount of funds to finance the operation; that is, the reserve in working capital will not be nearly so great since the business risk has been reduced considerably. Not only can the firm decrease the amount of funds required to finance the project but it can also employ more debt capital because the insolvency risk has been substantially reduced. Remember, the firm can afford financial risk (variation in earnings per share resulting from increased debt in the capital structure) since its value is not directly affected by variations in per share earnings. An example depicts this strategy. Assume that a small manufacturing firm could price its products in such a way as to create an expected annual earnings before interest and taxes (EBIT) of $20,000 but that there would be a 10 percent probability of loss. On the other hand, the firm could contract with a larger firm to take all of its output for a guaranteed EBIT fo $15,000. Since the firm would be contracting away its business risk, it could offset the lower profit margin by reducing its investment and increasing the use of debt capital. The reduced investment would offset the loss in return on investment, and the increased use of debt would offset the loss in return to equity.

The reader should note the relationship among goals, strategies, and policies. In the above case the goals were the same; i.e., use the correct level and proportion of capital for the project under consideration so as to optimize the value of the firm. The strategy was different and so were the capital investment policies. In the former case the firm assumed a certain level of business risk and in so doing required a greater volume of capital. Moreover, since a certain business risk was assumed, it had to use a limited amount of debt since debt increases the variation of earnings. Due to the adoption of a different strategy (avoiding all business risk) the firm increased its turnover of capital by decreasing the amount of capital used to produce the sales as well as increasing the amount of debt. Even though the EBIT was smaller, the firm optimized its return both on total and equity capital.

It is the writers' opinion that strategies are specific in much the same way as policies. That is, while all strategies relate to the risk that the firm encounters, each strategy pertains to a specific area of activity; e.g., there are strategies covering capital structure, procurement of funds, investment decisions, etc. The following depict the interrelationships among the various components of planning:

1. Goals are the functions of society and individuals within that society.
2. Strategies are the functions of goals.
3. Policies are the functions of strategies.
4. Procedures are the functions of policies.

Policies

The third phase of the planning process is the determination of policies that make it possible for the firm to achieve its objectives. Policies generally fall into several general classifications: (1) capital structure policies, (2) capital procurement policies, (3) income distribution policies, (4) capital synchronization policies, and (5) asset mix policies. The writers believe that these classifications tend to overlap; for example, income distribution policies may also be classified as capital procurement policies. Therefore, it is necessary to identify the specific policies that the small businessman should be familiar with so he can formulate and promulgate only those policies that will fulfill the firm's strategies and goals. The following policies are vital to the welfare of the firm, and each small business should specifically define each:

1. Policies determining volume of fixed capital.
2. Policies determining sources of funds.
3. Policies determining asset mix.
4. Policies determining debt–equity mix.
5. Policies determining debt mix.
6. Policies determining income and its distribution.
7. Policies determining credit and collection policies.
8. Policies determining investment in receivables, cash, and inventories.

It is highly recommended that each business regardless of size have a formal policy manual. In this manual not only should the policies be specifically detailed but the firm's goals and strategies identified. The principal purpose of this is to have a guide in operating the business as well as a basis for replanning when and if it is needed.

Organization

It was mentioned above that the owner-manager is responsible for the efficient use of capital resources. To fulfill the responsibility, he must see that in addition to being planned the financial activities are coordinated. Coordination requires that each function and subfunction be performed at the proper time; the achievement of this requires the functions to be organized. Organization in all firms regardless of size includes two primary phases: (1) organizing all activities into identifiable functions and (2) delegating adequate authority to the individuals who have been assigned the responsibility for their performance.

The organization structure of the business enterprise is nothing more than the hierarchy of its functions. The size and nature of the structure is dependent on the size and nature of the various functions; that is, as a general rule, each function increases in size as it increases in complexity. To minimize waste and inefficiency, the managements of large firms subdivide each function into various subfunctions and assign them to specialists, thereby creating a system.

The organization of a closely held company also has a system; however, the organization differs from that of a larger company; in fact, it changes at various stages of growth. We believe that the dynamic small firm goes through three distinct stages. The first stage begins when the entrepreneur invests his funds in an idea and lasts until the firm has gained a foothold in the market place. This is the most dangerous stage since it is the time when the firm is faced with the greatest risk, such as inadequate capital and markets. The goal of the organization is survival; that is, the owner feels that he has achieved his goal if he doesn't "go broke" and has really succeeded when he reaches and exceeds the break-even point. The second period is characterized by success and growth in the same market as determined at the beginning of the business. Many small businesses remain in this stage and only emerge from it when they move into the third phase, which often is to merge with another firm. The third stage is described as that stage in which the firm operates in several markets. As a general rule this stage is reached by either aggressive growth from within or by acquiring firms that operate in other lines through the process of merger. For the most part firms in the last group are not classified as closely held and do not concern us as much as the firms in the first two classifications.

The organization of firms in the first category is very simple in that the entrepreneurs usually make all the decisions regarding strategies and policies. This is not to deny the importance of the organization at this stage. As a matter of fact, it is as important, if not more so, than at any other stage in the life of the firm primarily because there is usually more conflict as to goals at this time. For example, investors in this stage are usually of two types: First, there is the individual who wants to develop the product in such a way as to cause the firm to achieve a prominent place in the total market. Second, there is usually an entrepreneur who wants to get his investment back plus a very high return. Once this is accomplished he wants to get out and invest the funds in another venture. If management is not very careful, there will arise a conflict of motives which may have serious repercussions; therefore, the identification of major goals and functions is vitally important in order to avoid conflicts that could cause failure. It should be remembered that small businessmen have characteristics different from those of the managers of large organizations. For the most part they are aggressive, decisive, commercially oriented, operations oriented, and authoritarian and have little patience with business politics. Obviously, if you have two or more individuals with these characteristics, you have potential conflict; therefore, it is essential that all goals, functions, and authority be well established.

The second stage also has many risks, but the managers do not have so many conflicts as are generally found in the primary stage. That is, exploiters generally leave the firm during the early part of the second phase, thus reducing the possibility of conflict. This period is commonly characterized by expanding functions as well as adding specialists. That is, as the firm grows there is a greater need for specialists and more funds to hire them. It is especially important for the owner-manager to create an organizational system that will define in absolute terms the duties and responsibilities of each manager. It should be pointed out that many individuals are hired at this stage who do not have any proprietary interest in the organization and therefore require definitive guidelines in order to operate at their greatest level of efficiency.

Control

Financial control consists of two steps: developing standards of performance and comparing activities with these standards. The former, although difficult to determine, are especially significant since they serve as a basis for the replanning process. Previously, standards were derived primarily from past experience, but with improved knowledge in the area of statistics and mathematics it is becoming easier for managers to look into the future and develop standards that directly relate to future activities. Moreover, with the use of computers it is easier for management to maintain accurate and up-to-date records of activities. As a result, it is possible for the owner to compare today's activities with predetermined standards. This not only allows management to ascertain early any discrepancies that occur but enables it to take remedial action before deviations become too great.

The most difficult task in the control process is the establishment of standards. This is particularly true in small firms because many are operated for personal rather than depersonalized goals. The latter are largely financial in nature, but personal goals take many forms and are nearly impossible to define. The writers wish to emphasize that owners should state their goals in terms which can be measured in financial units since they are the easiest to identify and measure.

Replanning

The replanning process is the last step in the planning process performed by the owners of the small firm, and it, like each of the other functions, is vital to the ultimate success of the business process. If the evaluation of performance (control) reveals that the end results of the firm's activities will not meet predetermined standards, it may be assumed that either the firm's policies or personnel are not effective. If it is the former, management must first ascertain whether it is the strategy or the policies that are ineffective and, second, make changes in either or both. This process is called replanning.

Replanning should not be undertaken unless there is positive knowledge that either the strategy or policies are ineffective. To establish proof of this requires that owners examine performance continuously since the economic environment in which the policies operate is constantly changing. Whereas evaluation is a continuous function, replanning is undertaken only when it has been proved that changes in strategy or policies are warranted.

Stages of failure

Fortunately there are many signals that indicate to owners when a firm's policies are ineffective and in need of replanning, long before complete financial embarrassment becomes a fact. That is, there are various stages of failure, and by careful examination management can detect failure symptoms and ascertain and correct their causes before it is too late. A word of warning: The causes must be determined and corrected if management wishes to avoid a recurrence. If only the symptoms are corrected and not their cause, most likely the difficulty will reappear, probably more severely the second time. To illustrate, suppose a firm is constantly short of cash. If management borrows additional funds without ascertaining the real cause for the cash shortage, the firm will probably experience a serious cash shortage within a very short time. On the other hand, if the cause is ascertained and corrected, management can raise the necessary cash and be reasonably certain that in the future the cash flow will not be interrupted in such a manner as to create a similar problem.

Financial failure may be divided into three phases: economic, financial, and legal. Economic failure exists when the rate of return realized on assets falls below expectations, causing the firm to drift toward the second and third stages of failure. Failure should be detected at this stage for several reasons;

two of the more important are the following : (1) Replanning is much more effective if it is initiated at this time, and (2) the actions required to eliminate the causes for economic failure are not nearly so drastic as those required to "cure" the causes usually present in the financial and legal stages of failure.

Economic failure, unlike financial and legal failure, does not mean that a firm is insolvent in the usual sense. That is, creditors have not incurred a loss. In fact, if management is able to reshape its policies, the firm will most likely be able to meet all maturing obligations as they come due. If, however, the "causes" are not removed, the firm will be called upon to refund existing obligations, ultimately defaulting because sufficient funds will not be available to satisfy the obligations. If management initiates action at this stage to eliminate the problem areas, the creditors are generally willing to renew their obligations and even to make available additional funds for operational purposes.

If the causes for economic failure are not ascertained and corrected, the firm can be expected to move into the second stage of failure, which may be referred to as financial failure. A firm in this phase is insolvent in that it is unable to meet its maturing obligations, but is is not insolvent in the bankruptcy sense; that is, liabilities do not exceed assets. We should point out that although drastic action is usually necessary to restore the firm to a sound position, it is not necessary to liquidate the business endeavor. A number of remedies in a wide range are available to management to aid in the correction of financial insolvency. Included among these remedies are readjustments, extensions, out-of-court composition settlements, and reorganization under the Bankruptcy Act.

The ultimate stage of financial embarrassment may be referred to as legal failure. The firm is said to be legally bankrupt when its liabilities exceed its assets. To correct this situation, usually management must reorganize under the Bankruptcy Act or enter into voluntary or involuntary liquidation. The latter is accomplished through the courts and under the jurisdiction of the Bankruptcy Act.

Action taken in the replanning process

Effective management cannot wait until the firm has experienced legal failure to take action, since in most cases the only remedies then available are reorganization or liquidation. In either case creditors generally lose, and ill will results. To avoid insolvency and at the same time to realize the highest possible return on investment, management must engage in continuous analysis for the earliest possible detection of causes for financial embarrassment. Corrective action taken when failure is imminent not only can be effective but in most instances is less drastic than that called for if the symptoms remain undetected until either the financial or the legal failure stage. The following example shows the importance of this approach.

The XYZ Company, a corporation operating in the midwestern and eastern parts of the United States, is engaged in the manufacture and sale of communication and navigation equipment for aircraft as well as electronic equipment and component parts. These products are sold directly to manufacturers, with no contact with the public. Mr. Wilson, the vice-president for finance, is very cost conscious and maintains cost records on all phases of the firm's operations. Past history shows that the board of directors has adopted the policy that return on investment should be equal to at least 15 percent. That is, investment should not be made in projects unless they return at least 15 percent, except when the investment is made for strategic reasons; in these cases, the directors reason that the low return would be offset by projects with returns exceeding 15 percent.

Wilson realizes that the rate will fluctuate above and below this standard; therefore, he maintains a record in graph form of the movement of the overall rate in order to determine any downward trends at the earliest possible time. Figure 3-1 depicts the movement of the firm's rate of return during the past 12 months.

Wilson had observed that since February the rate of return had declined steadily; furthermore, the forecast for the next 3 months indicates that the rate will not rise above 12 percent. The analysis also revealed the following: Sales had declined 10 percent during the past 9 months; cash had increased 15 percent over the level previously established by policy; receivables and inventories accounts had declined by approximately 12 percent during the past 12 months; turnover of capital had declined from 2.5 times to 2.1 times; and earnings as a percentage of sales also declined.

Wilson reasoned that immediate steps were necessary if the firm was to regain its previous position and achieve the goals that had been established. Also, he recognized that to initiate effective changes, an analysis should be made to isolate the cause or causes for the present condition. Wilson made the analysis and found the following conditions. The firm's prices were in line with those of its competitors, but earnings as a percentage of sales had declined below the average for the industry. In studying costs, he determined

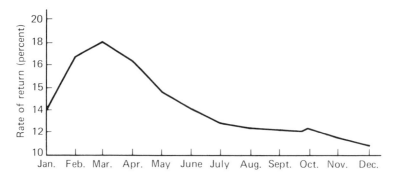

FIGURE 3-1. XYZ Company rate of return

that although variable costs were in line with those of other firms in the industry, fixed costs were excessive. In addition, the study revealed that the demand for three of the firm's major products had declined steadily over the past year. As a result, the firm was producing at less than full capacity, causing the per unit cost to increase. In determining the reasons for declining inventories, Wilson discovered that inventory levels had been tied directly to sales, and since sales had declined, he had reduced the level of inventories. As a result, the flow of funds had been interrupted, allowing cash to build up to a level exceeding that which had been established by policy.

Wilson concluded that the decline in the rate of return was the result of overexpansion of fixed assets and buildup of idle working capital. He knew that temporary changes could be initiated that would cause the firm's rate of return on investment to rise, but it would be necessary to institute permanent changes if the required return were to be maintained. The following temporary and permanent policy changes were recommended to eliminate these two basic problems.

First, the funds should be found for a crash research program with the primary objective of finding substitutes for the three products for which demand had declined. Once this program was under way, the firm should initiate a permanent research program for the development of new products that could be introduced as quickly as the demand for existing products tended to soften.

Second, if it became apparent to management that the new products could be developed within a short time, management could invest its idle cash in short-term government securities and convert them into cash whenever the need to build up inventories reappeared. Investments of this nature have the effect of improving the firm's rate of return and, at the same time, of providing flexibility. On the other hand, if management concluded that the new products could not be introduced within a reasonable time, it could use the excess cash to liquidate short- and intermediate-term loans, thus reducing the level of investment. Such action would have two effects: (1) The operating ratio would improve, and (2) investments would decline, thus causing the rate of return to improve.

Finally, if possible, the owners would want to reduce the size of their plant until products were found that would cause production to increase. This might be accomplished by not replacing existing equipment until demand increased or by selling idle equipment. If this policy were followed, investment turnover would increase, thus causing the rate of return to improve.

Wilson might have found other causes that would have had the same effects as those listed above. For example, the decline in inventories might have been caused by failure to follow consistently sound purchasing policies, and the decline in sales might have resulted from inadequate inventories. On the other hand, prices might have been entirely out of line with those of comparable producers. Also, incorrect credit terms might have forced buyers to look elsewhere for their supplies. Furthermore, the analysis might have indicated that the sales effort was concentrated on unprofitable lines, thus causing total demand as well as profits to decline, or that cash was increasing because the firm retained excessive funds in relation to need.

The discussion above shows how important it is for owners to approach the problem of replanning logically; that is, before replanning is undertaken, management should follow the same steps taken when plans were first developed. Briefly, the decision-making process as it applies to replanning includes five steps: (1) Seek out the real causes for the failure of present strategies and policies, (2) analyze the critical factors that influence the areas concerned, (3) develop alternative courses of action, (4) select and initiate the best course of action available, and (5) check the solution after it has been installed in order to determine its effectiveness.

Summary

It is believed that the planning function has been given little or no consideration in the management of small businesses, yet it may be the most important function that the manager performs.

All firms perform certain value-creating functions. While authorities disagree as to the titles of these functions, most, if not all, agree that production and distribution create value directly, whereas finance creates value indirectly. Also, management performs certain functions in each of these areas. For example, management should plan, organize, control, and replan the activities of each.

It is our belief that planning is absolutely essential if the firm is to operate efficiently and effectively. To accomplish this function in the most efficient manner we have recommended that planning include the following steps or phases: (1) establishing the objectives of the firm, (2) formulating strategies, (3) determining operating policies, and (4) creating procedures. While each of these steps is separate and distinct, they are interrelated. For example, procedures are the function of policies, and policies are the function of strategies, and strategies are the function of objectives. Stated differently, management must first determine its objectives and then develop its strategies and policies. It was also emphasized that strategies in small firms are fundamentally different from those in large companies, which means that operating policies in small firms are usually different from those in large firms.

The replanning function is extremely important since effective management cannot wait until the firm has experienced legal failure to take action. To avoid insolvency and at the same time realize the highest return on investment, management must engage in continuous analysis for the earliest detection of causes for financial embarrassment. The authors wish to express the importance of first determining the *cause* for failure before action is taken. If action is predicated on symptoms rather than causes, the firm will usually suffer additional harm, even though failure may be delayed temporarily.

QUESTIONS

1. Discuss generally why small businessmen fail to plan.

2. Explain the relationship between the production of values and business functions.

3. What should be the objectives of a small firm? What are the financial objectives of the firm's owners-managers?

4. Explain how strategies differ in large and small firms.

5. Explain the organization of the small firm in each of its periods of development.

6. Discuss the two steps involved in effective control.

7. Discuss the various stages of failure.

8. Discuss the action that should be taken by owner-managers in order to prevent failure.

PROBLEMS

3-1. Mr. Smith, owner-manager of the Jones Company, is extremely aggressive; that is, he never fails to assume risk when there is an opportunity to increase the firm's net worth. In explaining his aggressiveness, Mr. Smith stated that "the level of risk a manager can assume is directly related to the care which is exercised when monitoring existing strategies and policies." Specifically, he stated that the following should be noted and chartered monthly:

1. Rate of return on total investment.
2. Rate at which fixed (tangible) assets are turned each quarter.
3. Rate at which inventory and receivables are turned each quarter.
4. Earnings as a percent of sales.
5. Cash ratios (cash to current assets and cash to current liabilities).
6. Operating ratio.

Requirements:
    Obtain quarterly statements of a firm of your choice, and evaluate its policies by comparing the firm's actual operations with its stated goals, strategies, and policies. In your analysis, use the six ratios mentioned above by Mr. Smith. What changes would you recommend?

3-2. XYZ, Inc. was incorporated in September 1962 for the purpose of selling athletic devices. The authorized stock consisted of 250,000 shares of $1.00 par value common stock. The company issued 127,330 shares of its stock to three members of the Jones family for cash and equipment. The following balance sheets and profit and loss statements are supplied for your information. Evaluate the firm's strategies and policies, and make recommendations regarding both. Incidently, the owner-manager is extremely optimistic regarding the future of the firm's product. In fact, a major department store (the chain has at least 500 stores) has agreed to sell the devices exclusively.

XYZ, Inc.
Profit and Loss Data
1974–1978

	1978	*1977*	*1976*	*1975*	*1974*
Net sales	$525,000	$470,000	$300,000	$200,000	$180,000
Cost and expenses:					
Cost of sales	283,500	270,720	133,080	122,400	115,200
Operating expenses	231,000	179,540	114,840	70,600	55,260
Interest expense	950	625	65	352	174
Life insurance prem.	913	903	827	978	827
Income before taxes	$ 8,637	$ 18,212	$ 51,188	$ 5,670	$ 8,539
Less: Income taxes	1,727	3,642	5,732	-0-	-0-
Income after taxes	$ 6,910	$ 14,570	$ 45,456	$ 5,670	$ 8,539
Dividends	-0-	-0-	-0-	-0-	-0-
Retained earnings brought forward	28,928	22,018	7,448	(38,008)	(43,678)
Ending earned surplus *Add:* Back cash value of insurance	913	815	1,084	677	765
Ending retained surplus	$ 29,841	$ 22,833	$ 8,532	$(37,331)	$(42,913)

XYZ, Inc.
Balance Sheet
1974–1978

	1978	*1977*	*1976*	*1975*	*1974*
Assets					
Current assets:					
Cash	$ 35,000	$ 3,300	$ 12,375	$ 3,150	$ 3,050
Petty cash	50	50	-0-	-0-	-0-
Accounts receivable	60,350	75,150	50,350	42,525	38,850
Inventories (at cost)	68,750	95,225	67,485	20,375	12,875
Total current assets	$164,150	$173,725	$130,210	$66,050	$54,775
Fixed assets:					
Office equipment	3,600	3,180	2,325	2,020	1,610
Manufacturing equipment	23,400	14,280	7,740	6,800	2,665
Automobiles	14,060	14,060	11,205	8,725	8,725
	$ 41,060	$ 31,520	$ 21,270	$17,545	$13,000
Less: Accumulated depreciation	25,400	17,090	13,775	9,495	6,630
Total fixed assets	$ 15,660	$ 14,430	$ 7,495	$ 8,050	$ 6,370

XYZ, Inc.
Balance Sheet (Continued)
1974–1978

	1978	*1977*	*1976*	*1975*	*1974*
Other assets:					
Patents (at cost less amor.)	16,900	20,240	23,580	26,920	30,255
Organizational expense	-0-	-0-	-0-	-0-	-0-
Cash surrender value of life insurance	5,963	5,050	4,235	3,150	2,475
Total other assets	$ 22,863	$ 25,290	$ 27,815	$ 30,070	$ 32,730
Total assets	$202,673	$213,445	$165,520	$104,170	$ 93,875
Liabilities, Capital Stock, and Surplus					
Liabilities:					
Current liabilities					
Accounts payable	$ 40,167	$ 55,343	$ 22,070	$ 10,148	$ 6,835
Notes payable	-0-	-0-	-0-	-0-	-0-
Payroll taxes payable	1,490	1,180	620	1,673	273
Income tax payable	1,495	4,409	5,618	-0-	-0-
Total current liabilities	$ 43,152	$ 60,932	$ 28,308	$ 11,821	$ 7,108
Capital stock:					
Capital stock—250,000 shares authorized; 127,330 outstanding;					
$1 par	$127,330	$127,330	$127,330	$127,330	$127,330
Paid-in surplus	5,850	5,850	5,850	5,850	5,850
Earned surplus	29,841	22,833	7,532	(37,331)	(42,913)
Total equity	$163,021	$156,013	$140,712	$ 95,849	$ 90,267
Less: Treasury stock	3,500	3,500	3,500	3,500	3,500
Total	$159,521	$152,513	$137,212	$ 92,349	$ 86,767
Grand total	$202,673	$213,445	$165,520	$104,170	$ 93,875

chapter 4

PROFIT PLANNING

The term profit planning has come to represent a host of activities, extending from the preparation of a budget to an in-depth forecasting of the company's long-term future earnings. Profit planning may also be used in either a passive or an active sense in that the plan may comprise a summary of what management merely expects to occur or an indication on the part of the firm's owners as to their profit goals. In the first sense, the plan is basically an indication of management's perception as to what will occur in a future time period. At the conclusion of the period, the plan simply represents a historical comparison of what actually occurred relative to prior anticipations. Management does little to react to the developing circumstances to ensure that the expectations become reality. In the latter instance, the profit plan sets forth the necessary ingredients for achieving what should happen. Accordingly, the company's owners are particularly interested in periodic feedback as the planning period unfolds, with the hope of being able to react to any negative deviations.

The foregoing comments are descriptive of the two extreme concepts of formalized profit planning. Ideally, the firm's executives should work toward the more comprehensive framework in which the plan constitutes a well-devised statement of goals, operating strategies, financial plans of action, and a management information system. Thus, the profit plan comprises the firm's objectives as set forth by the owners, the avenues for achieving these objectives, and a system for providing continuous feedback as to the organization's progress in reaching these objectives. The operating plan provides explanation of the actions to be taken during the planning horizon in an effort to reach the company's goals. In turn, the financial plan reflects the company-wide expected profits resulting from the operating plan. The management information system simply includes "progress reports" required in assessing the actual results at interim points in time relative to the profit goals.

In this chapter, several aspects of the profit plan are provided. First, the justification of profit planning for the small business is explained. Second, the requirements for developing a viable profit-planning system are cited. Third, the procedural development of the plan, with an emphasis on content, is set forth. Finally, break-even analysis, a valuable tool in the profit-planning process, and the closely related concept of operating leverage are presented.

The Reasons for Profit Planning

Business leaders, both for large and small companies, have long been engaged in planning. However, the need for more formal and comprehensive planning has only in recent years come to be recognized by many larger organizations as representing an essential element for contributing to the continued growth of their firm. This requisite for planning includes profit planning. The basis for justifying the increased time and effort to planning has largely been related to the greater size and diversity of businesses. However, planning, especially profit planning, should not be restricted to the larger corporations in that profit planning is easily adaptable to the smaller firm's needs. In other words, the benefits accruing from the adoption of a profit plan are not strictly a function of the business entity's size.

Regardless of the asset size or the number of departments within the company, the profit plan affords a readily available criterion for decision making. By providing meaningful direction, a decision is no longer an isolated event requiring the initiation of extensive analysis. Stated differently, the decision-making process is taken out of a crisis atmosphere and placed into the overall context of company goals.

A second reason for profit planning being of importance to the firm is its merits as a communication link between the company's owner-management echelon and the employees. This requisite for informational flows is largely recognized by the upper levels of management within large corporations. However, the receipt of information by employees of the small business is usually relegated to informal, and possibly haphazard, discussions. Yet, the level of communication effectiveness regarding the profit objectives of the company is equally critical for the small firm. The profit plan, if administered correctly, facilitates the flow of information within the small organization in a systematic manner, which should further improve the firm's probability of reaching its financial goals.

In a sense related to the profit plan affording an essential communication vehicle, the plan should be of particular assistance as a motivational factor for the company's personnel. Only if the employees are effectively challenged and have a measurable goal against which their performance may be measured will the maximum contribution be achieved.

The last reason that might be given for the importance of the profit plan is the increased competitiveness experienced by all firms in recent times. While exceptions could be noted, businesses are increasingly subjected to competitive pressures. The response to this marked increase in competition has naturally been diverse. However, the small operation is somewhat limited in its options. For instance, the large organization has greater opportunity to reduce the risk of competition through diversification of investments or by operating in an industry having a high barrier of entry. In contrast, the small firm may only be able to respond to increased competition by being sharper in its existing operations. If so, the profit plan becomes an invaluable tool in consummating the firm's objectives.

The Requirements for Effective Profit Planning

The planning process has often existed more in form than in content, with a number of unmet requirements explaining the difficulties being encountered. The complexity of profit planning incorporates both conceptual and practical issues, ranging from the behavioral aspects necessary in effectively implementing the plan to the quantification of future events.

Behavioral factors

The primary behavioral concern in formulating the profit plan is the total involvement and commitment of all personnel having access to information that could be instrumental in improving the reliability of the plan. The tendency of most entrepreneurs is to be relatively self-reliant, attempting to structure the company plans single-handedly. Such an approach fails to capture the insight of individuals close to the operational aspects having a bearing upon the company's profitability. In addition, this involvement must be accompanied by effective communications among the respective groups within the company. The provision for instructions and procedures, in an understandable format, should permeate throughout the organization. Otherwise, the entire process is thwarted by lack of appreciation for the import of the profit plan on the part of the employees, which could cause the plan to be completely dysfunctional.

Quantitative requirements

As to the prerequisites that are quantitative in nature, the profit objectives established by the firm's management-owners must not be plagued by generalities. These goals should specifically cite the amounts to be achieved by particular product-service areas and the time frame within which the objectives are to be reached. When feasible, management should establish priorities for the objectives, with the criterion for ranking the individual goals being their contribution to the overall company profitability. Such a priority system should not be construed so as to maximize short-term profits at the expense of long-range earnings. Instead, the profit objectives should extend at least several years into the future, with detailed profit planning being maintained for the forthcoming fiscal year. Only in the context of the enterprise's long-term plans may the short-term goals have any validity. Finally, the key persons within the company should not be averse to changing the objectives as justified. Company needs and priorities change, and these changes should be reflected in the profit plan.

Another primary difficulty in profit planning, particularly in the long-term context, is the availability of data, both historical and futuristic. The source of the data may be classified as internal or external. The principal internal source for the historical data comes from the firm's accounting records or from the use of statistical techniques in sampling from the accounting data. External information might come from trade association publications or governmental documents. As to the information required for future estimates, two complementary resources may be employed. First, management may provide valuable inputs, based on their experience. Second, "scientific techniques" have increasingly been used within the business community, particularly by the executives of large diversified organizations. Such tools as break-even analysis, probability concepts, regression, and simulation are being used with increased frequency by large firms. Certainly, the larger businesses do not have exclusive rights to these techniques. However, seldom do small firms find these quantitative techniques appropriate, although a definite exception to such a disclaimer for quantitative tools for the small firm is the use of break-even analysis.

With respect to the quality of data included in the profit plan, some means for testing the reasonableness of the inputs should be incorporated into the plan. These tests of reasonableness should be performed both in terms of the consideration of alternatives available and the plausibility of the figures. The first requirement, the inclusion of multiple alternatives, stipulates that sufficient options have been considered in arriving at the final decision. After making a particular choice, an in-depth financial analysis should be performed to ascertain if all revenue and cost elements have been appropriately reflected. The examination may be taken from several reference points. First, the projected relationships should be compared with the historical performance of the company. Although differences would be expected, these dissimilarities should be explainable. A second set of benchmarks in effecting the financial analysis may come from competitive data. Information regarding businesses having similar operational characteristics offer significant insight into the acceptability of the data being used in the profit plan. However, for the small closely held concern, this information may be difficult to acquire in that privately owned organizations are extremely reluctant to divulge financial results.

The last requirement for an effective profit plan is the existence of timely and relevant feedback for an indication of the progress being made toward the company's goals. The system should be based on responsibility accounting, providing critical information to the appropriate managers. Only through such a framework may the firm's owners respond to the changing circumstances in a timely fashion.

The Development of the Profit Plan

In actually developing the profit plan, two issues have to be resolved. Who is to be given the responsibility of formulating the plan, and what should the content of the plan entail? For the large firm, the response to the first question generally takes one of two forms. A permanent planning staff may be formed, with the complete efforts of these individuals being restricted to corporate planning. Alternatively, an ad hoc planning committee made up of personnel and management normally concentrating upon other functions may be designated. The first alternative is typically infeasible for the small company. The limited staff within the smaller business simply precludes the allocation of key personnel on a full-time basis to company planning. The planning process via the committee approach, either formally or informally, is more compatible within the small business setting. The nature of the committee depends largely on the organizational structure and the size of the firm. For extremely small companies having only a minimal number of employees, the committee makeup will essentially include all key employees. For the small company having several departments, the committee would involve persons having a leadership function within their department.

With respect to the elements of the profit plan, Table 4-1 sets forth a general outline. The specifics and extent of detail will be somewhat dependent on the length of the planning horizon. However, the general content should be similar whether the perspective of the plan is short-term or long-term. The plan is initiated by establishing the firm's statement of objectives. The time periods could be quarterly if the profit plan is applicable for the forthcoming year or annual for a long-term profit plan. The outline is deceptively easy. In reality, extensive time and effort are required in developing the profit goals.

Having identified the profit objectives, management should explicitly provide the definitions and explanations necessary for establishing the parameters of the planning process (II in Table 4-1). For instance, is the profit plan only to apply to operating income, excluding interest received from securities? Is the asset base used in calculating return on investment to be measured on a replacement value or at book value? What types of constraints are to be imposed to prevent an increase in profits in the current year by excessively sacrificing larger income in later periods? Only by predetermining these factors may the profit-planning process flow smoothly.

The next phase of the plan (III, Table 4-1) is the structuring of the operational plans for the respective departments. This portion of the profit

TABLE 4-1

Profit Plan

I. Statement of operating profit objectives
  A. Indication of profit goals

Time period	Target return on investment	Total investment	Profit objective for period n
1	S%	$UUU	$AAA
2	T%	VVV	BBB
⋮	⋮	⋮	⋮
N	Z%	$ZZZ	$PPP

  B. Explanatory remarks

II. Basic guidelines
    The underlying assumptions being made throughout the profit plan should be identified, e.g., a precise definition of the asset base upon which the profits are to be generated or limitations on acceptable risk levels.

III. Operational plans for each department
  A. Department 1
  B. Department 2
    ⋮
  n. Department n
    1. Identification of alternatives
    2. Revenue and cost estimates for the various alternatives
    3. Selection of a specific option and a corresponding statement of objectives
    4. Plan of action for achieving objectives

IV. Financial plan for the company
  A. Anticipated earnings contribution for each department summarized
  B. Projected capital investments for the departments
  C. Cash budget statement
  D. Proforma profit and loss statement
  E. Proforma balance sheet

V. Management information system
    Establish procedures and timing for analyzing the progress being made toward the stated company objectives.

---

design encourages the personnel closest to the situation to investigate and consider the various alternatives that could potentially contribute to the firm's earning power. From these possible choices, a decision is made as to the alternative offering the largest potential benefit while not violating any basic guidelines established by management. Upon completion of these operational plans, the financial plan (IV in Table 4-1) may then be formulated. This segment of the plan is typically the part receiving the greatest, if not the entire, attention of the decision makers of the organization. However, to do so is an unquestionable mistake in that the quality of the output is completely reliant upon the care taken in the earlier stages of the plan's preparation.

The remaining section of the profit plan, management information systems, is the mechanism for affording seasonable and relevant feedback subsequent ot the initiation of the plan. As frequently noted, the quantity of data should not be the benchmark, but rather the reports should represent information upon which action is required.[1]

With the preceding recommendations for formulating a profit plan, attention could justifiably be directed toward any number of supporting techniques in the profit-planning process. However, the tool having the greatest potential for identifying cost-profit-volume relationships is break-even analysis. For this reason, the next section centers upon the concept and applications of break-even analysis.

Break-Even Analysis

Break-even analysis represents an important tool in profit planning. Basically, the benefit comes from affording the decision maker a means for structuring the key relationships. This technique is readily adaptable to the small firm in that the data requirements and the computational procedures are within the reach of most small firms. In other words, if the management of the small company has developed an effective accounting system and has a thorough grasp of the cost structure within the firm, break-even analysis should be an avenue for better understanding the cost-volume-profit relationships prevailing within the firm.

The concept of break-even analysis

Break-even analysis is familiar to most individuals having even minimal exposure to economics, accounting, or finance. The concept is normally explained and demonstrated by use of an illustration. For instance, Figure 4-1 depicts a typical break-even chart for the data shown in Table 4-2. For this manufacturing entity, five expense categories are set forth, with direct labor and direct materials being defined solely as variable costs. The remaining expenses (factory overhead, administrative expenses, and distribution expenses) envelope both fixed and variable expenses. Assuming the analysis relates to a new product line under consideration, the company ownership

---

[1]Credit for several thoughts presented in these sections should be given to Dale D. McConkey, *Planning Next Year's Profits*, (New York: American Management Association, Inc., 1968), and to Ernest H. Weinwurm and George F. Weinwurm, *Long-Term Profit Planning*, (New York: American Management Association, Inc., 1971).

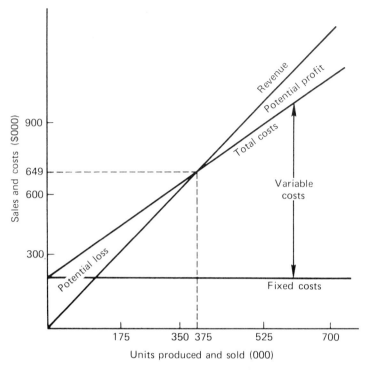

FIGURE 4-1. Break-even chart: Small Manufacturing, Inc.

TABLE 4-2

Price and Cost Data: Small Manufacturing, Inc.

Fixed costs:	
Factory overhead	$100,000
Administrative expenses	75,000
Distribution expenses	80,000
Total fixed costs	$255,000
Variable costs (per unit)	
Direct labor	$ .40
Direct material	.30
Factory overhead	.15
Administrative expenses	.10
Distribution expenses	.10
Total variable cost (per unit)	$1.05
Production capacity	700,000 units
Anticipated sales price per unit	$1.73

may have decided that $1.73 would be an appropriate selling price, given the competitive nature of the product.

Without extensive elaboration, Figure 4-1 graphs company revenue and costs relative to the sales and production level as expressed in units. Visual inspection suggests that the break-even points in units and dollar sales are 375,000 units and approximately $649,000, respectively. As long as the linear functions prevail without any discontinuities in the relationships, these break-even figures may easily be ascertained as follows:

1. a. Break-even in units: defined as the production level in units where revenues equal total costs (fixed and variable) or

   Unit sales price $\times$ Quantity of units sold $=$

   $$\text{Fixed costs} + \text{Unit variable cost} \times \text{Quantity of units sold} \quad (4\text{-}1)$$

   b. Solving for quantity of units sold (produced),

   $$\text{Quantity} = \frac{\text{Fixed costs}}{\text{Unit sales price} - \text{Unit variable cost}} \quad (4\text{-}2)$$

   which for the present example equals

   $$\frac{\$255,000}{\$1.73 - \$1.05} = 375,000 \text{ units}$$

2. a. Break-even in sales dollars: defined as the sales level in dollars where revenues just equal total costs or

   Dollar sales at the break-even point $=$

   $$\text{Fixed costs} + \text{Total variable costs} \quad (4\text{-}3)$$

   b. If the unit variable costs remain constant relative to the sales price, the foregoing equation may be redefined as being

   $$\text{Dollar sales at the break-even point} = \text{Fixed costs} + \left(\frac{\text{Unit variable cost}}{\text{Unit sales price}} \right) \left(\begin{array}{l} \text{Dollar sales at} \\ \text{the break-even} \\ \text{point} \end{array} \right)$$

   $$(4\text{-}4)$$

   c. Restructuring 2.b provides

   $$\text{Dollar sales at the break-even point} = \frac{\text{Fixed costs}}{1 - \dfrac{\text{Unit variable cost}}{\text{Unit sales price}}} \quad (4\text{-}5)$$

   which in the illustration becomes

   $$\frac{\$255,000}{1 - \dfrac{\$1.05}{\$1.73}} = \$648,750$$

The break-even concept from a practical perspective

The foregoing concept of break-even analysis, while being concise on a conceptual basis, is not so clearly definable in practice. The primary reason for this partial "ineptness" of the analysis is the failure of costs to adhere to a well-defined relationship with sales, as suggested by the traditional break-even framework. Figure 4-2 demonstrates two exceptions to the standard format. First, discontinuities in the fixed-cost line may be expected. In other words, fixed costs are generally not the same over the entire range of possible activity levels. As a result of these breaks, more than one break-even point could conceivably develop. In the figure, the break-even points occur both at sales levels *A* and *B*. Additionally, the graph represents decreasing revenues per unit within the upper range of productivity. Thus, a second modification in the usual graphical presentation that more closely represents reality is the change in the slope in the revenue line. In Figure 4-2, the slope of the sales function is reduced slightly at units level *C* and even farther at *D*. An explanation for these gradual reductions in slope might be quantity discounts being offered as large amounts of the product are sold. However, regardless of the impetus, a problem arises as the relationship between sales and variable costs is no longer constant.

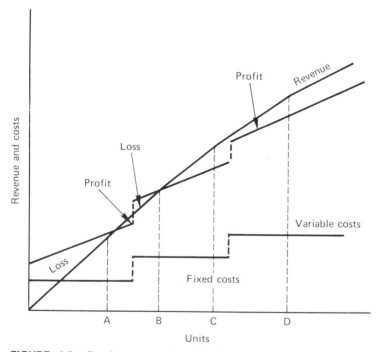

FIGURE 4-2. Break-even graph: violations of conventional analysis

Other measurement problems in constructing the break-even analysis, not shown in Figure 4-2, may be encountered. One such complication arises in the multiproduct case. In a later section, the analysis is examined for determining the cumulative break-even point for more than one product. In this context, the end result is specifically dependent on the underlying assumption regarding the mix of the products comprising the amalgamation. Stated differently, as the product mix is varied the break-even point also changes. Finally, the break-even results are often a function of the accounting process for allocating costs not specifically assignable to an individual product or product line. To illustrate, factory overhead, administrative expenses, and distribution costs typically are not related solely to a particular product, but rather the expenditure is beneficial to several separate product lines. In practice, any material change in the sales for a given product relative to the sales of other product lines usually impacts the benchmark for allocating costs. In turn the break-even point is altered.

Uses of break-even analysis

The potential applications of break-even analysis are both far-reaching and diverse. However, in the profit-planning context, three primary uses are easily recognizable.

1. *Measurement of the responsiveness of operating profits to sales changes.* The basic concept being examined in this type of investigation is the *business risk* of the firm in total or with respect to an individual product. As frequently noted, business risk is defined as the variability of the company's return on assets and is quantitatively measured by the *degree of operating leverage*. Break-even analysis affords invaluable information regarding the firm's level of business risk. Such data are particularly meaningful for the small business concern in light of the generally greater risks imposed upon the small firm relative to the large organization. In view of its importance, this facet of break-even analysis is deferred until a later section offering a further explanation of operating leverage.

2. *Evaluation of new product decisions.* Break-even analysis in this frame of reference seeks to facilitate the investigation of a new product by two means: (1) identify relationships that enhance the business executive's ability to estimate the revenues and expenses relating to the project and (2) determine, subject to the inherent approximations, the level of sales required for reaching the profitability break-even point. In the present illustration, the desirability of the project would depend on the company owners' expectations of the spread between sales and the break-even point of 375,000 units, frequently defined as the *margin of safety*. Although the difference between sales and costs may be negligible or even negative during the early years of the investment, the final decision should rest primarily upon the net present value of the benefits generated throughout the life of the investment.

3. *Examination of the impact of a general expansion in company operations.* For the small growth firm, the feasibility of an expansion is a never-

ending question. In this regard, the requirement for computing the break-even point in terms of sales dollars rather than units should become apparent. Essentially, the break-even analysis may be constructed in terms of units only for a single-product evaluation. For multiple products, the volume measurement must be expressed in units that are additive, which requires relying upon dollar sales. Hence, the simultaneous ability to compute break-even points in terms of both units and dollars, as done in Figure 4-1, does not exist in the total firm context. Accordingly, for graphical representation of the break-even point, the horizontal axis of Figure 4-1 would have to be converted from units of production to dollar sales.

While the determination of a dollar break-even point is beneficial in analyzing the sensitiveiy of the aggregate company profits to an expansion, the computations are at times difficult to derive. The problem comes from the variable costs being a function of different influences. For example, variable manufacturing costs relate more precisely to the production level, as compared to selling expenses being correlated with sales dollars. Hence, the accuracy of a dollar break-even analysis depends on the closeness in fit of the average variable expenses to the sales dollars. The estimation process for determining this fit may take one of several forms. In its simplest form, the fixed costs are identified, with any remaining expenses assumed to be variable. At the other extreme, satistical analysis may be employed for segregating the key relationships.[2]

Operating Leverage

An integral part of the informational content of break-even analysis relates to the sensitivity of operating profits to an increase or decrease in sales. In other words, if sales change 1 percent, what may we expect to be the consequence in terms of the variation in operating earnings? The answer to this question depends on the fixed-variable cost relationship existing within the firm, that being *operating leverage*, and represents a partial indication of the business risk being incurred by the company. Figure 4-3 offers a natural flow of the interpretation of operating leverage.

As observed in Figure 4-3, *business risk*, the counterpart to profitability, is the basic phenomenon being analyzed via operating leverage. If the variability in the firm's return on investment is deemed to be an indicator of business risk, the identification of the causes for such volatility becomes an

[2]For an indication of the possible options for approximating variable and fixed costs, see Carl L. Moore and Robert K. Jaedicke, *Managerial Accounting*, 3rd ed., (Cincinnati: South-Western, 1972), Chapter 10.

inportant issue. Figure 4-3 cites two inherent causes for business risk, these being changes in the level of sales and operating leverage. (The assumption is being made that asset size is held constant.) Certainly as sales rise and fall, the profitability of the firm would be expected to move in a like direction. However, the relative magnitude of the responsiveness of profits will vary depending on the operating leverage being utilized by the company owners, with *operating leverage* being defined as the use of fixed operating costs to magnify a change in profits relative to a given change in sales. To illustrate, assume that sales for Lyttle Corporation increase from $100,000 to $120,000, representing a 20 percent rise. If all related costs are variable with respect to sales, an equal percentage change may be expected in profits. For instance, if variable costs equal 70 percent of sales, with no fixed costs being encountered, the profits would be enlarged from $30,000 to $36,000, which again represents a 20 percent change. On the negative side, if sales decrease, profits should be diminished by a like percent.

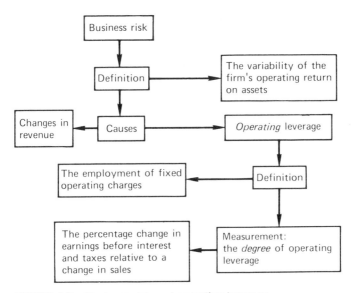

FIGURE 4-3. Business risk and operating leverage

If, however, the total costs for Lyttle involve both fixed and variable expenses, a certain percentage change in sales would result in an even greater modification in profits. Returning to the illustration, if the cost makeup is $35,000 in fixed expenses and 35 percent variable costs, the previous 20 percent change in sales would produce a 43 percent deviation in operating profits. This earnings change is determined as follows:

					Percent increase
Sales		$100,000		$120,000	20%
Expenses:					
Fixed	$35,000		$35,000		
Variable	35,000	70,000	42,000	77,000	
Profits		$ 30,000		$ 43,000	43%

Thus, the use of fixed operating costs yields greater variability in profits as the firm's sales move. If the economy has improved significantly, the use of operating leverage has a favorable impact upon profits. In contrast, if a downturn in the economy occurs, extensive operating leverage can be materially detrimental to profits.

The concept of operating leverage is quantified in terms of the *degree of operating leverage*. This term is defined as the percentage change in operating profits resulting from a 1 percent change in sales. In other words,

$$\text{Degree of operating leverage (DOL)} = \frac{\left(\dfrac{\text{Increase in operating profits}}{\text{Operating profits}} \right)}{\left(\dfrac{\text{Increase in sales}}{\text{Sales}} \right)}$$

As evident from the calculation, a base sales level must be specified prior to calculating DOL. In fact, the degree of operating leverage is not constant but rather is greater at sales levels close to the break-even point. As would be expected, a 1 percent change in sales near the break-even point produces a large percentage impact upon the small profits.

The actual computation of the DOL for the Lyttle Corporation at the $100,000 sales level under the two assumptions would be

$$\text{All variable costs:} \frac{\dfrac{\$16,000}{\$30,000}}{\dfrac{\$20,000}{\$100,000}} = 1.000$$

$$\text{Variable cost of 35\% plus \$35,000 fixed costs:} \frac{\dfrac{\$13,000}{\$30,000}}{\dfrac{\$20,000}{\$100,000}} = 2.167$$

As would be expected, a DOL of 1.0 prevails when all costs are variable, indicating that a 1 percent change in sales yields an equivalent 1 percent shift in operating profits. However, when the costs involve $35,000 in fixed expenses and a 35 percent variable costs/sales ratio, a 2.167 percent variation in operating income ensues from a 1 percent change in sales.

In summary, operating leverage is an important concept in finance, with the underlying measurement being reflective of the business risk associated with an individual project, an expansion, or an entire firm. The operating leverage premise is definitely germane for any management team. However, the investors and managers of the small firm frequently fail to make any serious effort to analyze carefully the risk inherent in the business. Although the subjective element in the decision-making process continues to be important for managers, regardless of the size of the enterprise, executives in small organizations all too often rely excessively upon their "gut feel." The operating leverage concept affords the management of a small company an instrument for systematically evaluating the riskiness of an investment.

Summary

Several reasons may be given for the need of profit planning within the small company. A key issue faced by small firms is the need for direction. A profit plan, if appropriately employed, offers such guidance, including a means for motivating empolyees. Second, the plan provides a natural avenue for communications between the owners-managers and the personnel within the business. Last, the profit plan is a meaningful response to increased competition for the small business entity. However, for these benefits to be realized, the construction and implementation of the plan has to be undertaken with care. Numerous requirements, as identified in this chapter, have to be met in order to ensure a reasonable probability of success.

The content of the profit plan would vary from company to company. Yet, one possible format would be the inclusion of (1) profit objectives by product and/or service areas and for the firm in total, (2) operational strategies, (3) financial plans, and (4) intermittent feedback associated with the progress being made. In developing these elements of the profit plan, several approaches may be taken in performing the analysis. A key technique used in this regard is break-even analysis. Although some difficulty may be encountered in actually making the application in practice, the benefit in terms of increased understanding of the profit-cost relationships is significant.

QUESTIONS

1. List three reasons why profit planning is important to the firm.

2. What are the two extreme concepts of profit planning that one is likely to encounter in actual practice?

3. What effect, if any, do behavioral factors have upon profit planning?

4. List the primary sources of historical and future information that would be useful for profit planning.

5. Why have smaller firms traditionally ignored formal profit planning?

6. What are the basic assumptions of traditional break-even analysis?

7. What uses would a firm have for break-even analysis?

8. What limitations are associated with break-even analysis?

9. What is operating leverage?

10. Briefly explain how operating leverages can be used to predict changes in operating profits.

PROBLEMS

4-1. Kilo Corporation processes sugar beets into refined sugar. Administrative salaries, insurance, rent and depreciation are considered to be fixed in amount and annually total $300,000. Kilo sells its sugar for $.24 per pound, and incurs labor costs of $.04 per pound. The beets are processed in such a manner that the cost of beets to Kilo is about $.12 per pound of refined sugar. Find the break-even point for Kilo Corporation in terms of pounds of sugar, both graphically and algebraically.

4-2. Amalgamated Widgetworks, Incorporated (AWI) is a medium-sized manufacturer of widgets. Each widget requires two pounds of raw material and twenty minutes of machine time, including start-up and take-down time. AWI has a long term contract for the purchase of its raw materials and can obtain any amount it needs at $.50 per pound. Machine operators are paid $4.50 per hour, and are paid double-time for any hours in excess of 40 per week. The labor market is such that AWI can use workers for less than a full week, if necessary. AWI has an average of fifty machines available for production. Fixed costs amount to $10,000 per week.

AWI has developed a very narrowly-defined market over the years, and this market will absorb up to 5000 widgets per week, at a price of $5 per widget. A foreign buyer has agreed to purchase additional widgets at a rate of $3 each, but AWI will sell only after they have satisfied the domestic market. Find the break-even point (or points).

4-3. Last year, XYZ Corporation had sales of $4,000,000 and operating profit of $200,000. This year, profits rose to $400,000 on sales of $5,000,000. What is the implied degree of operating leverage?

4-4. a. Using the information in problem #1 (above), calculate the degree of operating leverage for Kilo Corporation, assuming that the firm is producing and selling 6,250,000 lbs. of sugar.

b. What should the level of operating profit be if sales increase by 10%?

4-5. Nonstandard Oil Company had sales last year of $200 million, and operating profits of $30 million. The company has a corporate goal of 12% growth in operating profits each year. If the firm has a current degree of operating leverage of 3.0, what sales level will have to be achieved for the firm to reach its goal?

chapter 5

FORECASTING
ASSET REQUIREMENTS

The preceding chapter centered upon the profit-planning mechanism for the small business concern. An immediate follow-up question after determining the firm's future profitability concerns the potential stipulation for further investments in the organization. If the amount of profits is relatively static, only a minimal investment commitment is incurred, that being in terms of replacement expenditures. However, if significantly larger profits are anticipated, it is only reasonable to expect the operation to face major obligations in the form of incremental asset requirements. Consequently, moderate to large increases in earnings impose a concurrent need for additional financing, possibly exceeding the company's ability for generating funds from operations.

The Financial-Forecasting Process

The departure point for forecasting a firm's asset size and the corresponding financial requirements is the determination of the expected sales levels during the planning horizon. Essentially, the firm's underlying asset base is largely a function of the enterprise's sales volume. The operation of any business other than an extremely simplistic arrangement (e.g., an independent salesman distributing products on a consignment basis) requires a substantial investment in assets. Simply stated, an enterprising small businessman cannot expect to produce sales of $5 million without a major commitment to asset purchase. Thus, a reasonably close relationship exists between sales and assets, and management should expect to function within this latitude. Accordingly, the growth rate in the company's sales governs the increase in assets, which in turn dictates the financial requirements of the organization.

After projecting a business entity's sales during the planning horizon, the relationships between sales and the respective asset categories can then be approximated. With these estimates, a projection of the required asset level may be made. With the foregoing information, and with supplemental analysis, the financial needs of the business should become relatively evident. Hence, three phases are involved in forecasting the company's financial requirements: (1) ascertain the sales volume to be expected within the planning horizon, (2) estimate the asset base necessary to support the projected sales activities, and (3) determine the potential sources for financing the incremental investment in assets. As to the methodology for forecasting these variables, a variety of techniques is available.

Forecasting Techniques: State of the Art

A large number of forecasting techniques are available to the firm's management, with the appropriate choice being a function of the nature of the problem. The following presentation, while certainly not intended to be all inclusive, simply highlights the more popular types of forecasting tools.

Regression

Regression methods attempt to explain or predict movements in a dependent variable, such as sales, on the basis of its relationship with an independent variable, possibly advertising. The result is an equation derived by finding a linear line that best fits the data. Thus, the equation is merely a linear expression of the *predicted value* of the dependent variable in light of the value of the independent variable. This analysis is widely used and is frequently effective for short- and medium-term forecasting requirements. However, its success naturally depends on the strength of the relationship between the two variables. *Multiple regression* is used when a strong predictive relationship exists between a dependent variable and two or more independent variables. Both types of regression are explained in greater detail later in the chapter.[1]

Exponential smoothing

One of the simplest forecasting methods is that of the *moving average*. In its most basic form, a moving average is calculated each time period by deleting the earliest values and adding the lastest ones. Thus, the average changes over time with changes in the underlying data. As a result of its nature the technique generally requires a large data base and offers little flexibility in giving more recognition to more recent events. Accordingly,

[1]See Richard C. Clelland, Francis E. Brown, John S. deCani, J. Parker Brusk and Donald S. Murray, *Basic Statistics with Business Applications* (New York: John Wiley and Sons, 1966), pp. 418-470.

exponential smoothing enables a user to avoid the necessity of maintaining all the information which goes into the calculation of the average. Thus, inputs into the model are greatly reduced. Furthermore, more recent data points are given greater weight than old data. A common expression of the basic rule of exponential smoothing is given as:

$$\text{New average} = X \text{ (new information)} + (1 - X)(\text{old average}), \qquad (5\text{-}1)$$

where X is a fraction known as the *smoothing constant*. The primary application of this method is in short-term forecasting. However, the tool also has moderate capabilities for recognizing seasonal and cyclical variation in long-term forecasting.[2]

Box-Jenkins method

A newer technique, known as the *Box-Jenkins method*, is primarily limited to short-term forecasts. This methodology does not actually develop a forecast itself, but enables the user to identify the technique which would be most useful in deriving the forecast. By combining the best features of the *moving average* with another time series technique, *autoregression*, a special case of regression is developed where the independent variable is a prior value of the dependent variable. The result is the development of a model which is *optimal* for the problem being considered. For example, the use of the Box-Jenkins approach might ultimately result in a forecast via exponential smoothing, but the selection process in this instance is based on a rational, structured approach to the development of the most suitable model, rather than by an arbitrary trial-and-error approach.[3]

Econometrics

The most widely known econometric models are those used to estimate national economic factors, especially the Gross National Product (GNP). Basically, in predicting the GNP, a series of equations are developed from regression analyses, representing the variables in the economy and the relationships among these influences. The equations are then solved simultaneously for the key variables, such as GNP or consumer spending. These models may be extremely complex. For example, the econometric systems of the Wharton School of Finance and the Brookings Institute contain hundreds of equations. However, simpler models can be used to forecast less complex

[2]See Robert G. Brown, "Less Risk in Inventory Estimates," *Harvard Business Review* (July–August, 1959), pp. 104–115.
[3]See Vincent A. Mabert and Robert G. Radcliffe, "Forecasting—A Systematic Modeling Methodology," *Financial Management* (Autumn, 1974), pp. 59–67.

variables, such as sales for a firm. Even so, this method in its simplest context is quite complicated, and its application is difficult and expensive for the majority of small- or medium-sized firms. Yet, if economically feasible, econometric modeling may prove to be relatively accurate in its results.[4]

Input-output analysis

The input-output model is a specific application of matrix algebra, and is used to identify transactions between economic sectors and to determine the magnitude of such transactions. Each activity in the sector has only one primary input and only one primary output. The output may be a final product or an intermediate product serving as an input for other sectors. If the assumption is made that the basic input-output relationships between activities will remain constant in the future, forecasts can be obtained as to the amount of each activity's output required to reach a specified goal. The model can then be used to stimulate different situations by varying the inputs of the activities in the model. Alternatively, by specifying a desired result, the necessary inputs can be generated. Input-output analysis has been used for modeling several national economies, and is most useful for medium- to long-term planning.[5]

Delphi method

The previous techniques have at least one common factor, their quantitative nature. However, meaningful *qualitative analyses* are available. In this regard, a relatively flexible method which lends itself to all types of time frames and situations is the *Delphi method*. This technique draws on the collective opinions of a panel of experts, each of whom is queried apart from the other members of the panel. A series of questionnaires are normally used, and the responses to each question form the basis for each succeeding questionaire, thereby developing consensus or a range of opinions for use in forecasting expected events.[6]

The preceding overview of forecasting techniques, while recognizably limited in scope, hopefully serves to stimulate interest in the almost unlimited options available for forecasting purposes. However, at this point more information is to be provided regarding two specific approaches: (1) the percent-of-sales method, and (2) regression.

[4]See Steven C. Wheelwright and Spyros Makridakis, *Forecasting Methods for Management*, (New York: Wiley, 1973), pp. 135–140.
[5]See John Leslie Livingstone, "Input-Output Analysis for Cost Accounting, Planning and Control," *The Accounting Review* (January, 1969), pp. 48–64.
[6]See Steven C. Wheelwright and Spyros Madridakis, *Forecasting Methods for Management*, (New York: Wiley, 1973), pp. 88–89.

Percent of Sales Method

As indicated earlier, the most important determinant in projecting a firm's asset requirements and the corresponding financial needs is the anticipated sales level during the company's planning horizon. The sales projection may come from one of several sources, although most frequently in small businesses, this sales estimation comes from an informal, if not haphazard, "guesstimate" on the part of the company's owners. Ideally, such a figure will come through the firm's profit-planning mechanism, in which the *budgets* from each department are summarized to develop a company-wide profit plan. Alternatively, or even in conjunction with the profit plan, statistical forecasting techniques could be employed. More specifically, regression analysis may prove to be quite beneficial in forecasting sales. Since this process is explained in the next section, we shall defer the discussion regarding the sales forecast, assuming that management has by some means developed the sales forecast.

Recognizing the tendency of sales and assets to follow a similar pattern and the inclination for certain sources of financing also to be responsive to changes in sales, a natural approach for forecasting financial requirements is the *percent of sales method*. This method portrays the firm's assets and selected liabilities as a percent of sales. Given a sales projection, these percentages may be applied to the *change in sales* to estimate the expected modifications in the asset/liability balances. As an example, financial data for Lyttle Corporation are provided in Table 5-1. Although the company incurred a loss in 1977, the problem areas have been corrected, and a 10 percent after-tax profit margin is expected to be achieved in 1978 on a projected sales level of $910,000, representing a sales increase of $149,230. The present policy of the company is to pay 50 percent of the after-tax earnings in dividends. However, if possible, the annual dividends are not permitted to fall below $40,000.

With the information set forth in Table 5-1 and the foregoing profit/dividend expectations, projections may be made regarding the future asset levels and certain counterbalancing financial sources. Table 5-2 isolates the assets and liabilities that could be expected to vary with sales and reflects these accounts as a percentage of sales. Specifically, for the past three years, cash, accounts receivable, inventories, fixed assets, and other assets have been maintained at a relatively constant percent of sales. Deferred taxes and investments have not been sensitive to changes in sales and are not included in the computations. In addition, accounts payable and accrued expenses generally represent sources of financing that vary closely with sales. For Lyttle Corporation, these two sources are quite large relative to sales and have even increased in importance on a relative basis during the most recent three years. Adding taxes payable to accounts payable and accrued expenses,

Lyttle Corporation

Financial Statements

1968–1977

	1968	1969	1970	1971	1972	1973	1974	1975	1976	1977
Assets										
Current assets:										
Cash	$ 52,220	$ 68,300	$ 73,215	$ 91,806	$105,001	$100,892	$ 94,430	$ 75,767	$ 85,383	$ 91,300
Accounts receivable	114,420	89,320	95,263	125,032	180,100	129,285	145,704	175,104	183,425	192,430
Inventories	129,460	117,973	102,563	165,010	231,300	213,245	259,934	305,318	316,205	347,018
Deferred taxes	9,470	7,438	4,356	-0-	-0-	-0-	641	26,640	27,018	-0-
Property, plant, & equip.	73,970	74,370	75,460	130,034	131,200	150,092	187,592	247,843	282,437	271,627
Investments	7,976	20,380	33,780	3,041	5,608	4,508	6,765	4,008	84,509	93,974
Other assets	13,460	24,616	19,523	13,320	7,432	16,626	13,352	29,250	31,372	28,651
Total assets	$ 400,976	$ 402,397	$ 404,160	$ 528,243	$ 660,641	$ 614,648	$ 708,418	$ 863,930	$ 1,010,349	$ 1,025,000
Liabilities and Stockholder's Equity										
Accounts payable	$ 87,956	$ 91,286	$ 61,233	$144,281	$152,642	$148,116	$184,179	$278,341	$ 315,947	$ 366,656
Accrued expenses	22,809	5,139	39,370	50,632	56,322	50,263	68,849	68,420	94,182	115,885
Taxes payable	4,761	6,895	4,123	4,341	4,366	5,509	11,670	9,784	7,726	3,821
Notes payable	55,547	24,875	6,213	4,988	83,320	16,572	-0-	-0-	34,270	3,070
Total liabilities	$ 171,073	$ 128,195	$ 110,939	$ 204,242	$ 296,650	$ 220,460	$ 264,698	$ 356,545	$ 452,125	$ 489,432
Stockholder's equity:										
Capital stock	$ 37,460	$ 39,109	$ 39,271	$ 40,960	$ 42,240	$ 42,328	$ 45,167	$ 48,911	$ 49,479	$ 49,659
Paid-in capital	93,967	96,840	97,360	100,341	101,320	104,137	114,736	128,494	129,529	128,639
Retained earnings	98,476	138,253	156,590	182,700	220,431	247,723	283,817	329,980	379,216	357,270
Total equity	$ 229,903	$ 274,202	$ 293,221	$ 324,001	$ 363,991	$ 394,188	$ 443,720	$ 507,385	$ 558,224	$ 535,568
Total liabilities and equity	$ 400,976	$ 402,397	$ 404,160	$ 528,243	$ 660,641	$ 614,648	$ 708,418	$ 863,930	$ 1,010,349	$ 1,025,000
Sales	$ 375,000	$ 340,000	$ 320,000	$ 547,440	$ 647,070	$ 603,310	$ 640,770	$ 691,370	$ 747,690	$ 760,770

TABLE 5-2

Lyttle Corporation

Balance Sheet as a Percent of Sales

	1977	1976	1975	3 Year average
Assets				
Current assets:				
Cash	12.0%	11.4%	10.9%	11.4%
Accounts receivable	25.3	24.5	25.3	25.0
Inventories	45.6	42.3	44.4	44.0
Deferred taxes	NA[1]	NA	NA	NA
Property, plant, & equip.	35.7	37.8	35.8	36.4
Investments	NA	NA	NA	NA
Other assets	3.8	4.2	4.2	4.1
Total assets	122.4%	120.2%	120.4%	120.9%
Liabilities and Stockholder's Equity				
Accounts payable	48.2%	42.3%	40.3%	43.6%
Accrued expenses	15.2	12.6	9.9	12.6
Taxes payable	.5	1.0	1.4	1.0
Notes payable	NA	NA	NA	NA
Total liabilities	63.9%	55.9%	51.6%	57.2%
Stockholder's equity	NA	NA	NA	NA
Total liabilities and equity	63.9%	55.9%	51.6%	57.2%

[1]NA = not applicable.

we find that these three sources jointly represented 63.9 percent of sales in 1977 and average 57.2 percent for the 1975–1977 time period.

In projecting the company requirements, the results of Table 5-2 suggest that approximately $1.21 (three-year average) must be expended for assets for each $1.00 increase in sales. This amount does not reflect any changes in the investments and deferred-taxes accounts. Only by knowing the objectives of management with respect to company investment and the firm's accounting practices may these items be projected. Thus, for our purposes these accounts are disregarded. If sales do increase by $149,230 during 1978, the expansion in the company's assets, excluding investments and deferred taxes, should approximate $180,568 ($149,230×$1.21). The financing of these assets will come partly through the "spontaneous" sources of financing, which for Lyttle should be approximately 57.2 percent of sales. These sources should facilitate the asset growth by providing $83,360 ($149,230×$.572), requiring $95,208 to come from profits less any dividend payments and external financing. The funds generated internally after the 50 percent dividend payment should further decrease the financial requirements by $45,500 ($910,000 sales × a 10 percent profit margin × a 50 percent earnings retention rate), leaving $49,708 to be acquired by new financing. This remaining amount would have to come from debt or from issuing common stock if the firm has access to the equity markets. In summary, the percent of sales approach affords relevant information for forecasting asset requirements. Although not done in the current illustration, a proforma balance sheet could easily be constructed from the relationships being identified. Finally, the strength of the percent of sales method primarily relates to short- and intermediate-term forecasting. Since this technique implicitly assumes that the asset/liability sales relationship will remain constant, the accuracy of the results tends to dissipate in the long-term context. Accordingly, regression analysis would appear to be more applicable as the firm's planning horizon is lengthened.

Regression

Another approach to forecasting the asset and financial requirements for the firm is regression analysis. This technique would appear quite appropriate for the small business entity in that the level of sophistication would typically result in a material improvement in the accuracy of forecasts; also, the costs are reasonable and should be within an acceptable price range for many small business concerns. The only possible constraint that might prohibit the small firm's application of regression is the necessity for adequate historical data. For instance, a minimum of eight years of annual data would be essential in constructing the simplest possible forecast.

Regression analysis is a statistical model having as its primary objective the identification of the relationship between two or more quantitative variables. Although the technique specifies the historical comovement between variables, no suggestion of causal relationships is intended. The tool simply notes the *statistical* relationships but affords no proof of cause and effect. Only through an understanding of the phenomena represented by the variables may a judgment be made as to whether the events are related causally. The statistical analysis, however, does provide insight for the analyst in supporting a conviction regarding the existence of a cause-and-effect relationship between the variables selected for investigation.

The regression methodology is generally separated into two components for presentation purposes. A bivariate inquiry is defined as *simple regression*, representing the application of regression to two variables, one dependent and one independent. If, however, the variability of a certain factor is only nominally related to a single independent variable, the need for *multiple regression* may exist.

Simple regression

The attempt to estimate the value of a dependent variable as a function of a second variable stipulates that the relationship between the two variables be estimated either graphically or by deriving a mathematical equation that quantitatively sets forth the interaction. The first approach has come to be known as a *scatter diagram*, while the mathematical equation is termed a *least-squares regression line*.

scatter diagram

As the name implies, the scatter diagram simply graphs the two variables relative to each other. Drawing upon the accounting information for Lyttle Corporation, as contained in Table 5-1, a scatter diagram for sales and accounts receivable is depicted in Figure 5-1. The distribution of the observations in the figure offers an indication as to the functional relationship between the two variables. The line drawn through the points in the exhibit is a geometric representation of a linear equation that "best fits" the data by visual inspection. Thus, if sales in the forthcoming year have been projected to be $850,000, the investment in accounts receivable should be approximately $200,000.

The scatter diagram is particularly useful in two instances. First, if the relationship can be easily identified visually, the additional time and effort to compute an equation may not be warranted. Second, and more importantly, the visual examination assists in the choice of the most appropriate form of the mathematical function, that being linear versus curvilinear.

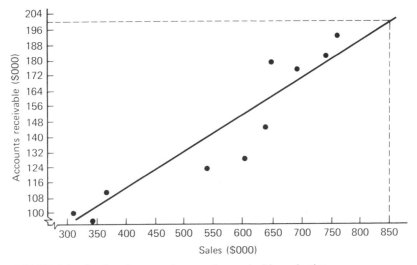

FIGURE 5-1. Scatter diagram of accounts receivable and sales

the regression line

In graphically positioning a line through the data comprising the scatter diagram, the purpose is to specify a function that best fits the observed points. In this regard, the *best fit* is defined as the equation that minimizes the sum of the squared differences between the regression line and the observations. For the linear regression estimation, the form of the equation is

$$Y_i = \alpha + \beta X_i + \varepsilon_i \qquad (5\text{-}2)$$

where Y_i = value of the dependent variable for the ith observation,
α = predicted value of Y when X equals 0,
β = predicted change in Y relative to a unit change in X.
X_i = value of the predictor variable,
ε_i = random error term for which $E(\varepsilon_i) = 0$.

In this format, the dispersion from the regression line would be measured by the error term as

$$\varepsilon_i = Y_i - (\alpha + \beta X_i) \qquad (5\text{-}3)$$

The minimization objective is accomplished by jointly computing the α and β terms that minimize Φ, the sum of the squared deviations, where

$$\Phi = \sum_{i=1}^{n} (Y_i - \alpha - \beta X_i)^2 \qquad (5\text{-}4)$$

For this objective, the parameters, α and β, may be calculated directly as follows:

$$\beta = \frac{\sum_{i=1}^{n} (X_i - \bar{X})(Y_i - \bar{Y})}{\sum_{i=1}^{n} (X_i - \bar{X})^2} \qquad (5\text{-}5)$$

$$\alpha = \frac{1}{n} \left(\sum_{i=1}^{n} Y_i - \beta \sum_{i=1}^{n} X_i \right) \qquad (5\text{-}6)$$

While the foregoing computations are relatively straightforward and represent standard output in most computer packages, several limitations of the regression model should be recognized as affecting the validity of the results. All too often these conditions are ignored, thereby causing one to rely completely upon the robustness of the model. These assumptions may be cited as follows:

1. The model is assumed to have been correctly specified, with the *linear* function adequately describing the relationship between Y and X.
2. The dependent variable is assumed to be normally distributed.
3. An assumption is made that homoscedasticity, or equal variance for all variables, prevails.
4. The independent variable is defined as being fixed or predetermined, as opposed to being random. This condition frequently does not apply. However, since no inference is generally made regarding the independent variable, this violation would not appear to be serious.
5. The error term is assumed to be normally distributed with an expected value of zero.

Reliability of forecast

Any number of tests may be performed for drawing inference as to the predictability of the foregoing regression model. Two such analytical measurements are the *coefficient of determination* and the *standard error of the estimate*. The coefficient of determination is associated with the correlation coefficient, which may be expressed as

$$r_{jk} = \frac{\text{cov}(X_j, X_k)}{\sigma_j \sigma_k} \tag{5-7}$$

where r_{jk} is a measure of the degree of association between the variables j and k, $\text{cov}(X_j, X_k)$ is the covariance between the two variables, and σ_j denotes the standard deviation for variable j. The value of the correlation coefficient varies from -1.0 to $+1.0$, with -1.0 reflecting a perfectly inverse linear relationship and $+1.0$ denoting a perfectly positive association. An r_{jk} of $.0$ indicates that the variation of variable j is completely independent of the variability of variable k.

The relationship between variables can be further depicted by examining the variation of the dependent variable associated with the dispersion of the independent variable, which may be measured by the coefficient of determination, r_{jk}^2. The total variation of the response variable may be measured as the *total sum of squares*, $\Sigma_{j=1}^n (Y_j - \bar{Y})^2$. If there is a perfect linear relationship between Y and X, in which $(Y|X) = E(Y|X)$ for all X, all values for Y would lie on the regression line, and the *associated sum of squares*, $\Sigma_{j=1}^n (Y_{jc} - \bar{Y})^2$, would equal the total sum of squares. (Y_{jc} represents the *calculated value* for Y from the regression equation for the jth observation.) In this case, the *unassociated sum of squares*, $\Sigma_{j=1}^n (Y_j - Y_{jc})^2$, would equal zero. Furthermore, when the $Y:X$ relationship is not perfect, certain values of

$(Y|X)$ are not equal to $E(Y|X)$, and the unassociated sum of squares would be greater than zero. Accordingly, a measurement of the degree of association is defined as

$$r_{jk}^2 = \frac{\text{Associated sum of squares}}{\text{Total sum of squares}} = \frac{\sum\limits_{j=1}^{n} \left(Y_{jc} - \overline{Y} \right)^2}{\sum\limits_{j=1}^{n} \left(Y_j - \overline{Y} \right)^2} \tag{5-8}$$

which is termed the coefficient of determination and identifies the percentage of variation in Y that may be associated with X.

A second indicator of the reliability of the regression line as a prediction model is the *standard error of the estimate*. Similar to the standard deviation statistic in a univariate analysis, the standard error of the estimate is a measure of dispersion. However, the latter statistic depicts the variability about the regression line rather than the dispersion around the expected value. An unbiased estimate of this statistic, σ_{YX}, may be computed as follows:

$$\sigma_{YX} = \sqrt{\sum\limits_{j=1}^{n} \frac{(Y_j - Y_{jc})^2}{n-2}} \tag{5-9}$$

The interpretation of σ_{YX} may best be demonstrated by an example. Assume that sales have been predicted for next year via a regression model, resulting in a projected $100,000, with the standard error of estimate being $10,000. If the prediction errors are independent and distributed normally about the regression line, confidence intervals may be specified. For instance, approximately two-thirds of the time the sales estimate should fall between $90,000 and $110,000 ($\pm$$10,000 from the predicted value), and a 95 percent confidence level may be assigned to the $80,000–$120,000 interval.[7]

Simple regression: an illustration

Returning to Lyttle Corporation, the simple regression model may be employed for projecting the firm's sales for the forthcoming 1978. Additionally, the asset accounts, accounts payable, and accrued expenses may be regressed against sales. With these regression equations and the estimated sales in hand, the asset requirements for 1978 as well as the financial needs may be approximated.

In forecasting sales, one of several predictor variables could be used. However, the management of the company anticipates the historical increases

---

[7]The 67 percent and 95 percent confidence levels are taken from a normal probability distribution table.

in sales to continue and considers the extrapolation of the sales trend line over time to be the most important single independent variable. Regressing sales relative to time yields the following characteristic line:

$$S_{ct} = \$286,704 + \$51,024 X_i$$

where S_{ct} = the *calculated* sales in period t as estimated by the trend line,
X_i = an integer designating the year number, with $1968 = 1, \ldots, 1977 = 10$.

Thus, the projected sales for 1978 would be

$$S_c(11) = \$286,704 + \$51,024(11) = \$847,068$$

As to the confidence that could be assigned to this estimate, the standard error of the estimate is $65,025, indicating that two-thirds of the time we could expect sales to be within the $782,943–$912,993 range. Thus, management's previously quoted $910,000 sales for 1978 is quite doubtful if the trend line provided by the previous year's sales is indicative of the future.

As to forecasting the balance sheet items relative to sales, Table 5-3 depicts the regression equations when the relevant asset/liability accounts are regressed against sales. As with the percent of sales method, the difference between the change in total assets and the increase in the spontaneous sources indicates the amount to be financed either internally or externally.

TABLE 5-3

Lyttle Corporation

Regression Equation for
Asset/Liability: Sales Relationships[1]

Independent Variable: Sales

Dependent variable	=	α + (β)	$\begin{pmatrix} Projected \\ sales \end{pmatrix}$ =	$\begin{pmatrix} Calculated \\ value \end{pmatrix}$	Standard error of the estimate
Cash	=	$47,537 + (.0639)	($847,968) =	$101,722	$13,100
Accounts receivable	=	4,532 + (.2386)	(847,968) =	206,857	13,520
Inventories	=	−70,657 + (.5102)	(847,968) =	361,976	25,320
Fixed assets	=	−91,906 + (.4484)	(847,968) =	288,323	34,640
Total assets				$958,878	
Accounts payable	=	−13,111 + (.4790)	(847,968) =	393,066	50,090
Accrued expenses	=	−4,080 + (.1727)	(847,968) =	142,364	15,650
Spontaneous sources				$535,430	

[1] Accounts are omitted if no relationship exists with sales or if the account is insignificantly small. For example, investments are apparently independent of sales and other assets, and deferred taxes represent only a small percentage of total assets.

With the simple regression analysis, the assets bearing a relationship with sales would be forecasted to be $958,878, an increase of $56,503 from the balance at the conclusion of 1977. Furthermore, the anticipated change in the spontaneous sources of financing from 1977 to 1978 would be $535,430 less $482,541, or $52,889. Hence, the additional funding required is only $3,614, which may easily be met through the retention of profits.

Multiple linear regression

The regression equation and correlation estimates in the preceding section may be employed to identify the statistical association between two variables. If a strong relationship prevails between the response variable and a single predictor variable, a bivariate regression function affords a meaningful estimation of this interaction. However, most generally the explanation of the dispersion for a given variable requires the simultaneous examination of two or more independent variables. The multiple linear regression model provides such a mechanism. The technique restricts the functional relationship to be linear in terms of the equation parameters, with the general format of the equation appearing as follows:

$$Y_i = \alpha + \beta_1 X_{1i} + \beta_2 X_{2i} + \ldots + \beta_n X_{ni} + \varepsilon_i \tag{5-10}$$

where α and the β's represent the parameters of the linear regression of Y on the X_i's and ε_i continues to denote the random error term. As with the bivariate analysis, α is the point of intercept on the Y axis, i.e., the expected value of Y when all X_i's equal zero. Also, the $\beta_1, \ldots, \beta_n$, designated as the *partial regression coefficients*, indicate the expected change in Y associated with a unit change of an individual predictor variable, with the remaining independent variables being held constant. Thus, multivariate regression is a stepwise process in which the dependent variable is regressed or correlated successively on the independent variables.[8] This procedure tests for the relationship between the response variable and the first independent variable. Next, the remaining variation of the dependent variable *not* explained by the first predictor variable is regressed against the variability of the second independent variable. This process is continued until the residual variation is examined with respect to the last variable. The order of the variables entering the analysis varies depending on the preference of the analyst. For example, a stepwise process could be employed in which the selection criterion is defined in terms of the capability of the variables to reduce the unexplained variance of the dependent variable.

[8]The term *multivariate* in this chapter is used only to indicate multiple independent variables. In the strictest sense, multivariate analysis relates to multiple dependent variables.

The estimation process for the equation parameters and the correlation coefficients involving multiple independent variables is similar to the simple regression model. However, an additional question might be raised in the multivariate case that did not exist in the bivariate framework. The analyst may have a need to know the relative importance of the respective variables in explaining the variability of the dependent variable. To illustrate, assume that management has constructed a regression model, with the dependent variable being sales and the independent variables being

$$X_1 = \text{Gross national product}$$
$$X_2 = \text{Interest rates} \qquad\qquad (5\text{-}11)$$
$$X_3 = \text{Disposable income}$$

In regressing sales on these variables, the relative contribution of each of the variables in predicting sales should be of interest to management. Several avenues for determining the relative importance of the independent variables are available. One such technique is the use of stepwise regression in which the variables are entered in accordance with the incremental variance explained in sales. Another means for ascertaining the relative predictability of the independent variables is through an examination of the coefficients comprising the regression equation. However, the mere fact that the regression coefficient is larger for gross national product than for interest rates yields no informational content in assessing the relative importance since the variables comprise different measurement units. For this reason, only if the individual coefficients are normalized relative to the standard deviation of the corresponding variable will any meaning be provided. In other words, if the transformed coefficients, β_j/σ_j, were to be (1) gross national product, .415, (2) interest rates, .277, (3) disposable income, .830, management would have evidence to support the position that disposable income is twice as important (.830/.415) as gross national product and three times as significant (.830/.277) as interest rates in predicting company sales. However, whether or not any of the independent variables are of material significance depends on the amount of variance relating to sales that is being explained by the predictor variables, either individually or jointly. For example, if only 40 percent of the variation in sales is being accounted for by the three independent variables, the thought that gross national product is more important than interest rates is meaningless.

As to the assumptions and limitations of the multiple regression model, the same limiting conditions that existed for simple regression continue to apply. However, one additional problem area may arise in multiple regression analysis. A primary purpose of most regression models, particularly for multiple regression, is the estimation and interpretation of the regression coefficients. Despite such a place of importance in the analysis, the reliability of the interpretation of these coefficients is potentially subject to bias and should be examined with extreme care. For example, if a high degree of correlation exists between the independent variables, the coefficients become unstable and misleading.

Multiple regression: the illustration continued

As a means for demonstrating the use of multiple linear regression, the sales forecast for Lyttle Corporation when employing only time as the dependent variable could be expanded to recognize multiple independent variables. Other factors could potentially yield meaningful information in an attempt to project 1978 sales. In other words, management's contention that the time element is the paramount factor may be tested by incorporating other potential determinants into the examination process. To illustrate, management may believe that disposable income per capita, construction starts within the community, and interest rates have a direct bearing upon the firm's sales volume. Accordingly, the data relating to these variables have been compiled in Table 5-4. Also, the previous year's sales have been included as a predictor variable in light of the proven relationship in the simple regression analysis.

The findings from the examination are reflected in Table 5-5. The relative importance of the independent variables is denoted by the incremental variance explained. As management had expected, the previous year's sales explain practically all of the variance, with the remaining three variables accounting only for an additional 7 percent of the variation. Furthermore, the standard error of the estimate is reduced from $65,025 to $52,347.

TABLE 5-4

Lyttle Corporation

Multiple Regression Independent Variables

Year	Disposable income	Construction starts	Interest rates	Last year sales
1968	5,060	1,470	.090	304,000
1969	5,240	1,560	.070	375,000
1970	7,970	1,870	.065	340,000
1971	9,980	1,340	.105	320,000
1972	5,470	1,640	.975	547,440
1973	7,600	1,730	.800	647,070
1974	9,840	1,900	.115	603,310
1975	9,540	2,140	.105	640,770
1976	9,980	1,470	.120	691,370
1977	8,340	2,400	.125	747,690

TABLE 5-5

Lyttle Corporation

Stepwise Regression

Variable to enter	Cumulative percentage of variation explained	Standard error of the estimate
Previous year's sales	86.39%	$65,025
Interest rates	90.70	57,484
Construction starts	93.39	52,347
Disposable income	*	*

*Not significant.

Summary

Forecasting a firm's financial requirements is not an easy task. This difficulty is particularly troublesome for *growth businesses* and firms subject to considerable uncertainty, which is often characteristic of the small company. Without any question, regardless of the approach taken for forecasting, an underlying knowledge of the business must exist. This basic understanding complemented with the appropriate forecasting methodology should go far in constructing meaningful estimates of the organization's financial requirements.

Of the numerous techniques available for use, many must be deemed as unfit for the small company, due to their cost and the technical expertise stipulated. However, the percent of sales method and regression analysis may well be viable analytical techniques for a small firm. Testing of the relationships prevailing within the company as well as relevant external factors should provide an indication of the relative efficiency of these two methods.

QUESTIONS

1. What is the single most important variable when attempting to forecast asset requirements?

2. List six methods of forecasting and indicate the time frame that is most useful for each.

3. For the percent of sales method of forecasting to be useful on a consistent basis, what condition must exist?

4. What is a scatter diagram? How is it related to simple regression?

5. Discuss the critical assumptions that must be met before a regression model can be used.

6. What is the standard error of the estimate?

7. When would multiple linear regression be used rather than simple regression?

8. Why might a forecaster prefer regression analysis to the percent of sales method in a given situation?

PROBLEMS

5-1. Fulcrum Brothers, Inc., is a small manufacturing firm which has been operating at or near capacity for the past five years. Sales have been growing at a modest rate and were $2,500,000 for the year just completed. The firm hopes to increase sales by 20 percent during the coming year, but realizes that the goal will require increased investment in assets. The balance sheet for the year just ended is presented as follows:

Fulcrum Brothers, Incorporated

Balance Sheet
for Year Ended December 31, 1977

Assets:	
Cash	$ 25,000
Accounts receivable	275,000
Finished goods inventory	500,000
Supplies	100,000
Plant and equipment	1,100,000
Total assets	$ 2,000,000
Liabilities and owner's equity:	
Accounts payable	$ 175,000
Accrued liabilities	225,000
Common stock	200,000
Other contributed capital	600,000
Retained earnings	800,000
Total liabilities and owner's equity	$ 2,000,000

All asset and liability accounts vary directly with sales. After-tax earnings on sales are normally 8 percent, of which 40 percent are paid out in dividends. Assuming that all external required financing would be borrowed from a local bank, calculate the amount of debt that will be necessary to reach the desired level of sales.

5-2. From the information in Problem 1, prepare a proforma balance sheet for the end of the coming year, assuming:
  a. target sales figures were reached
  b. all percentages held constant
  c. no payments have been made on repayment of debt.

5-3. Sam's Restaurant is trying to determine what to expect in sales for the next year. The owner has a rough idea that the more he spends on advertising, the more he should be able to expect in sales. Examining the financial statements over the last ten years, he extracts the following information:

Year	Sales (000)	Advertising Expenses
1	$15	$200
2	25	100
3	30	200
4	25	250
5	30	275
6	40	300
7	25	325
8	35	350
9	50	400
10	35	500

  a. Construct a scatter diagram and use linear regression to determine a line of best fit.
  b. If Sam's Restaurant incurs advertising expenses of $500 again this year, what will be the expected sales level?

5-4. Using the data in Problem 3 above, compute the standard error of the estimate. Then calculate the *approximate* upper and lower boundaries for expected sales, if advertising expenses are $500 this year, and the owner desires a 95% confidence level.

chapter 6

CASH FORECASTING:
PLANNING AND CONTROL

Cash forecasting has been defined as the process of estimating the sources and uses of corporate cash for a designated period of time into the future. The objective of such a procedure is twofold, with the first goal being to afford a basis for planning the firm's cash requirements and the second to control the company's cash flows. Furthermore, the planning phase is divisible into either long-range cash projections or short-term forecasts of the cash position. This chapter centers upon the more immediate time frame, such as a one-year planning horizon. Within this context, two approaches are generally taken in projecting corporate cash needs:

1. A cash flow forecast based on a proforma income statement in which the income statement is adjusted for noncash items. The resulting end figure would be the funds provided by operations. Additional consideration would then be given to cash flows not recognized in the income statement to arrive at the final *funds position* for the company.
2. A cash receipts and disbursements statement, or the *cash budget*, reflecting the initial cash balance, the receipts for the period, the expected disbursements, and the ending cash balance. Typically, this statement is segmented into *subperiods*, possibly either in terms of weekly or monthly time intervals.

The second objective assigned cash management is the provision for control. More specifically, the subsequent comparison of predicted cash flows with the actual amounts provides at least two benefits. First, the learning experience should enhance management's ability in accurately projecting future cash flow streams. Second, examinations of disparities from expectations on a regular basis permit the executive to react more quickly to developing problems. Stated differently, a continued awareness of how goals and objectives are actually materializing is essential.

In presenting the material relating to cash management, emphasis will be placed upon the planning segment of cash management as opposed to the control aspects. First, the importance of cash planning, particularly as it relates to the management of the small company, is addressed. Second, an overview of the cash flow cycle is provided. Third, a detailed illustration of a cash budget for a small firm is set forth.

Importance of Cash Planning for the Small Firm

The necessity of cash planning, whether for the large publicly owned corporation or for the small business, has long been recognized. The increased awareness that reported earnings, while being an indispensable indicator of the firm's progress, simply do not tell the complete story has resulted in more *funds* or cash-oriented statements.[1] This fact is of particular relevance for the company encountering change. No doubt, the "mature" organization has a need to know its cash requirements. For example, a frequent examination of the cash inflows and outflows by Consolidated Edison's management during the months preceding their decision to discontinue the payment of dividends would have been important in their decision. However, the requirement generally is not so critical for the large stable corporation as for a small growth firm. First, the environment in which the latter operations function frequently makes cash planning particularly significant. For instance, a circumstance often faced by small firms is undercapitalization. An undercapitalized enterprise results in a working capital shortage, such that the turnover of working capital from the point of investing in raw materials to the final collection of receivables continues to plague the management of a small company. In such an atmosphere, the company executive is compelled to "keep close tabs" on the organization's flow of cash.

The second factor associated with many small corporations that stipulates the implementation of a cash plan is the *growth* element. The ownership of a small business facing an expansion in size has to be more cognizant of the cash inflows and the necessary outflows. Contrary to the belief of many small businessmen, growth is not synonymous with financial prosperity. A growth firm is especially susceptible to financing difficulties, thereby requiring greater perceptiveness of the entity's funds flows.

A third instance in which the small firm may find cash planning essential is in approaching parties who represent potential sources of financing. Normally, for the small business the financing comes from the banker. Thus, in requesting from the bank a loan that entails any substantial amount, the cash plan becomes an important tool in two ways. First, the small businessman is in better touch with the realities of the loan request, especially

---

[1]See Joel M. Stern, "Earnings Per Share Don't Count," *Financial Analysts Journal*, (July–Aug. 1974), pp. 39–76, and Pearson Hunt, "Funds Position: Keystone in Financial Planning," *Harvard Business Review*, (May–June 1975), pp. 106–115.

in having a better understanding as to how the loan is to be repaid. This issue is generally a key concern on the part of the banker. Second, and of equal importance, is the increased credibility of the small business owner with the banker if the person requesting the loan has explicitly set forth the detailed cash flows. In this respect, the banker may not communicate any strong conviction to the prospective loan recipient concerning the influence of a well-developed cash budget upon the acceptance or rejection of the loan request. However, if specifically questioned, we believe most bankers would be in agreement that the preparation of a cash forecast is an instrumental tool in the acquisition of funds from a financial institution.

In summary, the amount of benefit derived from a cash plan for either the small or large business is a function of the extenuating circumstances, and the cash plan should not be considered as being critical to success for all firms regardless of the situation. Yet, despite such a prerequisite for the cash budget being a *strategic* planning tool, the small organization is probably more often found to be in a setting requiring a formal cash forecast than would be the case for large corporations. However, if our experience is any indicator, a relationship prevails, with large companies making more extensive use of the cash plan than do small businesses. In response, the manager of the small firm will often reply that he simply does not have the time to spend on forecasting. Besides, he considers himself close enough to the events that he is able to plan adequately in a mental fashion, without having to prepare a written budget. Such an argument may actually prove true for a minority of individuals. However, for most business executives time has a way of making financial details become hazy. As a result, the benefit of past experience is not nearly so beneficial. Furthermore, as already noted, in certain circumstances, a cash plan may possibly mean the difference between success and failure. Accordingly, an understanding of the cash flow cycle as well as the process for implementing a forecast are relevant issues for the executive assigned financial decisions in the small company.

The Cash Flow Cycle

The corporate cash flows may be divided into two basic categories. First, the *short-term operating cash cycle*, represents the outflows and inflows associated with the conversion of raw materials into finished goods and finally into the collection of receivables. Second, the liquidity level is impacted by the *nonoperating cash flows* involving distributions to investors and the government, receipts from new financing, and disbursements relating to capital expenditures. We shall review both of these segments of the underlying cash flow patterns.

Short-term cash cycle

In considering the short-term operational cash flows, the primary issue is the length of time that is required between purchasing raw materials and the final collection of receivables.[2] This period is then further divisible into several meaningful shorter time intervals. As a means for providing an overview, Figure 6-1 depicts the respective segments of the cash cycle. (The

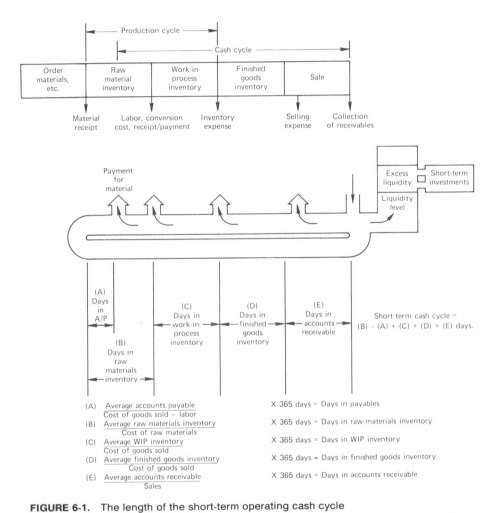

FIGURE 6-1. The length of the short-term operating cash cycle

SOURCE: Adaption from an article by Hampton C. Hager, "Cash Management and the Cash Cycle," *Management Accounting*, (March 1976), p. 20.

[2]The structure of this section draws upon Hampton C. Hager, "Cash Management and the Cash Cycle," *Management Accounting*, (March 1976), pp. 19–21.

nonoperating cash flows are assumed to be nonexistent for the moment.) In the figure, the cash cycle is seen to begin at the point of payment for raw materials and to continue through the collection of receivables, with funds being invested in raw materials, the labor for converting the materials into finished goods, the maintenance of the finished goods, and the required investment in extending credit. Moreover, as shown in the bottom portion of Figure 6-1, the time period for supporting these various investments may be specifically calculated. As a result of these computations, at least two advantages ensue. First, the quantitative determination of the individual time components assists management in ascertaining the relative significance of each of the subperiods and provides a means for realizing an interrelationship within the cycle. For instance, a decrease in the "days in raw materials," while initially appearing favorable, may result in a significant increase in the time that work-in-process inventory would have to be maintained due to bottlenecks when shortages in raw materials develop. A second advantage should result in terms of improved forecasting capabilities. After having developed a historical data base, the executive should be in a better position to specify anticipated cash flow trends.

While the analysis of the short-term cash cycle is of assistance, a misconception often results, particularly within the management of small growth businesses. The cycle, as described above, applies only to short-term cyclical variations in investments in net working capital. For instance, any "permanent" increases in accounts receivable will have to be financed through long-term financing and profits without being able to rely to any large extent upon the cash flows generated at the conclusion of the cycle. In essence, the collected funds are applied toward the financing of new receivables so that if the original funds were borrowed, the loan repayment cannot be met fully out of the receipts.

To clarify the application of the foregoing suggested format, a limited illustration is given in Tables 6-1 and 6-2. Based on the financial information for the Griggs Corporation (Table 6-1), the *net* cash cycle is calculated in Table 6-2. As set forth in the latter table, the firm maintains an average 40-day investment in raw products, extending 10 days beyond the credit terms being extended the company for purchases. An additional 30 days is taken for holding the inventory in the intermediate work-in-process phase, with an average 40-day period being sustained for the finished goods inventory. When the sale does occur, credit is typically provided to approved customers for 35 days. In summary, the beginning investment of cash for the raw materials culminates 115 days later through the receipt of cash from the customer.

Long-Term Cash Flows

The second type of cash flow is of a less "spontaneous" nature in that these flows do not occur automatically as a result of the production-sales

TABLE 6-1

Financial Statements

Griggs Corporation

Income statement—1977

Sales		$ 2,000,000
Cost of goods sold:		
Raw material	$400,000	
Labor	600,000	
Other costs	200,000	1,200,000
Gross profit		$ 800,000
Operating expenses:		
Marketing	$250,000	
Administrative	150,000	
Depreciation	100,000	500,000
Earnings before interest and taxes		$ 300,000
Interest		60,000
Taxable income		$ 240,000
Taxes (50%)		120,000
Net profit		$ 120,000

Balance sheet

	1976	1977
Current assets:		
Cash and marketable securities	$ 125,000	$ 175,000
Accounts receivable	175,000	209,000
Inventory:		
Raw materials	38,000	50,000
Work-in-process	95,000	103,000
Finished goods	125,000	137,000
Other current assets	12,000	26,000
Total current assets	$ 460,000	$ 700,000
Net fixed assets	840,000	1,300,000
Total assets	$1,300,000	$2,000,000
Liabilities and equity:		
Accounts payable	$ 45,000	$53,000
Short-term notes (9%)	240,000	400,000
Total current liabilites	$ 285,000	$ 453,000
Long-term debt (12%)	100,000	200,000
Total debt	$ 385,000	$ 653,000
Common stock	915,000	1,347,000
Total liabilities and equity	$1,300,000	$2,000,000

TABLE 6-2

Griggs Corporation

Operating Short-Term
Cash Flow Period (nearest days)

Days in raw material inventory:

$$\frac{\text{Average raw material inventory}}{\text{Cost of raw materials}} \times 365$$

$$\frac{\$44,000}{\$400,000} \times 365 \qquad\qquad = \qquad 40 \text{ days}$$

Less days in payables:

$$\frac{\text{Average accounts payable}}{\text{Cost of goods sold—labor}} \times 365$$

$$\frac{\$49,000}{\$600,000} \times 365 \qquad\qquad = \qquad (30 \text{ days})$$

Plus:

(1) Days in work-in-process inventory:

$$\frac{\text{Average work-in-process inventory}}{\text{Cost of goods sold}} \times 365$$

$$\frac{\$99,000}{\$1,200,000} \times 365 \qquad\qquad = \qquad 30 \text{ days}$$

(2) Days in finished goods inventory:

$$\frac{\text{Average finished goods inventory}}{\text{Cost of goods sold}} \times 365$$

$$\frac{\$131,000}{\$1,200,000} \times 365 \qquad\qquad = \qquad 40 \text{ days}$$

(3) Days in accounts receivable:

$$\frac{\text{Average accounts receivable}}{\text{Sales}} \times 365$$

$$\frac{\$192,000}{\$2,000,000} \times 365 \qquad\qquad = \qquad \underline{35 \text{ days}}$$

Total days for cash cycle   115 days

process. Such inflows and outflows are portrayed in Figure 6-2. Two elements are of particular interest to small-firm management in its efforts to forecast long-term cash flows. First, as already noted, the outflows relating to the "permanent" portion of working capital have to be financed with a long-term source of financing or through profits. Failure to recognize this principle has been a "trap" for many small businesses. Second, the small businessman often times fails to allow adequately for cash flows relating to essential replacements of capital equipment. For some reason, the ownership of a small business is relatively sensitive to the potential disbursements associated with an expansion but becomes somewhat unrealistic in forecasting replacement needs.

In review, in implementing a formal cash plan, management has to be cognizant of two types of cash flows. The first of these is the recurring inflows and outflows. Adequate sychronization of these cash movements is a basic need for most small organizations. Without thorough forethought in planning these flows, the firm may incur a severe liquidity crisis. The second pattern of cash streams involves the less spontaneous sources and uses of funds. The amounts are generally much larger in this category on a per transaction basis and are of a more "lumpy" nature. Due to the significant size of these cash receipts and payments, failure to plan may quickly place the company in a

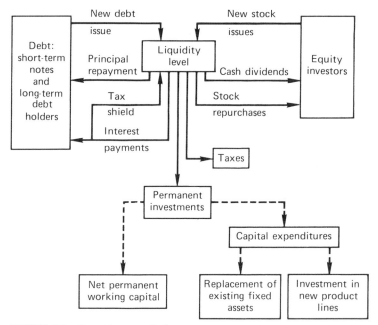

FIGURE 6-2. Long-term cash flows

financially hazardous position. However, the fact that this latter category may appear larger in dollar terms per event should not be permitted to minimize the seriousness of insufficient planning of the more routine cash flows. Either oversight can be fatal to a small operation.

With an understanding of the cash flows within the firm, attention is now directed to the actual planning process.

The Cash Budget

In view of the importance of cash budgeting to the small- to moderate-sized enterprise, particularly at select times, the subsequent material relates to the actual construction of a budget. First, the development of a cash budget is demonstrated. Second, attention is given to the need for recognizing risk in the analysis. In the first regard, an explanation of the process for structuring a cash budget is best accomplished by an illustration.

Cash budgeting: a case illustration

The Felt Tip Pen, Inc., (FTP), a maker of felt tip and nylon tip writing pens, was founded in 1972 and has proven to be relatively profitable. However, problems have recently arisen, with the firm coming up short of funds for maturing obligations. The difficulty has been attributed to fluctuating sales. James Menielle, vice-president and controller, is attempting to plan ahead by determining the firm's cash needs prior to conferring with the banker on forthcoming loan requirements. The primary objective of the analysis is to reflect the net cash gain (loss) during each month and the cash balance at month's end for 1977.

FTP's balance sheet and sales forecast is set forth in Tables 6-3 and 6-4. Other relevant information includes:

1. *Collection of Sales*: All sales during a given month are billed to customers on the first day of the next month. A 2 percent discount is allowed if the bill is paid on or by the tenth day of the month. Experience shows that 10 percent of all sales are paid by the tenth, 80 percent of all sales are paid within 30 days, and 8 percent are paid within 60 days.
2. *Dividend Income*: Dividends are received quarterly beginning in the month of January on the marketable securities. The dividend yield approximates 5 percent annually.
3. *Materials*: The amount of materials purchased in one month is based on the following month's forecasted sales. The materials' cost per unit is $.1250. Payments for materials are made in the month subsequent to the purchase.
4. *Salaries and Selling and Administrative Expense*: These expenses are paid during the month incurred, and are estimated in Table 6-5.

TABLE 6-3

Felt Tip Pen, Inc.

Balance Sheet, Dec. 31, 1976

Assets

Current assets:		
Cash[1]		$ 10,000
Marketable securities		10,000
Accounts receivable		58,000
Inventory[2]		41,000
Total assets		$119,000
Fixed assets:		
Land and building		$100,000
Equipment	$120,000	
Less: depreciation	60,000	60,000
Total fixed assets		$160,000
Total assets		$279,000

Liabilities and net worth

Current liabilities		
Accounts payable		$ 30,000
Short-term notes payable—7%, due May 1977		30,000
Long-term liabilities		
Notes payable—8%, due 1979		40,000
Total liabilities		$100,000
Capital stock		
Common—par value $1		$125,000
Retained earnings		54,000
Total net worth		179,000
Total liabilities and net worth		$279,000

[1]The firm seeks at all times to maintain minimum cash or cash equivalents of $20,000.
[2]A minimum inventory of $20,000 is maintained at all times.

5. *Dividend Payments*: Dividends are paid quarterly in February, May, August, and Novenber, at the quarterly rate of $.04 per share.
6. *Taxes*: Taxes are paid quarterly in January, April, July, and October. Earnings before taxes are assumed to be 20 percent of the total forecasted sales for the year. The quarterly payments are based on the total estimated taxes for 1977, divided into equal payments.

TABLE 6-4

Unit Sales Forecast for 1977
(units)

January	168,000	July	312,000
February	192,000	August	264,000
March	240,000	September	168,000
April	192,000	October	168,000
May	240,000	November	288,000
June	288,000	December	312,000

November 1976 actual sales—$270,000

December 1976 actual sales—$298,000

Sales price per unit—$.25

TABLE 6-5

Salaries and Selling & Administrative Expenses

Forecast for 1977
(dollars)

	Salaries	*Selling & admin.*		*Salaries*	*Selling & admin.*
January	$6,300	$ 6,300	July	$9,000	$13,200
February	7,000	7,400	August	8,600	12,000
March	8,000	10,000	September	6,400	7,000
April	7,000	7,410	October	6,400	7,000
May	8,000	10,100	November	8,600	12,840
June	8,600	12,840	December	9,200	13,460

7. *Equipment*: A $10,000 machine is to be purchased in September, 1977, paying $1,000 down with three equal monthly installments beginning the following month.

Initially assuming that no new debt is acquired during the year, and that any interest expense is paid monthly, a suggested cash budget for the company is presented in Table 6-6. In developing the budget, the point of departure is the forecasted sales, as provided in Table 6-4. Converting the figures from units to dollar sales (at $.25 sales price per unit), the sales are shown in line 1 of Table 6-6. Based on the company's collection experience,

TABLE 6-6

Felt Tip Pen, Inc.

Cash Budget 1977

(a)	Jan.	Feb.	March	April	May	June	July	August	Sept.	Oct.	Nov.	Dec.	Total sales
(1) Sales	$42,000	$48,000	$60,000	$48,000	$60,000	$72,000	$78,000	$66,000	$42,000	$42,000	$72,000	$78,000	$708,000
Cash receipts													
(2) Paid by the 10th (net of discount)	7,301	4,116	4,704	5,880	4,116	5,880	7,055	7,644	6,468	4,116	4,116	7,055	
(3) 30 day collection of Accounts receivable	59,600	33,600	38,400	48,000	33,600	48,000	57,600	62,400	52,800	33,600	33,600	57,600	
(4) 60 day collection of Accounts receivable	5,400	5,960	3,360	3,840	4,800	3,360	4,800	5,760	6,240	5,280	3,360	4,200	
(5) Dividends	125	—	—	125	—	—	125	—	—	125	—	—	
(6) Total receipts	$72,426	$43,676	$46,464	$57,845	$42,516	$57,240	$69,580	$75,804	$65,508	$43,121	$41,076	$68,855	

Cash disbursements

(7) Material payments	$21,000	$24,000	$30,000	$24,000	$30,000	$36,000	$39,000	$33,000	$21,000	$21,000	$36,000	$39,000
(8) Salaries (Table 6-5)	6,300	7,000	8,000	7,000	8,000	8,600	9,000	8,600	6,400	6,400	8,600	9,200
(9) Selling & administrative (Table 6-5)	6,300	7,400	10,000	7,410	10,100	12,840	13,200	12,000	7,000	7,000	12,840	13,460
(10) Dividend payments	—	5,000	—	—	5,000	—	—	5,000	—	—	5,000	—
(11) Taxes	$13,167	—	—	$13,167	—	—	$13,167	—	—	$13,167	—	—
(12) Pay back loan	—	—	—	—	30,000	—	—	—	—	—	—	—
(13) Interest expense	442	442	442	442	442	267	267	267	267	267	267	267
(14) Purchased equipment	—	—	—	—	—	—	—	—	1,000	3,000	3,000	3,000
(15) Total disbursements	$47,209	$43,842	$48,442	$52,019	$83,542	$57,707	$74,634	$58,867	$35,667	$50,834	$65,707	$64,927
(16) Net cash gain (loss) during month	$25,217	(166)	(1,978)	5,826	(41,025)	(467)	(5,054)	16,937	29,841	(7,713)	(24,631)	3,928
(17) Beginning of month cash and marketable securities	$20,000	$45,217	$45,051	$43,073	$48,899	$7,874	$7,407	$2,353	$19,290	$49,131	$41,418	$16,787
(18) Ending of month Cash and marketable securities	45,217	45,051	43,073	48,899	7,874	7,407	2,353	19,290	49,131	41,418	16,787	20,715

the monthly cash receipts from sales are computed. To demonstrate this process, the February cash receipts from sales are calculated as follows:

January, 1977 sales collected by February 10, 1977	10% of January sales ×(100% − 2% discount) =	$ 4,116
January, 1977 sales collected from February 11, 1977 to Feb. 28, 1977	(80 % of January sales)	= 33,600
December 1976 sales collected during February, 1977	(8% of December sales)	= 5,960
		$43,676

In addition to sales related receipts, other receipts are then added to ascertain total collections for the firm. For FTP, the only remaining receipts include dividend income from investments in securities.

Having determined the anticipated receipts for the respective months, attention may be directed to the forecasted cash disbursements. Looking first at material payments (line 7), we are required to estimate the cost of these payments by simply taking the $.1250 cost per unit times the number of units in the ensuing month. For instance, January payments are estimated at 192,000 units (February sales) times $.125, or $24,000. However, since the material payment is not made for 30 days, this purchase is shown as a disbursement in February. Salaries and selling and administrative expenses (lines 8 and 9) are taken directly from Table 6-5. Dividend payments (line 10) are calculated at $.04 per share times the 125,000 shares outstanding. The tax payments (line 11) represent one-fourth of the company's anticipated tax liability for 1977. If 2,832,000 units are sold for $.25 per unit, the total sales revenue would be $708,000. Furthermore, if the firm's before-tax profit margin is 20 percent, taxable income from operations is $141,600. The tax liability on this amount of income would be $54,468. (We are ignoring the tax consequence of the dividend income, since 85 percent of the dividend income is tax exempt for a corporation.) Per the firm's balance sheet, $30,000 in short-term notes mature in May, 1977 (line 12). The interest expense (line 13) is based on the notes payable shown in the balance sheet (Table 6-3). Finally, the equipment purchase (line 14) reflects the planned acquisition of equipment in September, 1977.

The net result of the cash receipts and disbursements is specified as the net cash gain (loss) during the month. However, the final product of concern to the company management is the balance in either cash or the combined cash and marketable securities accounts. In examining these amounts, the firm's minimum desired level for cash and marketable securities, that being $20,000 (footnote to the balance sheet in Table 6-3), is violated in May, 1977 as a result of having to retire the short-term note. The cash balances continue to deteriorate until August, 1977. At that point in time, the increased sales volume for May through July, 1977 counter the downward trend, with the cash and marketable securities approaching the $20,000 minimum requirement. In September, 1977, the liquid balances peak at $49,131 and then begin another cycle, with a year-end balance of $20,715. In brief, the firm may expect excess liquidity for the first four months of the year. Then for the three-month period ending in July, 1977, short-term financing would be required up to approximately $17,650. A smaller amount of financing would be necessary in November if the $20,000 safety stock in liquid assets is to be maintained.

The cash budget and risk analysis

A number of conceptual proposals have been made for determining the optimal level of cash. Probably one of the more pragmatic approaches has been the incorporation of simulation into the cash budget.[3] Even so, most small businessmen would have difficulty in justifying the time necessary in simulating the cash budget. Also, the necessary assessment of probabilities in the model may prove to be more than the small firm's executives choose to attempt, either as a result of the circumstances or due to a mental disinclination to make such determinations. For these reasons, we would suggest "sensitivity analysis" as a preference in most instances. Simply expressed, the financial executive would want to know the response of the final outcome to a change in a specific parameter. For FTP, Inc., management may wish to know how the monthly cash balances would change in response to a different collection rate. Although not as sophisticated as a complete simulation, the foregoing recommendation for sensitivity analysis may be greatly facilitated by the computer in order to analyze the needed number of possible combinations. However, with the increased accessibility of the small company to computer systems, no major problem should exist.

Summary

The proper planning and control of corporate cash is an important aspect of financial management whether the firm is small or large. However, as a result of the environment in which a small growth corporation operates, cash planning may take on additional importance. In making cash flow projections, the proprietorship of the small concern must distinguish between short-term recurring patterns and the more "lumpy" type of cash inflows and outflows. In other words, the success of efforts to predict future cash balances is dependent on an understanding of the firm's cash flow cycle. With a grasp

---

[3]See Eugene M. Lerner, "Simulating a Cash Budget," *California Management Review*, Vol. XI, No. 2 (Winter, 1968), pp. 79–86.

of these relationships, cash planning for most small enterprises either entails the *adjusted net income* approach or the cash budget. Due to the intricacies of the cash budget, extensive time was devoted to this technique. Yet, some effort should be given to coming to grips with the uncertainty associated with the one-point estimates of cash flows generated in a cash budget. To resolve this issue, the management may employ simulation to ascertain a range of possible cash flows or at least perform a more limited analysis in terms of knowing the sensitivity of the cash balances to a change in various key parameters.

QUESTIONS

1. What are two approaches for projecting cash flow?
2. State the two objectives of cash management.
3. Explain the meaning of Figure 6-1.
4. What problems are cited in the chapter as being frequently encountered by managements of small firms in predicting cash flow?
5. Distinguish between short-term or "spontaneous" cash flows and long-term cash flows.
6. Interpret Figure 6-2.

PROBLEM

6-1. The Goodwrench Tool Company is a manufacturer and distributor of precision tools for use in the maintenence of air conditioning and refrigeration systems. The tools are sold in kit form to retailers, from whom Goodwrench receives $40 per unit. Founded in 1960, the firm has acheived significant growth in sales and earnings, and four years ago the firm went public in order to finance needed expansion. Since the expansion, sales and earnings figures have corresponded reasonably closely with expectations; however, the seasonal nature of the industry has created serious cash flow problems from time to time.

In an effort to control this problem, the firm has created the new position of Financial Director, for which you have been hired. The President has asked you to develop a cash budget for the current year, 1978, so that the firm can take adequate steps to supplement cash shortage through borrowing, or effectively utilize cash when it is in excess of needs. In January of the current year, you have assembled all of the available information upon which to base your estimates. Some of the information will be drawn from the financial statements contained in the following tables. Table 1 is Goodwrench's balance sheet as of December 31, 1977. Table 2 includes income statements for both 1976 and 1977. Table 3 is a sales forecast by units for each month of 1978, on which the level of purchases will be based.

In developing your cash budget, you may assume that the cost-volume-profit relationship of the two preceding years will hold constant in 1978. Other relevant information includes:

1. *Collection of Sales:* Twenty percent of all sales are for cash. For the sales on account, 70 percent are collected in the month following the sale, 20 percent in the second month following the sale, and 9 percent in the third month. One percent of the accounts receivable will be written off as uncollectable.
2. *Direct Materials:* Materials are purchased two months prior to sale to allow time for machining and other servicing. The amount purchased is based on the forecasted sales figures, and payments for materials are made in the month subsequent to the purchase.
3. *Direct Labor:* Direct labor is applied to the purchased materials during the month prior to sale, and is paid during the month incurred.
4. *General and Administrative Expense:* These expenses are paid during the month incurred and are estimated to be $5,500.00 per month.
5. *Dividend Payments:* Dividends are paid quarterly in February, May, August, and November; quarterly dividends are expected to be $.11 per share.
6. *Taxes:* Taxes are paid quarterly in January, April, July, and October. Quarterly payments are based on the total estimated taxes for the year divided into equal payments. Use current corporate tax rates.
7. *Insurance:* An $8,000 insurance premium is due to be paid in June.

TABLE 1

Goodwrench Tool Company

Balance Sheet
December 31, 1977

Assets:	
Cash	$ 75,840
Accounts receivable	240,000
Inventory	250,000
Equipment (net of depreciation)	109,000
Land and building	230,000
Total Assets	$904,840
Liabilities and net worth:	
Accounts payable	$100,000
Accrued payroll	55,500
Taxes payable	105,465
Common stock ($1 par)	100,000
Retained earnings	543,875
Total liabilities and net worth	$904,840

TABLE 2

Goodwrench Tool Company

Income Statement
For Years Ended December 31, 1976 and December 31, 1977

			1976		1977
Sales			$3,300,000		$3,700,000
Less:	Direct materials	$1,650,000		$1,850,000	
	Direct labor	825,000		925,000	
	Cost of goods sold		2,475,000		2,775,000
			825,000		925,000
Gross Margin					
Less:	General & administrative expense	$66,000		$ 66,000	
	Insurance expense	8,000		8,000	
	Depreciation expense	24,000		24,000	
	Bad debt expense	26,400		29,600	
	Total other expense		124,400		127,600
Income before Taxes			700,600		797,400
Less:	Income tax		322,788		369,252
Net Income			$ 377,812		$ 428,148
	Earnings Per Share		$3.78		$4.28
	Dividends Per Share		.36		.40

TABLE 3

Unit Sales Forecast for 1978

January	5,000	July	12,000
February	5,000	August	13,000
March	6,000	September	12,000
April	7,000	October	9,000
May	9,000	November	6,000
June	11,000	December	5,500
		January, 1978	5,500

October 1977 actual sales—$340,000
November 1977 actual sales—$220,000
December 1977 actual sales—$200,000

American Management Association, Inc., Special Report No. 26, *Control of Non-Manufacturing Costs*, Times Square, New York: American Management Association, Inc., 1957.

BECKER, BENJAMIN M., and FRED A. TILLMAN, *The Family Owned Business*, Chicago, Ill.: Commerce Clearing House Inc., 1975.

BETANCOURT, RICHARD C., "Plan Your Own Cash Flow System," *Financial Executive*, Jan. 1975, pp. 28–37.

BLANK, SEYMOUR, "Small Business and Tight Money," *The Journal of Finance*, Vol. XVI, No. 1, March 1961, pp. 73–79.

BROULES, J. E., C. J. BUNTON, and J. R. FRANKS, "A Decision Analysis Approach to Cash Flow Management," *Operational Research Quarterly*, Vol. 25, No. 4, pp. 573–585.

BROWN, ROBERT G., "Less Risk in Inventory Estimates," *Harvard Business Review*, July-Aug. 1969, pp. 104–115.

BUMP, JACK A., "Profit Planning and Budgeting," *Finance Executive Handbook*, Homewood, Ill.: Irwin, Inc., 1970, pp. 417–430.

CLELLAND, RICHARD C., FRANCIS E. BROWN, JOHN S. DECANI, J. PARKER BRUSK, and DONALD S. MURRAY, *Basic Statistics with Business Applications*, New York: Wiley and Sons, 1966, pp. 418–470.

COHEN, KALMAN J., "Strategy: Formulation Implementation and Monitoring," *Journal of Business*, University of Chicago, July 1973, pp. 349–367.

DENNING, BASIL W., *Corporate Planning: Selected Concepts*, New York: McGraw-Hill, 1971.

DUDRICK, THOMAS S., ed., *How To Improve Profitability Through More Effective Planning*, New York: Wiley and Sons, 1975.

ELLIOTT-JONES, J. F., "Economic Forecasting and Corporate Planning," *Conference Board Report*, No. 585, New York: National Industrial Conference Board.

ELLIOTT, M. R., "Long Range Corporate Planning," *Conference Board Record*, New York: National Industrial Conference Board, Feb. 1973, pp. 47–50.

ELTON, EDWIN J., and MARTIN J. GRUBER, "On the Cash Balance Problem," *Operational Research Quarterly*, Vol. 25, No. 5, Dec. 1974, pp. 553–572.

FELLER, JACK H., "Is Your Cash Supply Adequate?" *Management Aids for Small Manufacturers*, Washington, D.C.: Small Business Administration, No. 174, March 1974.

FORBES, A. M., "Long Range Planning for the Small Firm," *Long Range Planning*, April 1974, pp. 43–47.

FORSYTHE, W. E., "Strategic Planning in the Seventies," *Financial Executive*, Oct. 1973, pp. 96–102.

GALDE, ROGER A., "Practical Planning for Small Business," *The Dynamic Small Firm: Selected Readings*, ed. by Ernest W. Walker, Austin, Texas: Lone Star Publishers, Inc., 1975, pp. 75–92.

GILMORE, FRANK F., "Formulating in Small Companies," *The Dynamic Small Firm: Selected Readings*, ed. by Ernest W. Walker, Austin, Texas: Lone Star Publishers, Inc., 1975, pp. 93–109.

GOODMAN, SAM R., *Techniques of Profitability Analysis*, New York: Wiley and Sons, 1970.

HUNT, PEARSON, "Fund Position: Keystone in Financial Planning," *Harvard Business Review*, May-June 1975, pp. 106–115.

HUSSEY, D. E., "Approach to Financial Planning," *Accountant*, April 4, 1974, pp. 422–423.

IRWIN, PATRICK H., *How To Make A Profit Plan*, Hamilton, Ontario, Canada: The Society Of Industrial and Cost Accountants, 1964.

JOPLIN, BRUCE, and JAMES W. PATTILLO, *Effective Accounting Reports*, Englewood Cliffs, NJ: Prentice-Hall, 1969.

LEASURE, J. WILLIAM, and MAJORIE SHEPHERD TURNER, *Prices, Profits, and Production*, Albuquerque, NM: University of New Mexico Press, 1974.

LIM, ROBIN, *Scientific Management for Small Business*, New York: Oceana Publications, Inc., 1973.

LINES, JAMES, *Profit Improvement*, London: Business Books Limited, 1973.

LIVINGSTONE, JOHN LESLIE, "Input-Output Analysis for Cost Accounting, Planning and Control," *The Accounting Review*, Jan. 1969, pp. 48–64.

LOCAISCO, VINCENT R., "Financial Planning Models," *Financial Executive*, March 1972, pp. 30–34.

MABERT, VINCENT A., and ROBERT C. RADCLIFFE, "Forecasting—A Systematic Modeling Methodology," *Financial Management*, Autumn 1974, pp. 59–67.

McCONKEY, DALE D., *Planning Next Year's Profits*, New York: American Management Association, Inc., 1968.

MEYER, ROBERT F., "Strategy Formulation and Implementation," *Financial Executive Handbook*, Homewood, Ill.: Irwin, Inc., 1970, pp. 12–26.

MORINE, JOHN F., "Corporate Planning: The Role of the Team at the Top," *Accountant's Journal*, June 1974, pp. 438–440.

MURPHY, JOHN F., "Sound Cash Management and Borrowing," *Small Marketers Aids*, No. 147, Washington, D.C.: Small Business Administration, Jan. 1972.

PFLOMM, NORMAN E., "Managing Company Cash," *Studies in Business Policy*, No. 99, New York: National Industrial Conference Board, Inc., 1961.

RACHLIN, ROBERT, *How To Use Return-On-Investment Concepts and Techniques for Profit Improvement*, New York: Pilot Books, Inc., 1974.

SCHABAKER, JOSEPH C., *Cash Planning in Small Manufacturing Companies*, Washington, D.C.: U.S. Government Printing Office, 1960.

SEED, ALLEN H., "Needed: Strategies To Improve Cash Flow," *Management Review*, March 1975, pp. 11–18.

SNGHVI, SURENDRA S., "Financial Planning and Analysis," *Managerial Planning*, July-Aug. 1974, pp. 35–40.

STERN, JOEL M., "Earnings Per Share Don't Count," *Financial Analysts Journal*, July-Aug. 1974, pp. 39–43.

SUMMERS, EDWARD L., *Profits, Growth, and Planning Techniques of Modern Financial Management*, Homewood, Ill.: Dow Jones-Irwin, Inc., 1974.

THRUN, WALTER J., "A Systems Approach to Cash Flow Determination," *Management Accounting*, Feb. 1973, pp. 29–31.

VAN HORNE, JAMES C., "A Risk-Return Analysis of a Firm's Working-Capital Positions," *The Engineering Economist*, Vol. 14, No. 2, Winter 1969, pp. 71–89.

WALLEY, B. H., *How To Make and Control a Profit Plan*, London: Business Books Limited, 1969.

WEINWURM, EARNEST H., and GEORGE F. WEINWURM, *Long-Term Profit Planning*, New York: American Management Association, Inc., 1971.

WELSCH, GLENN A., *Budgeting: Profit Planning and Control*, Englewood Cliffs, NJ: Prentice-Hall, 1964.

WHEELWRIGHT, STEVEN C., "Strategic Planning in the Small Business," *The Dynamic Small Firm: Selected Readings*, ed. by Ernest W. Walker, Austin, Texas: Lone Star Publishers, Inc., 1975, pp. 111–122.

WHEELWRIGHT, STEVEN C., and SPYROS MADRIDAKIS, *Forecasting Methods for Management*, New York: Wiley, 1973, pp. 135–140.

WOELFEL, CHARLES J., *Guides for Profit Planning*, Washington, D.C.: Small Business Administration, 1975.

part III

ACCOUNTING
AND DATA PROCESSING
SYSTEMS

chapter 7

ACCOUNTING SYSTEMS
AND INTERNAL CONTROL

An accounting system is generally defined to be the composite of the activities, operations, and procedures, with the related records and devices, necessary to accomplish the accounting function. The accounting function as expressed by the American Institute of Certified Public Accountants is the provision for "quantitative information, primarily financial in nature, about economic entities that is intended to be useful in making economic decisions —in making reasoned choices among alternative courses of action."[1] Thus, the effective accounting system should furnish *timely* and *useful information* in the decision-making process.

Although "inexperience" and "incompetence" of small business managers have been cited as the cause of more than 90 percent of the small company failures,[2] these statistics fail to indicate the source of such "incompetence" and "mismanagement." However, experience would suggest that ineptness in the accounting system is a prime factor for failure among small enterprises, due to a failure to provide financial information necessary in the decision-making process. In addition, attorneys active in bankruptcy proceedings verify that the large majority of small firms encountering financial distress have inadequate accounting records. Appropriately, the organization's financial data base must be organized so as to afford relevant and meaningful information for the decision maker. In brief, the term *incompetence* may only be a symptom of a more basic defect in the company, that being an insufficient accounting information system.

As a business increases in assets and sales, decentralization may become a necessity, with the authority and responsibility for operational decisions no longer resting with the ownership of the firm. No doubt as this process matures, the complexity and the intricacies of the accounting systems could

[1]*Statement of the Accounting Principles Board No.4*, (New York: AICPA, Oct., 1970), p. 17.

[2]*The Business Failure Record: 1972*, (New York, Dun and Bradstreet, Inc., 1973), pp. 11–12.

also be expected to become more involved. However, the conclusion that the small businessman, although intimately involved in all phases of the day-to-day operations, is less reliant upon sound financial information is not only incorrect but dangerously deceptive. For these reasons, the proprietors in the small business entity should have an understanding of the accounting system within their firm. In this respect, the following sections of this chapter provide basic principles related to systems design, followed by an overview of the design process. Subsequently, two elements of these principles are further described, within the small business context, those being cost accounting and internal control.

Principles of System Design

In the systems design process, adherence to certain underlying principles regarding the accounting design should be maintained.[3] First, the accounting system should not be cumbersome to the firm. Specifically, the system should be structured in order to provide the needed information *at a reasonable cost*. Otherwise, the accounting system may be highly sophisticated and yield intricate detail, but the cost of the process may be prohibitive. In contrast, the design should be commensurate with the small company's ability to finance the development and operation of the accounting segment of the firm. Furthermore, procedures should be sufficiently adaptable to changing conditions, whether the nature of the change in indigenous or exogenous to the organization. On the other hand, this flexibility should not be whimsical, resulting in inconsistencies and lack of uniformity.

A second feature of the accounting unit, effective reports and summarizations, should enhance the decision-making process within the firm. If several activities are performed within the company, the modus operandi of the accounting system should have the capability of identifying the strengths and weaknesses in the respective areas through the reporting system. The specific avenue through which these reports are normally constructed is the cost accounting process. Contrary to the frequently encountered opinion that cost accounting is of minimal benefit to the small organization, cost accounting procedures may be quite worthwhile to a firm of even moderate size. The advantages should accrue without having to build a system that overpowers the user. Stated briefly, the accounting entity should be developed in compliance with the organizational structure of the company and should be evident in the final reporting format.

The last major element of a sound accounting system is often referred to as *internal control*. Basically, this factor relates to the requisite checks and

---

[3]For an in-depth presentation of the development of an accounting system, see James Beardsley Bower, *Principles of Accounting System Design*, an unpublished Doctoral Dissertation at the University of Texas, Austin, 1960.

balances within the process to ensure accuracy and reliability of the accounting output. Also, the safeguarding of assets and the discouragement of potential fraudulent actions on the part of employees are involved. These characteristics have often been neglected by the small firm management, believing that the controls being prescribed are either unnecessary or infeasible within the small business concern. With the foregoing generic description of the accounting base, attention is now turned to the actual design of a system.

The Accounting System

Designing an effective and efficient system is not a simple matter. Construction of the system requires an ability to analyze management's problems and to understand the precise information needed for their solution. Furthermore, system design rests upon a thorough knowledge of accounting procedures, effective accounting reports, and internal control. Thus, the basic elements in designing a viable accounting system would include the following:

1. Classifying and summarizing data for the purpose of *assessing the current position* of the business.
2. Maintaining adequate *control* of corporate operations.
3. Providing suitable *financial statements* for use by prospective creditors and by company management.
4. Developing information essential to determining future courses of action, that is, *planning*.[4]

While the accounting system is of key importance to any firm, small or large, the structure of an effective system does not come spontaneously. In fact, experienced accountatnts and financial advisors find systems design to be a relatively difficult art to master. This knowledge and capacity to determine the effectiveness of the accounting base usually comes only after years of experience in working with a variety of systems. In this regard, if the ability to design effective accounting systems is difficult to develop, the question has to be raised as to how the small businessman can begin to cope with the problem. In response, recognition of the potential danger would have to be an important first step. Given this congnizance, the small entrepreneur has to acquire assistance, either by attracting the required expertise into the company either as an employee or as an external reference.

[4]See Nathan H. Olshan, "Recordkeeping Systems," *Small Business Bibliography No. 15*, (Washington, D. C.: Small Business Administration, October 1973), p. 1.

Sources of assistance

The entrepreneur-executive who knows he does not possess the expertise necessary for establishing a strong system has several sources of assistance available. First, if the resources of the business permit, a qualified internal accountant should be employed. However, care should be taken in the selection process of locating and attracting an accountant. Not infrequently an accountant may become "bound to tradition and inflexible and unyielding to the requirements" of the owners being served.[5] To be useful and effective, the accountant must be adaptable to a new environment both in terms of the system and management. Also, the ability to adjust to needed changes is essential in a small growth firm.

Depending on the size of the community, a second avenue of assistance to the small firm executive is a systems analyst within a data-processing company. If resources are limited, this alternative may be the least costly. Since the systems analyst is a specialist in the design of information systems for businesses, he generally should be able to render worthwhile services. However, the analyst's services are usually available only to the enterprise considering the purchase of an accounting system from a data-processing firm and typically are available only at a predetermined fee. Also, if the operations of the small business are relatively unique, a "packaged" system previously developed by the analyst for other businesses may not be appropriate.

The third source of assistance for not only developing but also maintaining the accounting system is the certified public accountant (CPA). In addition to tax consultation and audit responsibilities for the small company having a need for certified financial statements, the CPA may be called upon for a *client write-up*. This procedure constitutes the development of the basic system as well as the processing of the data through this framework in order to provide financial statements. As a result of exposure to a variety of businesses and typically a strong desire to work with the small business community, the qualified CPA has proven to be of significant benefit to most small firms. In general, the professional accountant frequently represents the most actively involved external consultant to the small firm, with these activities being centered around the firm's accounting system but extending deeply into the various operations of the business.

In summary, regardless of the eventual source of collaboration in designing the accounting system, the manager of the small enterprise has to at least be able to communicate with the particular professional regarding the basic needs of the concern's decision makers in terms of accessibility to

[5]See J. A. O'Brien, "Do Accountants Make Good Managers?" *The Accountants Digest*, (Sept. 1974), pp. 30–33.

financial data within the firm. Without such an awareness, the system may represent only a general "package" and may not be responsive to the needs of the business. Hence, an awareness of the underlying procedures of systems design is essential for the owners of a small company.

The accounting systems design process

Four phases of design construction may be identified: a *survey* of company needs, the *design* of the accounting base in view of management's informational requirements, the *installation* of the system, and the *follow-up*.[6] The *survey* represents the investigation into the decision-making process both in terms of the staff being responsible for these decisions and the specific flow of key data inputs. For the large firm, the survey comprises interviews with both top and middle managers in an effort to determine needs, charting the organizational aspects of the company, examining products and processes of production, and gathering data about the procedures already in use by the company. One of the primary goals of systems design for the large firm is to integrate the different levels of the organization and the different functions within the organization. Integration is vital within the large organization in order to foster adequate control at the respective levels of the operation.

In the small firm where management and ownership are generally in the hands of a few individuals, control over the organization and the supervision of employees are usually direct and personal. Normally, a complex system for these organizations is neither needed nor desirable. Thus, for the small business with a limited number of managers, the survey stage involves an inquiry into their specific informational needs. The key issue becomes the ascertainment of the information required by the manager in finalizing the necessary decisions. At first glance, the question may appear to be amenable to an easy answer; however, upon closer scrutiny the resolution of the problem may become immensely more difficult for a number of reasons. First, the owner of the small business entity may not have sufficient experience by which to identify the information that could be of assistance in making financial decisions. Second, a danger frequently occurring in the developmental process is the generation of an excessive number of reports. As a result, the owner becomes inundated with data, to the point of concealing the critical issues. In essence, the primary factor is not the *amount* of information but rather the *efficacy* of the communiqué in revealing the key issues. Finally, management should be careful not to fall into a trap of superficially copying the system of another company. In short, only through self-analysis may the executive have any assurance that the accounting data being provided satisfies the needs of the enterprise.

[6]Heckert J. Brooks and Harry D. Kerrigan, *Accounting Systems*, 3rd ed., (New York: Ronald, 1967), pp. 34–49.

Based on a thorough examination of the firm's needs, the actual design of the accounting system may then be undertaken. This facet of the systems construction involves (1) the specification of the format and types of financial summaries, (2) the detailing of a chart of accounts, (3) the design of the ledgers, and (4) the formulation of the procedures circumscribing the processing of the foregoing documents. For the large operation, the numerous divisions, or even departments, involving a multiplicity of product lines or services may compel financial summaries for the respective operational segments of the firm. This requisite for frequent and probing analyses is obvious for the large business. In contrast, the consensus that the small business has no such need is misleading. Although the complexity of the reports may be less, the fewer complications within the small firm should not be thought to negate the importance of well-conceived financial summaries. While the large firm is partitioned into a number of divisions with personnel having narrowly defined responsibilities, the small company owner-manager's functions are more diverse, covering more fronts. For this reason, management within a small firm has a significant requirement for lucid summaries of the financial activities of the business. Therefore, regardless of size, a need exists to compare the results of the operations against predetermined standards, with the deviations being analyzed as a basis for corrective action.

In developing financial reports, a supporting chart of accounts serves as the framework through which the data must flow. The classifications, as well as the subclassifications, of the accounts should be logically arranged and linked to the summaries. The criterion as to the adequacy of the chart of accounts is whether or not the codification yields the desired and needed information in a manner highlighting the critical elements for a successful operation. Any greater detail may cloud the important relationships by the maze of superfluous accounts; anything less conceals important data. As a practical matter, a CPA should be able to recommend a viable set of accounts, or, alternatively, trade associations frequently publish charts of accounts, making them available to their membership.

As a means for drawing the data together, ledgers, both general and special in nature, are employed in the accounting process. These ledgers represent the final step in the classification process, with the transactions being summarized in a chronological order by account and subsequently transferred to the general ledger in summary form. For instance, a cash disbursements journal categorizes the company's expenditures into the various defined accounts. At the conclusion of the *interim period*, usually defined as one month for accounting purposes, these accounts are closed, and the totals are carried to the general ledger.

When the systems design is completed the installation is then initiated. Although the installation may be substantially easier for the small firm, advance planning is still essential. New equipment, supplies, and work-space arrangements are necessary. Also, for the already existing small business changing over to a new system, the new procedures should be tested prior to company-wide adoption. If possible, the old technique should be continued in parallel until the effectiveness of the new processes is evaluated.

The remaining step in systems construction is the follow-up. The importance of comparisons of planned benefits with actual benefits cannot be overemphasized. Gradual return in an informal way to at least a portion of the old conventions may be expected. Thus, a follow-up is necessary as an assessment of the effectiveness of the system in contributing to the decision-making process.

The Cost Accounting Process

An important segment of the accounting system is the cost accounting procedures incorporated into the analysis. Cost accounting has been broadly defined as "a quantitative method that accumulates, classifies, summarizes, and interprets information for three major purposes: (1) operational planning and control, (2) special decisions, and (3) product (or service) costing."[7]Cost accounting techniques have proven particularly beneficial in the management and administration of a business, affording essential information in ascertaining the cost of producing a certain product or in rendering a service. In the past, these cost accounting applications were primarily associated with manufacturing operations; however, any business activity involving monetary exchanges represents a potentially beneficial area of usage for cost accounting, whether the organization is a wholesale concern, a retail outlet, a nonprofit or governmental unit, a financial institution, or a firm providing professional services. In addition, the size of the firm does not necessarily preclude cost accounting. Accordingly, a basic review of cost accounting will be provided in terms of the objectives as well as the types of systems. Finally, a justification of these applications for the small firm will be presented.

In a planning and control context, cost accounting may be linked to the following aims[8]:

1. Planning profit by means of budgets.
2. Controlling costs via responsibility accounting.
3. Inventory costing for measuring profit.
4. Assisting in pricing goods and services.

Cost accounting functions are intended to provide a measurement of budgeted material costs, wages and salaries, and other expenses of producing

[7]Charles T. Horngren, *Cost Accounting*, 3rd ed., (Englewood Cliffs, N. J.: Prentice-Hall, 1972), p. 944.

[8]Adolph Matz and Othel J. Curry, *Cost Accounting*, 5th ed., (Cincinnati: South-Western, 1972), pp. 41–44.

and marketing the firm's goods or services. These contemplated costs are examined in an effort to establish the relationship between such costs and the levels of business activity, requiring an indication of the variable and fixed costs. With this information, an operating forecast may be constructed that defines the cost-volume-profit relationships, which represent an essential ingredient in making major profit-planning decisions.

If budgets are to be effective, planning must be followed by effective controls. The fundamentals of controlling costs involve (1) assigning responsibilities for the control of costs by establishing lines of authority, (2) restricting the individual's control efforts in accordance with the controllable costs, and (3) reporting the person's performance.

Measuring company profit involves separating the costs applicable to units sold (cost of goods sold) from the costs applicable to the units remaining in inventories. This classification procedure is fundamental to the process of matching expired costs with revenues in order to determine profit.

To establish rational sales prices, managers must have a knowledge of both costs and their relationship to volume. The contemplated costs budgeted for normal capacity permit management to price goods and services for the recovery of costs and a normal profit.

Types of cost accounting systems

Managerial problems differ from industry to industry and from firm to firm. For this reason, cost accounting systems must be designed to meet the needs of the particular firm. Two major types of systems have evolved over the years: job order cost systems and process cost systems.

Job order costing is defined as a "system of applying manufacturing costs to specific jobs or batches of specialized or unique production in proportion to the amounts of materials, attention, and effort used to produce each unit or group of units."[9] Thus, a "job" may comprise one unit of any product (a house or airplane), or it may refer to many units of identical or similar products covered by a single production order, e.g., the production of a textbook, or it may be a service being rendered, such as a legal case.[10] The key factor is the collection and representation of costs related to a specific undertaking as opposed simply to determining aggregate costs.

Process costing is the cost accounting procedure for continuous or mass production industries, providing a method for costing products with the average cost being measured on the basis of total costs relative to the equivalent units of work performed. Since output for companies in mass production industries consists of like units being processed in the same manner, the assumption is made that the same amount of materials, labor,

[9]Horngren, *Cost Accounting*, p. 947.

[10]John C. Booth, Jr. "Your Accounting System: Is It Out of Date," *Texas Business*, (Sept. 1976), p. 26.

and overhead is charged to each unit of production. The emphasis is given to the accumulation of the costs for producing a designated number of units during a specific process, operation, or department for a given period of time.

Costs may be recorded on a historical and/or a predetermined basis under either job order or process costing. After operations have taken place, the actual costs incurred are accumulated on a *historical cost* basis. Also, a *standard cost* representing a predetermined cost may be calculated in advance of the operations for comparison with the actual costs. Both historical costs and predetermined costs may be utilized in a cost system. For example, a job order cost system generally uses historical costs for the material and labor while using standard costs for the overhead.

The logic of cost classifications needed for the development of cost data for management can best be illustrated by the chart in Figure 7-1. As may be observed, direct materials and direct labor are combined into the *prime cost*. Prime costs are basically the costs to be charged directly to specific units, jobs, or products. *Factory overhead*, the remaining component of factory costs, is composed of the cost of indirect materials, indirect labor, and all other manufacturing costs that cannot *conveniently* be charged directly to specific products or services. Factory overhead and prime costs are then combined with marketing and administrative costs to ascertain the total cost of the output.

With the foregoing synopsis of cost accounting, attention will now be given to the role of cost accounting for the small business.

Cost accounting and the small enterprise

The benefits ensuing from the application of cost accounting are not limited to large corporations. Undoubtedly, the complexity of the large multidivisional firm with operations in different localities makes cost accounting an absolute necessity for functioning. Yet, cost procedures are of significant importance to the small firms. Although the absence of cost accounting may not result in the small enterprise being dysfunctional, as might occur for the multifaceted major corporation, the analysis does permit the executive of the small entity to *fine-tune* the decision-making mechanism. In essence, from a positive side, the small-firm manager may expect a better understanding of the underlying relationships affecting profitability if appropriate cost accounting practices have been instigated. A large number of proprietors for small organizations make decisions with only limited information. For instance, pricing decisions are frequently determined largely upon competitors' actions, with only a restricted understanding of the cost of producing a product or providing a service. Although this style of operation may not cause business failure, the small-firm management is functioning with inadequate information unnecessarily.

In response to the foregoing contention, the executive of the small enterprise may question the merit of a cost system, citing the ability to assess

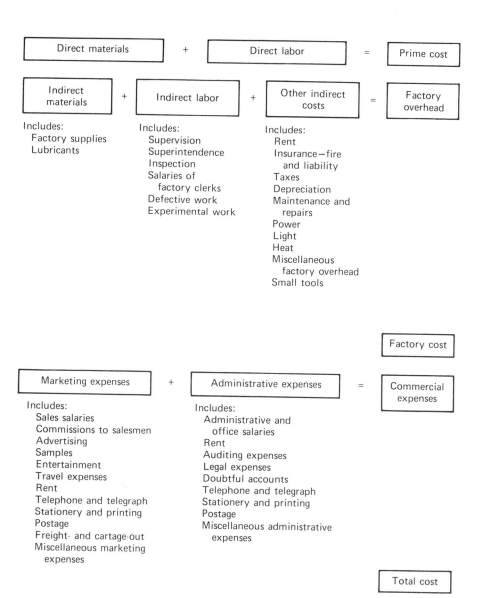

FIGURE 7-1. Analysis of total cost

SOURCE: Adapted from Adolph Matz and Othel J. Curry, *Cost Accounting*, 5th ed., (Cincinnati: South-Western, 1972), pp. 41–44.

costs without a formal mechanism. For certain small companies, the owners may be quite adept in assessing costs; however, for many small entities of even moderate complexity calculating costs of providing a unit of merchandise or service with a high degree of confidence does require more than "seat of the pants" estimates. In these instances, the small businessman has a distinct advantage if costs have been developed systematically and carefully.

In addition to using the cost accounting process, the leadership of the small organization should comply with the need to implement and maintain internal accounting controls. Only through these controls can management have any assurance regarding the accuracy of the accounting information being provided. Without such confidence, the entire financial decision-making process is jeopardized.

Internal Control

As already noted, the accounting system represents the financial data bank on which the vast majority of business decisions have their basis. Without this basic information, sound financial decisions become a matter of chance rather than design. Likewise, serious misjudgments may occur when the "information" is available but contains bias and/or inaccuracies. For this reason, internal control, while being important in safeguarding the firm's assets, also plays a key role in enhancing the quality of the financial output employed in the decision-making process. As set forth by the accounting profession, internal control is "the plan of organization and all of the co-ordinate methods and measures adopted within a business to safeguard its assets, check the accuracy and reliability of its accounting data, promote operational efficiency, and encourage adherence to prescribed managerial policies."[11] Within this general definition, two primary areas are included. The first two objectives of internal control, safeguarding assets and the accuracy and reliabiltiy of the data, pertain to *accounting controls*. In this context, accounting control is defined as

> ...the plan of organization and the procedures and records that are concerned with the safeguarding of assets and the reliability of financial records and to provide reasonable assurance that:
>
> a. Transactions are executed in accordance with management's general or specific authorization.
> b. Transactions are recorded as necessary (1) to permit preparation of financial statements in conformity with generally accepted accounting principles or any other criteria applicable to such statements and (2) to maintain accountability for assets.

[11]*Statement on Auditing Procedures, No. 33* (New York: American Institute of Certified Public Accountants, 1963), p. 27.

   c. Access to assets is permitted only in accordance with management's authorization.

   d. The recorded accountability for assets is compared with the existing assets at reasonable intervals and appropriate action is taken with respect to any differences.[12]

The second aspect of controls, incorporating operational efficiency and managerial policies, is associated with *administrative* or *managerial controls*. In this regard, administrative controls involve

> ...the plan of organization and the procedures and records that are concerned with the decision processes leading to management's authorization of transactions. Such authorization is a management function directly associated with the responsibility for achieving the objectives of the organization and is the starting point for establishing accounting control of transactions.[13]

The foregoing segregation is helpful in gaining an overall perspective of internal controls, particularly for the small firm, since the administrative portion of the checks and balances usually has to represent a larger segment of the controls for the small business due to fewer employees having accounting-related functions. In presenting internal control, the importance of the procedure within the small company will be highlighted. Second, the elements of internal control will be identified. Third, a brief view of the evaluation of the internal control system will be given. Last, ownership involvement in implementing internal control will be presented.

Importance of internal control in the small firm

Internal control has long been recognized as important in the large corporation. As cited in a major auditing text, "...internal control has developed into a technique of vital importance in enabling management of large complex enterprises to function efficiently."[14] Despite such prominence as a technique for large firms, the management of the small company should be able to reap benefits from developing effective internal controls. Without any question, maintaining internal control within the small business is difficult. The absence of a diverse staff makes the division of responsibilities impractical at times. However, this hardship should not minimize the significance of internal control within the small company relative to the large corporation.

Several reasons suggest that the equity holders of a small organization should be attuned to the internal control provisions within their firm. First, as

[12]*Statement of Auditing Standards*, No. 1, Section 320.28 (New York: American Institute of Certified Public Accountants, November, 1972).

[13]*Ibid.*

[14]Walter B. Meigs, E. John Larsen, and Robert F. Meigs, *Principles of Auditing*, 5th ed., (Homewood, Ill.: Irwin, 1973), p. 124.

already mentioned, the reliability and timeliness of accounting information in making financial decisions are indispensable. Although this applies to all businesses, whether large or small, an extra dimension exists for the small firm in which the owner has invested a large portion of his net worth. A faulty decision for this individual can materially impact an entire life-style for many years, if not for a lifetime. In other words, the decision maker who is also a major stockholder subjects himself to greater risk on a relative basis as important decisions are being made than may be the case for the corporate executive within the large business. Accordingly, having valid and timely imputs in the form of accounting information is essential, thereby minimizing the probability of poor judgments.

In addition to reducing the risk exposure of the firm through greater precision in the information base, internal control may have an indirect impact upon the availability of external financing. Frequently, the bank or other prospective lenders may include a provision in the loan agreement that certified financial statements are to be provided annually. Such a stipulation calls for audits by an independent certified public accountant. However, for an accountant to publish an unqualified opinion regarding the financial statements, internal controls must exist. As a part of the audit process, the accountant relies upon the existence of internal controls in examining the financial records. Since the audit normally is based on a sampling of the financial transactions rather than testing every event, the confidence of the auditor is in part a function of the level of internal controls prevailing during the time period under examination. If these procedures are nonexistent, the accountant may not be prepared to offer an opinion or at least may feel required to qualify the opinion. In turn, the confidence of the prospective supplier of capital has to be affected, possibly resulting in more restrictions in the contract accompanying the loan or even possibly the rejection of the loan itself.

A last benefit accruing to the firm through internal controls is the possible decrease in the expenses associated with the audit. If inadequate controls become apparent to the accountant, developing the basis for certified financial statements may require an extension of the examination. Simply stated, the more insufficient the controls, the more in-depth the auditing procedures become. As the investigation is extended, the costs naturally have to increase. "The ability of management to adopt sound accounting policies, maintain an adequate and effective system of accounts, safeguard assets, and devise a system of internal control that will help assure the production of proper financial statements is an important goal to containing audit costs."[15] Hence, the injection of sound internal controls into the system should result in lower expenses for the firm.

[15]Cindy H. Nance and William W. Holder, "Planning for the Audit: Logical Steps Toward Cost Containment," *Financial Executive* (May 1977), p. 47.

Elements of internal control

Certainly no single plan may be given for all firms in constructing an internal control program. The optimal plan would be a function of the nature of the operation, the size of the firm, the type of accounting system, and the philosophy and modus operandi of the management. However, some basic elements have come to be recognized as essential ingredients in most firms. These would include

1. An *organizational plan* constituting clear lines of authority and responsibility, while segregating the operating, recording, and custodial functions.
2. An *accounting structure* that sets forth the flow of transactions and provides reasonable accounting control over assets, liabilities, revenues, and expenses.
3. *Personnel* having ability and experience commensurate with their responsibilities.
4. An *internal auditing staff* charged with the surveillance and improvement of internal controls.[16]

These factors are investigated by the external accountant, with the intent being to verify that the company personnel do in reality observe these guidelines in the day-to-day operations.

the organization plan

An underlying principle of internal control would require that no one individual should be permitted to maintain sole oversight of a transaction from beginning to end. This separation of functions should occur along three lines whenever feasible:

1. Authorization to execute a transaction. This authorization refers to the person who has authority and responsibility to initiate record keeping of a transaction. Authorization may be general, referring to a class of transactions (e.g., all purchases), or it may be specific (e.g., sale of an important asset).
2. Recording of the transaction. This duty refers to the accounting and record-keeping function (bookkeeping) which in some organizations may be partially delegated to an electronic data-processing system. If EDP is in use, then an additional level of control over the machine system is required.
3. Custody of assets involved in the transaction. This duty refers to the actual physical possession or effective physical control of property.[17]

---

[16]Minor variations exist within the accounting literature regarding the characteristics of a control system. See Jack C. Robertson, *Auditing*, (Homewood Ill.: Business Publications, Inc., 1976), pp. 212–213, and Roger H. Hermanson, Stephen E. Loeb, John M. Saada, and Robert H. Strawser, *Auditing Theory and Practice*, (Homewood, Ill.: Irwin, 1976), p. 124.

[17]Jack C. Robertson, *Auditing*, p. 214.

The first item of accountability, the execution of the transaction, should be placed with operational management, while the second duty falls to the individuals having record-keeping responsibilities. Last, a party other than these two persons should be given the "effective" physical control of the property.

Without any question, the small-business executive who has had any measurable experience would quickly question the practicality of such isolation of functions for many small operations. When an organization has a limited number of employees, the strict application of this stipulation may not be attainable. When such a difficulty arises, the involvement of the owner becomes all the more important. Only through such activity on the part of the ownership may this deficiency be effectively countered. Suggestions in this regard are offered later in the chapter when viewing the contribution of management in developing internal control.

accounting structure

The accounting system has been referred to as the *media*, first, in terms of controlling the records of the operations and, second, in classifying the data into a formal structure of accounts. In constructing the system, minimal requirements would include (1) a chart of accounts identifying not only the nature of the account but also the responsible individuals; (2) a procedural manual; (3) proforma statements of operation, including a comparison of actual with predicted; (4) a cost accounting system, if appropriate; and (5) control of supporting documents, such as invoices and checks, by prenumbering the instruments.

In contrast to the previous factor, the organizational plan, no rationale exists for the small firm to be any less effective than a large company in developing a viable accounting system. A company, regardless of size, may implement procedures that expedite a sound accounting structure. These guidelines would include, but not be limited to, the following:

1. Record all cash receipts immediately.
   a. For over-the-counter collections, utilize cash registers easily visible to customers. Record register readings daily.
   b. Prepare a list of all mail remittances immediately upon opening of the mail, and retain this list for subsequent comparison with bank deposit tickets and entries in the cash receipts journal.
2. Deposit all cash receipts intact daily.
3. Make all payments by serially numbered checks, with the exception of small disbursements from petty cash.
4. Use an imprest petty cash fund entrusted to a single custodian for all payments other than by check.
5. Reconcile bank accounts monthly, and retain copies of the reconciliations in the files.
6. Use serially numbered purchase orders for all purchase transactions.

7. Maintain a receiving record, preferably by means of serially numbered receiving reports.
8. Issue checks to vendors only in payment of approved invoices which have been matched with purchase orders and receiving reports.
9. Prepare serially numbered sales invoices for all shipments to customers.
10. Prepare and mail customers' statements monthly.
11. Balance subsidiary ledgers with control accounts at regular intervals.
12. Prepare comparative financial statements monthly in sufficient detail to disclose significant variations in any category of revenue or expense.[18]

personnel

An extremely important, if not the *most* important, element in the firm's internal control has to be the quality of the personnel. The most well-conceived and intricate control system cannot be an effective mechanism in the hands of incompetent employees. The owner needs to be cognizant of the significant impact, either negative or positive, that the staff can have upon the reliability of the accounting information being received by management. Experience would suggest that the small business entity is especially suscept-ible to this potential difficulty. Frequently, the proprietor, in an effort to hold down overhead, selects an individual not because of exceptional capabilities but rather as a result of a "cheap" salary. Also, the inaccessibility to the major sources of qualified applicants may be a limiting factor in the small firm attracting the needed personnel. Even so, the small company should be as concerned as its larger counterpart about its selection process, the training system for present employees, and the evaluation of employee performance.

internal audit

Internal auditing, the process of examining the internal checks and balances by an accountant indigenous to the company, is normally under-taken only in the larger corporations. The internal auditor is responsible to top management and is more concerned with the efficiency of operations, as opposed to determining whether or not the financial statements fairly repre-sent the financial condition of the company. Although the small company may not be able to justify economically an internal auditing staff, the chief accountant in the small concern may be able to perform limited examinations and evaluations of the accuracy of the accounting data base.

Examining the internal control system

Although the small business does not require the same degree of complexity in evaluating the internal control, a formal procedure should be undertaken if for no other reason than the establishment of a "good habit." For some reason, even though the internal control for an extremely small

---

[18]Walter B. Meigs, et. al, *Principles of Auditing*, pp. 155–156.

business could currently be evaluated informally, the transition to a formalized examination when needed often lags the growth of the company. Also the provision of a permanent record is of value.

Methods for perusing the internal control vary; however, a popular analysis is the questionnaire approach. Such a questionnaire is illustrated in Figure 7-2. The questions are not all-inclusive but are provided as a means for depicting the nature and the extent of the investigation within the small company. A more detailed analysis would certainly be expected in a similar document for larger businesses.

The role of management in internal control

Without regard to the size of the organization, the responsibility for a trenchant internal control system rests with management. As asserted in the *Statement of Auditing Standards*, "the establishment and maintenance of a system of internal control is an important responsibility of management.... The system of internal control should be under continuing supervision by management to determine that it is functioning as prescribed and is modified as appropriate for changes in conditions."[19] In other words, the structuring of an internal control system is viewed as being an integral part of management's total responsibility, with the accountant playing a supporting role in the design, installation, and modification of the system.

While the size and diversity of a large corporation may have advantages in the control process, the ownership of a small business has a distinct advantage usually not available to the executive of the large firm. Active participation in the control system by an alert and interested owner represents a dimension normally not achievable in a large business. Such involvement on the part of key personnel within the small company assists greatly in overcoming the difficulty of maintaining separate functions within an operation. For instance, if necessity deems that the same employee is to serve as cashier and bookkeeper, the interaction of the owner in certain select functions may be a valid means to prevent fraud and/or to serve as a check in the accuracy of the information being processed. Examples of activities of the owner that would contribute to the validity of the internal control mechanism would be the following:

1. The approval of certain key documents on a current basis.
2. The inspection of the incoming mail.
3. A perusal of the bank statement prior to forwarding it to the employee assigned the task of reconciliation.
4. A critical review of the monthly trial balances of the firm's accounting records.
5. The inspection of accounts receivable statements prior to mailing.

[19]*Statement on Auditing Standards, op. cit.,* Section 320.31.

		Yes	No
1.	General		
	a. Are accounting records kept up to date and balanced monthly?	___	___
	b. Is a chart of accounts used?	___	___
	c. Does the owner use a budget system for watching income and expenses?	___	___
	d. Are cash projections made?	___	___
	e. Are adequate monthly financial reports available to owner?	___	___
	f. Does the owner appear to take a direct and active interest in the financial affairs and reports which should be or are available?	___	___
	g. Are the personal funds of the owner and his personal income and expenses completely segregated from the business?	___	___
	h. Is the owner satisfied that all employees are honest?	___	___
	i. Is the bookkeeper required to take annual vacations?	___	___
2.	Cash receipts		
	a. Does the owner open the mail?	___	___
	b. Does the owner list mail receipts before turning them over to the bookkeeper?	___	___
	c. Is the listing of the receipts subsequently traced to the cash receipts journal?	___	___
	d. Are over-the-counter receipts controlled by cash register tapes, counter receipts, etc?	___	___
	e. Are receipts deposited intact, daily?	___	___
	f. Are employees who handle funds bonded?	___	___
3.	Cash disbursements		
	a. Are all disbursements made by check?	___	___
	b. Are prenumbered checks used?	___	___
	c. Is a controlled, mechanical check protector used?	___	___
	d. Is the owner's signature required on checks?	___	___
	e. Does the owner sign checks only after they are properly completed? (Checks should not be signed in blank.)	___	___
	f. Does the owner approve and cancel the documentation in support of all disbursements?	___	___
	g. Are all voided checks retained and accounted for?	___	___
	h. Does the owner review the bank reconciliation?	___	___
	i. Is an imprest petty cash fund used?	___	___
4.	Accounts receivable and sales		
	a. Are work order and or sales invoices prenumbered and controlled?	___	___
	b. Are customers' ledgers balanced regularly?	___	___
	c. Are monthly statements sent to all customers?	___	___
	d. Does the owner review statements before mailing them himself?	___	___

FIGURE 7-2. The Smalltime Company's internal control questionnaire

	Yes	No
e. Are account write-offs and discounts approved only by the owner?	___	___
f. Is credit granted only by the owner?	___	___

5. Notes receivable and investments
   a. Does the owner have sole access to notes and investment certificates? ___ ___

6. Inventories
   a. Is the person responsible for inventory someone other than the bookkeeper? ___ ___
   b. Are periodic physical inventories taken? ___ ___
   c. Is there physical control over inventory stock? ___ ___
   d. Are perpetual inventory records maintained? ___ ___

7. Property assets
   a. Are there detailed records available of property assets and allowances for depreciation? ___ ___
   b. Is the owner acquainted with property assets owned by the company? ___ ___
   c. Are retirements approved by the owner? ___ ___

8. Accounts payable and purchases
   a. Are purchase orders used? ___ ___
   b. Does someone other than the bookkeeper always do the purchasing? ___ ___
   c. Are suppliers' monthly statements compared with recorded liabilities regularly? ___ ___
   d. Are suppliers' monthly statements checked by the owner periodically if disbursements are made from invoice only? ___ ___

9. Payroll
   a. Are the employees hired by the owner? ___ ___
   b. Would the owner be aware of the absence of any employee? ___ ___
   c. Does the owner approve, sign, and distribute payroll checks? ___ ___

10. Brief narrative of auditor's conclusions as to adequacy of internal control

_____

_____

_____

_____

_____

FIGURE 7-2. Continued

SOURCE: Herbert J. Steizer, "Evaluation of Internal Control in Small Audits," *Journal of Accountancy*, (Nov. 1964), pp. 58–59.

In short, internal control can be effectively administered in the small enterprise, and the importance of doing so should not be minimized. The procedures may be somewhat different from those that would be observed in a large company with separate divisions, but this does not mean its effectiveness in the given circumstances is reduced.

Summary

To be able to make sound financial decisions a firm's management must have a strong accounting system as a foundation. The use of the most sophisticated analytical financial techniques is meaningless if the data are either inaccurate or not available. This basic concept is applicable whether the firm is large or small. Hence, the ownership of the small company should avoid the temptation to operate without timely and accurate financial data simply because the smallness of the organization appears conducive to informal accounting practices.

The structuring of the accounting system should follow several principles. In developing a viable accounting framework, the trade-off between the benefits of additional information and the costs of compiling these data has to be kept in perspective. Management should avoid having insufficient inputs or expending large amounts of time and effort in compiling marginally beneficial data. A second guideline for building the accounting system is the requisite for responsibility accounting. The financial reports being generated from the accounting data base should fall along the lines of responsibilities of the respective personnel. The last principle is the requirement for internal control. These controls are of key importance in ensuring the accuracy and reliability of the accounting output and in safeguarding the firm's assets.

In designing the accounting system as the basis for financial decisions, superficial analysis in the form of predeveloped packages should be endorsed carefully, if at all. The construction process should be founded upon a survey of the firm's needs and not upon some standard package. Given these needs, the design may then be undertaken, with procedural aspects being clearly set forth, complemented with the specification of the format and types of financial summaries to be generated. Subsequent to the design, the installation is initiated; however, the mere fact that the system is well conceived and that installation has been completed does not ensure continued compliance with the intent of management. For this reason, follow-up is essential in guaranteeing personnel adherence to the plan.

Procedures for affording information regarding the cost of providing a unit of product or service can be instrumental in sound planning and control for any company, regardless of its size. The owner of the small enterprise should investigate the feasibility of cost accounting. If the system is initiated, the executive of the small operation has a strong need for understanding the cost accounting procedures. In an environment stipulating a thorough knowledge of most facets of the company, as is the case for most small entrepreneurs, cost data are particularly meaningful.

Another sector of accounting often not understood by the small firm executive, both in terms of intent and procedures, is internal control. Such controls, long recognized as essential in the large corporation, should not be slighted in importance in the small firm. Several reasons were cited for the owners of the small company taking seriously the implementation of internal controls for their organization. As to purpose, internal control facilitates the safeguarding of assets, improves the accuracy and reliability of financial statements, promotes operational efficiency, and encourages adherence to prescribed managerial policies. Having a grasp of the objectives of internal controls, the elements constituting these controls are to be identified, with management assuming prime responsibility for ensuring that these factors exist within the company.

In summary, while accounting and finance are separated for pedagogical reasons, in practice this segregation does not exist. Only by having a thorough understanding of the makeup of the accounting system can the proprietor react appropriately in making effective financial decisions.

QUESTIONS

1. Explain the principles given in the chapter relating to the design of the firm's accounting system.

2. Evaluate the three sources of professional assistance available for constructing an accounting system.

3. What difficulties might be encountered in the survey portion of designing the accounting system for the small company?

4. Evaluate the following statement: "The small business organization does not require an accounting system to the extent of the large firm since the smaller organization does not have so many departments and decentralized decisions."

5. Explain the benefits that may result from effectively implementing internal controls.

6. Contrast the level of difficulty the small-firm management might encounter in developing (a) the plan of organization and (b) the accounting structure for improving internal control.

7. Explain the importance of management in the accounting function in the small company.

8. a. What is meant by *responsibility accounting?*

   b. Is the *responsibility accounting* concept identical to *accountability?*

   c. How should the concept of responsibility accounting affect systems design?

PROBLEM

7-1. As an assignment external to the class, visit a small company in your local community. The purpose of the visit is to become familiar with the company's accounting system. Request the opportunity to (a) view the chart of accounts, (b) observe the flow of information through the system, and (c) examine the final reports generated for management. Finally, attempt to determine how the information is used by company personnel. Prepare a report of your visit according to the specifications of your instructor. (Note: You may wish to use the questions in Figure 7-2 as a guideline for your review. Yet, do not permit such a format to discourage creativity.)

chapter 8

ELECTRONIC DATA PROCESSING
IN THE SMALL COMPANY

In the preceding chapter, the accounting process was presented, with an emphasis being placed upon the needs of the small firm. In this regard, the accounting system was observed to involve the capturing of data, the processing and recording of the information, and finally a structuring of the quantitative results in a format supportive of the decision-making process. In each of these phases of processing the information, potential time delays and inaccuracies become critical. These difficulties have been relieved to a major extent by the advent of the computer. Although the transition has not occurred without problems, corporate managements have come to rely upon the computer in almost every facet of their operation. However, the benefits accruing from these applications have largely been restricted to the large business entity, simply due to the substantive fixed costs associated with the computer. These costs arise not only from the expenditure for the hardware but also for peripheral needs in terms of programming packages and trained personnel.

Although historically electronic data processing has been limited to large firms, more recently the owners of small businesses have begun investigating the applicability of the computer for their firms. The impetus for such interest has been the significant reduction in the costs of the computer, either through ownership or by having access to a system owned by a second party. More specifically, at the lower end, entire systems, including both hardware and the related software packages, are selling for amounts in the $5,000 to $10,000 range or may be leased for less than $500 per month. Installations generally no longer require additional air conditioning or false floors. Furthermore, programming languages have been simplified. If the present direction continues, particularly in terms of reductions in prices and increasing performance, the population of small businesses making use of the computer may be expected to increase significantly. Indicative of a conviction on the part of computer vendors that such a trend may be anticipated is the continued increase in the number of suppliers of small business computers.

The number of companies providing computer equipment compatible with small-firm requirements increased from 46 to 96 between 1975 and 1976, a 108 percent increase. In brief, the computer has become a potentially beneficial tool in the financial decision-making mode for many small companies.

In examining the feasibility of a computer system, the analysis should be taken through several phases. As highlighted in Figure 8-1, the investigation is initiated by establishing objectives in order to afford operational criteria by which to evaluate the equipment under consideration. Subsequently, but still a part of the early review process, an understanding must be developed of the various system specifications, both in terms of hardware and software. With a grasp of the specifications, management is then prepared to review the underlying options available, these being time sharing, service

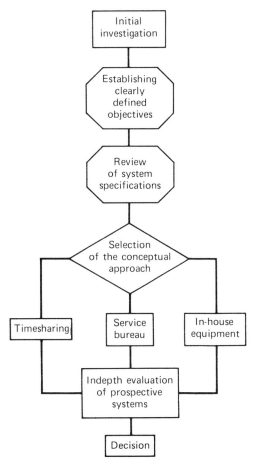

FIGURE 8-1. Computer selection process

bureaus, and an in-house computer. Finally, the small-firm executive, in conjunction with individuals having expertise in these areas, should perform a thorough evaluation of the hardware and software packages still being considered. The foregoing description provides a flow for the subsequent sections.

The Initial Investigation

The decision on the part of small-company management to rely upon electronic data-processing equipment should not be the result of a superficial analysis. As already noted, since the early 1950s innumerable computer applications within large corporations have been developed. As an extension of this phenomenon, and as the costs of computer applications have decreased, the potential utilization of the computer has come within range for many small businesses. Yet, along with this significant movement has come the possible tendency to overstate the usefulness of the computer in the small organization. The conviction that the computer can solve the company's problems has generally proven to be deceiving. An illustration of such an assertion would be as follows:

> If the price of your product cannot be increased, if you have difficulty controlling the cost of resources, and if your labor costs keep spiraling, greater management efficiency is the only answer to increase the figure on the profit line. In our dynamic economy, the best and perhaps only way this can be accomplished is through the use of a computer.[1]

Although advantages may be realized from the implementation of a computer-based system, these benefits must be prefaced with certain conditions. Otherwise, the initiation of the use of a computer, either owned or through an external group, may cause more problems than it resolves. The first prerequisite in this effort is the need for having well-defined objectives.

Setting objectives

Prior to deciding whether to adopt a particular computer arrangement, management should establish definite objectives. These goals should be sufficiently clear, even to the point of specifically determining the data to be stored, the desired manipulation of the information, and the format of the reports to be generated. Yet, to delineate these goals, the firm's needs have to be identified, as well as having an indication as to the feasibility of the application being analyzed. The feasibility of electronic data-processing equipment relates to the duties and responsibilities of the personnel within the

---

[1] Lee O. Cier, "Small Computers in Small Business," *Data Management*, (Nov. 1972), p. 27.

firm and the volume of transactions being encountered. In general, the more extensive the paper flow for both planning and control purposes and the greater the requisite for timeliness, especially if not attainable manually, the more likelihood that the computer may be beneficially used by the decision makers of the firm. Only after an in-depth review of these requirements, thereby establishing realistic objectives in accord with these needs, can a meaningful evaluation be made as to the effectiveness of the computer. However, normally the staff within the small business entity is not trained for performing this analysis. Also, reliance upon a single computer equipment firm in resolving these questions, while often tempting, is hazardous due to the natural bias these company representatives may be expected to possess. For this reason, several computer firms should be contacted in an effort to receive different viewpoints. Also, as a consequence of this potential bias, the company may be well advised to employ an external consultant in order to receive an unbiased perspective. In brief, the technical expertise available through the consultant is critical.

Although an exhaustive listing of the possible areas in which the computer might be of benefit within the small firm would be prohibitive, five basic functions are often executed through the use of electronic data-processing equipment[2]:

1. *Accounts payable.* The accounts payable program provides a timely analysis of the status of the payables outstanding. The reports facilitate the recognition of discounts and a current review of expenditures and liabilities. The output could be comprised of an invoice register, an aging report, an exhibit of amounts payable in the next cash cycle, and the actual production of checks to be forwarded to the creditors.
2. *Accounts receivable.* The primary objectives of this subsystem are to afford an aging of the receivables and furnish individual billing statements. Depending on the nature of the business and the informational needs of the company ownership, additional analysis could be performed. For instance, the firm's managers might want a classification in terms of the types of sales transactions being conducted in the operation.
3. *Payroll.* The purpose of this program is to eliminate the repetitive type of computations associated with salaries. The procedure is of particular benefit when these calculations are further complicated by commissions or payrolls based on productivity. After the salaries have been determined, net of any deductions, checks may then be generated by the program. Finally, the storage of the payroll data permits a summary of the information necessary in completing the quarterly payroll tax report.
4. *Inventory.* With the goal being to develop and maintain adequate inventory control, this subroutine yields an inventory availability statement. In conjunction with this material, reports might also include data for each inventory item with respect to sales (both in terms of units and dollars), costs, gross

[2]The presentation of these functions is taken from W. W. McKee, "Small Businesses Can Be Computerized," *Management Accounting*, (April 1972), pp. 49–52.

profit in dollars and as a percent of sales, average inventory expressed both in quantity and dollars, and turnover rates.

5. *General ledger*. The timeliness of the company's financial results in a framework compatible with the decision-making process is dependent on the completion of the general ledger within sufficient time to react to the information being compiled. Although a variety of reports may be prepared, typically a profit and loss statement, a balance sheet, and a sources and uses of funds statement are incorporated into the results. These summaries may be reflected on a monthly and year-to-date basis, either in dollars or in relative terms. Also, a comparison of results between periods could be made available.

Having designated the key requirements for the firm and the corresponding objectives for using the computer, attention should be given to the systems specifications. Based on these specifications, management may then evaluate the various competing systems, both in terms of concept (time sharing, service bureau, or in-house equipment) and the benefit and costs related to the respective systems. Accordingly, questions relating to system specifications are reviewed in the next section.

System specifications

The analysis of the system characteristics is divisible into the two basic categories, an examination of the computer *hardware* and an inquiry into the *software* accompanying the system.[3]

hardware evaluation

The proprietors of small firms have a tendency to be overly impressed with computer hardware and as a result fail to allocate adequate time and effort to this portion of the examination. As a consequence, a critical evaluation in matching needs with computer hardware capabilities is often not performed, but rather management's decision is based largely, if not completely, on the interaction with a single hardware manufacturer. In this regard, comparisons are essential in selecting the equipment that most satisfactorily meets the company's requirements. These requisites should be viewed in terms of the particular hardware capabilities and the equipment supplier's dependability in servicing the machinery. While a large number of questions may be raised regarding hardware specifications, two key concerns should be (1) the trade-off between processing and input/output speeds and (2) equipment expandability. With respect to the dichotomy between processing and the input/output capacity, computer facilities of the small business operation normally have a greater need for the ability to handle large

---

[3]This section is taken from Ronald C. Blankenship, and Carol A. Schaller, "The CPA, the Small Company and the Computer," *The Journal of Accountancy*, (Aug. 1976), pp. 4–49.

volumes of information rather than long computational procedures. In addition, equipment versatility is particularly significant to the small growth company. The small organization generally implements the system with only a few applications; however, as the size and complexity of the firm increases, the requirements placed upon the computer could be expected to increase manyfold. If the hardware is not conducive to such growth, the expansion may require new equipment, possibly even in a different series. If this conversion becomes necessary, an abrupt and disruptive transition may have to be made.

The second underlying criterion relating to the computer hardware is the vendor's ability to service the equipment. This benchmark is critical for any enterprise but particularly for the small company. Due to its size, the small business generally has to rely upon expertise external to the firm in maintaining the system. For this reason, what may have been thought to be a "bargain" may prove to cause frequent crises in terms of hardware malfunctions. A large number of small firms have been caught in this pitfall, despite efforts to avoid the problem. For this reason, in addition to receiving "promises" in the service contract, an arrangement should be made for specifying alternative systems in the event of extended hardware failure.

software evaluation

If the objectives for employing the computer have been sufficiently explicated, including the desired end product of the output, an evaluation of the software should be relatively straightforward. Concern, however, should be given to determining the stage of development and adaptability of the needed subroutines. Development costs of these application procedures would probably be prohibitive for the small company both in terms of costs and time. Having to expend extensive time and efforts to adapt a subsystem to the company's requirements could represent a major deterrent in achieving a relatively painless installation.

If a firm is considering an in-house computer, the user should give attention to the programming languages available on the system as well as the utility programs and the operating systems. As to the languages, two criteria should be followed, these being the convenience of application and the merits of the language with respect to documentation. In brief, the languages available on the system should be easy to learn and to apply in a business setting. Also, the operating system should be adequate for storing, sorting, and merging the data as needed to accomplish the desired results.

After establishing the underlying objectives and having determined the systems specifications, a decision as to the basic type of arrangement needs to be made. This decision may be an inherent part of the final evaluation, which is presented later in the chapter. Prior to explaining the nature of the evaluation process, the basic approaches available to the manager of a small firm will be explained.

The Alternative Approaches for Computer Facilities

Although a broad spectrum of options exist in terms of computer facilities available to the small business entity, one of three general approaches may be taken. These alternatives include time sharing, service bureau, and in-house equipment. The choices involved represent significant conceptual dissimilarities and may prove to be critically important. Selection of the appropriate approach, followed by a well-conceived implementation period, could make the difference between increased efficiencies, resulting in savings, and disproportionate expenses and/or ineffective operating procedures.

Time sharing

The "sophistication" of time sharing has been sufficiently simplified so as to afford a means for automating information processing within the small business. Time sharing involves accessing a central computer located at a site external to the firm through a remote terminal. In this fashion, the central equipment may be utilized simultaneously by a number of clients, with these users having to pay only for the computer time and peripheral equipment actually used. The terminal may be in the form of a typewriter or a cathode-ray tube, with a telephone line providing the communications link between the terminal and the computer. The primary costs associated with time sharing involve rental of the terminal and charges for computer time and memory requirements in processing transactions, updating files, and maintaining historical data in the memory units.

As to an evaluation of the time-sharing approach, several advantages and disadvantages exist. In terms of advantages, time sharing affords relatively quick turnaround time, particularly if the output requirements are not extensive. A second potential advantage comes in the form of costs. Time sharing does avoid the expenses related to procuring and maintaining highly trained computer operators and analysts. In essence, the training requirements are relatively simple for the terminal operation. Also, the costs of equipment rental and computer time may be relatively cheaper, especially for the small organization not having the volume of transactions to justify an in-house system. Last, time sharing is quite efficient for special jobs, including such reports as the examination of budget variances and sales reports. On the other hand, some serious limitations may be encountered in this concept. Specifically, if the program requires a large amount of output, the deficiency in the printing speed in most terminals may counter the benefit of having entry to large and efficient equipment. If the center does have a high-speed printer, an option may be exercised to have the information printed out at the central location. This alternative is especially appealing if the center is situated in the same community. A second limitation arises in effectively employing the predesigned programs available from a computer facility having terminal operations. Most service centers do have program libraries, but typically the users must be self-reliant in converting these programs to their specific applications, which may prove difficult for small businesses. Last, provisions may have to be made for a utility area in which the terminal may be located. Otherwise, the noise level may be quite distractive to the personnel in the same work space.

Service bureau

Service bureaus represent a second mode by which the small firm may make use of the computer. The material to be processed is forwarded to the center, usually on a monthly basis. Upon receipt of the data, the service center personnel process the information, with reports being generated in accordance with the programs developed for the firm's management. Typically these programs are general in nature, with only slight modifications required in adapting to the company's accounting system. However, specialized reports may be developed if the company's ownership believes the additional costs are justifiable in terms of providing key financial information for decision making. The procedure for processing the data is generally in a *batch* mode in that only one program at a time is utilized for a number of clients. Upon completing this phase of the processing, each of the remaining stages is initiated until the ultimate reports have been produced for all users.

In selecting a service bureau, two references may be helpful, the company's banker and/or accountant. The objectivity of these professionals is usually quite beneficial; however, not infrequently, the accountants may have a natural bias if they provide computer services within their organization. Yet, even so, if the accountant's data-processing equipment is compatible with the small firm's needs, having the firm's accountant and the computer staff within the same organization can prove to have favorable synergistic effects.

As to the criterion for selecting a bureau, the reputation of the service center is of key importance. In investigating the reputability of the center, the financial stability of the organization is to be closely scrutinized. In this regard, reference to other users may be informative in determining the company's reputation. Also, a review of the company's financial statement as well as a credit check may be desirable. A second benchmark that should be considered in the choice of a service bureau is reliability both with respect to the personnel and the equipment. Although difficult to ascertain, the qualifications of the center's staff should be reviewed. In addition, the reliability of the equipment should be of primary concern, with provisions being made for backup equipment. Also, as mentioned earlier, the service capabilities of the bureau should be commensurate with the objectives and needs of the small firm, avoiding both excessive and insufficient capacity. For instance, using a computer that provides greater speed than needed will result in higher costs.

The last standard for selecting a service center is the cost, with two types of charges being encountered: the costs of designing or adapting programs and repetitious expenses for processing. The amount of the fee for program design is a function of the extent of adaptation. For most small companies, these costs may vary from $300 to $1,000 for substantive program developmental costs. In contrast, if the firm's management decides to use a standard programming package, the costs are relatively small and are incorporated into the monthly charges; however, the user may have to modify the company's accounting system to comply with the program specifications. As to the monthly charges, the rates typically fall within a $100 to $300 range, depending on the volume of reports being generated. Also, if the volume of transactions is sizable, a cost reduction might be achieved by having employees within the small business develop the input records. For example, the keypunching of data by the small firm's staff may be economically advantageous.

In-house computer

The last option available to the small firm is to acquire an in-house computer. The feasibility of this alternative historically has been limited to the larger organizations within the small-firm classification. The volume and storage requirements simply exceeded the needs of most smaller organizations. More recently, the age of the smaller electronic data-processing equipment has brought the self-contained system within the reach of many small firms. However, unlike the service bureaus and time sharing, internal computerization requires significant expertise relating to the system. Considerably more care and thought must be given to this approach. Failure to accomplish an orderly implementation may result in the entire financial accounting system becoming dysfunctional.

The costs of these systems are naturally divergent, depending on the requirements of the firm. These systems are priced at a minimum of $5,000, including software, and may be as high as $100,000. Alternatively, the equipment may be leased via a service contract. In this regard, the average annual budget for data-processing machinery among small organizations averages $1\frac{1}{2}$ percent of sales,[4] with $400,000 representing an approximate minimum sales level for a firm contemplating the acquisition or lease of a computer.

In selecting the hardware, two fundamental choices rest with the company's management, the on-line system and the batch system. As to a comparison between the two options, the on-line configuration has greater versatility in terms of modifying and updating data files. In contrast, batch processing is straightforward, brute-force approach, with data being entered

---

[4]Malcom Stiefel, "Small Business Computers," *Mini-Micro Systems*, Vol. 9, No. 7, (July 1976), pp. 50–57.

and stored vial punched cards, punched tape, magnetic tape, or, more recently, small disks or diskettes.[5] However, the costs associated with the on-line arrangement are greater than the expenditures incurred in adopting the batch system. This cost advantage comes from the complexity of the equipment of the on-line system and the disk requirements having to be met in compiling and executing the various reports. In contrast, while the project-cost disparity favors batch processing, a disadvantage linked to this approach is the substantial increase in scheduling and processing time. For the small firm, the batch system imposes a substantial responsibility upon the company's personnel in procedure evaluation and scheduling. For this reason, if the indirect costs are recognized, the batch system may prove to be as expensive as on-line equipment. Furthermore, the lag in receiving the information with batch processing may result in the decision-making process being delayed by several days. Whether or not such a time element is critical depends on the type of decision as well as on the nature of the business. Hence, the choice basically relates to the trade-off between equipment costs versus processing costs, with the timeliness of the feedback being a possible concern.

With the foregoing overview of the approaches that may be taken in meeting the company's requirements for computerization, attention will now be given to the evaluation process in selecting a particular system.

The Evaluation Process

At this point in time, management has identified the objectives to be achieved by the installation of a computer facility. Also, the general philosophy regarding the choice of time sharing, or of a service center or company ownership of a system, has been resolved. Finally, the equipment specifications, both in terms of hardware and software, have been tentatively established. With this information, the company's owners should submit a proposal to a carefully selected group of computer manufacturers. This selection process should be based on personal interviews and references, by which management evaluates the credentials and general qualifications of each manufacturer. In cooperation with these suppliers, cost estimates for the installation and implementation of the system may be constructed. The firm's owners must then give specific attention to the acceptance or rejection of an investment in data processing equipment.

An overview of the analysis

In answering the question whether or not to make a relatively substantial dollar and time investment in computer facilities, the firm's management should conduct an in-depth examination of the benefits relative to the cost of

[5]Fonnie H. Reagan, "The Big Promise of Small Business Systems," *Infosystems*, Vol. 23, No. 5 (May 1976), pp. 36–39.

the investment. Although frequently more difficult to measure, the assessment of the benefits of a new facility is *at least* of equal importance with determining the cost. A clear understanding of the probable benefits to be derived from the investment is of critical importance to both the selection process and the control of operational costs subsequent to the initiation of the system. Certainly, not all benefits are easily quantifiable. In fact, the most important advantages are often the most difficult to measure. In these instances, only a description of the benefit, without actually assigning numerical values, may be necessary. Even so, management should not fail to recognize the potential significance of these *qualitative variables*, realizing that the final decision may have to rest upon their judgment as to the importance of these benefits for their firm.

Specific identification of the benefits accruing from the installation of a computer is simply not possible, without having a thorough understanding of the situation. However, at least five general areas representing potential benefits may be specified.[6] First, *equipment displacement* is a frequently cited benefit for installing a new computer system. The elimination of the need for existing accounting machines or an earlier generation computer represents a measurable benefit flowing from the decision to adopt a new computer. However, this effect is generally not a significant factor. Second, *direct cost displacement* may be realized, where savings result from a reduction in the personnel costs associated with a designated task. For example, the release of clerical time in the preparation of invoices, or more importantly, the relief of management from computational efforts in a market analysis, could be a significant reward of computerization. This benefit is particularly evident if the removal of a given task from management is supplemented with a more meaningful task, heretofore slighted. Third, *indirect cost displacement*, while being more difficult to measure precisely, generally comprises a significant element in the justification of a system. This result comes from more timely information for decision making, thereby permitting the company leadership to react more quickly to the changing environment. Illustrations would include closer surveillance of product costs, and improved management of inventory levels and credit extension. This facet is particularly important to the small business, in that the small firm frequently maintains a competitive edge relative to the large corporation by being able to respond more quickly to recent developments. Without the timely access to the company's financial data base, the opportunity to adapt to changing conditions quickly evaporates. A fourth possible advantage that could conceivably ensue from implementing a computer system would be the increased profitability from *additional sales*. The computer, if utilized to its potential, can possibly provide valuable marketing information, both in terms of identifying opportunities within the market place and in isolating the ability of the business entity to

---

[6]For further explanation, see K. Eric Knutsen and Richard L. Nolan, "Assessing Computer Costs and Benefits," *Journal of Systems Management*, (Feb. 1974), pp. 32–34.

fulfill these needs. Finally, the computer may facilitate *control* within the organization, which otherwise might be extremely difficult to enforce. To illustrate, management's policy regarding credit standards may not concur with the firm's credit personnel. As a result, strict compliance may not be met by lower level employees. However, routine computer checks could be implemented to verify the adherence to management's policies.

The preceding observations, while being general in nature, should afford an insight into the appropriate analysis for making the final accept/reject decision. In addition, a hypothetical illustration should prove useful in further clarifying the process.

An illustration of the evaluation process

The D. F. Scott Corporation is currently investigating the desirability of a computer. The firm's owners have visited extensively with Computer, Inc. to determine the costs of the installation and the operation expenses. After numerous on-site meetings with the Scott management, the systems analyst has projected the costs for a system that should be conducive to Scott's current and intermediate-term needs for data processing services. In fact, the equipment is expected to serve Scott's data processing requirements for approximately eight years, at which time a projected salvage value of $7,000 should be realized.

The costs were presented to the vice president of Scott in the format below, with a distinction being maintained between installation costs and recurring annual operational expenses.

If the computer is purchased, several benefits are anticipated. First, the present accounting equipment, having a book value of $10,000, could be sold

Installation cost (including hardware, software, and the renovation of the building to facilitate the structural and electrical requirements)	$75,000
Operational costs (annual)	
Personnel costs (operator-programmer)	$15,000
Site costs	
Utilities	2,000
Additional depreciation (depreciation on computer and related improvements less depreciation on accounting equipment)	7,250
Maintenance	2,000
Supplies	
Paper and printer ribbons	1,500
Magnetic tapes and disk packs	2,000
Miscellaneous	500
Total operational costs	$30,250

for $9,000. In addition to this immediate cash inflow, several favorable effects are expected to be realized throughout the life of the investment. Specifically, clerical assistance should be reduced by $6,000 annually. Furthermore, management currently expends a substantial amount of time in investigating cost overages, which could be readily programmed into the system. Thus, a search routine would automatically submit a warning if these excess costs arose. This analysis, along with several additional programmable options, has been roughly estimated to have a yearly opportunity cost with respect to management's time of $15,000. Finally, the principal reason, as viewed by management, for considering the installation of a new system relates to a potentially significant reduction in the time lapse of providing financial and marketing information. Although the company's owners view the advantage to be of prime importance, they also have difficulty in assigning a reasonable quantitative estimate to this benefit. The advantage is considered to represent a subjective decision on management's part. However, after extensive questioning, the company's vice-president estimated that the improved decision-making process could realistically increase profits by $20,000 in a given year.

With the foregoing information, the analysis might be approached in a format similar to Table 8-1. The initial objective of the calculations is to ascertain the net cost of the outlay on an after-tax basis. This computation requires taking the gross payment for the computer, $75,000, less the $9,000 selling price of the accounting equipment and less the tax savings from selling the old machinery at a $1,000 loss. The final after-tax cost is $67,520. Having determined the net cost of the facility, attention is given to the effective cash flow after taxes generated either directly or indirectly from the investment. This amount is $12,840, which constitutes the incremental earnings after tax from the project plus the additional depreciation, $7,250, to be recorded if the facility is installed. Finally, the net present value of the investment, assuming 8 percent to be the appropriate discount rate, is $10,051.48, which suggests that the data processing equipment should be purchased.

Summary

As a result of the continued decrease in costs and the reduced technical requirements, computer systems are coming within the economic reach of many small- and medium-sized businesses. Indeed, electronic data processing may reasonably be expected to facilitate the financial decision-making process within many small business operations. However, the investigation should be done with care, recognizing that the computer is not an automatic solution to every company problem. In fact, without management progressing in a logical and methodical manner, a computer may produce more problems for a small business than it solves.

A natural departure point of the investigation into a computer system is the establishing of definite objectives. As a basis for these objectives, the

TABLE 8-1

D. F. Scott Computer Analysis

I   Net cost of the replacement

Cost of the computer		$75,000
Selling price of the accounting machines		(9,000)
Tax consequence from the sale of the accounting machinery:		
Sales price	$ 9,000	
Book value	10,000	
Tax loss	($1,000)	
Marginal tax rate	48%	
Tax savings		(480)
Net cost of replacement		$67,520

II   Net additional cash flow after taxes per year

Reduction in clerical expenses	$ 6,000
Opportunity cost of managerial time	15,000
Potential increase in profitability resulting from improved information systems	20,000
Projected gross benefits	41,000
Computer operational expenses	30,250
Incremental earnings before tax	10,750
Taxes (48%)	5,160
Incremental earnings after tax	$ 5,590
Plus: additional depreciation	7,250
Cash flow after taxes (years 1-8)	$12,840
Computer salvage value	$ 7,000

Years	Cash flow after taxes	*III Net present value computation* Present value interest factors at 8%	Present value
1-8	$12,840	5.747	$73,791.48
8	7,000[1]	.540	3,780.00
		Present value of benefits	$77,571.48
		Cost of investment	67,520.00
		Net present value	$10,051.48

[1]Salvage value

company's owners must identify those of the firm's needs that may be facilitated by the installation of computer equipment. Thus, the entire investigation must be based on a thorough understanding of the firm's needs as well as a sound grasp of the functions that may be served by the computer. Otherwise, misconcepts will deter the entire process. With these objectives in mind, management should next determine the specifications of the system, with respect to both hardware and software, that are essential in satisfying the operational requirements. Moreover, an integral part of the investigation is an understanding of the differences with respect to capability and cost among a time sharing facility, a service bureau and an in-house system. Finally, with the foregoing information as the foundation for a decision, a thorough examination of the benefits relative to the cost of the system should be performed. If the key variables can be measured with any meaningful degree of accuracy, the analysis may be made in the form of a capital-budgeting problem.

QUESTIONS

1. Describe a logical flow of events to be taken in investigating the feasibility of a computer installation.

2. Explain the applications that are frequently made of computers in business.

3. What considerations should be recognized in selecting computer hardware?

4. What factors are important in identifying an appropriate software package?

5. Distinguish between time sharing, service bureau, and an in-house computer.

6. What determinants should be included in the evaluation of a service bureau?

7. Distinguish between an on-line system and a batch system.

8. Explain the five general areas that may provide economic benefits, either directly or indirectly, from installing a computer system.

PROBLEM

8-1. Either individually or as a small group identify a small local firm that is actively involved in the use of a computer. Request permission to have an opportunity to visit their facility for the express purpose of discovering how they have come to use the computer. During the interview learn how their firm initially began to use the computer and the problems encountered in the process.

"Accounting and EDP," *The Journal of Accountancy*, Vol. 138, Oct. 1974, pp. 40–46.

BENNINGER, L. J., "A Tool for Modern Management," *Cost and Management*, Vol. 47, July-Aug. 1973, pp. 20–25.

BLANKENSHIP, RONALD C., and CAROL A. SCHALLER, "The CPA, the Small Company and the Computer," *The Journal of Accountancy*, Aug. 1976, pp. 46–51.

BOBICK, STEVE A., EDMUND J. ARMON, and ARTHUR W. YERKES, "The Survey of Small Business Computers, *Datamation*, Oct. 1976, pp. 91–92.

BOWER, JAMES BEARDSLEY, *Accounting Systems Design*, Ann Arbor, Michigan: University Microfilms, 1968.

BURNS, DAVID C., and JAMES L. LOEBBECKE, "Internal Control Evaluation: How the Computer Can Help," *The Journal of Accountancy*, Aug. 1975, pp. 66–70.

CIER, LEE O., "Small Computers in Small Business," *Data Management*, Nov. 1972, pp. 27–31.

COUGER, DANIEL J., and LAWRENCE M. WERGIN, "Systems Management: Small Company MIS," *Infosystems*, Vol. 21, No. 10, Oct. 1974, pp. 30–33.

GIBSON, JAMES L., and W. WARREN HAYNES, *Accounting in Small Business Decisions*, Lexington: University of Kentucky Press, 1963.

GREER, GEORGE G., "The Increasingly Important Role of the Internal Auditor," *Retail Control*, Vol. 40, 1971, pp. 33–50.

GREGG, MAURICE W., "Accounting Control Systems for Inventory Shortage," *Retail Control*, Vol. 40, 1971, pp. 53–64.

HECKERT, J. BROOKS, and HARRY D. KERRIGAN, *Accounting Systems: Design and Installation*, 3rd. ed., New York: Ronald, 1967.

HORNGREN, CHARLES T., *Cost Accounting: A Managerial Emphasis*, 3rd. ed., Englewood Cliffs, NJ: Prentice-Hall, 1972.

"How To Succeed in Small Business," *Datamation*, June 1972, pp. 40–46.

KNUTSEN, K. ERIC, and RICHARD L. NOLAN, "Assessing Computer Costs and Benefits," *Journal of Systems Management*, Feb. 1974, pp. 28–34.

"Management Advisory Services," *The Journal of Accountancy*, Jan. 1976, pp. 90–91.

MATZ, ADOLPH, and OTHEL J. CURRY, *Cost Accounting: Planning and Control*, 5th ed., Cincinnati: South-Western, 1972.

MCKEE, WAYNE W., "Small Business Can Be Computerized," *Management Accounting*, April 1972, pp. 49–52.

MOORE, CARL L., and ROBERT K. JAEDICKE, *Managerial Accounting*, 3rd. ed., Cincinnati: South-Western, 1972.

O'BRIEN, J. A., "Do Accountants Make Good Managers?" *The Accountant Digest*, Sept. 1974, pp. 30–33.

REAGAN, FONNIE H., "The Big Promise of Small Business Systems," *Infosystems*, Vol. 23, No. 5, May 1976, pp. 36–39.

"Small Business Computers," *Mini-Micro Systems*, Vol. 9, No. 7, July 1976, pp. 50–64.

"Small-Scale Computing," *Modern Data*, Vol. 8, No. 6, June 1975, pp. 43–49.

SWALLEY, RICHARD W., "The Benefits of Direct Costing," *The Accountant Digest*, Dec. 1974, pp. 75–79.

part IV

FINANCIAL LEVERAGE

chapter 9

FINANCIAL LEVERAGE
AND CAPITAL STRUCTURE

Debt is relatively more important in small than in large businesses; to illustrate, during the first quarter of 1975 all manufacturing, mining, and trade corporations with less than $5 million in assets employed slightly more than 50 percent debt in their capital structure—50.4 percent for firms with $1 to $5 million in assets and 53.7 percent for firms with under $1 million in assets.[1] On the other hand, companies with more than $1 billion in assets used only 43.5 percent debt. Table 9-1 depicts the debt/equity ratios of small (under $5 million in assets) and large corporations (assets above $250 million) for the period 1967–1973. Included also are the standard deviation and coefficient of variation of these ratios.

It is interesting to observe that while both groups increased debt in their structure during the period, large firms increased debt at a faster rate, e.g., 18.4 percent compared to 14.3 percent for small firms. Also, the increase was constant throughout the period even though interest rates rose considerably. One explanation for the increased growth of debt in large firms is the depressed state of the stock market during this period, and management of these firms believed that interest rates would remain high; therefore, there was no reason for them not to enter the debt market. While small firms do not use the equity markets as a primary source of funds, they still feel the pressure of the market place. Remember, too, that small firms experienced difficult times during this period; that is, profits for retention purposes were adversely affected, thus forcing them to rely more heavily on debt capital.

Debt or Equity: That Is the Question

A firm may decide to use a financial mix consisting of both debt and equity capital for several reasons. The most important reasons are (1) the use

[1]Federal Trade Commision, *Quarterly Financial Report: Manufacturing, Mining and Trade Corporations, 1st Quarter, 1975,* (Washington, D.C.: U.S. Government Printing Office, 1975), p. 59.

TABLE 9-1

Leverage Position of Small and
Large Companies—Percentage
1967–1973

Year	Small firms [1]		Large firms [2]	
	Debt	*Equity*	*Debt*	*Equity*
1967	45.5	54.5	40.2	59.8
1968	46.2	53.8	43.0	57.0
1969	47.0	53.0	44.5	55.5
1970	48.0	52.0	46.0	54.0
1971	49.0	51.0	46.0	54.0
1972	50.4	49.6	46.8	53.2
1973	42.0	48.0	47.6	52.4
1967–1973 average	48.3	51.7	44.8	55.2
Standard deviation	2.16	2.16	2.37	2.37
Coefficient of variation	.045	.042	.053	.043

[1]Small firms are defined as manufacturing, mining, and trade corporations with assets of less than $5 million.
[2]Large firms are defined as manufacturing, mining, and trade associations with assets of more than $250 million.
SOURCE: Federal Trade Commission, *Quarterly Financial Report*: *Manufacturing, Mining, and Trade Corporations*, (Washington, D.C.: U.S. Government Printing Office, 1967–1973).

of debt capital tends to increase the return on equity capital; (2) debt capital is cheaper than equity capital; (3) debt capital is easier to obtain than equity, principally because the lender can look to the personal assets of the owners as well as to the cash flow of the company; (4) debt capital does not disturb the voting position of existing shareholders; and (5) debt provides flexibility during certain economic periods.

Financial leverage

Financial leverage, or trading on equity, is the process of using senior (debt or equity capital with a fixed return) capital to increase the rate of return on junior securities. That is, if capital obtained from debt sources is used in projects that produce a higher return than their cost, equity will benefit advantageously. The following example illustrates this concept. Assume that (1) $100,000 is invested in assets, (2) the rate of return on all capital is 10 percent, (3) all earnings (after taxes) are paid out in the form of cash dividends, (4) assets may be increased up to 100 percent without a change in costs or revenue, and (5) flotation costs are ignored for the sake of simplicity. The following financial data depict the firm's present position.

Total capital	Equity capital	Debt capital	Rate earned on capital	Interest costs	Taxes 20%	Dividends 100%	After-tax return on equity
$100,000	$100,000	0	10%	0	$2,000	$8,000	8.0%

Assume that management decides to double the firm's investment. Two alternatives are available: First, it could raise $100,000 through the sale of common stock, or second, it could raise the funds from a group of creditors at an average cost of 8 percent. The net effects of these two methods of financing are shown in the following example:

All equity funds used to finance the expansion

Total capital	Equity capital	Debt capital	Rate earned on capital	Interest costs	Taxes 20%	Dividends 100%	Return on equity
$200,000	$200,000	0	10%	0	$4,000	$16,000	8.0%

Assume management raises the additional capital from debt sources:

Equal mix of debt and equity capital

Total capital	Equity capital	Debt capital	Rate earned on capital	Interest costs	Taxes 20%	Dividends 100%	Return on equity
$200,000	$100,000	$100,000	10%	$8,000	$2,400	$9,600	9.6%

It can be seen that there was an increase of 20 percent in the return on equity capital primarily because debt rather than equity was used in the expansion process. The size of the increase resulting from the use of debt is determined by (1) the amount of debt used relative to equity and (2) the differential between the return on capital (K) and the cost of debt capital (K_i). Table 9-2 illustrates the effect of increasing or decreasing debt relative to equity.

It may be seen that a change from all equity to 75 percent equity and 25 percent debt caused the return to equity to increase 6.25 percent; a change to a 50/50 debt/equity ratio resulted in an increase of 20 percent, and a 75/25 debt/equity structure caused the return to equity to increase 60 percent. An important concept is that a constant increase in leverage causes return on equity to rise at an increasing rate. Conversely, a constant decrease in leverage causes the return to equity to decline at an increasing rate.

It was mentioned above that a change in the differential between the borrowing rate and the return on capital will also cause the return to equity to rise or fall. If the differential narrows, the return to equity will decline; on the other hand, if the differential becomes greater, the return to equity will

TABLE 9-2

Effect of Changing Debt Levels on Return to Equity

Total capital	Equity capital	Debt capital	Return on capital	Interest cost	Taxes 20%	Dividends 100%	Return to equity
$200,000	$200,000	$ 0	10%	$ 0	$4,000	$16,000	8.0%
200,000	150,000	50,000	10%	4,000	3,200	12,800	8.5%
200,000	100,000	100,000	10%	8,000	2,400	9,600	9.6%
200,000	50,000	150,000	10%	12,000	1,600	6,400	12.8%

increase. Incidentally, the change in the return to equity can result from a change in the interest rate or a change in the rate of return or both. Table 9-3 depicts the changes which result from a change in the differential between K_i (cost of debt) or K (return on capital).

It may be seen from Table 9-3 that when the return on capital (K) rose from 10 percent to 15 percent (a 50 percent increase), return to equity increased 83.3 percent. When the differential between K and K_i declined, the decrease in the return to equity was greater than the decrease in the differential; e.g., the differential decreased $66\frac{2}{3}$ percent, but the rate of return declined 90.9 percent.

The concept that the rate of return fluctuates more than either a change in the debt/equity ratio or a change in the differential between K and K_i is of utmost importance to the small businessman. First, in most cases the return on total capital (K) of the small firm is more sensitive to economic changes than in large companies, thus causing the rate of return to equity of small

TABLE 9-3

Impact on the Return to Equity
when the Differential Between K and K_i Changes

Total capital	Equity capital	Debt capital	Return on capital	Interest cost	Taxes 20%	Dividend 100%	Return to equity
$200,000	$100,000	$100,000	10%	$8,000[1]	$2,400	$9,600	9.6%
200,000	100,000	100,000	15%	8,000[1]	4,400	17,600	17.6%
200,000	100,000	100,000	5%	8,000[1]	400	1,600	1.6%
200,000	100,000	100,000	10%	10,000[2]	2,000	8,000	8.0%
200,000	100,000	100,000	10%	12,000[3]	1,600	6,400	6.4%

[1]Average interest rate, 8 percent.
[2]Average interest rate, 10 percent.
[3]Average interest rate, 12 percent.

companies to fluctuate more widely than in larger firms.[2] We know that the greater the variation, the greater the risk and vice versa. We also know that risk adversely affects the value of the firm; that is, the value of a dollar of earnings will be less for a firm whose earnings fluctuate than for one whose earnings are stable. Second, the small firm's cost of debt capital is very sensitive to changing economic conditions, thus accentuating the variation between K and K_i. In other words, not only do poor economic conditions cause the return to fall, but they also affect the firm's cost of debt adversely. The adverse impact of depressed economic conditions on the small firm's rate of return and cost of capital tends to cause the return to equity to fluctuate even more widely than when only one of the two is affected. The dual impact is often more than a firm can withstand, thus bringing about financial disaster. It is for this and other reasons that managers should be extremely careful when developing capital structure policies.

Cost of debt capital

The cost of capital is a very important aspect of financial management and many financial managers of middle-sized and large firms use it as the basis for accepting or rejecting investment projects. We believe that the concept is of lesser importance to the managers of small firms due to its difficulty in computation. Nevertheless, it should be remembered that debt is cheaper than equity capital not only because of the relative absence of risk from the viewpoint of the investor when compared to equity capital but also because interest charges are tax deductible. Under the present income law, corporations pay a 20 percent tax on the first $25,000 of income, 22 percent on the next $25,000, and 48 percent on all income in excess of $50,000. Since interest expense is deductible, the effective cost of debt capital is reduced by the amount of the firm's tax rate. To illustrate, if a firm's income is $25,000 or less, the cost of debt is reduced by 20 percent; that is, debt capital with an interest rate of 10 percent has an effective cost of 8 percent. In most instances the cost of equity capital is much higher than debt even when the effects of taxes are not considered. However, when the two are taken together, there is a decided cost advantage to the firm that employs debt capital in its capital structure provided, of course, that it is not used excessively.

Nonfinancial reasons for debt

Several nonfinancial reasons explain why firms use debt rather than equity capital; chiefly these are (1) debt may be the only source available regardless of cost, (2) debt does not disturb the voting position of existing

---

[2]As a general rule, small companies are less diversified than large firms, and any change in economic activities will have a larger relative change in total output than for their larger counterparts that are highly diversified.

shareholders, and (3) debt instruments provide flexibility that may not be possible when equity securities are employed.

There are times during the life cycle of many firms when additional equity funds are not available at reasonable costs, but the same firms may have assets that could serve as security for either long- or short-term credit. In such cases, it is advantageous for the firm to accept the more "risky" funds since these funds would be less expensive, thus allowing the firm to accept projects with lower "returns."

It should also be remembered that many financial institutions are severely limited or completely prohibited from providing equity funds, e.g., banks. Firms wishing to use these institutions as a source of funds must use debt in their capital structure. Finally, institutions that have been created or sponsored by the government to aid small businesses make available, at least in the beginning, only debt capital. For example, the Small Business Investment Corporations may ultimately take an ownership position, but they rarely do so at the outset. That is, they provide funds through the use of convertible debentures; if the firm succeeds, these securities are converted into common or preferred stock.

Many small- and middle-sized firms employ debt capital in order to preserve control. If equity capital is secured through the sale of stock, existing shareholders are required to increase their stockholdings proportionally if they wish to maintain their control. The problem of dilution does not occur if debt securities are issued since they do not enjoy the same voting privilege as equity securities.

It should be emphasized that the problem of control is of little consequence to "managers" of firms whose stock is widely distributed; however, for the small firm where the stock is concentrated, control is of major consequence since in many cases the right to be an officer rests with the amount of stock held.

Every firm operates in a constantly changing economy; therefore, financial managers must constantly plan for financial flexibility. Flexibility is secured when management is able to contract or expand the amount of capital invested in current or fixed assets as the need arises. As a result of the firm's flow of capital, all funds invested in either current or fixed assets will ultimately be converted into cash. A problem arises when cash cannot be reinvested in profitable projects; that is, if these funds remain idle, the rate of return on invested capital will decline. If the firm is able to return the *excess* capital to the original investors, the rate of return is unaffected. If a certain portion of debt is used in the firm's financial mix, management can reduce the excess by repaying the debt obligations, thus preserving the firm's return on investment.

Debt instruments also provide flexibility by allowing management to take advantage of changing *costs* of capital. For example, suppose the market for equity securities is weak; in this case, management can use short- or intermediate-term debt to finance the firm's asset requirements and replace the debt through retained earnings or from the proceeds of stock sold when the market rights itself.

Capital Structure

To avoid confusion, capital structure is defined as including all forms of debt and equity capital, not just long-term instruments. It was pointed out above that although the use of debt will, in most cases, cause the rate of return on equity capital to increase, it also increases the financial risk of the firm. That is, the use of debt increases the possibility of insolvency as well as variability in the earnings available to equity. A large majority of small business firms are perfectly capable of assuming a certain amount of risk and should be interested in employing a level of debt commensurate with their ability to assume risk. If this level is exceeded, it is generally believed that the value of the firm will be adversely affected and the firm may actually experience insolvency. A paradox exists in small business since in many cases the major source of funds is debt oriented, yet many small businesses cannot afford debt because they cannot stand the risk. For this reason all owners and managers should be extremely careful when determining their capital structures.

Small businesses, unlike large firms, cannot follow the traditional theory governing capital structure. While the average small firm will not use the traditional concept when developing capital structure policies, it is well for the managers of small businesses to be familiar with the underlying theories.

Theories of Capital Structure

There have been several major contributors to a theory of capital structure. Among the more important are Durand, Modigliani and Miller, Donaldson, Solomon, and Schwartz. The following is a brief description of two opposing concepts. The so-called traditional theory states that, up to a certain point, debt added to the capital structure will cause the market value of the firm to rise and the cost of capital to decline; however, after the optimum point has been reached, any additional debt will cause the market value to decrease and the cost of capital to increase. The second approach states that the cost of capital is unaffected by the amount of debt employed. One of the foremost advocates of the traditional concept is Ezra Solomon; the latter approach is defended by Modigliani and Miller.

Traditional theory

Considerable differences exist among the followers of the traditional school, but all are in substantial agreement that the judicious use of debt will increase the value of the firm and reduce the cost of capital. The optimum structure is the point at which the value of the firm is highest and the cost of capital is lowest.

Solomon, in his interpretation[3] of the traditional view, concludes that there is a definite impact on a firm's total market value as leverage is increased; moreover, this impact can be divided into three distinct stages as leverage is increased from zero:

1. In the first phase, the following are discernable: (a) The market value increases as leverage increases; (b) the cost of equity (K_e) rises as debt is added but does not rise fast enough to offset the increase in the net earnings rate achieved through the increased use of lower-cost debt capital; and (c) the cost of debt (K_i) remains constant or rises only slightly. Each of these factors contributes to a condition that permits the market value of the firm to increase and the average weighted cost of capital (K_o) to decline.
2. In the second phase, the addition of debt after a certain degree of leverage has been reached will produce only a moderate increase in market value. As a consequence, K_o remains relatively constant.
3. Finally, the addition of debt to a firm's capital structure after a critical point will cause a decrease in the market value as well as an increase in the K_o; that is, both K_i and K_e will rise at an abnormal rate.

These concepts are depicted in Figure 9-1. It may be noted that the cost of capital curve K_o is saucer-shaped rather than U-shaped as traditional theory would indicate. In the case of the saucer-shaped curve there is an optimum range extending over the greater range of leverage. This is not true in the case of the U-shaped curve, since there is a precise point at which the market value will decline and K_o will decrease. Solomon defines this point as that "precise point where the rising marginal cost of borrowing is equal to the average overall cost of capital."[4]

Variations on the traditional theory

In the main, there is little or no disagreement with the general concept underlying the traditional theory as described by Solomon; however, there is disagreement about the shape of the K_e curve, which, of course, affects the shape of the K_o curve.

[3]Ezra Solomon, *The Theory of Financial Management* (New York: Columbia University Press, 1963), pp. 93–98.

[4]Solomon, *Theory of Financial Management*, p. 97.

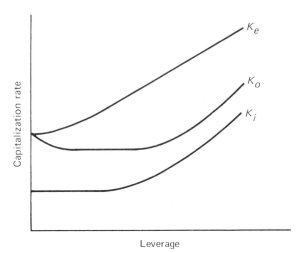

FIGURE 9-1. Traditional approach

The traditional theory suggests that the shape of the K_o curve is primarily, if not solely, the function of leverage. The authors are in substantial disagreement with this concept.[5] The major point of difference is that the slope of the K_e curve, rather than being solely the function of leverage, is also dependent on (1) the asset mix combination as reflected in earnings before interest and taxes (EBIT) and (2) the relation between K_i and K (return on total capital).

There is no doubt in our minds that K is a function of a firm's asset mix, which in turn is an important variable in the determination of capital cost. In other words, K_e and K_o are affected not only by the amount of debt that a firm employs but also by the asset mix. (The importance of a change in asset mix is explained thoroughly in working capital principle 1 in Chapter 13.)

Let us direct our attention to the impact that the relation between K and K_i has upon cost of capital. It may be concluded that the expected return on equity capital is greatly increased when a firm's cost of debt (K_i) is small relative to the return on total capital (K) (see Table 9-4 as well as p. 147.).

In the example, the return to equity in Firm A is much greater than for either B or C, yet all three use the same amount of leverage; therefore, the higher return of Firm A's stockholders is the direct result of the differential between K_i and K. It is difficult to believe that an investor would not pay more for an investment in A than in B or C; therefore, it is believed that the K_e curve of Firm A will be lower than the curve for either Firm B or Firm C.

[5]The following ideas are incorporated in Richard H. Pettway and Ernest W. Walker, "Asset Mix, Cost of Capital, and Capital Structure," *The Southern Journal of Business*, April 1968, pp. 34–43.

TABLE 9-4

Gain Derived from the Use of Debt When K and K_i Differ

| Firm | Total capital | Source of funds | | K | K_i | Percent return on equity | Percentage gain |
		Debt	Equity				
A	$200	$100	$100	12%	6%	18	50
B	200	100	100	10%	6%	14	40
C	200	100	100	8%	6%	10	25

Note: For simplification, debt is not categorized, and it is assumed that it has an average cost, as shown.

Also, the K_o curve of Firm A will be lower than for either of the other two firms (see Figure 9-2).

It is both interesting and important to note that at each level of debt the return to equity capital is greater in Firm A than in either of the other two (see Table 9-5). For example, Firm A's return to equity was 12.67 percent or 21.2 percent higher than B and 111 percent higher than that of C when debt amounted to only 10 percent of the total capital. Note that there was a gain of 42.1 percent in return to Firm A when debt was increased from 10 percent to 50 percent, but there was a gain of only 34.0 percent in B when debt was increased to 50 percent, and there was no gain for C. The significance of this is that shareholders in companies with the greatest differential between return on capital (K) and the cost of debt (K_i) can expect to gain more for each additional unit of debt that is added than can shareholders in companies whose differential is smaller.

It is also important to note that should the differential $(K-K_i)$ decrease

TABLE 9-5

Relation of Debt Equity and Spread
Between K and K_i to Return on Equity[1]

| Total capital | Debt/equity ratio | EBIT | | | Percent return on equity | | |
		A	B	C	A	B	C
$200	10/90	$24	$20	$12	12.67	10.45	6.00
200	20/80	24	20	12	13.50	11.00	6.00
200	30/70	24	20	12	14.57	11.72	6.00
200	40/60	24	20	12	16.00	12.67	6.00
200	50/50	24	20	12	18.00	14.00	6.00

[1]Taxes are not considered.

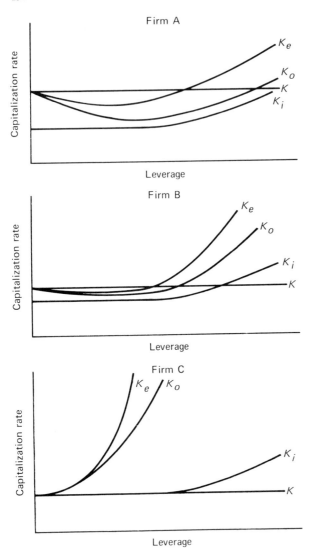

FIGURE 9-2.

as a result of a decline in K or K_i the resultant loss would be less in Firm A
than in Firm B or C (see Table 9-6). In other words, from a standpoint of
potential loss, there is less risk in a firm with a large differential between K
and K_i than in one with a small differential. Since stockholders in a company
with a large differential can expect to gain more from each additional unit of
debt employed in the financing process as well as assuming less risk in the
event that K declines, they are willing to pay a relatively larger price for the
stock. This being true, the weighted cost of capital will decline more than it

TABLE 9-6

Effect on Return on Equity when *K* Declines

Debt equity ratio	Percent return on equity			Percent return on equity			Percentage decline		
	A 12%	*B* 10%	*C* 6%	*A* 10%	*B* 8%	*C* 4%	*A*	*B*	*C*
10/90	12.97	10.45	6.00	10.45	8.22	3.78	17.5	21.3	37.0
20/80	13.50	11.00	6.00	11.00	8.50	3.50	18.5	22.7	41.7
30/70	14.57	11.72	6.00	11.72	8.86	3.14	19.6	24.4	47.7
40/60	16.00	12.67	6.00	12.67	9.33	3.00	20.8	26.4	50.0
50/50	18.00	14.00	6.00	14.00	10.00	2.00	22.22	28.6	66.7

would in a firm with a smaller differential between K and K_i as debt is added to the structure.

Another important aspect is that, according to the foregoing logic, both K_e and K_o will rise after the optimum has been reached, but the rate of increase will be smaller for the company with the greatest differential between K and K_i and more rapid for a company with a smaller differential (see Tables 9-5 and 9-6 and Figure 9-2).

The conclusion is that a change in K has as great an impact on both K_e and K_o as a change in leverage.[6] Therefore, the maximum advantage is achieved when management is able to increase K through an improved asset mix or by assuming more business risk and using the correct amount of leverage.

Modigliani-Miller position

Modigliani and Miller represent by far the most sophisticated support for the thesis that the total market value of the firm and the cost of capital are independent of the capital structure (except for tax considerations). If their thesis is accepted, it would seem that no capital structure is inherently more desirable than any other.[7] Their approach begins with the suppositions that (1) all firms are composed of equity capital; (2) they are divided into

[6]The presentation infers that the difference between K and K_i is the result of the changes in K only. It should be emphasized that the difference is also influenced by K_i; in fact, K_i frequently changes more radically than K.

[7]The description given here was taken principally from the following: F. Modigliani and M. A. Miller, "The Cost of Capital, Corporation Finance, and the Theory of Investment," *American Economic Review*, Vol. 48 (July 1958), pp. 261–97; A. Barges, *The Effect of Capital Structure on the Cost of Capital* (Englewood Cliffs, N.J.: Prentice-Hall, 1963), pp. 7–18, 77–90, 100–113; and J. Fred Weston, "A Test Of Cost of Capital Propositions," *The Southern Economic Journal*, Vol. 30 (Oct. 1963), pp. 105–112.

equivalent return classes with every firm in each class susceptible to the same degree of business risk; (3) the return on the outstanding shares of firms in any class is proportional to the return on the shares issued by any other firm in the class, so that the securities of each firm in the equivalent return classes are perfectly substitutable in the market; and (4) information about the market place is perfect, and all investors are presumed to act rationally, thus creating a perfect market.

Under the assumptions held by Modigliani and Miller, firms are not perfect substitutes when debt is introduced in the capital structure. Moreover, they contend that return to owners can be increased through the use of debt, but the increased returns are subject to more risk since there is an increased dispersion of the income. As a consequence, firms with different debt/equity ratios are no longer perfect substitutes.

The following propositions outline the Modigliani-Miller argument about the relation of capital structure to the cost of capital and the market value of the firm:

1. The cost of capital and the market value of a firm are independent of its capital structure. The cost of capital is equal to the capitalization rate of a pure equity stream of income for its class, and the market value is ascertained by capitalizing its expected return at the appropriate discount rate for its class.

2. The second proposition, little more than a restatement of the first, maintains that the expected yield on a share of stock (K_e) is equal to the appropriate capitalization rate for a pure equity stream for that class, plus a premium, related to financial risk, which equals the debt/equity ratio times the spread between the capitalization rate (K_e) and yield on debt (K_i). Stated differently, the impact that a smaller K_e would have on cost of capital (K_o) is offset by an increase in K_e.

3. The cutoff point for investment in the firm is always the capitalization rate, which is unaffected by the types of securities used to finance the investment.

The theoretical validity of these propositions is difficult, if not impossible, to counter; however, they have been attacked by numerous authorities. Some of the criticisms are much more sophisticated and comprehensive than others, but all seem to attack the perfect market assumption and the arbitrage argument.

Modigliani and Miller argue that, through personal arbitrage, investors would quickly eliminate any inequalities between the value of levered firms and the value of unlevered firms in the same risk class. The basic argument here is that individuals (arbitragers), through the use of personal leverage, can alter corporate leverage. This argument cannot be supported in a practical world, for it is extremely doubtful that personal investors would substitute personal leverage for corporate leverage, since they do not have the same risk characteristics. The writers believe that the criticisms lodged against Modigliani and Miller's thesis are valid, thus limiting its use in an actual situation. Nevertheless, the propositions and their criticisms should be carefully studied since they will aid in understanding capital structure theory.

The Choice Between Debt and Equity

The authors do not wish to get into an academic argument with the proponents of the traditional and Modigliani-Miller capital structure models as to their validity in determining the optimum levels of debt in large firms. We are convinced, however, that these tools are unacceptable as techniques which managers of small firms can use in this important decision since both use cost of capital prominently in the decision process. It has been pointed out that cost of capital cannot be calculated in small- and middle-sized firms with any degree of confidence; therefore, any technique using cost of capital to determine optimum levels is of questionable value for small- and middle-sized firms. As a consequence we would like to introduce a technique that does not use cost of capital when determining the optimum level of debt.

The tool that we consider to have the most validity for use is the indifference chart. The information in this chart does two things: First, it allows managers to calculate the return on equity and earnings per share at various levels of earnings before interest and taxes (EBIT). Second, it serves as a basis for determining the level of debt that a firm can *safely* employ. Before proceeding with this analysis it is important to note that the return to equity and EPS are influenced by any movement of EBIT as well as by the rate of interest that the firm is required to pay (unless of course each moves in the same proportion). An example illustrates this approach. Assume the manager of the Brown Company wants to know the level of debt that can "safely" be used to finance operations. After carefully studying the demand and supply conditions surrounding the firm's operation, the manager decided that EBIT could never fall below $5,000, nor would it be higher than $30,000 on an investment of $200,000 in assets.

Mr. Brown, the owner-manager of the firm, knows that the volume of debt would influence return on equity as long as the return on assets exceeded the cost of that debt. He is also aware that the level of debt employed would increase the risk that must be assumed and would adversely influence the cost of debt as well as equity, thus reducing the advantage of leverage. In the light of this knowledge, he decided never to employ more than 60 or less than 10 percent debt. The results of these debt/equity alternatives are calculated and included in Table 9-7 and Figure 9-3.

TABLE 9-7

Calculations Showing Varying Returns to Equity when Debt Levels Are Changed

	Plan A [1]			Plan B [1]			Plan C [1]		
EBIT	$5,000	$17,500	$30,000	$5,000	$17,500	$30,000	$5,000	$17,500	$30,000
Interest	4,800	4,800	4,800	8,000	8,000	8,000	9,600	9,600	9,600
PBT	200	12,700	25,200	(3,000)	9,500	20,000	(4,600)	7,900	20,400
PAT	160	10,160	20,160	(2,400)	7,600	17,600	(3,680)	6,320	16,320
Return on equity	.001	7.3%	14.4%	(24%)	7.6%	17.6%	(4.6)	7.9%	20.4%
EPS	$.01	$.73	$1.44	(.24)	$.76	$1.76	($.46)	$.79	$2.04

[1]$200,000 total capital; three plans: plan A, 30 percent debt and 70 percent equity; plan B, 50 percent debt and 50 percent equity; plan C, 60 percent debt and 40 percent equity.

Note: Interest cost, 8 percent.

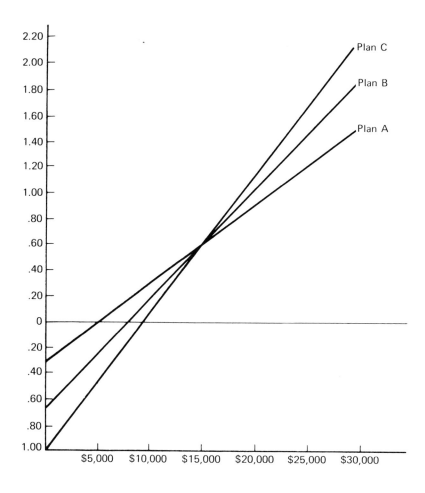

EBIT

Plan A: 30 percent debt and 70 percent equity; 14,000 shares of common stock outstanding.

Plan B: 50 percent debt and 50 percent equity; 10,000 shares of common stock outstanding.

Plan C: 60 percent debt and 40 percent equity; 8,000 shares of common stock outstanding.

FIGURE 9-3. Indifference chart

An examination of Figure 9-3 reveals an interesting phenomenon in that regardless of the debt used by the firm there is always one point on the EBIT curve that yields identical returns to equity and earnings per share. This point is called the indifference point since management is indifferent as to the level of debt employed as long as EBIT equals this amount. It was noted above that the indifference point is influenced by the interest cost; that is, if interest goes up, the indifference point moves upward and to the right and vice versa if the interest rate declines. Incidently, the indifference point is easy to calculate either by plotting various debt/equity plans on the EBIT chart or solving the following equation:

$$\frac{X-I}{S_1} = \frac{X}{S_2} \qquad (9\text{-}1)$$

where X = the indifference point,
$\quad I$ = interest cost in dollars,
$\quad S_1$ = number of shares when debt is used,
$\quad S_2$ = number of shares when only equity is used.

To illustrate this particular formulation, assume the facts as depicted in Table 9-7 and Figure 9-3:

$$\frac{X-\$9,600}{8,000} = \frac{X}{20,000}$$

$$8,000\,X = 20,000\,X - \$9,600(20,000)$$

$$8,000 = 20,000 - \frac{\$9,600(20,000)}{X}$$

$$\frac{\$9,600(20,000)}{X} = 20,000 - 8,000$$

$$\frac{\$192,000,000}{X} = 12,000$$

$$\$192,000,000 = 12,000\,X$$

$$X = \frac{\$192,000,000}{12,000}$$

$$= \$16,000$$

An examination of Figure 9-3 reveals that the indifference point is equal to $16,000; the proof is shown in Table 9-8.

Note that regardless of the debt/equity combination, earnings per share as well as return on equity equals 64.0 cents and 6.4 percent, respectively, when EBIT equals $16,000. However, the earnings per share and return on equity increase and decrease at a faster rate in those cases where larger amounts of debt are used. For example, when EBIT rose from $16,000 to $30,000 and debt equaled 60 percent, earnings per share increased from 64.0

TABLE 9-8

Indifference Point: $16,000

	Plan A	Plan B	Plan C
EBIT	$16,000	$16,000	$16,000
Interest	4,800	8,000	9,600
PBT	11,200	8,000	6,400
PAT	8,960	6,400	5,120
EPS	0.64	0.64	0.64
Return on equity	6.4%	6.4%	6.4%

cents to $2.04, a percentage increase of 219 percent. However, when debt equaled only 30 percent, earnings per share increased from 64.0 cents to $1.44 or 125 percent. The reverse is true when EBIT experiences a decline; e.g., if EBIT declines to $5,000, EPS under plan A would decline 98 percent, but under plan C it would decline 172 percent. The significance of this is obvious; that is, changes in EBIT have a greater impact on EPS and return on equity in firms that employ greater amounts of debt. Stated differently, the firm with a higher debt/equity ratio is more sensitive to change in EBIT than one with a lower debt/equity ratio.[8]

Consideration of risk

The manager of a small firm can use the indifference chart advantageously when selecting the "correct" level of debt. The first step is to calculate the degree of risk associated with EBIT by calculating the standard deviation from the expected EBIT. Assume in the Brown Company case that the standard deviation is $3,000 and that the expected EBIT is $16,000. If the manager had no capacity to assume risk, he would not choose plan C because it would be possible for EBIT to decline to $8,500, thus causing the firm to incur a loss of $1,100, or a tax-adjusted loss of 11 cents per share. Under these assumptions, management could choose plan B advantageously since EBIT would exceed interest payments by $500 at all times—this assumes a normal distribution. However, if the manager could afford some risk, it is possible to employ 60 percent debt (plan C) since 95 percent of the time he would expect EBIT to equal or exceed $11,500.

While there is no scientific method of "correctly" determining the exact level of debt, managers can use the indifference analysis very advantageously since they are able to calculate with a reasonable degree of accuracy the degree of variation that can be expected in EBIT. Given this fluctuation and the degree of risk which it can assume, management can calculate with a

---

[8]The sensitivity of earnings per share to changes in EBIT is frequently referred to as the *degree of financial leverage* in finance literature.

reasonable degree of certainty the level of debt that it can employ in its structure.

One final word of warning. In small companies, the most critical decision is not always the amount of debt but the type of debt that is employed. The solution of this problem requires not only that management ascertain the amount of dollars required to service the debt, but it must also synchronize the firm's flow of funds—see Chapter 13 for a more complete discussion.

Summary

During the last several years the use of debt in large firms has increased at a slightly faster rate than it has in small firms; nevertheless, debt is now and doubtless will remain a more important source of funds in small firms than in large firms. One major reason for heavy reliance of small firms on debt sources is that equity funds are not always available to them at a reasonable cost.

Not only do small businesses employ more debt than equity, but they also use more short- and intermediate-term debt than long-term debt. As a consequence the risk of insolvency is greatly magnified.

The traditional reasons for using debt are that (1) it tends to increase the return on equity, (2) debt is cheaper than equity, (3) debt is usually easier to obtain than equity, and (4) debt does not disturb the voting position of existing shareholders.

While the use of debt tends to increase the return on equity for firms of all sizes, it should be emphasized that its advantages are not as great for small firms as for large ones. This situation exists because the differential between the cost of debt and the return on total capital is generally less in small firms, thus reducing the leverage effect.

The traditional and more sophisticated methods of determining the level of debt to use in a firm's capital are not as applicable for small businesses as they are for larger companies; therefore, we recommend the use of the indifference point technique when determining the level of debt. It is also recommended that the manager use the standard deviation technique to measure the risk associated with the firm's EBIT. Once the degree of risk is known, the manager is more able to calculate the amount of debt that should be used.

QUESTIONS

1. Contrast the debt position of small and large firms. What trends, if any, are discernable?

2. What are the principal reasons firms employ debt in their capital structures?

3. Explain what happens to the return on equity when debt/equity ratios change. Also, explain what occurs when the differential between K_i and K changes.

4. Discuss several nonfinancial reasons small firms resort to the use of debt capital.

5. Explain the traditional approach to optimal capital structure decision making.

6. Explain the concepts underlying the indifference point chart.

7. What disadvantages do you associate with the indifference point technique?

PROBLEMS

9-1. The NOYB Company is contemplating an expansion program. After a study of the market for their products they decided to purchase a small firm for a cash price of $100,000. Since the acquired firm would increase the size of the NOYB Company by 50 percent, it was necessary to enter the market for the $100,000 purchase price. The firm had followed conservative financing policies in the past and had never employed more than 10 percent debt—all short-term. After a very careful evaluation of the proposed project, it was concluded that the following probability of sales would prevail during the next three years:

Probability	Sales
.10	$300,000
.25	450,000
.30	600,000
.25	750,000
.10	900,000

In determining the manner in which the $100,000 of assets could be financed, it was decided that two alternatives were possible. The first was to raise the $100,000 directly from existing shareholders. The second was to secure the funds from an insurance company. The insurance company indicated that it would be glad to finance the expansion with a $100,000, five-year note at an interest rate of 12 percent.

Exhibits 1 and 2 depict the balance sheet and profit and loss data resulting from the two proposals.

EXHIBIT 1

Balance Sheet Data—Proposal 1

Assets		Liabilities and net worth	
Cash	$ 30,000	Trade payables	$ 40,000
Receivables	50,000	Notes payable (10%)	15,000
Inventory	50,000	Common stock	200,000
Plant & equipment	160,000	Retained earnings	45,000
Other assets	10,000		$300,000
	$300,000		

Profit and Loss Data—Proposal 1

Probability	.10	.25	.30	.25	.10
Sales	$300,000	$450,000	$600,000	$750,000	$900,000
Operating cost	285,000	414,000	540,000	668,000	783,000
EBIT	$15,000	$ 36,000	$60,000	$82,000	$117,000
Interest	1,500	1,500	1,500	1,500	1,500
PAT	$13,500	$ 34,500	$58,500	$80,500	$115,500
Taxes	2,700	7,090	14,800	25,140	41,940
Earnings	$ 10,800	$ 27,410	$ 43,700	$ 55,360	$73,560

EXHIBIT 2

Balance Sheet Data—Proposal 2

Assets		Liabilities and net worth	
Cash	$ 30,000	Trade payables	$ 40,000
Receivables	50,000	Notes payable	15,000
Inventory	50,000	Long-term note (5 yr, 12%)	100,000
Plant & equipment	160,000	Common stock	100,000
Other assets	10,000	Retained earnings	45,000
	$300,000		$300,000

Profit and Loss Data—Proposal 2

Probability	.10	.25	.30	.25	.10
Sales	$300,000	$450,000	$600,000	$750,000	$900,000
Operating cost	285,000	414,000	540,000	668,000	783,000
EBIT	$ 15,000	$ 36,000	$ 60,000	$ 82,000	$ 117,000
Interest	13,500	13,500	13,500	13,500	13,500
PAT	$ 2,500	$ 22,500	$ 46,500	$ 68,500	$ 103,500
Taxes	500	4,500	9,730	19,380	36,180
Earnings	$ 2,000	$ 18,000	$ 36,770	$ 49,120	$ 67,320

Assumptions:
1. The probability distribution of sales shown above is reliable.
2. Operating costs vary as shown in Exhibits 1 and 2.
3. The total amount of funds from each source will remain constant regardless of sales.
4. The interest rates will not change during the next three years.
5. Industry averages show that (1) the debt/equity ratio is 60 percent equity and 40 percent debt and that (2) interest is earned six times.

Requirement:
Which method of financing should be employed? Why?

9-2. The Longhorn Corporation is seriously considering expanding its present assets by $100,000. The firm has several alternatives, but the owner has finally decided on one of the following plans. Plan One calls for borrowing the entire $100,000 from a major insurance company. The loan would be for five years at an annual interest rate of 10 percent. Plan Two is a combination of borrowing and private placement of common stock—a $50,000 five year loan at an annual interest rate of 10 percent and $50,000 in common stock at a price of $15.00 net (3,333 shares). Assume existing tax rates.

The existing capital structure of the corporation is as follows:

Assets		*Liabilities and net worth*	
Cash	$ 50,000	Accounts payable	$ 95,000
Accounts receivable	100,000	Notes payable (10%)	100,000
Inventory	100,000	Other	5,000
Fixed assets	350,000	Long-term note (10%)	100,000
	$600,000	Common stock (30,000 shares)	300,000
			$600,000

The capital structures of the two plans are as follows:

Plan one		*Plan two*	
Accounts payable	$ 95,000	Accounts payable	$ 95,000
Notes payable (10%)	100,000	Notes payable (10%)	100,000
Other	5,000	Other	5,000
Long-term note (10%)	100,000	Long-term note (10%)	50,000
Long-term note (10%)	100,000	Long-term note (10%)	100,000
Common stock (30,000 shares)	300,000	Common stock (33,333 shares)	350,000
	$700,000		$700,000

Requirements:

1. Calculate earnings per share and return on equity capital for both plans when earnings before interest and taxes (EBIT) are $0, $40,000, $60,000, and $80,000.
2. At what level of EBIT will earnings per share and return on equity be equal for the two plans of financing? Why did earnings per share decline (for both plans) after EBIT reached a certain level?
3. Assume that the following probability estimates of future earnings before interest and taxes prevail for the next five years. Calculate the expected EBIT and EPS.

Probability	EBIT
.10	$25,000
.15	50,000
.50	70,000
.15	90,000
.10	115,000

4. Using the above data, calculate the standard deviation of distribution. How can this technique be used to assist management in selecting the correct method of financing?

PART IV SELECTED REFERENCES

ALTMAN, EDWARD I., "Corporate Bankruptcy Potential, Stockholder Returns, and Share Valuation," *Journal of Finance*, December 1969, pp. 887–900.

ARDITTI, FRED D., "Risk and the Required Return on Equity," *Journal of Finance*, March 1967, pp. 19–36.

BARGES, A., *The Effect of Capital Structure on the Cost of Capital*, Englewood Cliffs, N.J.: Prentice-Hall, 1963, pp. 7–18, 77–90, 100–113.

DONALDSON, GORDON, "New Framework for Corporate Debt Capacity," *Harvard Business Review*, March–April 1962, pp. 117–131.

Federal Trade Commission, *Quarterly Financial Report: Manufacturing, Mining and Trade Corporations, 1st Quarter, 1975*, Washington, D.C.: U.S. Government Printing Office, 1975, p. 59.

FLINK, SOLOMON J., *Equity Financing for Small Business*, New York: Simmons-Boardman Publishing Corp., 1962.

GHANDI, J. D. S., "On the Measurement of Leverage," *Journal of Finance*, December 1966, pp. 715–726.

HASLEM, JOHN A., "Leverage Effects on Corporate Earnings," *Arizona Review*, March 1970, pp. 7–11.

HELFERT, ERICH A., *Technique of Financial Analysis*, 3rd ed., Homewood, Ill.: Irwin, 1972.

MODIGLIANI, F., and M. A. MILLER, "The Cost of Capital, Corporate Finance, and the Theory of Investment," *American Economic Review*, July 1958, pp. 261–297.

SOLOMON, EZRA, "Leverage and the Cost of Capital," *Journal of Business*, October 1955, pp. 240–252.

SOLOMON, EZRA, *The Theory of Financial Management*, New York: Columbia University Press, 1963, pp. 93–98.

"Strategy for Financial Emergencies," *Harvard Business Review*, November–December 1969, pp. 67–79.

WESTON, J. FRED, "A Test of Cost of Capital Propositions," *The Southern Economic Journal*, October 1963, pp. 105–112.

WILLIAMS, EDWARD E., "Cost of Capital Functions and the Firm's Optimal Level of Gearing," *Journal of Business Finance*, 1971, pp. 78–83.

WIPPERN, RONALD F., "Financial Structure and the Value of the Firm," *Journal of Finance*, December 1966, pp. 615–634.

part V

VALUATION

chapter 10

VALUATION

For the most part, the value of firms in the United States is extremely difficult to calculate, yet each will have to be valued at least once, if not more often, during its existence. While there are numerous reasons a firm should be evaluated, we are concerned only with the value of a firm that is to be disposed of in whole or in part by sale or exchange. Furthermore, we shall discuss valuation both from the seller's and buyer's viewpoint. This statement suggests that there is more than one value for a firm at any given time. The writers are aware that there is an "economic value" of an item at any given time; however, we are also aware that in any sale there are at least two concerned parties and that it is extremely unlikely that both perceive value from the same viewpoint; therefore, for all practical purposes a business firm has a different value to different individuals. Generally speaking, the only way in which a sale can be consummated is for one or both of the parties to compromise its concept of value. It is this final price that we wish to establish in order that both buyer and seller will be satisfied that the price is close to his idea of value.

Techniques of Valuation

There are several techniques that may be used to ascertain the worth of the firm: book value, market value, and capitalization of earnings. We shall discuss each of these methods since each is applicable to different types of companies. For example, the book value method is particularly valid when evaluating companies in extractive industries as well as financial companies. Market value can be used in any company as long as there is a willing buyer and a willing seller, neither being under any compulsion to buy or sell and both having reasonable knowledge of relevant facts. This technique is most useful in establishing the value of large firms but has little use in ascertaining the worth of a small firm.

The capitalization of earnings technique is most useful for firms of all sizes which use and reuse their assets to create income. While the concept is simple, the determination of the earnings stream and its capitalization rate is extremely difficult. While book value and capitalization of earnings techniques are more useful to the small business firm, each method will be explored in some depth.

Book Value

The book value technique, while possessing many deficiencies, is often used by both buyers and sellers of small businesses. While its use is recommended for firms in extractive industries and financial institutions, the method is used by all firms primarily because market value and capitalization of earnings techniques cannot be used with any degree of confidence. The book value of a firm is equal to the value of its assets (in most cases intangibles are not included) minus its liabilities. If the book value of a firm's common stock is desired, then all that's necessary is to subtract the value of all stock issues (preferred) having a prior claim over common stock from this total and divide the results by the number of shares of common stock outstanding.

There is a good argument for including intangible assets in book value computations since in many cases the intangibles are purchased and are valuable. Since most authorities recommend that intangibles be deleted before book value is computed, it is recommended that two book values be computed, one including intangibles and one excluding them.

It has been argued that book value is not very dependable primarily because fixed assets are usually shown at depreciated cost and are often below replacement costs; therefore, it is usually necessary to reappraise the value of all assets in the light of today's prices and then subtract all liabilities. This value is then said to be the *present* book value of the firm's assets. If the value is to be used for liquidation purposes, then intangibles should be subtracted; however, if the firm is to be sold as a going concern, intangibles probably should be included.

The use of asset value is questionable for any firm that is to be sold as a going concern primarily because market value depends on earning power and the firm's ability to pay dividends; it is for this reason that the writers do not recommend the use of book value as a technique to ascertain the value of a firm.

Market Value

The writers cannot recommend the use of market value as a method of calculating the value of a small firm even though there may be an established price for the firm's securities. These prices may be speculative and as such do not reflect the present value of the firm. For this reason no further discussion of market value is included in this chapter.

Capitalization of Income

The capitalization of earnings technique simply means that the firm's value is determined by capitalizing its earnings by a rate that reflects the risk associated with that firm; that is, the greater the risk, the higher the discount rate. The readers know that small businesses are extremely risky and as a consequence would demand the use of a rather high capitalization rate. The size of the rate is influenced by the amount of risk that is inherent in a firm as well as the efficiency of a particular firm's management; therefore, it is useless to generalize as to the size of the rate used by small businesses. It should be pointed out, however, that the rate will usually be higher than for large established businesses. It may be concluded that if the business is small, highly competitive, and requires a small capital outlay, the discount rate used should range somewhere between 15 percent and 50 percent. Again, it should be pointed out that the rate is totally dependent on (1) the risk associated with the future earnings of the firm and (2) the efficiency of the operating management.

The earnings flow of a small firm is dependent on the abilities of owners as well as the policies of the firm. That is, the cash flows of the firm to be acquired as well as the capitalization rate which is to be used in the discounting process should reflect the policies of the acquiring company.[1] It is for this reason that we recommend the following technique be used when determining the level of earnings and capitalization rate of the firm to be valued.

Assume that the Smith Company is interested in acquiring the Jones Company and therefore wishes to establish the value of the firm's assets through the use of the capitalization of earnings method. To accomplish this requires that Smith calculate the level of future earnings as well as a capitalization rate satisfactory to both managements. The following data of the Jones Company were made available to the owners of Smith Company.

---

[1]This is true when the acquisition does not require changes in the policies of the acquiring company.

Data: Jones Company (1976)

Book value of current assets (net)	$300,000
Book value of fixed assets (net)	100,000
Notes payable (nontransferable)	50,000
Term loan (nontransferable)	20,000
Preferred stock (no call premium)	30,000
Common stocks (50,000 shares—book value)	100,000
Retained earnings	200,000
EPS (1976)	1.10

Sales Data by Years

	1973	1974	1975	1976
Actual sales	$300,000	$350,000	$410,000	$400,000
Profit after tax	24,000	43,750	61,500	55,000
	1977	*1978*	*1979*	*1980*
Projected sales	$405,000	$410,000	$400,000	$400,000
Profit after tax	60,750	61,500	60,000	60,000

The owner of Smith Company requested and received the following data from the accounting department. In addition to the 1976 financial data the controller stated that operating expenses and income data for the years 1972–1975 were similar to the 1976 data.

Data: Smith Company (1976)

Total assets	$ 600,000
Liabilities	100,000
Preferred stock	0
Common stock (average market price—100,000 shares)	1,560,000
Sales	836,700
Profit after tax	104,000
EPS	1.04
Price earnings	15/1

The owner of the Smith Company used the concepts set forth above and determined that he could pay one share of the Smith Company's stock for 4.21 shares of Jones Company stock. The following Smith data were used in the calculation of this exchange ratio: (1) Income as a percent of sales averaged 12 percent over several years, and (2) earnings on total assets averaged 17 percent during the same period. This being true, the value of Jones' firm was calculated as follows:

Average projected sales (annually)	$403,750
Income as a percent of sales	12%
Expected income annually	$48,450
Valuation of Jones' assets	
$48,450 ÷ 17%	$285,000
Liabilities (valued at par)	$70,000
Preferred stock	$30,000
Capitalized value of Jones' assets	$185,000
Market value of Smith's stock (average)	$15.60
Number of shares required to purchase Jones' assets	
$185,000 ÷ 15.60	11,859
Exchange ratio	
50,000 ÷ 11,859	4.21 to 1

The owner of Smith Company assumed that Jones Company's assets when used by Smith's personnel and operating under Smith's policies would produce an average of $48,450 after-tax income. This means that the net book value of Jones stock equaled $3.70 ($185,000 ÷ 50,000). Since Smith stock sold for an average of $15.60 in the market place, it requires 4.21 shares of Jones stock to have the same value as Smith's stock. Stated differently, the management of Smith Company could sell 11,859 shares of stock in the market place and pay Jones $185,000—this ignores the cost of flotation.

The net effect of this exchange would be that Smith would retain its relative position with regard to return on assets and sales, but earnings per share would rise. The increase in earnings per share is entirely the result of financial synergism, i.e., trading a high P/E share of stock for one that has a lower price.

Financial Conditions After the Merger

	1977	1976
Sales	$1,240,450	$836,700
Profit after tax	152,450	104,000
Profit (after tax) as percent of sales	12.2%	12.4%
Earnings per share	$ 1.36	$ 1.04
Earnings on assets	17.2%	17.2%
Assets	$ 885,000	$600,000
Liabilities	$ 170,000	$100,000
Preferred stock	-0-	-0-

It is highly unlikely that Jones would accept Smith's offer since its operations are more "efficient" than Smith's. The following is a comparison of the two firms:

	Smith[1]	Jones
Profit (after tax) as a percent of sales	12.4	13.8[2]
Profit (after tax) as a percent of total assets	17.3	13.7[1]
Earnings per share	$1.04	$1.10[1]

[1]1976 only.
[2]Average for three years of actual operation.

Viewing the value of the Jones Company from the position of its owner (seller) rather than the owner of Smith (buyer), the exchange ratio ought to be considerably better than what was offered. Using the operational characteristics of the Jones Company as a basis, we are able to calculate a different value for the Jones' stock. The following calculations indicate that the exchange ratio should be 2.57 to 1 rather than 4.21 to 1:

Average projected sales	$403,750
Income as percent of sales (Jones' average performance in 1975–76)	15%
Expected income annually (average for 1977–1980)	$ 60,563
Valuation of Jones' assets	
$60,563 ÷ 15% (average forecasted capitalization rate)	$403,753
Liabilities	$ 70,000
Preferred stock	$ 30,000
Capitalized value of Jones' assets	$303,753
Market value of Smith's stock	$ 15.60
Number of shares required to purchase Jones' assets	
$303,750 ÷ 15.60	19,471
Calculation of exchange ratio	
50,000/19,471	2.57 to 1

Given the above conditions and assuming the merger is accomplished by an exchange of one share of Smith's stock for 2.57 shares of Jones' stock, the following would prevail after the first year's operations:

Financial Conditions After the Merger

	1977	1976
Sales	$1,240,450	$836,700
Profit after tax	$ 164,563	$104,000
Profit (after tax) as a percent of sales	13.3%	12.4%
Earnings per share	$ 1.38	$ 1.04
Earnings on combined assets	16.4%	17.3%
Assets	$1,003,753	$600,000
Liabilities	$ 170,000	$100,000
Preferred stock	-0-	-0-

It is highly unlikely that either Jones' or Smith's assumptions will prevail. Also, it is highly unlikely that Jones will accept an exchange ratio of 4.21 to 1; it is equally unlikely that the owners of Smith will accept an exchange ratio of 2.57 to 1. Obviously, a compromise is necessary if the merger is to materialize. Since the management of Smith should not accept an investment that would jeopardize the equity position of its shareholders, it could afford to increase its offer to a point where the price/earnings ratio is equal to or exceeds 15 to 1. It may be assumed that if return on assets and sales remains constant or increases, the price/earnings ratio will not be jeopardized. If the exchange ratio of 4.21 to 1 is accepted by Jones, it may be assumed that the P/E ratio would remain constant or increase. In any event, the equity position of the shareholders would be preserved. If the P/E remained constant, the price of the stock would increase to $20.40. In this case Jones would enjoy a gain of $4.80 per share after one year's operation. At the time of the merger Jones' 11,859 shares of Smith stock would be worth $185,000; after the merger, the shares would have a market value of $241,924, an increase of 30.7 percent. Such a prospect would be difficult for Jones to refuse; however, Jones would argue that if his firm added $60,563 to the income of the merged companies, it should receive at least 19,471 shares of Smith's stock in exchange for its stock. They could also argue that at the exchange ratio earnings per share would be $1.38, and if the P/E of 15 to 1 remained constant, the market price of Smith's stock would rise to $20.70, slightly more than the $20.40 projected by Smith. Smith would probably argue that if only $48,450 in earnings were produced from Jones's assets, the P/E ratio may decline because earnings per share would increase only 23 percent while sales increased 48 percent. In the light of the above argument, it is reasonable to believe that a compromise could be reached that would be satisfactory to both groups.

It should be noted that in the above discussion the market value of Smith's stock is known. There are cases where two firms merge and neither has a market value. When this prevails, it is necessary for the principals to find a comparable firm whose stock is traded and use its P/E ratio as a basis. In selecting comparable companies it is essential that a valid comparison exist. That is, (1) the line of business must be the same or very similar; (2) growth in income and sales should be comparable; (3) similar accounting methods should prevail; (4) ratios such as return on assets, return on net worth, etc., should be similar; and (5) the capital structure should be comparable.

In summary, it may be concluded that the following concepts may be used effectively when determining the value of a firm's assets:

1. The purchase price of the assets should not equal an amount that would cause the value of the firm's equity to decline. An exception would be if the

decline is only for a short duration after which the return would increase at an acceptable rate.

2. The capitalization rate should not exceed the capitalization rate of the acquiring firm unless management can be assured that efficiency will be increased as a direct result of the merger.

The above discussion described a valuation process in which one firm sought to acquire another and the management did not follow the assets. If the management of the acquired firm is to be merged into the total operation, serious consideration should be given to the fact that management is often the most important element in the valuation process. Unfortunately, management is not easy to quantify. The authors know of one merger in which a firm with a history of losses was acquired along with its management. Under the new arrangement, the incoming management was used only in technical areas, and the merger was highly successful. This is true in many high-technology-type firms; that is, while management may be extremely capable from a technical standpoint, they are incapable of "managing" the entire process. If management of the acquired firm adds to the overall strength of existing management, then a premium should be added to the value of the firm to be acquired.

A final word of warning should be heeded when using the capitalization approach. Extreme care should be the underlying philosophy of the appraiser when projecting sales and earnings since a mistake in either will greatly distort the value of the firm. Not only is it important to ascertain the level of sales and earnings, but it is equally important to predict the variability of the sales. The reader remembers that the greater the variability of sales and earnings, the greater the risk and the greater is the discount rate. In other words, a volatile stream of earnings is not worth as much as a stable stream of earnings.

Summary

In all probability the assets of a small business will be valued some time during its life cycle. For this reason it is essential that managers know the various methods available to them to accomplish this function. It was pointed out that the authors believe that each asset has an economic value at any given time; however, we are also aware that in any sale there are at least two concerned parties and it is extremely unlikely that both perceive value from the same point of view. In light of this, we believe that a firm has different values to different individuals or groups of individuals.

There are three principal methods that may be employed when valuing a firm: (1) book value, (2) market value, and (3) capitalization of income.

Each of these methods is valid for certain types of firms or under certain conditions. For example, book value is an excellent method to use when valuing firms in extractive industries as well as financial institutions. Market value, on the other hand, is an acceptable technique in those cases where there is a willing buyer and a willing seller, neither being under any compulsion to buy or to sell and both having knowledge of relevant facts. The capitalization of earnings technique is most useful for all firms that use and reuse their assets to produce goods and services, regardless of the size of the firm.

The authors recommend book value and the capitalization of income technique for small firms. We do not recommend the use of market value because small firms rarely, if ever, meet the prerequisites necessary if this method is to be effective.

When using book value it is recommended that all assets, including intangible assets, be reappraised in the light of existing prices. The use of the capitalization of income technique requires the correct determination of (1) estimated income and (2) capitalization rate. The authors believe that both of these should be calculated using the characteristics of the buying firm. If the derived value does not satisfy the seller, the buyer and seller can negotiate a value acceptable to both. If this figure cannot be determined, it is reasonable to assume that the sale should not be consummated.

QUESTIONS

1. Briefly describe the three methods of valuing business firms.

2. In general, what types of firms should be valued by (a) market value, (b) book value, and (c) capitalization of income?

3. Discuss the philosophy that should be used by a buyer when valuing a firm to be acquired.

4. In what way does the P/E ratio of an acquiring firm influence the exchange ratio?

5. Using related knowledge, discuss several techniques that may be used to improve forecasted income and sales.

PROBLEMS

10-1. The president of the Simplex Company, a producer of advanced technological products, has asked you to determine the value of the firm's common stock. To aid you in this evaluation project he has supplied you with the accompanying financial information.

The Simplex Corporation

December 31, 1976 and 1977—in thousands

	1977	1976
Assets		
Current assets:		
Cash	$ 2,576	$ 260
Accounts receivable	3,877	1,617
Unreimbursed costs & fees under fixed price & cost plus fixed fee contracts	1,755	1,822
Inventories (at lower of cost or market)	3,199	1,701
Prepaid expense	303	86
	$11,710	$5,486
Other assets	191	141
Property, plant, & equipment:		
Land	404	—
Equipment & leasehold equipment	2,301	1,475
Less: Depreciation and amortization	699	503
	$ 2,006	$ 972
Intangibles:		
Excess of investment in assets over book value at date of aquisition	1,696	1,716
Patents and organizational expense, less amortization	126	59
Total assets	$15,729	$8,374
Liabilities and Net Worth		
Current liabilities:		
Notes payable to banks	$ 600	$1,906
Trade accounts payable	2,371	748
Payroll and related items	714	198
Accrued expenses	645	256
Federal income taxes	194	272
Current maturities of long-term debt	168	154
Total current liabilities	$ 4,692	$3,534
Long-term debt	$ 5,498	$ 391
Deferred federal income taxes	86	50
Shareholders' equity:		
Common stock (authorized 1,000,000 shares at $.50 par value)	301	245
Paid-in capital	3,361	3,330
Retained earnings	1,791	824
Total liabilities and net worth	$15,729	$8,374

Financial Data for 5 Years' Operation—in thousands

	1977	1976	1974	1973	1972
Sales	$ 17,489	$ 9,166	$ 5,215	$ 2,828	$ 1,802
Profit before tax	$ 1,413	$ 1,041	$ 708	$ 414	$ 209
Net income	$ 967	$ 647	$ 380	$ 215	$ 131
Earnings per share	$ 1.62	$ 1.32	$ 1.11	$ .67	$ .41
Average number of shares outstanding	598,456	491,868	342,868	318,701	318,701

Requirements:

1. Calculate the book value of the firm's common stock as of December 31, 1977.
2. Determine the value of the common stock using the capitalization method.

10-2. Mr. Cooper, one-half owner of Cooper Publishing Company, died on January 1, 1976. Mr. Thomas, owner of the remaining stock, decided to exercise the buy-out agreement that each had signed in the event of death. Incidently, the right of purchase extended four years after the death of either owner.

The corporate balance sheet as of December 31, 1975 was as follows:

Assets		*Liabilities and net worth*	
Cash	$12,000	Notes payable	$10,000
Receivables, net	4,000	Accounts payable	11,000
Inventories	30,000	Accruals	3,000
Fixtures & equip-		Common stock plus	
ment (net)	30,000	surplus	52,000
Total	$76,000	Total	$76,000

Pretax earnings during the past three years had equaled $8,000, $10,000, and $11,000. Pretax earnings had been forecasted to reach $16,000 by the year 1980.

Calculate the price that Mr. Thomas should pay the estate of Mr. Cooper.

PART V SELECTED REFERENCES

ACKERMAN, ROBERT W., and LIONEL L. FRY, "Financial Evaluation of a Potential Acquisition," *The Financial Executive*, October 1967, pp. 34–54.

EHBAR, A. F., "When Book Value Matters and When It Doesn't," *Fortune*, July 1974, p. 571.

FAIRCHILD, STEPHEN J., "Anticipated Replacement Cost Theory of Asset Valuation," *Managerial Planning*, July–August 1972, pp. 27–32, 40.

GELMAN, M., "Economist-Financial Analyst Approach to Valuing Stock of a Closely Held Corporation," *Journal of Taxation*, June 1972, pp. 353–354.

HARDY, D. J., "Valuation: A Financial Planning Tool for Closely Held Corporations," *Trusts and Estates*, September 1974, pp. 584–587.

JOHNSON, R. B., "Financial Change and Corporate Values," *Journal of Commercial Bank Lending*, September 1973, pp. 20–25.

LALL, R. M., "Valuation of Fixed Tangible Assets," *International Accounting*, July–August 1971, pp. 76–78.

"Look at Valuation of Stock in a Closely Held Corporation," *National Underwriter* (Life Ed.), December 23, 1972, p. 12.

MARONEY, R. E., "Most Courts Overvalue Closely Held Stocks," *Taxes*, March 1973, pp. 144–156.

OLSON, IRVING J., "Valuation of a Closely Held Corporation," *The Dynamic Small Firm, Selected Readings*, ed. by Ernest W. Walker, Austin, Texas: Lone Star Publishers, Inc., 1975, pp. 267–285.

REILLY, FRANK K., "What Determines the Ratio of Exchange in Corporate Mergers?," *Financial Analysts Journal*, November–December 1962, pp. 47–50.

SACKMAN, JULIUS, "Market Value Approach to Valuation," *Appraisal Journal*, January 1973, pp. 58–81.

WALKER, R. G., "Asset Classification and Valuation," *Accounting and Business Research*, Autumn 1974, pp. 286–296.

WARRELL, C. J., "Enterprise Value Concept of Asset Valuation," *Accounting and Business Research*, Summer 1974, pp. 220–226.

WHITTINGTON, G., "Asset Valuation, Income Measurement, and Accounting Income," *Accounting and Business Resources*, Spring 1974, pp. 96–101.

part VI

INVESTMENT
DECISION MAKING

chapter 11

THE CAPITAL BUDGETING PROCESS

It has been mentioned that generally firms should not make an investment unless it increases their value. While it is believed that managers of firms of all sizes accept this as a sound criterion, many firms, both large and small, do not follow sophisticated techniques that yield this desirable result. To illustrate, R. M. Soldofsky of Iowa State University made a study of 123 business firms in Iowa and found that 71, or 58 percent, of them used the payback method to evaluate investment projects. According to Soldofsky, none of the companies employed what may be considered to be the net present value or internal rate of return concept to evaluate investment projects. He also found that only "a very few of the firms computed a rate of return on investment or even the rate of return on net worth." It is worth noting that in 1955 only 9 percent of the Fortune 500 industrial corporations used the discounted cash flow concept but that by 1973 the percentage had increased to 50 percent. Even though the number of corporations using the discounted cash flow approach had risen considerably in that decade, those using payback had risen to 65 percent. In other words, many of the companies that were shifting to the more sophisticated approach were reluctant to give up completely on payback.[1]

Gray, Bird, and Scott surveyed 139 small- and medium-sized companies and found that the payback method was used by 51 percent of the firms, while 30 percent indicated they used some variation of an accounting return on investment. Only 10 percent used one of the "theoretically correct" capital budgeting techniques to evaluate investments.[2]

[1]Robert M. Soldofsky, "The What, Why and How of Capital Budgeting for Smaller Businesses," *Iowa Business Digest*, (January 1966), pp. 3–17. See J. William Petty, David F. Scott, Jr., and Monroe M. Bird, "The Capital Expenditure Decision-Making Process of Large Corporations," *The Engineering Economist*, Vol. 20, No. 3, (Spring 1975), pp. 159–172.

[2]Otha L. Gray, Monroe M. Bird, and David F. Scott, Jr., "Investing and Financing Behavior of Small Manufacturing Firms," *MSU Business Topics* (Summer 1972), pp. 29–38.

Another interesting fact observed by Gray, Bird, and Scott was that 61 percent of the firms interviewed used a basic standard of financial performance against which proposed uses of funds were appraised. The most popular procedure (37 percent) was to compare the expected rate of return on an investment proposal with the cost of a specific source of funds, such as borrowing or equity. As the writers would expect, only 13 percent of the respondents used some mix of financing costs such as an average overall cost of all sources of funds.[3] While Gray, Bird, and Scott did not offer an explanation for this very low percentage, the writers believe that the average weighted cost of capital is not used extensively because of the extreme difficulty of its computation. In fact, we believe that in those firms where it is used, it is actually an estimated cost rather than a computed one.

Not only do managers of small firms fail to use "sophisticated" investment decision techniques, many don't give any serious consideration to this process because they think they never have enough capital to invest and that any investment of capital is justified. Actually, small businesses should give at least as much, if not more, attention to the investment process as larger firms do, since they have less accessibility to capital.

The investment process in small and large companies actually differs only as to degree of analysis and consists generally of the following steps: project generation, project analysis, project selection, and project installation. Prior to a discussion of each of these, it is necessary to discuss exactly what is meant by investments.

Nature and Meaning of Investments

"Investment" means different things to different people. When investment is mentioned in social circles, it usually means an investment in stocks and bonds of companies listed on the New York Stock Exchange, the American Stock Exchange, or the over-the-counter market. That is, people usually think of an individual investing a certain sum of funds in a portfolio of stocks or bonds. In a business firm, however, although investment may include some stocks and bonds, for the most part it consists of current and fixed assets.

Current assets may be defined as cash and any assets that are expected to be converted to cash, sold, or consumed during the operating cycle. These may be short-term marketable securities, receivables, inventories, and prepaid expenses. Tangible fixed assets, on the other hand, are those physical items that represent future services to be used over a prolonged period of time; that is, the form of fixed assets is changed over more than one operating cycle. Included in these assets are investments in stocks and bonds that are expected to be converted into cash in the long run; however, these are not the ones

[3]Gray, et al., "*Investing and Financing Behavior...*", pp. 29–38.

with which we are concerned. The reader should remember that most investment decisions involve both fixed and current assets, since fixed assets must be accompanied by current assets in order to be productive.

Investment projects vary both in size and complexity. To illustrate, management may be considering the purchase of an entire firm, or it may be contemplating the replacement of a piece of equipment. In the former case, both types of assets are involved,[4] whereas in the latter only fixed assets may be involved, since the replaced equipment may not require additional current assets—in fact, there may be a reduction in the amount of current assets needed to operate the machine, as a result of the improved productivity of the investment.

Reasons for Investing

Generally speaking, an investment is made only if value is preserved and/or increased. While this statement is true, it is much too general; therefore, it is best to point out more specifically the reasons why investments are made. Some of the most common are:

1. To replace used or obsolete equipment.
2. To expand production of existing product lines.
3. To expand distribution facilities.
4. To expand vertically as well as horizontally.
5. To improve product quality.
6. To increase facilities designed to increase employee morale.
7. To expand for strategic purposes, such as (a) keeping up with the Joneses or (b) diversification to reduce risk.

Obviously the small firm will not encounter as many of these reasons as the larger and more complex firm; nevertheless, managements of the smallest companies find that they, too, invest for a variety of reasons.

While the classification of investments according to reasons is important, it is believed a classification of "projects" according to priority is of greater benefit to smaller companies, since they usually have a constant capital rationing problem. That is, most smaller companies have more projects than financial resources; therefore, a grouping according to priority would assist management in allocating funds to the areas of greatest need.

At least two groupings according to priority are possible. First, projects may be classified as those which are (1) not postponable, (2) postponable without deterioration, and (3) postponable but with some loss of opportunity. It is readily apparent that such a classification system will greatly aid management in selecting investments which will provide continuity to the

---

[4]Intangible assets, such as goodwill, may also be involved in this purchase.

firm's life. It should be pointed out that the use of this system may permit an investment that will produce lower yields in the short run, but if management has effectively classified projects, investment in the long run should be optimized.

A second grouping recognizing priority is related to profits. The first category would include those investments which affect profits directly; the second grouping would include only those which affect profits indirectly. Illustrative of the first grouping would be projects in which costs are reduced or sales are enhanced or both. Projects that affect profits indirectly are those that cause productivity to increase (i.e., labor-saving investments).

The authors recommend the first grouping system since it is believed that most of the managers of small firms experience a shortage of investment funds; therefore, projects that cannot be postponed should be given the first consideration, even though other opportunities may show a greater profit in the short run.

Organization for Planning and Controlling Investments

While we generally associate capital budgets with large firms since they have longer lines of internal communication and larger amounts of capital to invest, small businesses can also utilize capital funds more effectively by adopting a formalized capital budgeting procedure. Because of their highly individual nature, it is vital that each small business firm develop its own budgeting procedure. In formulating these procedures, there are certain common elements that must be taken into consideration. These factors are discussed below.

The planning period

The planning period for the investment process should encompass sufficient time that the future course of a firm will be orderly and to some degree predictable. It is true that due to the nature of the small business, its planning period cannot equal the five- to ten-year span usually covered by larger firms; nevertheless, it should be long enough to include the majority of replaceable assets. In some cases this may very well extend to five or more years.

The budget period for projects designed to improve operating efficiency should be shorter, since it is imperative that management consider all equipment that will give it a competitive advantage. Since such equipment is constantly being introduced, the capital budget should not be of such length and nature that management would be prevented from considering these newer innovations. In summary, the budgetary planning period should be of such length as to permit flexibility.

The level at which decisions are made

To assure the greatest degree of return from each dollar invested, it is suggested that all proposals be judged within the same framework and that the same criteria be used as the basis for each decision. In a large business such as a multinational firm, this suggestion is not possible; such firms find it necessary to decentralize the decision-making process so that several groups, some of which may be on different scalar levels, arrive at the final decision. Since most small companies operate in a much less complex environment, it is recommended that their major investment decisions be made at the highest possible level [i.e., a budgeting committee made up of the president, the major finance officer, the major officer in charge of distribution (marketing), and the major production officer]. Many of these functions are often combined, thus making the decision-making process less complicated.

In some cases investment decisions may be "pushed" down into the organization; however, this authority should be carefully granted and clearly defined. For example: (1) there should be a limitation on the total amount that could be committed to one project, (2) the total amount available to be spent during a given period should be designated, and (3) the types of expenditures to be considered should be defined in precise language. In other words, not only the amount but the purpose of each expenditure should be well defined and controlled by "top" administrative officials. The centralized control of the budgeting process cannot be overstressed. This necessity must be satisfied because in many cases it takes only one poor investment by the small firm to cause "total" failure.

Project generation

Small companies often conduct their search for potential investments in a rather unsophisticated way; yet, this procedure is probably one of the most important aspects of their capital budgeting program, primarily since most small firms are constantly faced with capital rationing. First priority should be given to projects that cannot be postponed. To illustrate, suppose that a firm is producing an important product insofar as survival is concerned, yet the product is not as profitable as some of the firm's other products. If the machines used in the production of this product are either worn out or obsolete, management should list this investment at the "top" of the investment program. Information relating to this type of project flows up to management from operating personnel. Since the number of scalar levels in the management hierarchy is much smaller in the small company than in the larger company, the investment process can be less formal. It should be emphasized, however, that if the process is too informal, effective evaluation may be impaired and poor investment decisions will result.

Projects designed to improve operating efficiency through (1) decreasing direct and indirect costs and (2) increasing profits directly or indirectly may originate at any level of the firm and should be placed in the second category of priority. In fact, some of these projects should be considered on a par with the nonpostponable projects. This is particularly true when the firm is changing its image.

It is emphasized that if a firm does not generate enough investment proposals to keep it at "the head of its class," it will surely suffer by becoming stagnate and losing its competitive position. With this as a warning, management of small companies should develop a system by which investment proposals can reach top management. This system doesn't need to be complicated, but it is imperative that it possess three characteristics: (1) it should be made known to all individuals in the firm, (2) the lines of communication through which the investment proposal is to flow must be constantly kept open, and (3) each investment should be evaluated in accordance to its priority, and the evaluation made known to the originator of the proposal. Remember, simplicity, not complexity, is an absolutely essential characteristic of any investment generation system.

The timing of project generation should be continuous; that is, employees should be allowed to submit projects for consideration at any time. However, to avoid decisions that may not be optimal, it is best that the evaluation process be done at specific times throughout the year (i.e., quarterly, semiannually, or annually). The only exceptions would be projects that fall into the category of improving profitability and those considered to be emergencies.

Project Evaluation

It has been suggested by some writers that small businesses cannot formulate an effective evaluation system since they do not have the time, money, or expertise to establish such a program. This assertion, in our opinion, is completely untrue. It is our belief that it is as important for small firms to develop a formalized program of evaluation as for larger firms. The principal reason for this statement is that characteristically the small firm is more risky than its larger cousin; therefore, any mistake, either of commission or omission, would probably have greater impact on the future welfare of the company than it would have in a larger company.

Criteria for investment decision making

It has been stated previously that there is only one theory of finance —and that theory holds for all firms regardless of size or type. This being the case, managers should use the same criteria for investment in small firms as are used for investment in larger firms. Since there is no definitive work on investment criteria for small firms, it is necessary to look to the investment literature of large firms in order to arrive at an acceptable investment criteria.

It was stated in Chapter 2 that the primary goal of a financial manager is to secure and employ capital resources in the amount and proportion necessary to increase the efficiency of the factors of production. Authors state this goal or criteria in various ways; for example, Van Horne thinks that the investment criteria "should be the rate of return on a project that will leave unchanged the market price of the stock." In this sense, the cost of capital is the required rate of return needed to justify the use of capital.[5] Brigham and Smith differ slightly from Van Horne in stating that the "investment theory of the firm contends that management should adjust the level of capital expenditure to the point where the marginal rate of return for investment projects is equal to the marginal cost of capital."[6] Many other writers could be quoted but for the most part they all refer to the concept of maintaining the value of the firm, and many use cost of capital as the criterion simply because it has been defined as investors' expectations. It is extremely difficult to use cost of capital as a criterion in either small or large companies, since it is extremely difficult to calculate. While there are those who say that they can compute an acceptable cost of capital for middle-sized and large firms, it must be concluded that it cannot be done with any degree of accuracy for smaller companies. In the light of this conclusion, it is necessary to approach the criterion problem from a different viewpoint.

The predominant reason why businesses invest funds in assets is to increase the present value of the firm's equity capital. This objective is achieved only if the return on all invested funds equals or exceeds the returns desired by the suppliers of both debt and equity capital. If the return is equal to these expectations, then there probably will be no change in the value of the firm; however, if it is above or below, a change in value may be expected. An example shows this relationship. Assume that the Jones Company has the following capital structure:

Assets		*Source of capital*	
Cash	$ 5,000	Trade payables	$ 20,000
Receivables	10,000	Notes payable[1] (8.332)	30,000
Inventory	20,000	Common stock[2]	50,000
Other current assets	1,000		
Fixed assets	64,000		
	$100,000		$100,000

[1]Due at the end of the year.
[2]*Market value* equals par value and *expected return* equals 30% before taxes or 24% after taxes.

[5]James Van Horne, *Financial Management and Policy*, 3rd ed. (Prentice-Hall, Inc., 1974), p. 101.
[6]Eugene F. Brigham and Keith V. Smith, "The Cost of Capital to Its Small Firm," *Engineering Economist*, Vol. 13, No. 1 (Fall 1967).

One way in which management can achieve its objective of maintaining or increasing the present value of its equity capital is to average the returns "expected" on debt and equity capital and use this rate as the minimum acceptable rate of return on investment. In the example above, the before-tax weighted average expected return of all capital is 17.5 percent and is computed in the following manner:

	Capital structure proportion (percent)	Expected return before tax (percent)	Weighted average expected return[1] (percent)
Trade payable	20	0	0
Notes payable	30	8.33	2.50
Net worth	50	30.00	15.00
			17.50

[1]Since cost of capital has been defined as the expected return on invested capital, this rate may be called the firm's weighted average cost of capital (K_o).

To prove that values are protected when the average expected return is received from the investment, the following example is given:

Funds available for investment (assets)	$100,000
Earnings before interest and taxes (EBIT)	17,500
Earnings paid out to creditors	2,500
Earnings before taxes	$ 15,000
Taxes at 20%	3,000
Earnings after taxes	$ 12,000

It may be noted that under the conditions above the firm's creditors received the return promised them (i.e., $2,500, or $8\frac{1}{3}$ percent on $30,000). Equity investors also received their expectations [e.g., 30 percent before tax ($15,000 ÷ $50,000), or 24 percent after taxes ($12,000 ÷ $50,000)].

In the event that the average return is not realized, the equity investor would "realize a loss in expectations" and would probably reduce the estimated value of the stock. On the other hand, if expectations were exceeded, the opposite would occur.

The investment decision would be greatly simplified if management could calculate its expectations prior to the time an investment is made. It is the opinion of the writers that such a computation is impractical since adequate information is not available; therefore, another approach must be employed which will yield the same results. The adjusted internal rate of return technique is the method recommended and will be explained thoroughly in Chapter 12. For the present, the use of the technique will be illustrated by the end results without explaining how it is derived.

In the case above, assume that management is able to forecast $17,500 in expected earnings before interest and taxes. It is easy to see that the interest cost of $2,500 is adequately covered, and earnings before taxes yield an internal rate of return of 30 percent on an equity investment of $50,000; or a 24 percent return after taxes.[7] In this case the return to equity satisfies the equity investor and the investment is made.

In summary, the minimum criterion for an acceptable investment is a return that meets the expectations of the suppliers of *all* types of capital. If the cost of capital can be calculated, it should serve as the investment criterion; however, if it cannot be measured, an alternative, presented in Chapter 12, such as the *adjusted internal rate of return* should be used so as to ascertain the required rate of return to all investors. Exceptions would be those projects that are made for prestige rather than for profit purposes.

Techniques of valuation

Any of several methods may be employed when choosing among alternative investment proposals. Each method is designed with a particular purpose in mind—to determine the rate of return that each project may be expected to yield, as well as ascertaining the degree of risk associated with the investment. The most common evaluation methods are payback, average rate of return, internal rate of return (IRR), and net present value (NPV). To be effective the last two methods require knowledge of a firm's cost of capital; and since this is extremely difficult if not impossible for the small firm to calculate accurately, the authors will adjust the internal rate of return in such a manner that it will assist in informing owner-managers when their required rate of return is obtained.

If any or all of the preceding techniques are to be effective, it is imperative that management be able to ascertain the firm's cash flow. Since the payback, internal rate of return, net present value methods, and adjusted internal return employ different cash flows in their calculation, it is necessary to define the type of flow that each uses. First, the cash flow used in the payback process includes cash that is available to repay the investment (principal but not return); it is defined as follows:

$$\text{Cash flow} = \text{Earnings} + \text{Depreciation} + \text{Working capital}$$
$$+ \text{Scrap value (if any)}$$

---

[7] The internal rate of return is found by (1) ascertaining the present value interest factor and (2) relating this factor to a percent rate of return; e.g., equity investment divided by cash flows received by the owners equals present value interest factor. Substituting, we have $50,000 \div $65,000 = .769. In the annuity table you will find .769 under the 30 percent column; that is, the internal rate of return on equity (IRR_e) of this project is 30 percent before taxes.

The cash flow that is used in NPV, IRR, and adjusted IRR calculations includes an amount that permits the investors to ascertain whether they will receive their original investment plus an *expected return* commensurate with the risk of the investment. For example, the creditors are able to calculate whether they will receive the contracted interest rate plus principal. The equity investors, on the other hand, use the cash flow in calculating whether they will receive their principal plus a return commensurate with the risk involved. To accomplish these goals the cash flow is defined as follows:

$$\text{Cash flow} = \text{Earnings} + \text{Interest (adjusted by the tax rate)}$$
$$+ \text{Depreciation} + \text{Working capital} + \text{Scrap value (if any)}$$

In order to explain these various techniques—payback, average rate of return on average investment, internal rate of return, net present value, and the adjusted internal rate of return—we shall apply each method to a single example. In pursuing this goal, assume that a small group of investors is considering forming a company to produce pollution equipment. Preplanning reveals certain information about the assets required and the manner in which they are financed, shown in Table 11-1. In addition, a marketing and production study, as reflected in Table 11-2, reveals the expected income from all projects undertaken by the firm during a five-year period.

TABLE 11-1

The White Company

Balance Sheet Data

Assets:	
Current assets:	
Cash	$ 10,000
Receivables	20,000
Inventories (all inventories)	20,000
Fixed assets:	
Plant and equipment	50,000
Total assets	$100,000
Liabilities and net worth:	
Current liabilities:	
Notes payable	$ 15,000
Accounts payable	15,000
Long-term note	20,000
Net worth	
Common stock	50,000
Total liabilities and net worth	$100,000

TABLE 11-2

The White Company

Income Data

	Year				
	1	*2*	*3*	*4*	*5*
Expected EBIDT[1]	$24,500	$25,000	$26,000	$25,500	$27,000
Expected interest payment[2]	4,600	5,200	5,000	5,400	5,800
Depreciation	9,000	9,000	9,000	9,000	9,000
Expected earnings before taxes	10,900	10,800	12,000	11,100	12,200
Taxes (20%)	2,180	2,160	2,400	2,220	2,440
Profit after tax	8,720	8,640	9,600	8,880	9,760

[1]EBIDT means earnings before interest, depreciation, and taxes.
[2]The change in totals resulted from changing interest rates, not amount borrowed.

payback method

Investments in assets are relatively large and generally take several years to recover. Investors usually consider the degree of risk that is assumed when making an investment directly related to the length of time required to recover the investment from the firm's cash flows. The payback method of evaluating investment proposals stresses the length of time that is needed for investors to recover their investment from operating cash flows rather than the return on their investment. The cash flows available to investors in the recovery of the original investment in the example above are computed as follows and are shown in Table 11-3.

It is easy to see that the investment in the example above will not be returned until the end of the fifth year. The method of calculation is simply

TABLE 11-3

The White Company

Cash Flows Used in Payback Calculation

Year	Earnings +	Depreciation +	Working capital +	Scrap	= Cash flow
1	$ 8,720 +	$ 9,000 +	$ 0	+ $ 0 =	$ 17,720
2	8,640 +	9,000 +	0	+ 0 =	17,640
3	9,600 +	9,000 +	0	+ 0 =	18,600
4	8,880 +	9,000 +	0	+ 0 =	17,880
5	9,760 +	9,000 +	50,000	+ 5,000 =	73,760
	$45,600 +	$45,000 +	$50,000	+ $5,000 =	$145,600

adding up the cash received by years until the investment is recovered. In the case above, $71,840 of the original investment was recovered by the end of the fourth year, leaving $28,160 of the $100,000 investment outstanding. Since the earnings of $9,760 in the fifth year would not cover the $28,160, management would have to wait until the end of the year to recover the difference of $18,400 from depreciation, working capital, and scrap.

The payback method has several advantages but ignores at least two primary considerations. First, it does not consider the manner in which income is received and therefore ignores the time value of funds; second, it ignores income beyond the payback period.

The advantages the payback method claims are: (1) the payback is easy to calculate; (2) if a firm is experiencing a shortage of cash, the payback method may be used to select investments that yield a quick return of cash funds; and (3) all factors remaining the same, the payback method permits calculation of the length of time required to recapture the original investment, thus determining the degree of risk of each investment.

As mentioned above, the time value of money and the amount of funds received after the asset has been "paid out" have been ignored. To illustrate, suppose that a firm compares the investment worth of two $700 projects with cash flows as follows:

	Cash flows	
Year	*Project 1*	*Project 2*
1	$500	$200
2	100	200
3	100	300
4	200	200

Both projects have a payout of three years, but Project 1 is more desirable from an investment standpoint because of the time value of money; that is, a dollar is worth more today than it would be if received at a later date. For example, Project 1 will return its investment plus a rate of return of 14.2 percent, whereas Project 2 will produce its investment plus a return of 10.6 percent, over the four-year period.

A second criticism of the payback method is that it ignores income that is produced beyond the payback period. Suppose that a firm is contemplating two projects. Project x has a payback period of two years and Project y is "paid out" in four years. If payback is the only criterion, the former would be accepted over the latter. However, suppose that Project y produced a stream of income over ten years but the stream of Project x's income ceased after two years. Obviously, Project y is more desirable, since it produces a higher average return on investment.

average rate of return on average investment

The payback method of computation does not take into consideration the relative profitability of the project. The average rate of return is designed with this purpose in mind and is computed by adding the total of all earnings after depreciation and taxes, and dividing this amount by the number of years the project will last. After the average "earnings" is determined, the average rate of return may be calculated by dividing average earnings by the average investment of the project. Referring again to the example illustrated in Table 11-2, the project yields 18.24 percent and is calculated as follows:

$$\frac{\$8,720 + \$8,640 + \$9,600 + \$8,880 + \$9,760/5}{\$50,000 + \$50,000/2} = 18.24\%$$

The average return method of selecting alternative uses of funds takes into consideration "savings" over the entire life of the project; nevertheless, it has a primary weakness in that the time value of funds is ignored. Since income may be reinvested time and again at some rate, it follows logically that current income is more valuable than future income. The methods that take this into consideration are commonly called discounted cash flow methods; the more common techniques are internal rate of return, net present value, and adjusted internal rate of return.

internal rate of return

In determining which investments to accept by ascertaining the discounted rate of various investment opportunities, the owners should first estimate the cash flow, which includes the "return" to *all types* of investors for each investment during its economic life; and second, ascertain a rate that equates the present value of these cash flows to the present value of the cost of the investment. If this rate equals or exceeds the required rates of return, the project is acceptable. As mentioned elsewhere, these required rates of return are equal to the firm's cost of capital of the *various kinds* of capital. If these costs can be calculated and weighted and summed together, the weighted average cost of capital may be compared to the internal rate of return. If the latter is equal to or greater than the former, the project will either sustain or increase the value of the firm.

Referring to Table 11-2, we are able to ascertain the cash flows that should be used in this process of evaluation as well as NPV (Table 11-4).

With these cash flows computed, we are now able to ascertain the internal rate of return of the project; stated differently, we are able to find a rate that will equate these cash flows to the present value cost of the investment required to produce them. In the example above, it is assumed that the investment is made in period zero (period prior to the time when a cash flow is created). It is further assumed that there will be no change in the

TABLE 11-4

The White Company

Cash Flows Used in IRR and NPV Calculations

Year	Earnings +	Interest (1 − TR) +	Depreciation +	Working capital +	Scrap =	CF
1	$ 8,720	$ 3,680	$ 9,000	$ 0	$ 0 =	$ 21,400
2	8,640	4,160	9,000	0	0 =	21,800
3	9,600	4,000	9,000	0	0 =	22,600
4	8,880	4,320	9,000	0	0 =	22,200
5	9,760	4,640	9,000	50,000	5,000 =	78,400
	$45,600	$20,800	$45,000	$50,000	$5,000 =	$166,400

investment. Although this is not a realistic assumption, it is done for purposes of simplicity. Later this assumption will be dropped and a technique that compensates for changing investments will be introduced.

The IRR is determined by solving the following equation:

$$\sum_{t=1}^{n} \frac{(CF)_t}{(1+r)^t} - \sum_{t=0}^{n} \frac{(CO)_t}{(1+r)^t} = 0$$

where CF_t is the cash flow received in period t; n is the last period in which cash flow is expected; CO_t is the cost of the investment in period t; and r is the interest rate that equates the present value of the expected future cash flows to the investment regardless of when it is made (i.e., r is the internal rate of return).

Since r is the only unknown element in the equation above, it must be ascertained by trial and error. If the cash flows are the same in each year, the process is quite simple; that is, the rate may be found by simply dividing the cash flow into total investment and determining the rate from the Present Value of an Annuity of $1 Table (see Appendix). Assume that a firm can expect a cash flow of $5,927 annually for four years from an investment of $18,000. To solve, simply divide cost by the receipts; the answer is a present value interest factor annuity ($PVIF_a$) of 3.037. The next step is to equate the $PVIF_a$ to the interest rate that it represents; to do so, move across the four-year column until you find 3.037, which, in this case, is under the 12 percent column. Thus, the internal rate of return equals 12 percent.

If the cash flows are unequal, r must be ascertained by trial and error. To accomplish this requires several steps. First, the manager estimates the interest rate he or she believes will equate the present value of the expected cash flows to the present value of the investment. Second, the manager ascertains the present value interest factors of the estimated rate and multiplies these factors by the expected cash flows. Third, these products are summed and compared to the present value of the investment. If the sum is less than the present value of the investment, the manager should select a set of higher present value interest factors (derived from a lower interest rate) that, when multiplied by the expected cash flows, will produce a value that will either equal or exceed the present value of the investment. If greater, the exact interest rate lies somewhere between these two rates and can be determined by interpolation.

We are now ready to solve for the rate that equates the predetermined cash flows of the White Company to the total investment required to produce them. Table 11-5 depicts this process with the internal rate of return equaling 15.56 percent.

The internal rate of return of 15.56 percent is now to be compared to the rate of return desired by all investors (i.e., their required rate of return or weighted average cost of capital). If either of the latter is greater, the project is said to be unacceptable, because the value of the firm will not be sustained if the project is undertaken; however, if the internal rate of return is equal to or above the desired rate, the project is said to be acceptable, since the value of the firm will be preserved or increased.

One weakness of the IRR method of evaluation is that it is extremely difficult if not impossible for management to specify a single rate of acceptance. Second, the internal rate of return represents the return to both creditors and equity investors, and it is difficult to know the specific manner in which this rate is shared. That is, what rate does equity receive and what rate do the creditors receive? Finally, there may be more than one IRR which equates the present value of cash inflows with the present value of cash

TABLE 11-5

The White Company

Determination of IRR of the Project

| | Cash flows | | | Present value | | |
Year	Out	In	PVIF at 14%	Cash flows	PVIF at 16%	Cash flows
0	$100,000	$ 0	1.000	−$100,000	1.000	−$100,000
1		21,400	.877	18,769	.862	18,447
2		21,800	.769	16,764	.743	16,197
3		22,600	.675	15,255	.641	14,487
4		22,200	.592	13,142	.552	12,254
5		78,400	.519	40,690	.476	37,318
				+$ 4,619		−$ 1,297

Interpolate: $\dfrac{\$4,619}{\$5,916} \times 2.0\% = 1.56\% + 14.00\% = 15.56\%$

TABLE 11-6

The White Company

Distribution of Cash Flows Between
"Income" and "Principal"

Investment[1]	IRR 15.56%	Theoretical return of investment	Cash flow[2]
$100,000	$15,560[3]	$ 5,840	$21,400
94,160	14,651[3]	7,149	21,800
87,011	13,539[3]	9,061	22,600
77,950	12,129[3]	10,071	22,200
67,879	10,562[3]	67,838[4]	78,400
41[4]	0	0	0

[1]Investment at the beginning of each period.
[2]Cash flow at the end of each period.
[3]Obtained by multiplying the investment for the period by the IRR, that is, by 15.56%.
[4]Does not equal, because of rounding.

outflows. This can result where there is abnormality in the timing and size of the cash flows; however, the existence of multiple internal rates of return is unusual.

The exact meaning of the IRR is that investors recapture their investment plus a certain return. It should be pointed out that the return is constant (relative to investment over time) throughout the life of the investment. Table 11-6 illustrates this concept.

net present value method

It was mentioned earlier that many authorities in the field of finance believe that the minimum investment criterion is the firm's weighted average cost of capital, and that no investment should be undertaken (at least theoretically) if the yield does not equal this minimum.[8] This being the case, it is only necessary to discount the cash flows resulting from the investment with the minimum acceptance criterion (average required rate of return). If the present value of the discounted flows are equal to or greater than the investment, the investment should be made, since the investors will receive their expectation (return plus principal).

[8] This method is applicable to those firms that can either calculate their weighted average cost of capital or select an accurate required rate of return. Many authorities believe that these criteria may be ascertained by large firms, but the writers do not believe that closely held firms can "compute" these criteria.

The following formula may be used to calculate the net present value of various projects:

$$NPV = \sum_{t=1}^{n} \frac{(CF)_t}{(1+k)^t} - \sum_{t=0}^{n} \frac{(CO)_t}{(1+k)^t}$$

where CF_t is the cash flow received by *all* investors in year t; k is the firm's required rate of return (usually the firm's weighted cost of capital); CO_t is the cost of the investment in period t; and n is the last period in which a cash flow is expected.

The calculation of net present value of the cash flow for the White Company, assuming a 12 percent required rate of return, is shown in Table 11-7.

In this case the net present value of the project equals $11,148, which means that the present value of the *return* exceeds the present value of cost by $11,148. Since equity investors are the recipients of these present value dollars, the market value of the firm will most probably increase. Stated differently, when the net present value of the cash flows equals or exceeds zero, the project is said to be acceptable in that the value of the firm will be preserved or increased. On the other hand, if the net present value is less than zero, the project is undesirable in that expectations will not be met and in many cases the firm will decline in value.

The usefulness of the net present value method in small firms is very questionable, since the small firm cannot ascertain a single required rate of return for all capital—weighted average cost of capital—with any degree of confidence. Even if it could calculate this rate, management would still have the problem of calculating the return on equity when NPV is greater than zero.

TABLE 11-7

The White Company

Net Present Value: Cost of Capital Equals 12 Percent

| Year | Cash flows | | Present value | |
	Out	In	PVIF of 12%	Cash flows
0	$100,000	$ 0	1.000	−$100,000
1		21,400	.893	19,110
2		21,800	.797	17,375
3		22,600	.712	16,091
4		22,200	.636	14,119
5		78,400	.567	44,453
			Net present value of cash flows = $	11,148

Summary

Capital budgeting (investment decision making) is as complex and important in small firms as in large firms; therefore, it is essential that owner-managers adopt a formalized capital budgeting procedure. Although each firm must develop its own budgeting procedure, certain common elements should be taken into consideration by all firms. For example, a budget should be developed to cover a certain period (e.g., five years). Decisions regarding investments should be made at the highest possible level for two vitally important reasons: (1) one bad decision may cause failure and (2) most small firms face a continuous capital shortage.

In deciding which projects to accept, managers of small firms should give high priority to projects that cannot be postponed, as well as to those which improve operating efficiency. The timing of project generation should be continuous; however, to avoid less than optimal decisions, the evaluation process should be done at a specific time (e.g., quarterly, semiannually, or annually).

There are several methods of project evaluation. In this chapter, payback, average return on average investment, internal rate of return, and net present value methods are discussed. Payback is an important technique but does not take into account the time value of funds in evaluating the return on a project after the investment is recovered. Average rate of return on average investment is an extremely weak technique and should not be used, even in conjunction with other methods. Internal rate of return and net present value consider the time value of funds but are weakened by the fact that small firms normally do not have the capacity to determine the required rate of return (weighted average cost of capital) that may be used as an acceptance criterion. It is believed that these weaknesses can be corrected by making certain adjustments to the internal rate of return concept. This method is presented in Chapter 12.

QUESTIONS

1. How do you account for the fact that so many companies continue to use unsophisticated investment decision techniques?

2. List several reasons why investments are made.

3. Classify investments according to priority. Why do you think this method of classification is sound?

4. What should be the budget planning period for small companies? Why are they shorter than for large companies?

5. "In some cases investment decisions may be 'pushed' down into the organization; however, this authority should be carefully granted and clearly defined." Explain.

6. Explain why the predominant reason that businesses invest funds in assets is to increase the present value of the firm's equity capital.

7. Explain the difference between the required rate of return that is used by small business as a criterion for investment decisions and the average weighted cost of capital.

8. Discuss the disadvantages associated with payback and average rate of return on average investment. Why should small firms use payback even though it has disadvantages?

9. Explain how the IRR and NPV is derived. What disadvantages do they have when used by managers of small businesses?

10. Define how cash flows are determined when using (a) payback and (b) internal rate of return, net present value, and adjusted internal rate of return.

PROBLEM

11-1. Compute the IRR and NPV of problems 12-1 and 12-2. Assume that the firm's required rate of return is 15 percent.

chapter 12

THE CAPITAL BUDGETING
PROCESS (CONTINUED)

It is believed that the internal rate of return technique can be adjusted in a manner that will overcome the objections levied against the IRR and NPV techniques. It may be remembered that the two primary disadvantages of these methods are: (1) the varying types of investors are unable to ascertain their rightful share of the calculated return; and (2) each method, to be effective as a decision-making tool, requires knowledge of a weighted average cost of capital, which, in most cases, cannot be ascertained with any degree of confidence. The following is a description of the technique, which we have chosen to entitle the "adjusted internal return."

Adjusted Internal Return Method

Computational procedures

The adjusted internal rate of return technique requires at least two adjustments to be made in the firm's data. First, the capital account should be divided into debt and equity sources. If leases are used in the financing process, they should be isolated from traditional sources of debt and the internal rate of return on this capital should be computed. To accomplish these adjustments requires knowledge not only of the capital structure of the firm but of the asset mix as well. Incidentally, a change in either the asset mix or debt/equity mix affects the flow of funds, which, in turn, causes the internal rate of return of each supplier to change. Moreover, a change in the firm's asset mix will cause the IRR on all capital either to increase or decrease, but a change in the debt/equity mix will not cause the IRR on total capital to change. Second, the firm's cash flows should be divided in such a way that management can ascertain the internal rate of return on (1) debt capital and (2) equity capital.

Employing the data of the White Company, we are able to illustrate these adjustments. Restating the cash flow and balance sheet data in Table

TABLE 12-1

The White Company

Balance Sheet Data

Assets:	
Current assets:	
Cash	$ 10,000
Receivables	20,000
Inventories	20,000
Fixed assets	50,000
Total	$100,000
Liabilities and net worth:	
Current liabilities	
Notes payable	$ 15,000
Accounts payable	15,000
Long-term note	20,000
Net worth:	
Common stock—50,000 shares	50,000
Total	$100,000

Expected cash flows—adjusted for taxes by years:

1	$21,400
2	21,800
3	22,600
4	22,200
5	78,400

12-1, the allocation of the cash flows between creditors and the owners is provided in Table 12-2. In viewing the table, the cash flows associated with the creditor's portion of the investment, CF_d, consists of interest adjusted by the tax rate of the firm plus the amount of the capital provided by the creditors. The latter amount is represented in the cash flow as depreciation, return of working capital, and scrap value. The amount of depreciation, working capital, and scrap allocated to each supplier is based on the contribution of each. In the example above, since the creditors financed one-half of the investment, it is presumed that the cash flow allocated to them will consist of one-half of the depreciation plus one-half of the working capital plus one-half of the scrap value. On the other hand, if the creditors had financed only one-third of the investment, they would have received only one-third of the depreciation, working capital, and scrap. It should be emphasized that while the principal owed to the creditors will not actually be repaid in this manner, it is "earned" in this way.

TABLE 12-2

The White Company

Allocation of Cash Flows
to Creditors and Owners

Cash flow allocated to creditors

Year	Interest $(1 - TR)$ +	.50 (Depreciation) +	.50 (Working capital)	+ .50 (Scrap) =	CF_d
1	$ 3,680	+ $ 4,500 +	$ 0 +	$ 0 =	$ 8,180
2	4,160	+ 4,500 +	0 +	0 =	8,660
3	4,000	+ 4,500 +	0 +	0 =	8,500
4	4,320	+ 4,500 +	0 +	0 =	8,820
5	4,640	+ 4,500 +	25,000 +	2,500 =	36,640
	$20,800	+ $22,500 +	$25,000 +	$2,500 =	$70,800

Cash flow allocated to owners

Year	Earnings	+ .50 (Depreciation) +	.50 (Working capital)	+ .50 (Scrap) =	CF_e
1	$ 8,720	+ $ 4,500 +	$ 0 +	$ 0 =	$13,200
2	8,640	+ 4,500 +	0 +	0 =	13,140
3	9,600	+ 4,500 +	0 +	0 =	14,100
4	8,880	+ 4,500 +	0 +	0 =	13,380
5	9,760	+ 4,500 +	25,000 +	2,500 =	41,760
	$45,600	+ $22,500 +	$25,000 +	$2,500 =	$95,600

CF_e, on the other hand, includes earnings plus the amount of funds provided by the equity investors. In this case they, like the creditors, receive one-half of the depreciation, working capital, and scrap. Again it is emphasized that the ratio of depreciation, working capital, and scrap received by creditors as well as equity investors coincides with their contribution to the investment (i.e., debt/equity ratio).

After CF_d and CF_e have been determined, we are able to calculate the internal rate of return (IRR_d) of debt capital by solving the following equation:

$$\sum_{t=1}^{n} \frac{(CF_d)_t}{(1+r)^t} - \sum_{t=0}^{n} \frac{(CO_d)_t}{(1+r)^t} = 0 \qquad (12\text{-}1)$$

where CF_d is the cash flow "earned" for the creditors in period t, CO_d is the amount of capital supplied by *all* creditors, and r is the rate that equates the present value of the future CF_d to the present value of investment provided by the creditors. In other words, r (IRR_d) is the internal rate of return on the amount of debt capital invested by all creditors.

The internal rate of return on equity capital (IRR_e) may be determined by solving the following equation:

$$\sum_{t=1}^{n} \frac{(CF_e)_t}{(1+r)^t} - \sum_{t=0}^{n} \frac{(CF_e)_t}{(1+r)^t} = 0 \qquad (12\text{-}2)$$

where CF_e represents the cash flow earned for the equity investors, CO_e is the amount of capital supplied by the equity investors, and r is the rate that equates the present values of future CF_e to the present value of the investment provided by the equity investors. That is, r (IRR_e) is the internal rate of return on equity capital.

Using the adjusted data of the White Company, we are able to calculate the IRR_d and IRR_e for the investors of debt and equity capital. Table 12-3 depicts these calculations.

TABLE 12-3

Calculation of IRR_d for
the White Company

Year	CF_d	CO_e	PVIF at 8%	$	PVIF at 10%	$
0	$ 0	$50,000	1.000	− $50,000	1.000	− $50,000
1	8,180	0	0.926	7,575	0.909	7,436
2	8,660	0	0.857	7,422	0.826	7,153
3	8,500	0	0.794	6,749	0.751	6,384
4	8,820	0	0.735	5,402	0.683	6,024
5	36,640	0	0.681	24,952	0.621	22,753
				$ 2,100		− $ 250

Interpolate: $\dfrac{\$2,100}{\$2,350} \times 2.0\% = 1.78\% + 8.00\% = 9.78\%$

$IRR_d = 9.78\%$

Calculation of IRR_e for
the White Company

Year	CF_e	CO_e	PVIF at 20%	$	PVIF at 22%	$
0	$ 0	$50,000	1.000	− $50,000	1.000	− $50,000
1	13,220	0	.833	11,012	.820	10,840
2	13,140	0	.694	9,119	.672	8,830
3	14,100	0	.579	8,164	.551	7,769
4	13,380	0	.482	6,449	.451	6,034
5	41,760	0	.402	16,787	.370	15,451
				$ 1,531		− $ 1,076

Interpolate: $\dfrac{\$1,531}{\$2,607} \times 2.0\% = 1.17\% + 20.00\% = 21.17\%$

$IRR_e = 21.17\%$

From the example above it may be seen that by determining the internal rate of return for debt and equity capital, we are able to provide management with information that is essential to a sound investment decision. First, the investment of $100,000 ($50,000 from debt and $50,000 from equity sources) is returned in full and is available for reinvestment. Second, the return of the total number of dollars paid to creditors is covered in excess of five times in total as well as annually. Third, the after-tax weighted average return on all types of debt equals 9.78 percent. Finally, equity investors know that the firm is earning a 21.17 percent on their investment. This knowledge makes it possible for them to compare this return with returns from other investment opportunities as well as their expectations. If the latter criterion is met, the investment is acceptable.

The adjusted internal rate of return has several advantages when compared to the NPV and IRR techniques. First and probably most important is that the equity investors are able to determine the return on their invested capital. This figure is unavailable in other methods. Second, it does not require a knowledge of the firm's "weighted cost of capital." Finally, it is a vehicle by which the internal rate of return on total capital will be calculated. For example, in the case above we know that the firm's IRR will be 15.47 percent ($21.17 \times .50 + 9.78 \times .50 = 15.47$ percent) if the project is undertaken.

Impact of a changing asset mix and capital mix

It was mentioned earlier that a change in the asset mix or capital structure will cause the "returns" to change. To illustrate, assume that the firm is able to produce the same EBIDT with an asset mix of 70 percent working capital and 30 percent fixed assets rather than 50 percent working capital and 50 percent fixed capital. The balance sheet and profit and loss data are given in Table 12-4.

The reader recalls that IRR_d and IRR_e may be determined by solving equations (12-1) and (12-2). Substituting the data from Table 12-5 in these

TABLE 12-4

The White Company

Balance Sheet Data

Assets		*Liabilities and net worth*	
Cash	$ 15,000	Notes payable	$ 15,000
Receivables	25,000	Accounts payable	15,000
Inventories	30,000	Long-term note	20,000
Fixed assets	30,000	Common stock	50,000
	$100,000		$100,000

TABLE 12-5

The White Company

Income Data

	Year				
	1	2	3	4	5
EBIDT	$24,500	$25,000	$26,000	$25,000	$27,000
Interest	4,600	5,200	5,000	5,400	5,800
Depreciation	5,400	5,400	5,400	5,400	5,400
PBT	$14,500	$14,400	$15,600	$14,700	$15,800
Taxes	2,900	2,880	3,120	2,940	3,160
PAT	$11,600	$11,520	$12,480	$11,760	$12,640

Cash Flows Allocated to Creditors

Year	$Interest(1 - TR)$	+	$.50(\$27,000)$	+	$.50(\$70,000)$	+	$.50(\$3,000)$	=	CF_d
1	$ 3,680	+	$ 2,700	+	$ 0	+	$ 0		$ 6,380
2	4,160	+	2,700	+	0	+	0	=	6,860
3	4,000	+	2,700	+	0	+	0	=	6,700
4	4,320	+	2,700	+	0	+	0	=	7,020
5	4,640	+	2,700	+	35,000	+	1,500	=	43,840
	$20,800	+	$13,500	+	$35,000	+	$1,500	=	$70,800

Cash Flows Allocated to Owners

Year	Earnings	+	$.50(\$27,000)$	+	$.50(\$70,000)$	+	$.50(\$3,000)$	=	CF_e
1	$11,600	+	$ 2,700	+	$ 0	+	$ 0	=	$ 14,300
2	11,520	+	2,700	+	0	+	0	=	14,220
3	12,480	+	2,700	+	0	+	0	=	15,180
4	11,760	+	2,700	+	0	+	0	=	14,460
5	12,640	+	2,700	+	35,000	+	1,500	=	51,840
	$60,000	+	$13,500	+	$35,000	+	$1,500	=	$110,000

equations, we find that IRR_d equals 9.18 percent and IRR_e equals 25.97 percent (see Table 12-6).

As a result of the changes in asset mix, the "return" on equity capital increased from 21.16 percent to 25.97 percent, an increase of 23 percent. The principal reason for the increase is the decrease in depreciation, which, of course, is an expense. Since expenses were smaller, earnings were greater, resulting in a higher return. This increase was reduced somewhat by the fact that a larger amount of the investment was in working capital rather than fixed capital. Since working capital is normally recovered later in the project's life than fixed capital (through depreciation), it has less value; however, the loss in value resulting from the time value of funds concept was insufficient to

TABLE 12-6

IRR$_d$ and IRR$_e$ Calculations

Year	\multicolumn{2}{c}{Cash flows}		Present value of CF_d		Present value of CF_e	
	CF_d	CF_e	At 8%	At 10%	At 24%	At 26%
1	$ 6,380	$14,300	$ 5,908	$ 5,799	$11,526	$11,354
2	6,860	14,220	5,879	5,666	9,243	8,959
3	6,700	15,180	5,320	5,032	7,954	7,590
4	7,020	14,460	5,160	4,795	6,117	5,741
5	43,840	51,840	29,855	27,225	17,677	16,330
			$52,122	$48,517	$52,517	$49,974
PV of investment			50,000	50,000	50,000	50,000
			$ 2,122	($ 1,483)	$ 2,517	($ 26)

$$IRR_d \text{ interpolation: } \frac{\$2,122}{\$3,605} \times 2.0\% = 1.18\% + 8.0\% = 9.18\%$$

$$IRR_d = 9.18\%$$

$$IRR_e \text{ interpolation: } \frac{\$2,517}{\$2,543} \times 2.0\% = 1.97\% + 24.00\% = 25.97\%$$

$$IRR_e = 25.97\%$$

offset the increase in the return resulting from reduced expenses (depreciation). It should be noted also that the risk in a firm with a relatively larger amount of working capital is probably less than in a firm with more invested in fixed assets.

The reader knows, of course, that a firm can increase the return to equity by employing more debt, provided that the return on total capital exceeds the borrowing rate. Not only will the return on equity increase, but IRR$_e$ will also increase. The following example reveals this fact. Assume that debt is increased to 60 percent and equity is decreased to 40 percent, but the asset mix consists of $50,000 in fixed assets and $50,000 in working capital. The debt mix remains the same; also, interest rates remain the same. Liabilities under these conditions are as follows: notes payable, $18,000; accounts payable, $18,000; and long-term debt, $24,000. Interest costs are $5,520, $6,240, $6,000, $6,480 and $6,960, respectively. CF$_d$ and CF$_e$ for each of the five years are as follows (see Table 12-7):

Year	CF_d	CF_e
1	$10,920	$11,584
2	11,640	11,408
3	11,400	12,400
4	11,880	11,616
5	45,360	34,232

TABLE 12-7

The White Company

Calculation of CF_d and CF_e
(Debt/Equity Ratio 60/40)

EBIDT	$24,500	$25,000	$26,000	$25,500	$27,000
Expected interest	5,520	6,240	6,000	6,480	6,960
EBDT	$18,980	$18,760	$20,000	$19,020	$20,040
Depreciation	9,000	9,000	9,000	9,000	9,000
EBT	$ 9,980	$ 9,760	$11,000	$10,020	$11,040
Taxes	1,996	1,952	2,200	2,004	2,208
EAT	$ 7,984	$ 7,808	$ 8,800	$ 8,016	$ 8,832
Effective interest	$ 4,416	$ 4,992	$ 4,800	$ 5,184	$ 5,568

Calculation of CF_d

Year	Interest$(1-TR)$ +	.60(Depreciation) +	.60(Working capital)	+.60(Scrap) =	CF_d
1	$ 4,416 +	$ 5,400 +	$ 0 +	$ 0 =	$ 9,816
2	4,992 +	5,400 +	0 +	0 =	10,392
3	4,800 +	5,400 +	0 +	0 =	10,200
4	5,184 +	5,400 +	0 +	0 =	10,584
5	5,568 +	5,400 +	30,000 +	3,000 =	43,968
	$24,960 +	$27,000 +	$30,000 +	$3,000 =	$84,960

Calculation of CF_e

Year	Earnings +	.40(Depreciation) +	.40(Working capital)	+.40(Scrap) =	CF_e
1	$ 7,984 +	$ 3,600 +	$ 0 +	$ 0 =	$11,584
2	7,808 +	3,600 +	0 +	0 =	11,408
3	8,800 +	3,600 +	0 +	0 =	12,400
4	8,016 +	3,600 +	0 +	0 =	11,616
5	8,832 +	3,600 +	20,000 +	2,000 =	34,432
	$41,440 +	$18,000 +	$20,000 +	$2,000 =	$81,440

Substituting the data above in Equations (12-1) and (12-2), we find that IRR_d equals 9.85 percent and IRR_e equals 23.91 percent, which is 13.0 percent higher than when the project was financed with 50 percent debt and 50 percent equity—see Table 12-8.

In summary, it can be said that the asset mix and debt–equity mix definitely affect the return on equity. That is, the return on equity capital increases in direct relation to an increase in working capital and debt capital. This is important to the small business manager, since small businesses employ more working capital and debt capital than their larger counterparts.

TABLE 12-8

The White Company

Calculations of IRR_d and IRR_e

Year	Cash flows		Present value of CF_d		Present value of CF_e	
	CF_d	CF_e	At 8%	At 10%	At 20%	At 24%
1	$ 9,816	$11,584	$ 9,090	$ 8,923	$ 9,649	$ 9,337
2	10,392	11,408	8,906	8,584	7,917	7,415
3	10,200	12,400	8,099	7,660	7,180	6,498
4	10,584	11,616	7,779	7,229	5,599	4,914
5	43,968	34,432	29,942	27,304	13,761	11,741
Present value of CF_d and CF_e			$63,816	$59,700	$44,106	$39,905
Present value of investment			60,000	60,000	40,000	40,000
			$ 3,816	($ 300)	$ 4,106	($ 95)

IRR_d interpolation: $\dfrac{\$3,816}{\$4,116} \times 2.0\% = 1.85\% + 8.00\% = 9.85\%$

$IRR_d = 9.85\%$

IRR_e interpolation: $\dfrac{\$4,106}{\$4,201} \times 4.0\% = 3.91\% + 20.00\% = 23.91\%$

$IRR_e = 23.91\%$

It should be emphasized that while return increases, the amount of risk also increases; therefore, management should compare the increase in return to the incremental risk before a decision is made to increase the proportion of debt capital. The reader should note also that the gain resulting from the increased use of debt was not very great (e.g., 13 percent). The primary reason for this low increase is the direct result of the small firm's extremely low tax rate (i.e., the larger the tax rate, the higher the increase in the return to equity). This point was developed in Chapter 9, which deals with capital structure.

Adjusting for Risk in Investments

It has been stated several times elsewhere in this book that small firms have greater business and financial risk than large firms and are usually more vulnerable to "poor" decisions than their counterparts. As a general rule, the large firm accepts projects which have the highest expected value provided that the discounted value of the future cash flows exceeds the cost of capital or a "hurdle" rate if the cost of capital is not known. Second, given several investment opportunities with approximately the same expected value, the large firm usually accepts the projects with the smallest relative dispersion of net operating income. That is, if projects are mutually exclusive, the large firm will accept those investment opportunities whose cash flows have the smallest standard deviation and coefficient of variation. The logic behind this strategy of risk evaluation is that the market value of the firm's stock is subject to this risk, and, all other things being equal, the greater the variation in net operating income, the smaller the price/earnings ratio (i.e., the greater the risk, the smaller will be value of the firm).

Risk: the small firm's perspective

Small businesses, on the other hand, are concerned with variations in cash flows and return on equity, but they are much more concerned with insolvency. The risk associated with dispersion is relatively inconsequential to the small firm, since the "price" of its stock is usually not affected by variations in earnings. They are very sensitive to losses since they (1) have less equity to serve as a buffer against losses, (2) do not generally have the same credit status or assets to offset losses, and (3) are not very well diversified; therefore, losses of any size may cause failure. To avoid insolvency as well as fluctuations in cash flows, small business managers should carefully evaluate the risk associated with each project under consideration.

Methods of evaluating risk

There are many techniques available to management to evaluate the risk associated with investment decisions. These techniques range from the simple to the very complex. The latter group is usually so costly that small businesses cannot afford to employ it in their evaluation process. It is for this reason that the greatest emphasis is placed on the discussion of the less complicated methods.

risk-adjusted discount rate method

Many owners will arbitrarily select the project with the least risk. That is, when there are two investments that are mutually exclusive, the manager will select the one that he believes will not result in a loss that would cause .nsolvency. In fact, he may turn down the project with the highest return if he believes that there would be a greater chance of loss in that particular project.

Another informal method of risk adjustment is to adjust upward the discount rate used in determining the net present value of a project. For example, if the manager has been using a hurdle rate of 15 percent he may increase this rate to, say, 20 percent if he believes the project to be more risky than the average project. If the net present value is still positive (equal to or exceeding zero), it will be compared with other alternative investment opportunities; or, if it is the only investment that is being evaluated, it will be accepted. This method involves adjusting the denominator in the equation;

TABLE 12-9

The White Company

Calculation of Net Present Value of a
Risky Project When Minimum Rate of Acceptance Is 20 Percent

Year	Cash flow	PVIF 20%	PV of cash flows
1	$21,400	.869	$ 17,826
2	21,800	.756	15,129
3	22,600	.659	13,085
4	22,200	.571	10,700
5	78,400	.497	31,517
	Present value of cash flows		$88,257
	Present value of investment		100,000
	Net present value		($11,743)

that is, the higher the risk, the higher the denominator. Table 12-9 depicts this method of risk adjustment.

The perceived net present value of this particular project is negative and is therefore unacceptable; if the cash flows had been discounted at 15 percent, the project would have been acceptable since it would have had a NPV of $1,567.

probability distribution approach

A more sophisticated accounting for risk may be achieved by directly measuring the variability of returns. In most cases the projected cash flows of a particular investment are the best estimates of a single outcome in each period. We all know that there are many possible outcomes, but by knowing the probability of each, we can determine the most probable outcome. While this may not be the outcome for any single year, it will average over the long run. The authors are aware that it is impossible for most small companies to gather the necessary data that will produce objective probability distributions; therefore, in most cases it is recommended that only subjective probability distributions be determined. The simplest probability distribution is to forecast three estimates, these being: optimistic, pessimistic, and most likely. Usually, each of these estimates are associated with a particular state of the economy. For example, an optimistic estimate is associated with "good" times; a pessimistic estimate would occur during "bad" times; and the most likely estimate occurs during normal economic conditions. If the fluctuations in the state of the economy are the basis for our forecasts, then all we have to do is to estimate subjectively the probable conditions at given times in order

TABLE 12-10

The White Company

Determination of Expected Earnings Before
Interest, Depreciation, and Taxes

State of the economy	Probability of the event[1]	Year[1]				
		1	*2*	*3*	*4*	*5*
Recession	.25	$22,500	$23,000	$23,000	$22,500	$25,000
Normal	.50	24,500	25,000	26,000	25,500	27,000
Boom	.25	26,500	27,000	29,000	28,500	29,000
Expected value by year		$24,500	$25,000	$26,000	$25,500	$27,000

Note: To find the expected value of the events multiply each event by the probability of that event [e.g., ($22,500).25 + ($24,500).50 + ($26,500).25 = $24,500].
[1]Subjectively determined.

to determine an expected cash flow. Table 12-10 illustrates this technique of determining the expected earnings before interest, depreciation, and taxes that were used in the White Company examples.

The reader should note that a normal distribution was assumed in the example above. Had our subjective evaluation been skewed to the left, the expected cash flow would have been below the most likely or normal estimate, thus causing the expected value to be less than those calculated. Likewise, the greater the spread between the estimated cash flows as well as the greater the spread between the estimates of the events occurring (probabilities), the more risky the project. The techniques used to measure the risk characteristics of various projects is the standard deviation and/or a relative risk measurement, the coefficient of variation. The standard deviation is easy to compute provided that we are able to ascertain the probability distribution of future cash flows. The first step is to calculate the expected value of the outcomes in each year by solving the following equation:

$$\bar{R}_t = \sum_{i=1}^{n} R_{it} P_{it} \tag{12-3}$$

where $\bar{R}_t$ is the expected value in year t; R_{it} is the ith possible cash flow associated with each period; P_{it} is the probability that R_{it} will occur.

The standard deviation, σ_t, for period t is computed by solving the following formula:

$$\sigma_t = \sqrt{\sum_{i=1}^{n} \left(R_{it} - \bar{R}_t \right)^2 P_{it}} \tag{12-4}$$

Below is the calculation of the standard deviation for each of the five years:

Year 1

$(R_{ir1} - \bar{R_1})$	$(R_{i1} - \bar{R_1})^2 P_{i1}$
$22,500 - \$24,500 = -\$2000$	$(\$4,000,000).25 = \$1,000,000$
$24,500 - 24,500 = 0$	$(0).50 = 0$
$26,500 - 24,500 = 2000$	$(4,000,000).25 = \underline{1,000,000}$
	$\$2,000,000$

$$\sigma_i = \$1,414$$
$$cv_i = \sigma_1 / \bar{R_1} = .058$$

Year 2

$23,000 - \$25,000 = -\$2000$	$(\$4,000,000).25 = \$1,000,000$
$25,000 - 25,000 = 0$	$(0) \quad\quad\quad 0$
$27,000 - 25,000 = 2000$	$(\$4,000,000).25 = \underline{1,000,000}$
	$\$2,000,000$

$$\sigma_2 = \$1,414$$
$$cv_2 = \sigma_2 / \bar{R_2} = .057$$

Year 3

$23,000 - \$26,000 = -\$3,000$	$(\$9,000,000).25 = \$2,250,000$
$26,000 - 26,000 = 0$	$(0).50 = 0$
$29,000 - 26,000 = 3,000$	$(\$9,000,000).25 = \underline{2,250,000}$
	$\$4,500,000$

$$\sigma_3 = \$2,121$$
$$cv_3 = \sigma_3 / \bar{R_3} = .083$$

Year 4

$22,500 - \$25,500 = -\$3,000$	$(\$9,000,000).25 = \$2,250,000$
$25,500 - 25,500 = 0$	$(0).50 = 0$
$28,500 - 25,500 = 3,000$	$(\$9,000,000).25 = \underline{2,250,000}$
	$\$4,500,000$

$$\sigma_4 = \$2,121$$
$$cv_4 = \sigma_4 / \bar{R_4} = .083$$

Year 5

$25,000 - \$27,000 = -\$2,000$	$(\$4,000,000).25 = \$1,000,000$
$27,000 - 27,000 = 0$	$(0).50 = 0$
$29,000 - 27,000 = 2,000$	$(\$4,000,000).25 = \underline{1,000,000}$
	$\$2,000,000$

$$\sigma_5 = \$1,414$$
$$cv_5 = \sigma_5 / \bar{R_5} = .052$$

Having determined the expected returns and the standard deviations for the respective time periods, the net present value for the entire investment and the standard deviation of this value may be ascertained. The first element, the NPV, is computed by simply discounting the annual expected returns, $\bar{R}_t$, back to the present and deduct the investment cost. This process is essentially equivalent to the previously cited NPV calculations. However, instead of discounting at the cost of capital, the appropriate discount rate is the risk-free rate. The rationale for this departure is based upon the approach to be taken in analyzing the return and risk characteristics of an investment. In the present context, NPV is to be measured by finding the present value of the cash flows without incorporating any risk into the investigation. To do so requires discounting at a rate that accounts only for the time value of money, that being the risk-free rate. To discount the cash flows at a rate that includes a risk premium while simultaneously examining the variability of returns (standard deviation) would result in double counting for risk. Hence, the probability distribution approach computes the net present value at a risk-free rate to ascertain the benefit of the project, and determines the risk by measuring the dispersion of returns.

In the current example of the White Company, the net present value may be calculated. If the prevailing risk-free rate, i, is 8 percent, the net present value would be $26,150.80, as set forth in Table 12-11. Thus, the net present value is definitely positive when only the time value of money is given recognition. However, in a world of uncertainty, where the returns will most certainly depart from the expected value, acceptance of the investment is also dependent upon the risk associated with the returns.

In measuring the potential variability of the net present value, a key determinant is the relationship of the projected cash flows over time. Specifically, does the actual outcome in a particular year have an impact upon subsequent period returns? If a strong relationship exists, the cash flows are

TABLE 12-11

The White Company

Year	Expected cash flows $(\bar{R}_t)$	Present value interest factors at 8%	Present value
1	$21,400	.926	$ 19,816.40
2	21,800	.857	18,682.60
3	22,600	.794	17,944.40
4	22,200	.735	16,317.00
5	78,400	.681	53,390.40
		Expected present value	$126,150.80
		Cost of investment	100,000.00
		Expected net present value	$ 26,150.80

said to be highly correlated over time, which increases the aggregate variability of cash flows. However, if the resulting cash flows in a certain year have no bearing upon later returns, the total dispersion over the life of the project is not as great. Without becoming involved in the proof, the computation of the standard deviation of the net present value of an investment may be shown as follows:

1. *For a project with dependent cash flows over time:*

$$\sigma_{NPV} = \sum_{t=1}^{n} \frac{\sigma_t}{(1+i)^t}$$

2. *For an asset with independent cash flow over time:*

$$\sigma_{NPV} = \sqrt{\sum_{t=1}^{n} \frac{\sigma_t^2}{(1+i)^{2t}}}$$

where σ_{NPV} is the standard deviation of the net present value for the investment; σ_t is the standard deviation of the cash flow in year t, as provided earlier; and i is the risk-free rate.

Assuming the cash flows for the White Company investment to be independent relative to time, the project standard deviation would be

$$\sigma_{NPV} = \left[\frac{\$1,414.21^2}{(1+.08)^2} + \frac{\$1,414.21^2}{(1+.08)^4} + \frac{\$2,121.32^2}{(1+.08)^6} + \frac{\$2,121.32^2}{(1+.08)^8} + \frac{\$1,414.21^2}{(1+.08)^{10}} \right]^{1/2}$$

$$= [\$2,000,000(.857) + \$2,000,000(.735)$$

$$+ \$4,500,000(.630) + 4,500,000(.540) + 2,000,000(.463)]^{1/2}$$

$$= [\$1,714,000 + \$1,470,000 + \$2,835,000 + \$2,430,000 + \$926,000]^{1/2}$$

$$= \$3,061.86$$

With the foregoing information, the decision maker has access to two key elements in making a sound decision whether to accept the investment. In brief, the investors must evaluate the $26,150.80 expected net present value and the standard deviation of $3,061.86 in light of their attitude toward the risk–return trade-off.

It was pointed out above that the principal risk of a small firm is that of potential insolvency. The probability distribution is one technique that allows us to select the project with the least insolvency risk. In the case of the White Company there is only an insignificant chance of insolvency (this presumes that we have correctly selected our probabilities); therefore, we would make the investment if other opportunities were not better as measured by (1) return on equity capital and (2) risk of variation as shown by the standard deviation and coefficient of variation.

We may conclude that a manager of the small firm should first measure both the risk of insolvency and the risk associated with variation; however, the risk of insolvency is more important due to the characteristics of the small firm. If a project satisfies this requirement, management should test it from the viewpoint of variation and expected return.

The certainty-equivalent technique

The use of the certainty equivalent is another way in which management may evaluate a project riskwise. This method is directly associated with the manager's concepts regarding utility. Briefly stated, the utility theory states that the value of an investment is directly related to the manager's propensity to assume risk. As a general rule an individual may be classified as either a risk taker or a risk averter, although obviously there are degrees within these two classifications. Figure 12-1 depicts two possible positions. Curve *B* depicts an individual who is a risk taker, whereas curve *A* clearly reveals that this individual is a risk averter. Stated differently, the individual depicted by curve *A* also has a diminishing marginal utility for money (return), while the individual portrayed by curve *B* has an increasing marginal utility for money (return). As a consequence of the decreasing marginal utility the risk averter is not agreeable to "pay" much in terms of risk for each subsequent dollar in return (i.e., he will pay *OX* in risk for *OR* return, *OX'* for *OR'* return, and only *OX"* for *OR"* return). The risk taker is exactly the opposite, in that he will accept an increasing amount of risk for each subsequent dollar in return.

The certainty equivalent (CE) is directly related to utility theory in that it presumes that the rational investor has a diminishing marginal utility. To derive the certainty equivalents for an individual, it is necessary to construct his indifference curve. This task is done by ascertaining the amount of return required by the investor to make him indifferent to a choice between a return that possessed risk and a certain return. Suppose that you are indifferent to the four projects in Figure 12-2. Project *A* has a return of 10 percent but no

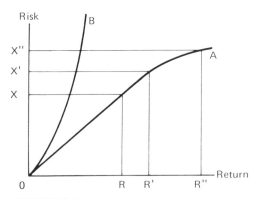

FIGURE 12-1.

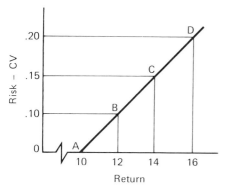

FIGURE 12-2

perceived risk; project B has a return of 15 percent but has a coefficient of variation (standard deviation/expected return) of .10; project C has a return of 20 percent with a coefficient of variation of .15; and project D has a return of 25 percent but its coefficient of variation is .175. Since the investor is indifferent between each project, a certainty-equivalent factor, α, may be calculated for each of the projects by dividing the risky projects (B, C, and D) into project A, whose return is certain (e.g., .833 for B, .714 for C, and .625 for D). Thus, the project with the *lowest* CE is considered to be the most risky.

Employing this concept, it is only necessary to adjust the cash flows of each project by a certainty-equivalent factor and discount the resulting amount at a risk-free rate of interest. If the appropriate factor for the cash flows of the White Company is determined by the decision maker to be .80, the revised net present value of the adjusted cash flows would be $6,656, as reflected in Table 12-12. Therefore, the firm's value will be maintained or improved.

TABLE 12-12

Adjusted Net Present Values
Using Certainty Equivalents

Year	Cash flows	$a = .8$ Adjusted cash flows	PVIF at 6%	PV adjusted cash flows
1	$21,090	$16,872	.943	$15,910
2	21,840	17,184	.890	15,294
3	22,260	17,808	.840	14,958
4	21,870	17,496	.792	13,857
5	78,040	62,432	.747	46,637

Present value of adjusted cash flow at 6%	$106,656
Present value of investment	100,000
Net present value	$ 6,656

In summary, the small businessman has available to him three methods that are fairly easy to use in adjusting for the risk that may be present in an invesment. First, he may adjust upward the rate used to discount the firm's cash flows. Second, the manager may adjust the cash flows (numerator) through the use of probability distributions. Finally, he may determine the certainty equivalents of projects with varying risk levels and then calculate the net present value of the projects. If the NPVs of the flows are equal to or greater then the present value of the costs, he can accept them without fear of losing value.

Review and Control

Unlike the large firm which may have several reviews of the decision resulting from one or more of the evaluation methods mentioned above before a final decision is made, projects in the smaller firm will more than likely not have any reviews. That is, the group doing the evaluation will also be the "reviewing" group. In the case of the "larger" small firms, projects usually go to the Board of Directors for final review and action.

In a large firm capital expenditure projects are combined into what is generally called the capital expenditure budget. This budget not only serves as the planning document but also acts as the control device. For example, any changes in this budget can be made only by the highest authority. Also, reports are constantly prepared regarding the expenditures and progress toward completion. If deviations are noted they must be explained and approved by the appropriate authority. In some cases requests for additional capital may be necessary, and occasionally projects may be "junked" even after the expenditures have been made.

The control process in the small firm, while much less complicated than in the large firm, is equally important. As in the large firm, the responsible person should follow the progress of the project from the time that it has been approved until its completion. Any deviations in costs should be noted and explained. If additional funds are required, it is necessary for the "controlling" officer to reevaluate the project to see if it continues to be justified. If it is justified, necessary corrections are made and the project is continued. However, if the existing and predicted "overages" are not justified and it is deemed excessive to the total welfare of the firm, it is better to take these early losses rather than create a situation that may cause the entire firm to fail.

After the project has been completed and placed in production, it is necessary for management to measure actual performance with expected results. The primary reason for this postaudit is to improve future capital budgeting processes so as to improve operating efficiency.

Summary

The authors believe that the internal rate of return and net present value methods have two primary disadvantages when used in the investment decision-making process: (1) the various types of investors are unable to ascertain their rightful share of the calculated return and (2) each method, if effective as a decision-making tool, requires knowledge of a weighted average cost of capital or required rate of return for use as an investment criterion. The authors do not believe that either can be effectively calculated in small companies. To overcome this difficulty, we have made certain adjustments to the internal rate of return method which we believe will provide the managers of small firms with an effective decision-making technique.

The method requires that two adjustments be made to the firm's data. First, the capital account should be divided into debt and equity sources. If leases are used in the financing process they should also be isolated from the traditional sources. Second, cash flows should be divided in such a way that management can calculate the internal rate of return on debt and equity capital. In this regard, total cash flow CF_t is divided into cash flows allocated to suppliers of debt capital CF_d and cash flows allocated to suppliers of equity capital CF_e. CF_d consists of interest (adjusted by the firm's tax rate) plus the amount of capital provided by the creditors. The latter is represented by the creditors' share of depreciation, working capital, and scrap value. The portion of depreciation, working capital, and scrap value allocated to the creditors is based on their contributions (i.e., the debt/equity ratio). CF_e consists of earnings (after tax) plus the amount of capital provided by the owners. Again this share is based on their contributions (i.e., the debt/equity ratio). Once the cash flows have been allocated to suppliers of equity and debt capital, we are able to solve for the IRR of each source by solving the following equations:

$$\sum_{t=1}^{n} \frac{(CF_d)^t}{(1+r)^t} = \sum_{t=0}^{n} \frac{(CO_d)^t}{(1+r)^t} t$$

and

$$\sum_{t=1}^{n} \frac{(CF_e)_t}{(1+r)^t} = \sum_{t=0}^{n} \frac{(CO_e)^t}{(1+r)^t}$$

It was observed that a change in the firm's asset mix would cause a change in the IRR_e and IRR_d as well as a change in total IRR. It was also observed that a change in the firm's debt/equity ratio would also cause IRR_e and IRR_d to change but total IRR would not change.

Several methods to evaluate risk were presented. It was suggested that the risk inherent in a project may be best observed by calculating the probability distribution of the firm's cash flows. Larger small businesses may possibly use the certainty equivalent method to evaluate the riskiness of projects.

Finally, the control process in the small firm, while much less complicated than in the large firm, is quite important. The owner-manager should follow the progress of projects from their approval until their completion. Also, management should measure actual performance with expected results. It is through this control process that future capital budgeting procedures will be improved.

QUESTIONS

1. Criticize the use of internal rate of return and net present value as a method of selecting investments.

2. Discuss the adjustments that are necessary to solve for IRR_e and IRR_d.

3. What impact does a change in asset mix and capital mix have on IRR_e, IRR_d, and IRR_t? Explain.

4. How many managers evaluate the riskiness of various projects? Which method do you recommend when using the adjusted internal return method of project evaluation?

PROBLEMS

12-1. Mr. Jones is contemplating the purchase of a small plant that manufactures pollution equipment at a price of $300,000. He requests that you decide whether the purchase is advisable. The following information is supplied for your evaluation:

Proposed Financing

Accounts payable	$25,000
Notes payable (12%)	50,000
Long-term note (5 yr, 10%)	75,000
Common stock (15,000 shares at $10 par)	150,000
	$300,000

Proposed Asset Mix

Fixed assets (fully depreciated in 5 yr)	$200,000
Cash	15,000
Inventory (at cost)	22,500
Accounts receivable	62,500

The following income and cost data have been verified by Mr. Jones:

Net sales	$750,000	$800,000	$775,000	$790,000	$805,000
Cost of goods sold	487,500	528,000	496,000	513,500	531,300
	262,500	272,000	279,000	276,500	273,700
Other expenses	210,000	220,320	228,990	221,500	221,697
Operating profit	52,500	51,680	50,010	55,300	52,003
Interest[1]	13,500	13,500	13,500	13,500	13,500
Profit before taxes	39,000	38,180	36,510	41,800	38,503
Taxes[2]	8,080	7,900	7,532	8,696	7,971
Profit after taxes	30,920	30,280	28,978	33,104	30,532

[1]Mr. Jones expects interest rates to decline slightly over the five-year period.
[2]The tax rate averages 20.7%.

Requirements:

Calculate payback, IRR_d, and IRR_e. Would you recommend the purchase? If so, why? If not, why not?

12-2. The President of the XYZ Company is attempting to determine whether he should purchase a small manufacturing plant for its book value of $125,000. His analysis reveals the following information:

Total investment	$125,000
Asset mix	
Cash	7,500
Receivables	32,500
Inventories	35,000
Plant & equipment	50,000
Financial sources	
Notes payable at 14%	12,500
Accounts payable at 0%	20,000
5-year note at 12%	50,000
Sale of common stock	42,500
EBIT	
Year 1	25,000
2	30,000
3	20,000
4	17,500
5	27,500
Depreciation (annually)	10,000
Assume the following:	
Tax rate	30%
No losses from bad debts of obsolete inventory	

Questions:
1. Should he purchase the plant for $125,000?
2. What are the IRR_d and IRR_e?
3. What would you recommend concerning the method of financing the acquisition?

12-3. The owner of NOYB is contemplating investing $100,000 in a firm that produces machine tools. The following two methods of financing the acquisition have been proposed, and he is interested in knowing which of the two is the best:

Financing Alternative 1

Total investment		$100,000
Asset mix		
Cash	$10,000	
Receivables	20,000	
Inventory	20,000	
Plant & equipment	50,000	
Financial sources		
Notes payable (15%)		15,000
Accounts payable (0%)		15,000
5-Year note (12%)		20,000
Common stock		50,000
Expected EBIDT		25,000 (annually)
Depreciation		10,000
Interest		4,650 (annually)
EBIT		15,000
PBT		10,350
Tax (20%)		2,070
PAT		8,280

Financing Alternative 2

Asset mix		*Financial mix*	
Cash	$10,000	Notes payable (12%)	$ 5,000
Receivables	20,000	Accounts payable (0%)	15,000
Inventory	20,000	5-year note (12%)	10,000
Plant	10,000	Common stock	30,000
($40,000 leased; annual payments			
of $10,440)			
EBIDT	$25,000		
Depreciation	2,000		
Interest payments	1,800		
Lease payments	10,551		
PBT	10,649		
PAT	8,519		

Questions:
1. Should the investment be made? (Show all calculations.)
2. Which method of financing should be employed?

PART VI SELECTED REFERENCES

ANDERSON, C. M., "Capital Budgeting Process," *Management Accounting*, September 1972, pp. 30–32.

ANG, JAS. S., "Weighted Average vs. True Cost of Capital," *Financial Management*, Autumn 1973, pp. 56–60.

ARDITTI, F. D., "Weighted Average Cost of Capital: Some Questions and Its Definition, Interpretation and Use," *Journal of Finance*, September 1973, pp. 1001–1007, and discussion, June 1975, pp. 879–892.

BERANEK, WM., "Cost of Capital, Capital Budgeting and the Maximization of Shareholder Wealth," *Journal of Finance and Quantitative Analysis*, March 1975, pp. 1–20.

BIERMAN, HAROLD, JR., "Survey of Capital Budgeting: Theory and Practice," *Journal of Finance*, May 1970, pp. 349–360.

BIERMAN, H., and J. E. HASS, "Capital Budgeting Under Uncertainty—A Reformulation," *Journal of Finance*, March 1973, pp. 119–129.

BIERMAN, HAROLD, JR., and SEYMOUR SMIDT, *The Capital Budgeting Decision*, New York: Macmillan, 1971.

BRENNAN, J. J., "New Look at the Weighted Average Cost of Capital," *Journal of Business Finance*, Spring 1973, pp. 24–30.

BRIGHAM, EUGENE F., and KEITH V. SMITH, "The Cost of Capital to the Small Firm," *The Engineering Economist*, Fall 1967, pp. 1–26.

CHATEAU, JEAN PIERRE D., "Capital Budgeting Problems under Conflicting Financial Policies," *Journal of Business Finance and Accounting*, Spring 1975, pp. 83–103.

FREMGEN, J. M., "Capital Budgeting a Survey," *Management Accounting*, May 1973, pp. 19–25.

FRIEDLAND, SEYMOUR, *The Economics of Corporate Finance*, Englewood Cliffs, N.J.: Prentice-Hall, 1966.

GRINYER, JOHN R., "Cost of Equity Capital," *Journal of Business Finance*, Winter 1972, pp. 44–52.

HINSON, D. R., "Time Adjusted Capital Budgeting Models," *Management Accounting*, July 1975, pp. 55–58.

KILLBOUGH, L. N., "Relevancy of Capital Cost for Decision Making," *Managerial Planning*, March–April 1973, pp. 26–30.

KLAMMER, T., "Association of Capital Budgeting Techniques with Firm Performance," *Accounting Review*, April 1973, pp. 353–364.

LEE, SANG M., "The Cost of Capital and the Structure of the Firm," *Journal of Finance*, March 1970, pp. 35–46.

LEE, SANG M., and A. J. LERVO, "Capital Budgeting for Multiple Objectives," *Financial Management*, Spring 1974, pp. 58–66.

MAO, JAMES C. T., "The IRR as a Ranking Criterion," *Engineering Economist*, Winter 1966, pp. 7–13.

MODIGLIANI, FRANCO, and MERTON H. MILLER, "The Cost of Capital, Corporation Finance, and the Theory of Investment," *The American Economic Review*, June 1958, pp. 261–297.

MORTON, W. A., "Investor Capitalization Theory of the Cost of Equity Capital," *Land Economist*, August 1970, pp. 248–263.

NANTELL, T. J., and C. R. CARLSON, "Cost of Capital as a Weighted Average," *Journal of Finance*, December 1975, pp. 1343–1355.

ROBICHEK, ALEXANDER A., and JAMES C. VAN HORNE, "Capital Budgeting: A Pragmatic Approach," *Financial Executive*, April 1969, pp. 26–38.

SCHWAB, B., and H. SCHWAB, "A Method of Investment Evaluation for Smaller Companies," *The Dynamic Small Firm, Selected Readings*, ed. Walker, Ernest W., Austin, Texas: Lone Star Publishers, Inc., 1975, pp. 211–230.

SCOTT, DAVID F., OTHA L. GRAY, and MONROE M. BIRD, "Investing and Financing Behavior of Small Manufacturing Firms," *The Dynamic Small Firm, Selected Readings*, ed. by Ernest W. Walker, Austin, Texas: Lone Star Publishers, Inc., 1975, pp. 167–184.

SPIES, R. R., "Dynamics of Corporate Capital Budgeting," *Journal of Finance*, June 1974, pp. 829–845.

STERN, J. M., "What Cost of Capital Means to Investors and Management," *Commercial and Financial Chronical*, August 31, 1972, p. 617.

VANDELL, R. F., "Capital Budgeting: Theory or Results," *Financial Executive*, August 1973, pp. 46–50.

VERNON, T. H., "Capital Budgeting and the Evaluation Process," *Management Accounting*, October 1972, pp. 19–24.

WALKER, ERNEST W., ed., "Investment and Capital Decision Making in Small Business," *The Dynamic Small Firm, Selected Readings*, Austin, Texas: Lone Star Publishers, Inc., 1975, pp. 185–210.

WESTON, J. FRED, "Investment Decisions Using the Capital Asset Pricing Model," *Financial Management*, Spring 1973, pp. 25–33.

WRIGHTSMAN, DWAYNE, and JOHN G. MCDONALD, "The Cost of Capital Concept: Potential Use and Misuse," *Financial Executive*, June 1965, pp. 2–8.

part VII

WORKING CAPITAL MANAGEMENT

chapter 13

WORKING CAPITAL THEORY AND MANAGING CASH

The management of working capital is one of the most, if not the most, important duties of the manager of the small firm. It has been said many times that large firms tend to be profit oriented, whereas small firms are cash flow oriented; that is, managers of the latter group are more concerned with the speed and regularity with which assets change their form than they are with the "bottom-line figure." This changing process is vital not only to the success of the small firm but to its survival. That is, if assets do not change their form at a desired rate, profit as well as the liquidity position of the firm are affected.

The primary purposes of this chapter are fourfold: (1) to discuss the various concepts of working capital, (2) to discuss the nature and importance of working capital in small businesses relative to their larger counterparts, (3) to discuss the principles that the authors believe to be the basis of a theory of working capital, and (4) to discuss the management of cash in the small firm.

Concepts of Working Capital

There are two general working capital concepts: net and gross. Net working capital is the difference between current assets and current liabilities. This concept is useful to some degree to groups interested in determining the amount and nature of assets that may be used to pay current liabilities. Moreover, the amount that is left after these debts are paid may be used to meet future operational needs. From the management of working capital viewpoint this concept has little or no relevancy.

Gross working capital refers to the amount of funds invested in *current assets that are employed in the business process.* This is a going-concern concept, since it is these assets that financial managers are concerned with if they are to bring about productivity from other assets. The gross concept is used here, since one of the principal functions of the manager is to provide the *correct amount* of working capital at the *right time* in order for the firm to realize the greatest return on its investment.

Working capital may be classified in two ways. The first classification is directly related to the gross concept of working capital; that is, working capital may be classified as captial invested in the various components of current assets, such as cash, inventories, receivables, and short-term unexpired costs. From the manager's viewpoint this classification is helpful, since it categorizes the various areas of financial responsibility. For example, funds invested in cash, inventories, and receivables require careful planning and control if the firm is to optimize its return on investment. (Since short-term unexpired costs account for such a small portion of capital invested in current assets, they are not considered.)

This classification is most important to management, but it is not completely adequate, since it makes no mention of *time*. And since time is vital in the formulation of procurement policies, a second classification alluding to time is necessary. *Using time as a basis, working capital may be classified as either permanent or temporary.*

Permanent working capital is that amount of funds required to produce the goods and services necessary to satisfy demand at its lowest point. Such capital possesses the following characteristics: First, unlike fixed assets, which retain their form over a long period of time, permanent working capital is constantly changing from one asset to another. Second, the fund of value representing permanent working capital never leaves the business process; therefore, suppliers should not expect its return until their need ceases to exist. Third, as long as a firm experiences growth, the size of the permanent working capital account will increase.

Temporary or variable working capital, like permanent working capital, changes its form from cash to inventory to receivables and back to cash, but it differs in that it is not always gainfully employed. *Businesses that are seasonal and/or cyclical in nature require more temporary working capital than firms that are not so influenced. Therefore, managers should obtain the capital that is temporarily invested in current assets from sources that will allow its return when not in use.* If this policy is followed, the turnover of investment will be more favorable, thus permitting *a more efficient use of capital.* It should be pointed out that although seasonal and cyclical working capital may be obtained from the same source, the contractual terms vary widely. For example, banks may be the principal suppliers of both types, but the charges may be different. Moreover, contractual restrictions on short-term loans differ considerably from those placed on term loans and long-term contracts.

Nature and Importance of Working Capital in Small Companies

It was mentioned above that working capital management is extremely important in small businesses since it is relatively more important in small companies than in large companies. The data in Table 13-1 tend to prove this important point.

While the relative importance of these assets changes slightly throughout the year as well as from year to year, these data do reflect the relative importance of each type of working capital. It is interesting to note that U. S. government and other securities are greater in the large companies than in the smaller companies. This is understandable since not only does it require a certain amount of expertise to invest in money market instruments, but it also requires quite large purchases. As a consequence the smaller companies, while having a relatively large amount of cash, do not have the total volume of dollars that would make it profitable to purchase these securities, nor do they have the specialized money managers.

While it is interesting to show that each of the current assets (except marketable securities) is relatively more important in small companies than in the larger companies, it is more significant at this juncture to note the size of total working capital. For example, companies under $5 million in assets have approximately two-thirds of their assets tied up in working capital, whereas the large companies have just slightly more than *one-third* of their assets invested in working capital. Obviously, then, working capital, while important in the larger companies, is a vital factor in the smaller companies, and any change in their total volume will have a major impact on return on investment.

TABLE 13-1

Investments in Working Capital—Manufacturing, Mining, and Trade Corporations: 1975

First Quarter (percent of assets)

Working Capital Components	Under $1	$1–$5	$50–$100	$250–$1,000	Over $1,000
	Assets (in millions of dollars)				
Cash	10.2%	7.1%	4.1%	2.8%	2.4%
U.S. government and other securities	1.0	1.1	2.1	1.4	3.2
Receivables	26.3	25.1	20.1	17.0	12.1
Inventories	24.5	30.8	29.8	27.0	18.3
Current assets not elsewhere stated	4.2	3.4	1.9	2.5	2.3
Total current assets	66.2%	67.5%	58.0%	50.7%	38.4%

SOURCE: Federal Trade Commission, *Quarterly Financial Report: Manufacturing, Mining and Trade Corporations, 1st Quarter, 1975*, Washington, D. C.: U. S. Government Printing Office, 1975, pp. 58–71.

A Four-Part Theory of Working Capital

A firm's fixed capital is determined by its scale of production; once committed, the capital remains invested regardless of production levels. Working capital, on the other hand, is employed only when actual production is undertaken, and the volume required is generally determined by the level of production. The precise level of investment in working capital is predicated on (1) management's attitude toward risk and (2) factors that influence the amount of cash, inventories, receivables, and other current assets required to support a given volume of output.

Risk as used here means the risk of not maintaining sufficient current assets to (1) meet all financial obligations as they mature and (2) support the proper level of sales. It is the writers' opinion that four principles invoking risk serve as the basis of a theory.[1]

First principle

The first principle is concerned with the relation between the levels of working capital and sales. Briefly, it may be stated as follows: *If working capital is varied relative to sales, the amount of risk that a firm assumes is also varied, and the opportunity for gain or loss is increased.* This principle implies that a definite relation exists between the degree of risk that management assumes and the rate of return. That is, the more risk that a firm assumes, the greater is the opportunity for *gain* or *loss*. An examination of Figure 13-1 reveals that when the level of working capital relative to sales decreases, the opportunity for gain from investment *increases*, but the opportunity for loss also *increases* and vice versa. (Here sales and output are considered equal.) It should be noted that while the gain resulting from each *decrease* in working capital is measurable, the losses that may occur are much more difficult to measure. For example, return on investment increased from 7.6 percent to 16.6 percent when working capital fell from $120,000 to $50,000 (see Table 13-2). Gains that would be reflected in reduced costs are also measurable, for example, savings resulting from a reduction in warehouse space when inventory is reduced. Moreover, it is believed that while the potential gain resulting from each decrease in working capital is greater in the beginning than potential loss, the exact opposite occurs if management continues to decrease working capital; that is, potential losses are small at first for each decrease in working capital but increase sharply if it continues to be reduced.

[1] This theory is taken from Ernest W. Walker, "A Theory of Working Capital Management," *Proceedings of the Southwestern Finance Association* (Austin, Texas: Bureau of Business Research, The University of Texas at Austin, 1966), and Ernest W. Walker, "Toward a Theory of Working Capital," *Engineering Economist*, Vol. IX, No. 2 (Jan.–Feb. 1964).

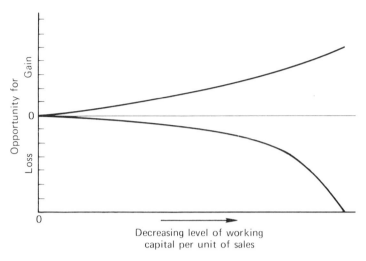

FIGURE 13-1.

TABLE 13-2

XYZ Manufacturing Company

Financial Data

	Working capital		
	$ 50,000	$ 90,000	$120,000
Fixed capital	$ 10,000	$ 10,000	$ 10,000
Liabilities	30,000	30,000	30,000
Net worth	30,000	70,000	100,000
Sales	100,000	100,000	100,000
Fixed capital turnover	10.0	10.0	10.0
Working capital turnover	2.0	1.1	0.833
Total capital turnover	1.66	1.0	0.761
Earnings (as percent of sales)	10.0	10.0	10.0
Rate of return (percent)	16.6	10.0	7.6

Obviously, it should be the goal of management to select the level of working capital that optimizes the firm's rate of return. This level is defined as *that point at which the incremental loss associated with a decrease in working capital investment becomes greater than the incremental gain associated with that investment.* It is emphasized that each company will have a unique set of curves, since the shape of each curve is determined by the risk associated with the firm as well as by the size of the working capital account relative to total assets.

It is presumed that by analyzing correctly the factors determining the amount of the various components of working capital as well as predicting the state of the economy, management can determine the ideal level of working capital that will equilibrate its rate of return with its ability to assume risk; however, since most managers do not know what the future holds, they tend to maintain an investment in working capital that exceeds the ideal level. It is this excess that concerns us, since the size of the investment greatly influences a firm's rate of return on investment.

As stated in the first principle, if the level of working capital is increased, the amount of risk is decreased, and the opportunity for gain or loss is likewise decreased. On the other hand, if the level of working capital is decreased, the exact opposite is true; therefore, management's attitude toward risk definitely affects the level of working capital maintained for a given volume of sales. That is, a more conservative management employs more working capital for a given volume of sales than one which can and is willing to assume more risk.

Up to this point we have been talking about industries in general. Now let us turn our attention to specific situations. Financial managers of certain industries have more to gain or lose by following aggressive working capital policies than do managers in other industries. That is, the rates of return caused by changes in working capital in such industries as chemicals, retail trade, and drugs are much larger than those in the steel and paper industries. To illustrate, the management of an average chemical firm can increase the rate of return on investment 100 percent by decreasing working capital 50 percent and holding everything else constant. On the other hand, a 50 percent decrease in working capital in the average steel firm would increase the rate of return only 24 percent.[2]

The obvious conclusion is that managers should determine whether they operate in businesses that react favorably to changes in working capital levels; if not, the gains realized may not be adequate in comparison to the risk that must be assumed when working capital investment is decreased.

Second principle

As mentioned above, management is faced with the problem of determining the ideal level of working capital. It is not our purpose in this section to develop techniques that may be used by management in the solution of the correct level; rather, we shall present a principle that will serve as a basis for its determination. In our opinion, the concept that each dollar invested in fixed or working capital should contribute to the net worth of the firm should serve as a basis for such a principle. If this is true, the following principle qualifies and is applicable for investments made not only in various components of working capital but in fixed capital as well. Stated succinctly,

[2]Walker, "Toward a Theory of Working Capital," p. 29.

it is as follows: *Capital should be invested in each component of working capital as long as the equity position of the firm increases.* More will be said about this principle in Chapter 14.

Third principle

Whereas the first principle dealt with the risk associated with the amount of working capital employed in relation to sales, the third principle is concerned with the risk resulting from the type of capital used to finance current assets. This principle may be stated as follows: *The type of capital used to finance working capital directly affects the amount of risk that a firm assumes as well as the opportunity for gain or loss and cost of capital.*

There is no question but that different types of capital possess varying degrees of risk insofar as the business firm is concerned. Moreover, investors relate the price for which they are willing to sell their capital to this risk; that is, they charge less for debt than for equity capital, since debt capital possesses less   risk. Since this is true, management is able to increase its opportunity for higher returns on its equity capital through the use of debt capital. A firm wishing to minimize risk will employ only equity capital; however, in so doing, it foregoes the opportunity for higher returns on equity capital. A word of caution is necessary at this juncture. It has been stated that return to equity capital increases directly with the amount of risk assumed by management. This is true, but only to a certain point. When excessive risk is assumed, a firm's opportunity for loss will eventually overshadow its opportunity for gain, and at this point return to equity is threatened. When this occurs, the firm stands to suffer severe losses.

Unlike rate of return, cost of capital moves inversely with risk; that is, as additional risk capital is employed by management, cost of capital declines. This relationship prevails until the firm's optimum capital structure is achieved; thereafter, the cost of capital increases, because not only will creditors increase the amount of interest charged, but also suppliers of equity will decrease the price they are willing to pay for various types of equity securities.

Fourth principle

As noted above, the use of debt is recommended, and the amount to be used is determined by the level of risk management wishes to assume. It should be noted that risk is not only associated with the amount of debt used relative to equity; it is also related to the nature of the contracts negotiated by the borrower. Some of the more important characteristics of debt contracts directly affecting a firm's operation are restrictive clauses of the contracts and dates of maturity. It is believed that maturity dates are the more important of the two insofar as solvency is concerned; therefore, particular attention is directed to this area.

Lenders of short-term funds are particularly conscious of this problem, and in an effort to protect themselves by reducing the risk associated with improper maturity dates, they are requiring firms to produce documents depicting cash flows. These documents, when properly prepared, not only show the level of loans necessary to support sales but also indicate when the loans can be repaid. In other words, lenders realize that a firm's ability to repay short-term loans is directly related to cash flow and not to earnings, and therefore a firm should make every effort to tie maturities to its flow of internally generated funds.

This concept serves as the basis for the final hypothesis of the presentation. Specifically, it may be stated as follows: *The greater the disparity between the maturities of a firm's short-term debt instruments and its flow of internally generated funds, the greater the risk and vice versa.* Incidentally, management is not compensated for assuming the risk referred to in this concept; therefore, under no circumstances should it be assumed.

To illustrate this concept, assume the following about X Company, a small manufacturer of toys: (1) Sales are highly seasonal, with 75 percent occurring between July 1 and August 30, (2) the firm relies on short-term bank loans and trade credit to finance seasonal inventory requirements, (3) credit terms are for 60 days, and (4) no cash discounts are given. Inventories and receivables were low relative to cash at the beginning of the year primarily because customers had liquidated last year's receivables and production had not begun for the year. In the first quarter, the firm, realizing that orders would start pouring in during July and August, began to manufacture for inventory. During this quarter, cash declined and inventories increased but receivables remained constant. In the second quarter a few sales were made, and as a result, accounts receivable increased slowly; however, cash outflow was greater than inflow, which meant that cash continued to decline. To offset this decline and to finance the continuing buildup in inventories, the finance manager negotiated a 60-day promissory note on May 15. As predicted, sales began to rise gradually in early July and increased rapidly during the latter part of the month and in August. The cash account began to increase due to the reversed flow of funds, but it did not reach its peak until the fourth quarter. The firm was therefore unable to meet its obligation with funds from internally generated sources.

This simple example shows how it is possible for a firm to face insolvency or embarrassment even though it might be making a profit. A word of caution is necessary at this point. It is extremely difficult to predict accurately a firm's cash flow in an economy such as ours. Therefore, a margin of safety should be included in every short-term debt contract; that is, adequate time should be allowed between the time the funds are generated and the date of maturity. If there is one weakness in the borrowing contracts of small companies, this is it.

Summary

The fundamental basis for a working capital theory is risk; that is, in most cases the opportunity for gain or loss varies directly with the amount of risk that management assumes. Briefly stated, the policies governing the amount and type of working capital are determined by the *amount of risk* management is prepared to assume. To illustrate, by increasing the amount of risk it is willing to assume, management can reduce the amount of working capital required and thus increase the efficiency of capital, resulting in an increase in total profits. Further, by employing more risk capital, management can increase the rate earned on equity capital, also reducing its cost of capital; and finally, management can employ more debt capital, provided it can accurately determine the firm's ability to repay its obligations and can schedule its maturity dates accordingly.

Cash Management

The management of cash flows is one of the most important functions of the management of small firms. While it is difficult to prove statistically, it is believed that the failure to manage cash flows effectively is a primary reason for the extremely high casualty rate among small- and middle-sized firms. Numerous examples could be cited but would serve no useful purpose because each firm is unique and cash flow problems result for many different reasons. Included below is a discussion of ways and means of optimizing the cash flows of the small firm.

All firms, regardless of size, type, or location, have the same types of motives for holding cash: transaction, precautionary, and speculative. The cash held for transaction motives is used to meet the normal cash requirements of the business. Although the majority of a firm's cash inflows and outflows are nonrandom and predictable, some are random and, in some cases, impossible to predict. If all flows were nonrandom, the cash position of the firm would be minimized; unfortunately cash flows in small companies can and are usually highly unpredictable. These random flows, along with abnormal cash needs, are provided for by precautionary cash balances and lines of credit. The size of the precautionary cash balance should be directly related to the firm's risk-taking ability and attitude. If management is adverse to risk, the precautionary balance will be larger than if management were willing to assume risk or if it possesses a strong credit rating at some financial institution such as a bank. As a general rule, the larger firms will invest this precautionary balance in such marketable securities as treasury bills and commercial paper in order to offset a complete loss of return. Small businesses, on the other hand, find it extremely difficult to invest their excess cash in such instruments and therefore "lose" the profit from these investments. This aspect of cash management is covered later in this chapter. The final reason for holding cash—speculative purposes—allows management to take advantage of profitable opportunities. For example, management may maintain large cash balances in order to be able to take advantage of an anticipated price increase. The ultimate in speculation occurs when production assets are exchanged for cash in anticipation of a major break in the economy. In general, a business should not speculate with cash balances; this being true, no further attention will be given to this particular reason for holding cash.

Cash Synchronization: The Fourth Principle Revisited

It will be remembered from above that the fourth principle stated that *the greater the disparity between the maturities of a firm's short-term debt instruments and its flow of internally generated funds, the greater the risk and vice versa.* It was further stated that this disparity is without question one of the central problems of the small business enterprise. The solution of this problem would go a long way in solving the failure rate for small businesses.

The "pot" of cash can be thought of as a set consisting of several subsets. See Figure 13-2. First, the set is divided into subset A and B. Subset A consists of all cash flowing into the firm, whereas subset B contains all the cash that flows out of the firm. Cash inflows are derived from such sources as (1) cash sales, (2) collection of receivables, (3) sales of securities to the public,

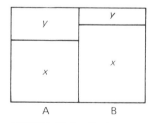

FIGURE 13-2. Cash Universe

and (4) borrowings from financial institutions. One basic characteristic of cash inflows of small firms is the lack of control that owners and managers have over them. As a consequence subset A can and should be divided into two additional subsets, i.e., X and Y. Subset X represents all inflows that management considers to be nonrandom, whereas subset Y represents random inflows.

Cash outflows, on the other hand, are more under the control of management and are therefore capable of being nonrandom. However, the small firms are often underfinanced and are somewhat dependent on inflows for funds to meet maturing obligations; therefore, cash outflows are also random and nonrandom. It should be emphasized that effective planning could, for all practical purposes, eliminate the amount of outflows that should be classified as nonrandom.

According to the fourth principle of working capital, the ideal situation would be when inflows coincide perfectly with outflows. Should this be the case, the amount of cash held in the form of precautionary balances would be near zero. While this ideal position cannot be accomplished, it can be approached through effective cash budgeting techniques. To avoid duplication, see Chapter 6 for a detailed discussion of the cash budgeting process.

Control of cash

The control of cash is mandatory since there is a moral, legal, and economic obligation on the part of management to meet its maturing obligations. The moral obligation alone should be sufficient reason management would want to be liquid. Generally speaking, management is vitally concerned with the legal and economic reasons for maintaining liquidity at all times, i.e., satisfying maturing obligations. From a legal standpoint managers know that if they don't pay obligations as they mature they will either be forced into bankruptcy or sued. Neither alternative is desirable.

There are many economic reasons managers want to be liquid. For example, suppose a firm receives a discount of 2/10, net 30. Assume further that it is unable to take advantage of these credit terms. Under these circumstances the firm increases its cost by an annualized rate of 36 percent; stated differently, it increases the cost of doing business, which in turn decreases its competitive advantage as well as decreasing the earnings of the firm.

Another economic reason for meeting obligations as they mature is the protection of the firm's credit standing. The authors know a small businessman who increased sales at a compounded rate of growth of 25 percent per year for four years. During this time he never made less than 27 percent before taxes, yet the bank refused to extend further credit. An investigation revealed that he had failed to synchronize cash flows and during the past two years had never met his loan commitments on time. An effectively developed cash budget would have allowed him to synchronize inflows with outflows, and more than likely the firm would still be in existence. Many other examples and reasons could be mentioned here that support the logic that a firm should be liquid.

The cash budget is not only a planning device, but it also serves as a basis for controlling cash. That is, it establishes a sound basis for controlling the cash position. For this purpose it is necessary to prepare a budget report, which is nothing more than a comparison of actual income and expenditures with planned income and expenditures. If deviations occur, revisions to the cash budget for the succeeding period should be made. It is emphasized that if effective budgeting is to be achieved, management must make a thorough analysis of the deviations before corrective action is taken. If the analysis reveals that the variation is the result of an ineffective policy instead of an error in the budgetary process, action should be taken to correct the policy. However, if the error is the result of an ineffective budgeting technique, the technique should be improved or the individual employing the technique should be given whatever guidance is necessary to prevent a recurrence of the variation.

The student should keep in mind that control of cash calls for a complete replanning process. For example, objectives are reviewed, strategies are studied, and existing policies are examined. If changes are needed, they are made, and finally management corrects its procedures to assure that the correct policy is properly executed. When this process has been accomplished, a revised cash budget is prepared as a part of the planning process, and as each period is terminated, a cash report is made to determine whether the cash plan is effective.

Management of cash balances

The time value of funds concept tells us that a dollar received in the immediate future has more value than one received at some later time; all other things remaining equal, management should make every effort to speed up cash flowing into the firm and delay cash flowing out of the firm. It should be emphasized that management should not fail to meet its obligations when developing policies that delay the outflowing of funds. Many techniques may be used in reducing the span between the time a customer renders payment and the time the funds are available for use by the firm; some of the more important are (1) the lock box system, (2) concentration banking, and (3) special handling of payments.

It is possible for management to reduce the time that funds are in transit (float) by creating postal boxes in post offices located near the customers. Customers send their payments to these boxes rather than to the company offices, thus saving several days. At regular times, daily or even more often, the firm has a bank pick up the checks and deposit them in a special checking account; after the checks are cleared locally, the bank remits by wire to the firm's bank of deposit. Such a system reduces float by several days, permitting the firm to use its cash more effectively.

A similar technique, referred to as concentration banking, also shortens the time that funds are in transit. To illustrate the process, a firm establishes one or more collection centers in areas close to a large number of customers. The centers bill the customers and collect the accounts. As soon as the payments are received, they are deposited in a local bank. At regular intervals, the funds in excess of compensating balances and local requirements are transferred by wire to a concentration bank or banks. The wire transfer technique is most frequently used, since it is much faster than a transfer of deposits by checks, which must be collected through the usual channels.

In some instances, firms expedite the movement of funds from the customer through the use of personal messengers or air mail. These techniques are generally employed only when there is a small number of accounts or when large payments are involved.

Obviously firms can reduce their cash accounts by the number of banks that are used, reducing the total amount required for compensating balances. In some instances the level of cash may be reduced by paying banks for services rather than maintaining compensating balances.

Finally, financial managers can reduce cash requirements by developing techniques that effectively control the disbursement of funds. Although the techniques used to accomplish this vary with each situation, the idea is to time the payments to coincide with the due dates. Any technique that delays payment beyond the due date is generally bad and should not be utilized.

Investment of idle cash funds

The majority of large companies invest their idle cash funds in marketable securities; unfortunately, however, this is not true with small firms. There are many reasons why smaller firms do not invest their surpluses in such instruments as government securities, commercial paper, state and municipal obligations, and obligations of financial institutions such as banks and savings and loan institutions.

Before exploring this subject, it is necessary to define the cash surplus. Surplus cash consists primarily of all cash in excess of those funds required to meet current operating requirements. The term "required to meet current operating requirements" has a different meaning to different firms. To the large sophisticated firm it often means any funds that are not needed within a very short period—a week or even a day. To the smaller firm it could mean the funds that are not required for a month or a quarter. In the first instance the larger firm could invest the funds profitably for this period primarily because it has the expertise; also the amount of funds may be quite large. On the other hand, the smaller company does not find it profitable to invest its surplus even though the period of time may be much longer. The principal reasons for this are the following: (1) a small firm doesn't have enough funds to invest in any of the above obligations except CDs of banks or savings and loan associations, (2) the cost associated with a small amount of funds would tend to reduce the gains to a point where it would not be worth the trouble involved, and (3) many banks require that the smaller companies maintain rather large deposit of funds in the form of compensating balances if they are to receive credit at a favorable rate of interest.

Even though small firms have difficulty in investing idle funds, there are times when they should take advantage of this technique so as to increase their rate of return of total capital. If the amount of cash required for current operations exceeds the compensating balances demanded by banks, the manager should consider the possibility of investing these funds in marketable securities. The investment policy relating to this important area should clearly establish the (1) minimum amount that should be invested, (2) minimum investment period, and (3) criteria for selecting investments.

Many large companies will not invest funds of less than $1 million. Obviusly most small companies could not afford such a high minimum; therefore, they should consider the profitability of much lower amounts. It is our opinion that serious consideration should be given to investing as little as $5,000 or $10,000. Excess cash in amounts of less than $5,000 or $10,000 should be left in demand deposits in order to improve the firm's credit status. That is, the gain from the improved credit status would be worth more than the interest earned from investments.

Due to the uncertainty associated with cash flow requirements, it would not be too wise to invest for periods of more than 30 to 60 days. It is true that businesses using minimum investment periods of 30 to 60 days are following a conservative policy; however, it is the opinion of the authors that this is an essential policy due to the amount of cash available for investment and the risk characteristics of the cash flow of small firms.

As with larger companies, there are three principal criteria that should be used by small companies when selecting the type of securities in which to invest their excess cash: (1) safety of the investment, (2) marketability of the investment, and (3) yield.

Of these three, the most important is safety. It may be remembered that one of the primary responsibilities of the manager is to protect the value of the firm. Obviously if the short-term investments result in a loss, not only would the firm lose the amount of the investment, but because cash is needed to pay maturing obligations it may suffer a serious loss in liquidity which could cause the firm to experience total loss.

Marketability, the ability of a security to be sold in a relatively short time without loss, is the next most important criterion when investing excess cash. This is particularly important for small firms since it is very difficult to anticipate changes in inflows of cash. If the firm is investing excess cash which has been earmarked to meet a certain obligation, then the firm will want to invest in repurchase agreements or prime finance company paper for which it can select securities whose maturity dates will coincide with its commitment.

Yield, the third criterion for selecting securities for investment, should be considered only after the safety and marketability criteria have been met. Yield is most important if a small firm is accumulating funds for expansion purposes from the profits of the firm since the manager will want the cash to produce as much as if it were reinvested in the operations of the firm. As a matter of fact, it is possible to substitute excess cash for normal bank loans, thus saving the interest charges that are normally paid. These funds should be used to finance inventory and receivables since these two assets change their form at a much faster rate than fixed assets and are available for reuse within a reasonable length of time.

After carefully formulating the policies governing (1) criteria, (2) minimum amount of the investment, and (3) the length of time funds will be invested, the manager is ready to select the types of securities that will be purchased.

Small companies should use only short-term government securities, high-grade commercial paper of *finance companies*, and certificates of deposits of banks and/or savings institutions. All other money market instruments should be excluded except in unusual circumstances. The principal reason for limiting investment securities to these three types is that the administration of the investment program is greatly simplified—plus the fact that the two primary criteria (safety and marketability) are satisfied.

The managers of most small firms do not have the time or knowledge to act as the buying and selling agent. It is therefore suggested that this function be delegated to the firm's banker. However, if CDs are used, then it is possible for the manager to perform the buying and selling functions rather than relying on the banker. While it is not the purpose of the authors to recommend specific sources of certificates of deposit, it should be remembered that a bank that is supplying the firm with operating capital would look more favorably on the firm that also purchased its CDs; moreover, it will also perform the buying and selling functions at a more favorable cost.

In summary, it should be emphasized that while small firms are often restricted from investing their precautionary cash balances in money market instruments, it is nevertheless important for those firms that do have cash in excess of their compensating balances to establish a set of policies that will govern this function.

Summary

There are two general concepts of working capital: net and gross. While the net working capital concept—current assets minus current liabilities—is useful to groups interested in determining the amount and nature of assets that may be used to pay current liabilities, it is believed that gross working capital—amount of capital invested in current assets that are employed in the business process—is of more importance to management, since it is obligated to provide the correct amount of current assets at the right time in order to realize the greatest return on investment.

It was pointed out above that working capital is relatively more important in small than in large companies, and that its control is vital, in that any change in the total volume will have definite impact on the firm's profitability.

A general theory of working capital, consisting of four principles, was presented. The theory, briefly stated, is that the policies governing the amount and type of working capital are determined by the amount of risk which management is prepared to assume. That is, by increasing the amount of risk it is willing to assume, management can reduce the amount of working capital and thereby increase the efficiency of capital. Through the use of debt capital, management can increase the rate earned on equity, and finally, management can use more debt capital as well as less working capital if it can accurately determine the firm's ability to repay its obligations and can schedule its maturity dates accordingly.

The management of cash flows is probably the most important function that managers of small firms perform. Small businesses have the same motives for holding cash as large firms; these are transaction, precautionary, and speculative. The latter motive is of less importance; therefore, management should concentrate on the transaction and precautionary reasons for holding cash. The degree of randomness of the firm's cash flows determines the level of precautionary balances, and it is in this area of cash management that owner-managers of small companies should concentrate their efforts; that is, management should make policies that will synchronize inflows with outflows.

The control of cash is absolutely essential if a firm wishes to optimize its efficiency. While the cash budget serves as both a planning tool and a control device, it should be emphasized that the budget only tells when something is wrong. To correct problems as they arise requires a complete replanning process rather than simply finding a solution to each symptom. In addition to the control of cash balances, management is charged with the initiation of activities that will assure the firm that cash will flow into the firm at the earliest time. Tools that have been developed and are available to the managers of small firms are (1) the lock box system and (2) concentration banking. Both methods tend to reduce the lapse between the time when a customer makes payment and the time when the funds are available for use by the firm.

One use of these funds is to meet the outflow requirements of the firm. Another is to invest the excess funds in profitable investments. As a general rule small firms do not have large cash balances for investment; therefore they don't always invest in the same types of securities. However, any investment they make should meet the following criteria, which, incidentally, are used by large firms as well: safety, marketability, and yield.

In the main, small firms invest primarily in certificates of deposit of banks and/or savings institutions, high-grade commercial paper of finance companies, and short-term government issues. The primary reason for limiting investment to these three is that the administration of the investment program is simplified, plus the fact that these securities are both safe and marketable.

QUESTIONS

1. Define net and gross working capital. Why is the latter concept more important to the financial manager than the first?

2. Explain why small firms tend to hold relatively more cash than their larger counterparts.

3. Why are receivables higher in the smaller firms than in the larger firms?

4. Explain briefly each of the four principles of working capital management.

5. Explain how the NPV and IRR formulas can aid management in ascertaining whether it should invest in working capital or not.

6. What are the principal reasons firms hold cash?

7. Discuss the characteristics of the so-called "pot" of cash.

8. Explain in general terms how an owner-manager can control his cash flows.

9. Discuss (a) lock box systems and (b) concentration banking.

10. Discuss the following elements of an investment policy which should be observed by small firms: (a) minimum amount to be invested, (b) minimum investment period, and (c) criteria for selecting types of securities that small firms may include in their portfolios.

PROBLEMS

13-1. Using the following information, prepare a cash budget showing cash flows for May, June, and July. Indicate when and how much borrowing will be necessary. The company has a line of credit with its bank for $25,000 and wishes to maintain a minimum of $5,000 as a cash balance.

Data as of April 30, 1978

Current assets

Cash	$10,000
Inventory	11,667

Actual sales		*Forecasted sales*	
January	$15,000	May	$35,000
February	20,000	June	40,000
March	25,000	July	55,000
April	30,000	August	60,000

Accounts receivable. All sales are for credit. Eighty percent of accounts receivable are collected in the month immediately following the sale, 10 percent in the second month, and 8 percent in the third month, 2 percent being charged off to bad debts.

Cost of goods sold. Eighty percent of sales. Eighty percent of purchases are paid for during the first month after the purchase, and the remaining 20 percent are paid for during the second month after purchase.

Sales and administrative expenses. $4,250 per month plus 10 percent of sales. Eighty percent of these expenses are paid during the month in which they are incurred, and 20 percent are paid in the following month.

Inventories. At the first of each month, inventories (at cost) should be one-third of the forecasted sales for that month. For example, inventory on April 1 should have been $10,000.

Capital expenditures. During July, the company will make a capital expenditure of $10,000 for two new delivery vans.

Requirements:

The manager of the firm wants to know what will happen to cash flows if he were to change certain policies which affect the inflows and outflows of the firm. To obtain this information he requests that you substitute the following policies for those that presently exist:

1. Tighten the credit policies by requiring that 90 percent of accounts receivable be collected in the month immediately following the sale, 5 percent in the second month, and 4 percent in the third month. Two percent would be charged off to bad debts.
2. Decrease inventory levels to 20 percent, but retain the same policy regarding accounts payable.
3. Pay accounts payable as follows: 50 percent of purchases paid during the first month after the purchase and the remaining 50 percent paid during the second month.
4. Change the credit policy so that 40 percent of the accounts receivable are collected in the month immediately following the sale, 50 percent in the second month, 9 percent in the third month, and 1 percent charged off as bad debts. This policy will cause the following change in the sales forecast:

May	$40,000
June	50,000
July	62,500
August	80,000

Note to Student: Replace only one policy at a time; that is, replace existing collection policy with policy change 1 above, but retain all other policies; replace existing inventory policy with policy change 2 while retaining all other original policies. In other words, don't cumulate your policy changes.

chapter 14

WORKING CAPITAL MANAGEMENT: RECEIVABLES

As mentioned in previous chapters, cash, receivables, and inventory are the three primary components of working capital. We have already discussed the various concepts of working capital essential to effective planning as well as the development of certain principles which serve as a basis for a theory of working capital. We are now concerned with those factors and techniques that should be considered when planning the level of receivables that management should maintain.

During the first quarter of 1975 all manufacturing, mining, and trade corporations with assets of less than $5 million employed 25.5 percent of their total assets to finance receivables.[1] The only other assets that exceeded receivables in importance were nonresidential fixed assets and inventories. It should be noted that while the relative importance of receivables has changed very little during the past several years the total volume has increased from $206.1 billion in 1970 to $321.8 billion at the end of the second quarter in 1976.[2]

Because of the importance of receivables both relatively and volume-wise, it is imperative that management formulate effective policies if it intends to protect shareholders' net worth.

Factors Influencing Investment in Receivables

The second principle of a theory of working capital clearly states that capital should be invested in each component of working capital as long as the equity position of the firm increases. This means that funds should not be

---

[1]Federal Trade Commission, *Quarterly Financial Report: Manufacturing, Mining and Trade Corporations, 1st Quarter, 1975,* (Washington, D. C.: U. S. Government Printing Office, 1975), p. 57.

[2]*Federal Reserve Bulletin,* Vol. 62, No. 12, (Dec. 1976), p. A41.

committed to receivables unless they cause the value of the firm to remain constant or to increase. To ascertain whether this goal is achieved requires that all funds invested in receivables yield their cost of capital (return expected from debt and equity capital). Since all receivables are received at some time in the future, the owner must include the time value concept in any valuation method used to determine whether the funds committed to receivables produce their "cost." The criteria used to ascertain whether the firm's goals regarding receivables investment are met are rather difficult to determine since the cost of capital is extremely difficult, if not impossible, to calculate. It may be recalled that we substituted the IRR_d and IRR_e evaluation approach for the internal rate of return and net present value techniques of selecting investment. When evaluating investment in receivables we can use the NPV technique provided management uses the average weighted IRR rate as the discount or hurdle rate. For example, assume the overall IRR_d and IRR_e of a firm equal 6 and 18 percent, respectively. Assume further that the debt/equity ratio is 50/50; in this case the discount or hurdle rate used in the NPV equation equals 12 percent annually or 1 percent per month if the firm's sales are spread evenly over the year. Again it should be noted that the cost of capital should be used as the discount rate in those instances where it is calculable.

Policies affecting sales, cash discounts, length of credit terms, credit risks, and volume of delinquent accounts directly affect the size of the receivables investment. The policies that affect sales, such as pricing, distribution, and advertising, will not be discussed here; however, factors influencing the remaining policies are explored in this section.

Cash discounts

Not only do cash discounts affect the level of the receivables account, but they also affect a firm's cost of capital in that they may cause it to increase or decrease. To illustrate, assume that a firm's cost of capital or internal rate of return is 1 percent per month but that its cash discount terms are 2 percent cash, net 30 days. If the discount is taken, the firm's cost of capital doubles—24 percent instead of 12 percent—and the net worth of the firm suffers. If the cash discount is taken, the present value of the sale will be less than it would have been if the account had been collected at the end of 30 days. A simple example illustrates this. Assume an article costing $0.92 sells for $1.00 with terms of 2 percent cash, net 30 days. If the cash discount is taken, the present value will equal $0.06:

Sales	$1.00
Cash discount 2%	.02
Cash or present value	$ .98
Cost (present value)	.92
Present value	$ .06

If the cash discount is not taken by the customer, the present value of the profit is equal to $0.07, a gain of $0.01; the computation is as follows:

Present value of sale 30 days hence, when cost
    of capital is 1% $0.99
Cost (present value)   − 0.92
                                          $0.07

Since the cost of capital is 1 percent per month and the cash discount is 2 percent, the firm will have sustained a loss of 1 percent (reduction in net worth) if the discount is taken. If the two are equal, it makes no difference to the credit manager whether the discount is taken; however, if the discount is less than the cost of capital and it is taken, the net result will be to raise the present value of the firm's net worth.

As mentioned above, cash discounts also affect the level of receivables that are required to be financed. For example, assume a firm's normal sales are $10,000 per month. If credit terms are 2/cash, net 60, the level of receivables (investment in current assets) is dependent on whether the cash discount is taken. If it is taken, there will be no investment in receivables; the $9,800 received each month could be used to finance inventories or any other expense of doing business, thus reducing the total amount of funds available to run the business. If the cash discount is not taken, the firm would have $10,000 invested in receivables (this is assuming all creditors paid on time), thus causing the total investment to increase. If these invested funds did not "return" their cost, then the value of the equity position on the firm would decline; on the other hand, if the cash discount exceeded the "cost" of funds, there would also be a decrease in the equity account. It is imperative that the cash discount policy be carefully formulated.

Credit terms

In most cases business firms sell on credit terms; that is, the business firms extend credit to their customers for varying lengths of time; the most prevalent terms are 30, 60, or 90 days. Some firms will actually sell on much longer terms, for example, automobile dealers and farm machinery dealers.

To illustrate the concepts involved and the impact that varying credit terms have on the equity position of the business firm, assume the following:

1. Weighted average IRR, 1 percent per month.
2. Terms, 90 days.
3. No cash discounts.
4. Sales of 100 units at $10 per unit.
5. Fixed and variable costs, $9 per unit.

The dollar value of the sale equals $1,000, but the present value of the firm's profit varies directly with the length of credit terms and the firm's weighted average IRR. These changes are depicted in Table 14-1.

TABLE 14-1

Illustration of Changing Value of
Receivables when Credit Terms Vary

Terms	Sales	PVIF of discount rate		Present value of sales		Present value costs	Gain or loss in the firm's equity	
		1%	2%	1%	2%		At 1%	At 2%
Cash	$1,000	1.000	1.000	$1,000	$1,000	$900	$100	$100
30 days	1,000	.990	.980	990	980	900	90	80
60 days	1,000	.980	.961	980	961	900	80	61
90 days	1,000	.971	.942	971	942	900	71	42
180 days	1,000	.942	.888	942	882	900	42	(18)
270 days	1,000	.914	.837	914	837	900	14	(63)
360 days	1,000	.887	.788	887	788	900	(13)	(112)

The data in Table 14-1 illustrate how the (average weighted internal rate of return equals the discount rate) discount rate and length of credit terms directly affect the firm's net worth. In the case where the discount rate equaled 1 percent per month, the firm's net worth increased only as long as the credit terms did not exceed 293 days. On the other hand, had the discount rate been 2 percent per month, the firm would have realized an increase in net worth only if the credit terms were for five months or less. It may be seen from Table 14-1 that the shorter the credit terms, the greater is the present value of the firm's equity capital; however, it should be remembered that the suppliers of capital only want their expectation; therefore, any credit terms that result in a zero gain in net present value are acceptable. In the above case where the discount rate equaled 1 percent, the value of the firm will not suffer until credit terms exceed 293 days. This is not to say that a firm should give credit for 293 days when everyone else is granting 60-day credit. It says only that you can compete effectively if your competition is granting terms of, say, 270 days.

Credit risk

The last major policy affecting receivables is the selection of credit risk (customers). Traditional theory states that the selection of credit risk is determined by relating bad debt losses to the profit margin; that is, the greater the firm's profit margin, the more risk it can absorb. If the firm's objective is to optimize profits, it will sell to customers in the lowest risk category for which profits on sales exceed bad debt losses. For example, the credit manager in one firm divides the customers into four categories. Each

TABLE 14-2

Profit Potential by Risk Categories

Risk category	Gross sales[1]	Expected bad debts Percent	Expected bad debts Dollar	Loss of profit from bad debt	Loss of profit from operating cost	Profit
A	$20,000	0	$ 0	$ 0	$ 0	$2,000
B	30,000	3	900	90	810	2,100
C	40,000	7	2,800	280	2,500	1,200
D	60,000	10	6,000	600	2,400	0

[1]Sales are arbitrarily selected.

group includes all customers with the same risk characteristics; that is, customers in group A always pay promptly, customers in group B are expected to have bad debt losses of 3 percent, group C's expected bad debt losses will be 7 percent, and group D's will equal 10 percent. If the firm's profits before bad debts equal 10 percent on sales, the theory says that the firm should sell to groups A, B, C, and D since no loss will result from sales. From a practical standpoint, management will probably not sell to group D since no profits will be realized (see Table 14-2).

This theory does not take into consideration the concepts of the "cost of capital" and the time value of funds. When both are considered, it is extremely doubtful that the firm would break even if it sold to customers in groups C or D. To understand why this is true as well as to ascertain correctly the type of customers acceptable from a risk standpoint, the following should be considered.

First, the amount of time required to collect an account increases directly with risk; that is, it takes more time to collect the accounts in group D than C, C than B, and B than A. Stated differently, the distribution of the collection experience will vary among groups. Second, the cost of collection increases as risk increases (in the example in Table 14-3, it is assumed that collection cost increases $1 per $100 of sales for each 15 days that an account is late). Third, the longer it takes to collect an account, the greater is the firm's investment in that account. Finally, the present value of the "return" on an account decreases in direct relation to the amount of time needed to collect the account. To incorporate these concepts into the theory that guides the firm in selecting credit risk, it is necessary to establish the collection characteristics of its customers.

In most cases it is possible to divide into groups those customers who have similar risk characteristics. Since each has different risk characteristics,

TABLE 14-3

Measuring the Expected Date of Collection

Groups	Probability	Days to collect	Expected number of days to collect	Increase in cost of collection
A	1.00	30	30	<u>0</u>
B	.40	30	12.00	
	.32	45	14.40	
	.25	75	18.75	
	<u>.03</u>	<u>0</u>	<u>0</u>	
	1.00		45.15	<u>$1</u>
C	.23	30	6.90	
	.30	45	13.50	
	.40	100	40.00	
	<u>.07</u>	<u>0</u>	<u>0</u>	
	1.00		60.40	<u>$2</u>
D	.05	30	1.50	
	.10	60	6.00	
	.25	75	18.75	
	.30	90	27.00	
	.20	105	21.00	
	<u>.10</u>	<u>0</u>	<u>0</u>	
	1.00		74.25	<u>$3</u>

the time to collect the accounts will vary. Table 14-3 depicts one method of determining the "expected" number of days required to collect the average account in each category.

A brief explanation of the preceding will be helpful to the analysis that follows. As previously mentioned, the amount of time required to collect an account increases directly with risk. To determine the expected amount of time that will be needed to collect the average account in each risk category, a probability distribution is established.

For example, there is a 100 percent probability that all customers in group A will pay within 30 days; therefore, the expected amount of time each account is outstanding is 30 days. The customers in group B will take more time to pay; i.e., 40 percent will pay in 30 days, 32 percent will pay in 45 days, 25 percent will pay in 75 days, and 3 percent will never pay. As a consequence, management can expect to use an average of 45 days to collect from customers in this category. Employing the same technique for each group, we find that it will take an average of 60 days to collect from the customers in group C and 75 days to collect from the customers in group D. Moreover, it will cost an additional $1 for each $100 of sales to collect from group B, $2 per $100 from group C, and $3 per $100 from group D. This information should not be difficult to accumulate but rather should be readily available from past experience.

Let us now apply the discounting and the time value of funds concepts to these collection data and see which of the risks can be accepted. You will recall that there is a cost associated with each dollar invested in receivables and that each sales dollar sold on terms will have a greater value if received in the immediate future than if received at a later date. Applying these concepts to the above data, we can ascertain the present value of the sales in each category (Table 14-4).

The data in the fifth column of Table 14-4 indicate that the present value of the sales that will be collected in 30 days will exceed the firm's direct cost and expectation by $1,800 and that the present value of the sales of group B will return direct cost and expectation plus $1,350. The present value of sales of groups C and D will be $2,646 *less* than direct cost and expectation, thus causing the present value of the firm's net worth to decline.

The following conclusions are obvious from Table 14-4: (1) If all sales were accepted ($150,000), the net present value of the firm's net worth would increase $504. (2) If sales were made to groups A, B, and C, the net present value of the firm's net worth would increase by $2,774. (3) If sales were made to groups A and B, net present value would increase $3,150.

Traditional and net present value theory both dictate that all groups should be accepted but for entirely different reasons. That is, traditional theory says that since no profits will be lost it is permissible to accept all groups, but it should be pointed out that this technique did not consider the "cost" of carrying the receivables. Net present value theory, on the other hand, took this "cost" into consideration and still revealed that the firm's

TABLE 14-4

Present Value of the Sales of a Firm
(by groups)

Group	Sales	Present value of sales	Present value of cost[1]	Expected present value of sales
A	$20,000	$19,800	$18,000	$1,800
B	30,000	29,550	28,200	1,350
C	40,000	39,224	39,600	−376
D	60,000	58,530	61,800	−2,270

[1]Includes losses from bad debt, cost of collection, and operating cost of 90 percent. All costs are assumed to be incurred at time 0.
Note: It is assumed that the firm's hurdle rate is 1 percent per month.

equity position would remain positive even after accepting all four groups. It should be emphasized that the firm should *not* accept groups C or D if they are mutually exclusive.

Adjusting for Risk

In the above example we assumed that there was a 100 percent probability of selling $150,000 to all groups. This is not a valid assumption; the risk associated with sales to each group should be recognized and adjustments made accordingly. There are several methods that may be used when adjusting for the risk related to sales; the best known techniques are (1) substituting expected revenues for revenues that are most likely to occur and (2) adjusting the discount or hurdle rate upward for those cash flows which are considered to be more risky.

In accomplishing the first technique management ascertains a probability distribution of sales to each group. That is, rather than assuming that $20,000 will be sold to group A, management would calculate expected sales by using a probability distribution that it believes will result. As mentioned elsewhere in this book, it is believed that it is best to calculate expected sales

TABLE 14-5

Expected Sales

Risk categories	Probability	Sales	Expected sales
Group A	.25	$15,000	$ 3,750
	.50	20,000	10,000
	.25	25,000	6,250
	1.00		$20,000
Group B	.30	$20,000	$ 6,000
	.50	30,000	15,000
	.20	40,000	8,000
	1.00		$29,000
Group C	.35	$30,000	$10,500
	.50	40,000	20,000
	.15	50,000	7,500
	1.00		$38,000
Group D	.40	$40,000	$16,000
	.50	60,000	30,000
	.10	70,000	7,000
	1.00		$53,000

TABLE 14-6

Present Value of Expected Sales

		Present value[1]				
Groups	*Expected sales*	*Expected sales[1]*	*Operating cost[2]*	*Bad debts[2]*	*Collection costs[3]*	*NPV*
A	$ 20,000	$ 19,800	$ 18,000	$ 0	$ 0	$1,800
B	29,000	28,565	26,100	870	281	1,314
C	38,000	37,240	34,200	2,660	738	(358)
D	53,000	51,198	47,700	5,300	1,544	(3,346)
	$140,000	$136,803	$126,000	$8,830	$2,565	$ (590)

[1]Discount is found by weighting IRR_i and IRR_e; e.g., weighted average of the IRRs of the example in Chapter 11 equaled 15.48 percent. For this problem a discount rate of 12% is used.
[2]Operating costs and debt losses are assumed to be incurred in period 0.
[3]Collection costs are assumed to be incurred at the end of 90 days (average of the 180 days at which time debts are written off).

by determining sales that (1) are most likely to occur, (2) would occur under the most adverse circumstances, and (3) could occur under ideal economic conditions. The first step in this determination is to divide the 100 percent potential among these three occurrences. Assume, for example, that 50 percent of the time sales representing "most likely" will occur, that 25 percent of the time the firm will experience ideal economic condition, and, finally, that the firm will experience poor economic conditions 25 percent of the time (see Table 14-5). It is generally conceded that variations from the norm will have a greater impact on marginal than on economically sound customers. For example, more customers in groups B, C, and D will be affected by "poor" times than in group A. The impact of this is that the more marginal the group, the greater will be the variation of expected sales from "most likely" sales.

Substituting expected sales for most likely sales and discounting these with the average weighted internal rate of return of an acceptable project, we find that their present value is less than the present value of costs by $590—see Table 14-6. Stated differently, the suppliers of capital would not receive their "expectations,"[3] and the firm should not sell to all groups unless it expects other advantages to accrue from these sales.

The second method available to management when adjusting for risk is to vary the discount rate, e.g., the greater the perceived risk, the greater the discount rate. For example, 1 percent (12 percent annual rate) may be used to discount sales in group A, 2 percent for sales in group B, and 3 percent for groups C and D. In this case the net present value of all groups is negative,

[3]Expectations include the expected return plus a return of the original investment.

TABLE 14-7

Present Value of Sales: Using Varying
Discount Rates[1]

		Present value		
Groups	Sales	Expected sales	Operating cost, bad debts, and collection costs [2]	NPV
A	$ 20,000	$ 19,800	$ 18,000	$1,800
B	30,000	29,100	28,174	926
C	40,000	37,704	39,532	(1,828)
D	60,000	55,728	61,647	(5,919)
	$150,000	$142,332	$147,353	$(5,021)

[1]Discount rates used: 1% for group A, 2% for group B, and 3% for groups C and D.
[2]Collection costs are assumed to be incurred in period 0.

which means that if all groups are accepted the value of the firm would be adversely affected. This being the case, it is suggested that customers in group D be eliminated. If this group is eliminated, the net present value will equal $898 and the value of the firm would be preserved—see Table 14-7. While this method is simple and should be given serious consideration, extreme care should be used in the selection of the higher discount rates. There are several other methods, but for the most part they are complicated and expensive to use.[4] It is for these reasons that the authors recommend the use of expected sales rather than "most likely" sales or increasing the discount rate for those groups of customers which are considered to be risky.

Summary

Receivable management is of utmost importance in small firms since receivables constitute approximately 25 percent of total assets. Several policies directly affect the size of receivables: (1) sales policies, (2) cash discounts, (3) length of credit terms, and (4) credit risks. The first set of policies was not discussed in this chapter, but factors affecting each of the other policies were.

Cash discounts affect not only the level of receivables, they also affect the firm's cost of capital or expected rate of return. Assume that a firm's cost of capital or expected rate of return is 12 percent per annum but that its cash discount terms are 2 percent cash, net 30 days. If the discount is taken, the firm's cost of capital received is 24 percent per annum. Stated differently, the present value of this particular sale will be less than if the discount had not been taken. It is true that the amount of investment in receivables is reduced,

[4]For example, the certainty equivalent method and simulation may be used to adjust for risk.

but the cost of capital as well as the net present value of the sale is decreased. A rule which, if followed, would preserve the firm's present value is for the cost of capital not to exceed the firm's average cost of capital (the required rate of return if the cost of capital cannot be determined).

Most business firms, large or small, sell on credit terms. There is no question that the length of the credit terms not only affect the size of the receivable account but also affect the equity position of the firm. That is, the longer the terms, the larger the receivables and the lower the present value of the sales. It is for this reason that management should carefully calculate the length of time that credit can be extended, and if the customer violates these terms, the seller must either absorb the loss to equity plus obtaining larger amounts of credit or find some way of shifting this burden to the purchasers. To accomplish this end is the primary reason why many sellers charge their customers an interest rate that approximates their cost of capital on any account that exceeds the firm's credit terms.

In the previous chapter, four principles of working capital theory were stated. The second principle stated that capital should be invested in each component of working capital as long as the equity position of the firm increases. This means that funds should not be committed to receivables unless they cause the value of the firm to remain constant or to increase. To accomplish this goal requires that all funds invested in receivables yield the required rate of return.

The net present value technique is recommended when determining whether to accept or reject an account or a group of accounts if management follows the practice of categorizing customers. To improve the decision, management should use expected days outstanding as well as expected sales. The next step is to determine the net present value of the sales (using the firm's required rate of return as the discount rate). If the present value of the sales is positive, the account or group of accounts is acceptable. If not, action should be taken that will produce the desired results, such as reducing the number of days the sales are outstanding or adding an interest rate equal to the firm's expected return to those accounts which exceed the firm's terms. If these actions will not work, the sales should not be made since the firm's equity position will deteriorate.

QUESTIONS

1. What criteria should management use as a basis for decisions to invest funds in receivables?

2. What principal policies have a direct influence on the volume of receivables that a firm will have outstanding at any one time?

3. Explain why the profit margin should not serve as a criterion for granting credit to a customer.

4. Explain how the NPV concept can assist management in selecting credit risk.

5. Discuss several methods that management can use to adjust for risk in receivables management.

PROBLEMS

14-1. The XYZ Company categorizes its customers into five risk groups. An analysis of past experience indicates that bad debts losses and average days sales outstanding for each category were as follows:

Category	Bad debt losses (percent)	Days sales (outstanding)
A	1%	20
B	2%	25
C	3%	30
D	5%	60
E	8%	90

The firm is presently extending unlimited credit to categories A, B, and C but is not accepting any sales from categories D and E. The sales manager estimated that the firm was losing $400,000 in sales from category D firms and $600,000 from category E firms. He recommended that these sales be accepted since the firm realized an 8 percent profit on each dollar of sales and the firm's internal rate of return equals 12 percent per annum.

Requirement:
Would you sell to category D? Category E?

14-2. The ABC Company has the following credit policy: discount of 2 percent for cash or 30 days net. In the event the account is not paid within 30 days, a charge of 1 percent is added to the total bill. Presently 80 percent of their customers pay cash and the remaining 20 percent pay by the end of the 30 days. The sales manager reported that one of his major competitors is giving 3/cash, net/60. He stated that he thought he could compete more effectively if the company adopted this policy. The financial officer made a study and found that if the new policy were adopted sales would increase from the present $600,000 to $750,000 but only 70 percent of the customers would take the discount. Assume the ABC Company presently earns 10 percent profit after all costs but after the change in policy the profit rate will be decreased by the incremental credit costs. Should the firm adopt the new policy?

14-3. The NYOB Company presently follows the policy of granting no cash discounts; that is, they sell on 30 days net. A recent analysis indicated that their average collection period is 60 days. The owner requested the financial officer to ascertain if the adopting of a cash discount policy would reduce days sales outstanding. The financial officer made a sample survey and found that sales would increase from $500,000 to $550,000 and that 50 percent of these customers would pay cash. The remaining 50 percent would continue to take 60 days to pay their accounts.

Requirement:

Assuming an investment criterion of 18 percent per annum, should the firm give the discount?

PART VII SELECTED REFERENCES

ABRAHAM, A. B., "Factoring—The New Frontier for Commerical Banks," *The Journal of Commercial Bank Lending*, April 1971, pp. 32–43.

ARCHER, STEPHEN H., "A Model for the Determination of Firm Cash Balances," *Journal of Financial and Quantitative Analysis*, March 1966, pp. 1–11.

BARRY, JOSEPH K., "Cash Management, A Sharper Focus," *Journal of Accountancy*, April 1967, pp. 82–85.

BAUMOL, WM. J., "The Transactions Demand for Cash," *Quarterly Journal of Economics*, November 1952, pp. 545–556.

BEAN, VIRGINIA L., and REYNOLDS GRIFFITH, "Risk and Return in Working Capital Management," *Mississippi Valley Journal of Business and Economics*, Fall 1966, pp. 28–48.

BEECHLER, P. J., "Cash Management: Forecasting for Profit," *Management Adviser*, July 1973, pp. 35–43.

CABATIT, JULIETT B., "Effective Approach to Accounts Receivable Management," *Accountant's Journal*, September 1972, pp. 150–152.

CARRUTH, E., "Importance of Being Liquid," *Fortune*, June 1972, pp. 49–50.

Cash Flow Analysis for Managerial Control, NAA Research Report No. 38, New York: NAA, 1961, pp. 2–10, 51–60.

EDICK, THOMAS B., "Credit Executive's Role in Cash Management," *Credit and Financial Management*, October 1975, pp. 16–17, 33.

EITEMAN, WILFORD J., and JAMES N. HOLTZ, "Working Capital Management," *Essay on Business Finance*, Spring 1971, pp. 37–42.

Federal Reserve Bulletin, 1976.

Federal Trade Commision, *Quarterly Financial Report*: *Manufacturing, Mining and Trade Corporations*, Washington, D. C.: U. S. Government Printing Office, 1975.

FREITAS, L. P., "Monitoring Accounts Receivable," *Management Accounting*, September 1973, pp. 18–21.

FROST, PETER A., "Banking Services, Minimum Cash Balances and the Firm's Demand for Money," *Journal of Finance*, December 1970, pp. 1029–1039.

HEYMAN, D. P., "Model for Cash Balance Management," *Management Science*, August 1973, pp. 1407–1413.

HORN, FREDERICK E., "Managing Cash," *Journal of Accountancy*, April 1964, pp. 56–62.

KNIGHT, W. D., "Working Capital Management—Satisficing Versus Optimization," *Financial Management*, Spring 1972, pp. 33–40.

LERNER, E. M., "Simulating a Cash Budget," *California Management Review*, Winter 1968, pp. 79–86.

LEWELLEN, WILBUR G., and ROBERT W. JOHNSON, "Better Way to Monitor Accounts Receivable," *Harvard Business Review*, May–June 1972, pp. 101–109.

LUDEMAN, D. H., "Corporate Liquidity in Perspective," *Financial Executive*, October 1974, pp. 18–22.

MA, J. C., "Accounts Receivable Financing," *Credit and Financial Management*, December 1974, pp. 28–31.

"Managing Company Cash," *Studies in Business Policy*, New York: National Industrial Conference Board, Inc., 1961.

"Managing Your Corporate Cash for Profit," *Dun's Review and Modern Industry*, June 1960, pp. 50–52.

MAO, JAS. C. T., "Controlling Risk in Accounts Receivable Management," *Journal of Business Finance and Accounting*, Autumn 1974, pp. 395–403.

MARRAH, GEORGE L., "Managing Receivables," *Financial Executive*, July 1970, pp. 40–44.

MEHTA, DILEEP R., "Optimal Credit Policy Selection: A Dynamic Approach," *Journal of Financial and Quantitative Analysis*, December 1970, pp. 421–445.

MEHTA, DILEEP R., *Working Capital Management*, Englewood Cliffs, N. J.: Prentice-Hall, 1974.

MURPHY, JOHN F., "Sound Cash Management and Borrowing," *Small Marketers' Aid*, Washington, D. C.: Small Business Administration, 1975.

ORGLER, YAIR E., *Cash Management*, Belmont, Calif.: Wadsworth Publishing Company, Inc., 1970.

PEACOCK, DUNDAS, "Cash Flow—A Management Tool," *Credit and Financial Management*, August 1963, pp. 18–21.

PETTWAY, RICHARD H., and ERNEST W. WALKER, "Asset Mix, Capital Structure and the Cost of Capital," *Southern Journal of Business*, April 1968, pp. 34–43.

SCHIFF, MICHAEL, "Credit Management," *Financial Executive*, November 1975, pp. 28–33.

SCHWARTZ, D. R., and R. M. SOLDOFSKY, "How Companies Manage Cash," *Financial Executive*, October 1972, pp. 40–46.

SMITH, KEITH V., "State of the Art of Working Capital Management," *Financial Management*, Autumn 1973, pp. 50–55.

SURYANARAYANAN, S. "Control of Accounts Receivable," *Management Accounting*, February 1, 1975, pp. 156–159.

TALENT, W. J. "Cash Management: A Case Study," *Management Accounting*, July 1974, pp. 20–24.

VAN HORNE, JAMES C., "A Risk-Return Analysis of a Firm's Working-Capital Position," *Engineering Economist*, Winter 1969, pp. 71–88.

VAN NORDEN, L, "Factoring: Cash for Your Receivables," *Administrative Management*, August 1972, p. 34.

WALKER, ERNEST W., ed., "Credit Policies: Factors To Be Considered in Their Formulation," *The Dynamic Small Firm, Selected Readings*, Austin, Texas: Lone Star Publishers, Inc., 1975, pp. 247–265.

WALKER, ERNEST W., *Essentials of Financial Management*, 2nd ed., Englewood Cliffs, N. J.: Prentice-Hall, 1971.

WALKER, ERNEST W., "A Theory of Working Capital Management," *Proceedings of the Southwestern Finance Association*, Austin, Texas: Bureau of Business Research, The University of Texas at Austin, 1966.

WALKER, ERNEST W., "Towards a Theory of Working Capital," *Engineering Economist*, January–February 1964, pp. 21–35.

WELTER, P., "How To Calculate Savings Possible Through Reduction of Working Capital," *Financial Executive*, October 1970, pp. 50–58.

WRIGHTSMAN, DWAYNE, "Optimal Credit Terms for Accounts Receivable," *Quarterly Review of Economics and Business*, Summer 1969, pp. 59–66.

part VIII

SOURCES
OF FINANCING

chapter 15

SHORT-TERM CAPITAL

The subject of capital procurement policies may be approached in several different ways. For example, they may be studied from the standpoint of internal versus external sources and debt versus equity financing, or they may be viewed in respect to the length of time that the capital remains in use by the firm before it is returned to the supplier. The latter method is generally preferred because the approach it represents is familiar to both the supplier and user. From the standpoint of the user, financial managers have specific uses for short-, intermediate-, and long-term capital and develop definite policies with regard to the time the capital is used. Suppliers, on the other hand, tend to specialize in either long- or short-term capital; to illustrate, banks, commercial finance companies, factors, and certain governmental agencies specialize in relatively short-term capital.

There are several disadvantages to this approach. Among the more important are these: First, each category tends to merge into the next; that is, short-term loans may really be long-term loans because of a prearranged contract between the supplier and user. This arrangement is especially prevalent among small business, for reasons to be explained later. Second, no clear line of demarcation exists between the various categories. One financial institution may classify all term loans as intermediate-term capital, and yet some may be for a 5-year period and others may have a 10- to 20-year maturity.

The format of this chapter is three basic sections. First, as a natural departure point, the relative importance of short-term credit for the small company is reviewed. In light of the significance of this form of financing for the small firm, an extensive presentation is offered regarding the relevant factors for determining the appropriate balance between short- and long-term debt capital. Finally, the sources providing short-term credit for the small company are presented.

The Importance of Short-Term Debt for Small Businesses

Short-term financing plays a vital role in the financing of assets, regardless of the size of the firm. However, this source is of particular significance to the small business. Having limited access to the capital markets, the smaller company has to place greater reliance upon short-term sources, particularly trade credit and short-term bank credit. In contrast, the large corporations, while utilizing trade credit extensively, employ short-term bank loans as a means for providing greater flexibility if the need arises. These basic differences are manifested in Table 15-1, in which organizations within the two small business categories, comprising firms with an asset size of less than $5 million, utilize more than twice as much trade credit on a relative basis than the large national corporations exceeding $1 billion in assets. Also, short-term bank loans account for less than 1 percent of the large company's total capital structure, as compared to at least 5.3 percent for smaller operations. Thus, for the large business entity, the importance of short-term bank credit comes in the form of increased discretion rather than as a result of the volume. The smaller organization has no such option. If after maximizing its use of trade credit additional funds are required, the smaller company, for the most part, must approach the banker for additional monies.

In addition to the observed disparity between large and small firms in the makeup of the short-term debt, the small operation is compelled to draw more heavily upon short-term sources vis-á-vis longer-term financing. This dissimilarity also may be readily observed in Table 15-1, with current liabilities constituting approximately 35 percent of the capital mix in contrast to only 20 percent for the largest companies. Finally, the small concern's disability to enter the long-term public markets places additional burden upon short-term financing. Thus, the small firm is restricted in its availability to long-term sources of financing. Accordingly, the significance of short-term funds takes on an extra dimension for the small organization.

The foregoing scarcity in long-term debt for the small enterprise has existed for several reasons. In the past, bankers were interested primarily in "self-liquidating" loans, not considering the nature of banking to be compatible with the extension of credit for extended periods of time. However, more recently bankers have altered this philosophy, providing intermediate-term loans to businesses. Yet, in spite of this trend, the bank loan officer remains hesitant to offer long-term capital to the small concern. Possibly one reason for this reluctance stems from the possibility of a death of a key executive within the small business, thereby threatening the entire continuity of the organization. While insurance may partially counter this loss, in many instances no amount of money will offset the loss of the leader in the small firm.

TABLE 15-1

Liabilities and Stockholders' Equity Expressed as a Percentage

First Quarter, 1976

			Asset size	
Capital structure	*Less than $1 Million*	*$1 Million– $5 Million*	*$25 Million– $50 Million*	*Over $1 Billion*
Short-term loans (original maturity of 1 yr or less):				
Bank loans	5.31%	7.17%	4.83%	.98%
Commercial paper	.08%	.21%	.07%	.79%
Other short-term loans	1.48%	1.50%	.45%	.30%
Advances and prepayments by U.S. government	.01%	.14%	.15%	1.20%
Trade accounts & trade notes payable	16.93%	15.81%	9.61%	6.15%
Income taxes accrued, prior & current years, net of payments:				
Federal	1.27%	1.80%	2.14%	2.10%
Other	.32%	.29%	.24%	.42%
Installments, due in 1 year or less, on long-term debt:				
Loans from banks	1.55%	1.31%	1.11%	.15%
Other long-term debt	1.02%	1.12%	1.03%	.53%
Current liabilities not elsewhere specified, including excise & sales taxes, & accrued expenses	6.20%	6.02%	6.35%	7.97%
Total current liabilities	34.17%	35.37%	25.98%	20.59%

Long-term debt in more than 1 year:				
Loans from banks	7.74%	6.18%	7.77%	2.02%
Other long-term debt	9.13%	7.67%	10.17%	15.24%
Noncurrent liabilities not elsewhere specified, including deferred income taxes	1.41%	1.84%	3.20%	6.00%
Minority stockholders' interest in consolidated domestic corporations	.01%	.04%	.24%	.32%
Total liabilities	52.46%	51.10%	47.36%	44.17%
Capital stock & other capital	18.76%	15.44%	18.60%	15.83%
Retained earnings	31.18%	35.43%	35.24%	40.72%
Deduct: Treasury stock, at cost	(2.40%)	(1.97%)	(1.20%)	(.72%)
Stockholders' equity	47.54%	48.90%	52.64%	55.83%
Total liabilities and stockholders' equity	100.00%	100.00%	100.00%	100.00%

Factors Influencing the Decision Between Short-Term and Long-Term Debt

In determining the financing policies of the firm, two underlying questions must be resolved: (1) What is the optimal debt/equity relationship, and (2) what should be the composition of debt in terms of short-term and long-term maturities? In this chapter, we are to assume the debt/equity mix has been ascertained, with the remaining question to be addressed being the determination of the debt-maturity structure. As already noted in Table 15-1, the small firm not only employs greater amounts of debt in the capital structure but also uses larger proportions of short-term debt relative to the long-term liabilities. In this regard, any attempt to analyze the differences between small and large firms with respect to debt-maturity structures should be done in the context of a general presentation of the key factors having an impact upon the decision. As depicted in Figure 15-1, these determinants may be segmented into two categories: (1) the advantages and disadvantages of the two respective choices without regard to firm characteristics and (2) the relevant factors coming to bear upon the decision when viewed strictly from the individual company's perspective. The nature of these various elements is presented in this section.

Advantages of short-term debt

With respect to the advantages of short-term credit, two considerations generally favor employing short-term credit, these being cost and flexibility. In viewing the cost element in Figure 15-1, dashed lines tie this factor to both the advantages of short- and long-term debt. As will be indicated shortly, this variable typically leans in favor of short-term debt, but exceptions do occur. Flexibility, however, comes to favor short-term credit without exception.

cost differences

As shown in Figure 15-1, the cost advantage does not unequivocally align with either short-term or long-term securities. Yet, a strong tendency has been proven for short-term indebtedness to have an advantage in terms of cost. In comparing the relative costs of short-term and long-term financial obligations, several factors are of concern. The primary issue is the respective interest rates with the objective being to select the financing instrument imposing the lower interest cost. The relationship between yields on comparable securities and the corresponding maturities is defined as the *term structure of interest rates* and is presented graphically by a yield curve. Figure 15-2 represents a typical yield curve in which the short-term securities carry a lower interest rate vis-á-vis the longer-term obligations. This upward-sloping curve has generally prevailed, with few exceptions, in the past 50 years. This association may be further demonstrated by comparing the interest rates for a

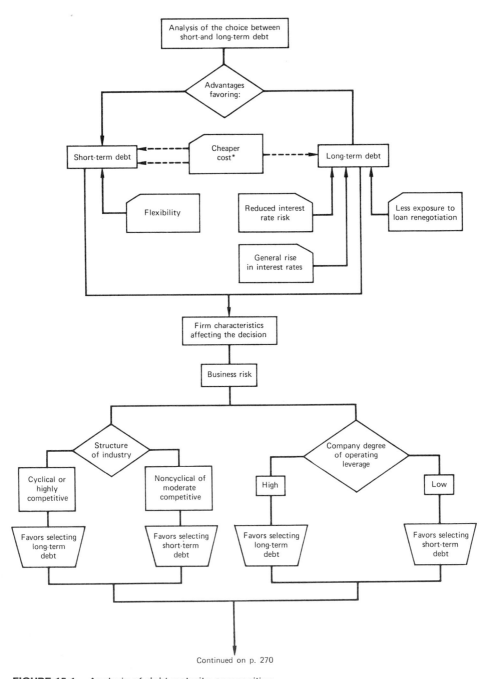

Continued on p. 270

FIGURE 15-1. Analysis of debt-maturity composition

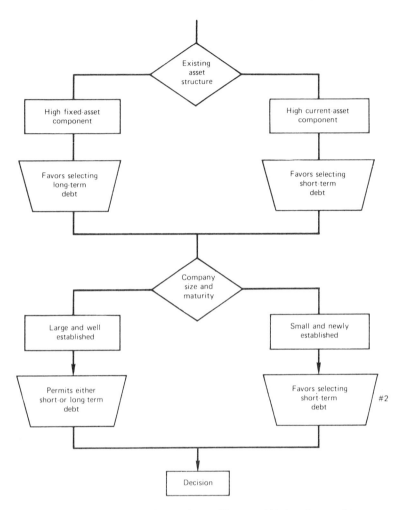

*The cost advantage varies between short and long term debt, depending upon the economic conditions. However, the cost of short term credit has usually been the cheaper source of financing.

FIGURE 15-1   (Continued)

long-term bond and a short-term money instrument over time. In Figure 15-3, the interest rate for an Aaa bond is graphically compared with the annualized rate for prime commercial paper. As evidenced in this figure, only in 8 years of the 50-year period being presented did the short-term rate exceed the long-term rate. However, the majority of these deviations during this time frame have occurred during the past decade.

In addition to the spread between the interest rates, certain peripheral costs must be recognized in order for the comparison to be complete. These further considerations may best be explained by an example. Assume that the

FIGURE 15-2. Yield curve

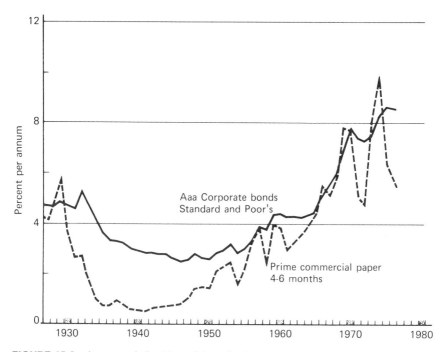

FIGURE 15-3. Long- and short-term interest rates

SOURCE: *Federal Reserve Chart Book*, Washington, D.C.: Board of
Governors, Federal Reserve System, 1976.

company has a need for supplementary funds. The decision has been made to issue debt, with one of two choices being contemplated: (1) issue a 10-year bond having a yield to maturity of 9.825 percent, or (2) acquire the capital by borrowing from the bank for 180 days at 8.5 percent. Thus, if the loan from the bank is finalized, a savings of 1.325 percent could be realized when compared to the long-term indebtedness.[1] However, the foregoing interest rate savings will not be completely realized due to other costs being incurred. First, issue costs may be incurred in floating certain types of financial obligations. These costs are typically lower for the long-term security. In the present illustration, the annualized issue cost might be .1 percent and .2 percent for the long-term and short-term debt instruments, respectively. A second possible cost is the compensating balance that may be required by the bank. For example, if a 10 percent compensating balance is stipulated by the bank, the effective cost for the short-term loan would be 9.444 percent, an incremental cost of .944 percent above the stated rate. This effective cost is computed as follows:

$$\frac{\text{Stated interest rate}}{1 - \text{Compensating balance}} = \frac{8.5\%}{1 - .1} = 9.444\%$$

In summary, the cost comparison between the foregoing illustrative long- and short-term debt would be

	Long-term debt cost	Short-term note cost
Stated interest rate	9.825%	8.500%
Issue costs	.100	.200
Adjustment for the compensating balance	0	.944
	9.925%	9.644%

Although a cost savings may result by acquiring the short-term loan, the benefit is not so large as might have originally been thought. Yet, even with the addition of these secondary costs, the short-term option generally is cheaper. Accordingly, if the explicit costs were the only factor coming to bear upon the decision, short-term debt would generally be favored. However, other considerations must be analyzed.

[1] In this example, the yield to maturity for the bond is assumed to include the issue premium that frequently must be granted to investors when issuing a new bond. If we were comparing the short- and long-term yields shown in Figure 15-3 for the purpose of estimating the potential savings by issuing a short-term security, the premium must be recognized by adding this incremental cost to the bond yield. In other words, the yield to maturity for a seasoned bond already being traded is not equivalent to a new bond, even though both instruments are considered to be in equivalent risk classes.

flexibility

If the fund requirements for the company are partially cyclical in nature, management should *not* finance these short-term needs through long-term debt. Short-run variations in the volume of assets held by a firm result largely from changes in the level of current assets that the firm maintains rather than changes in the volume of fixed assets, because fixed assets are determined insofar as possible by the anticipated optimum level of output and are seldom changed, whereas current assets vary with changes in the rate of production and may undergo radical changes in some firms. In addition to changes in production, current asset levels are also influenced by changes or expected changes in the supply of current assets. For example, a firm using large amounts of steel in production will increase its inventory if the output of steel is expected to be adversely affected in the short run. As a general rule, temporary changes in the level of current assets should be financed by short-term credit. In other words, the debt-maturity structure should be tied to the timing of the cash inflows resulting from the investments of the firm. Otherwise, if the short-term fluctuations in asset requirements are financed long-term, as these needs diminish the firm will be faced with excessive funds. When this situation develops, management, for the most part, has one of two alternatives: (1) retire the long-term debt prematurely or (2) invest the surplus capital in temporary marketable securities. As to the first choice, long-term financing can possibly be returned to its creditors at an early date. Nevertheless, the process is significantly more involved than when repaying short-term debt. In fact, to redeem long-term debt may contractually stipulate the payment of a penalty for early termination of the liability. For instance, premature retirement of a long-term debt could require a premium being paid between 1 percent and one year's interest, which could easily approach 10 percent. However, for the small firm not dealing in the capital markets this prepayment penalty is typically at the lower end of the 1 to 10 percent range.

The second reaction to a transitory excess in capital, in lieu of attempting to redeem the firm's long-term debt, is to shift the excess funds into marketable securities during the interim period. This response may minimize the impact of paying interest on the long-term indebtedness but will not counter entirely these interest expenses, simply because the interest rates on short-term marketable securities of reasonable quality are generally less than the interest having to be paid by the company for its long-term funds.

In summary, a key advantage of short-term debt has to be the *flexibility* afforded as cyclical variations in asset requirements are encountered. This flexibility permits the business to keep funds fully invested during slack periods by reducing company liabilities. In turn, capitalizing upon this ability to adapt quickly should yield greater profits for the organization.

Reasons for using long-term debt

Returning to Figure 15-1, three advantages are cited for using long-term debt. Although the effect would not be felt uniformly, these factors should have an impact upon any deliberation regarding the firm's debt-maturity structure. These three motivations for preferring long-term maturities are explained below.

reduced interest rate risk

As already noted, the expected interest rate for short-term financing has historically been less than the equivalent figure for long-term debt. However, as should be apparent from Figure 15-3, the short-term rates are subject to a significantly larger degree of variability. Hence, if a company finances extensively with obligations having short-term maturities, a concomitant condition to be expected is a greater volatility over time in the interest expense for a given amount of debt. Consequently, the company's earnings per share will be subject to larger variance, to which most managers and investors have a strong aversion. For this reason, long-term debt affords greater stability in earnings available to the owners. Whether this reduction in interest rate risk by employing long-term securities is attractive to the proprietors of the small organization is dependent on their attitudes toward the risk/return trade-off in that the reduction of the variability in interest costs typically comes only with an increase in the expected interest charges.

loan renegotiation

In addition to the risk of volatile interest expenses, a firm relying heavily upon short-term debt also faces the necessity of frequent renegotiation of its loans. This episode carries with it considerable uncertainty for the firm, not only in terms of the new interest rate but in potential restrictions included in the terms of the loan or, at the extreme, the denial of the credit for a subsequent period. The last concern, the lender's decision not to continue with the firm, usually need not be a concern, provided a recession and/or a discontinuity of the company's prosperity does not develop. If, however, problem areas arise that result in a reduction in earnings, the creditor will scrutinize closely the merits of the situation in deciding whether or not to grant the loan.

The difficulty arising from the inability to renegotiate on equivalently favorable terms or from the rejection of the loan proposal affects any firm, large or small. However, the problem is potentially more pervasive for a small firm that does not have access to the capital markets. For instance, all companies having to raise capital during the 1974–1975 recession were met with substantial obstacles. Since the recovery, the large corporations with excellent credit ratings are no longer encountering a major problem in the acquisition of credit. Even so, the smaller companies and the firms not considered as "prime" credit risks continue to have problems in recovering to prerecessionary levels. For many of these organizations, the liquidity and earnings ratios continue to fall. In addition, due to their own difficulties, many short- and intermediate-term financiers have become stricter in their credit standards, thereby compounding the problem. As a final result, smaller and less credit-worthy enterprises continued to have refunding problems even into 1976.

the general rise in interest rates

A final reason clearly favoring the issuance of long term debt vis-á-vis short-term liabilities is the general long-term pattern of rising interest rates. Again referring to Figure 15-3, in most years a company could have borrowed at a cheaper rate via short-term financing. Yet, due to the general rise in interest rates since 1945, a firm borrowing money at a stated percent for a 20-year period would normally pay greater amounts of interest in the earlier years but would have a cost advantage in later periods. To illustrate, if a business signed a 20-year note in 1954, the interest rates of this loan would have been larger for 9 years but less expensive in the remaining 11 years. This ability to benefit from being tied to a fixed rate for the long term could be demonstrated even more clearly subsequent to 1960. In summary, if the trend prevails, the immediate cost advantage from short-term borrowing may be offset by greater costs in later years.

Firm characteristics and the debt-maturity structure

A number of firm characteristics could be identified as impacting the decision between short- and long-term debt, with three key determinants being (1) the business risk of the operation, (2) the existing asset structure, and (3) the company size and maturity. These factors, as depicted in Figure 15-1, are explained below.

the level of business risk

Business risk has been defined as the variability of the firm's return on assets. This type of uncertainty is a function of the industry within which the business operates and the amount of fixed operating expenses incurred by the operation. If the industry is highly competitive and/or particularly sensitive to changes in the economy, the company's sales will be subject to wide fluctuations. Furthermore, if the organization is characterized by a high degree of operating leverage, the relative variability in earnings before interest and taxes is further magnified, thereby increasing the firm's business risk.

If the company's ownership attempts to maintain a "reasonable" level of total risk for the firm, the existing level of *business risk* has to be recognized in arriving at the debt-maturity structure decision. From the company's perspective, the greater the proportion of short-term debt relative to the concern's total debt, the greater the risk of insolvency. Thus, all else being constant, as business risk increases, the financing by short-term credit should be reduced. In summary, if an enterprise functions in a highly competitive industry, or an industry noted for its volatility, and/or the firm's operating leverage is substantial, short-term financing should be curtailed. If, on the other hand, these conditions are moderate, management has greater discretion in its employment of short-term debt.

existing asset structure

As mentioned previously, the nature of the assets being financed has to enter in to the determination of the "optimal" debt composition. The rationale cited earlier for this position is related to the need for distinguishing between secular and temporary investments. In a similar context, but from the creditor's perspective, the type of assets controls the financial terms to be offered. If the nature of the business is service or retail oriented, which normally requires larger investments in working capital as opposed to capital expenditures, long-term debt arrangements are not so readily available. For the lender, these current assets simply do not offer the collateral necessary for long-term protection. At the other extreme, capital-intensive firms by their nature have to rely more heavily upon long-term financing due to the necessity for synchronizing cash inflows and outflows.

company size and maturity

The size and maturity of a firm have a definite impact upon the company's financing strategy. For the new small business long-term debt funds are primarily available by mortgaging real estate, acquiring equipment through installment purchases, and/or by arranging for "off-balance-sheet" financing through long-term leases. When these funds are depleted short-term credit represents the only remaining origin for debt funds. Hence, for the relatively small firm, management's discretion between long- and short-term financing is not so great as observed for the larger and more mature corporation. For this reason, small firms normally are compelled to depend on the closer maturing obligations. This phenomenon is readily apparent in Table 15-2. For manufacturers, an inverse relationship clearly exists between the amount of short-term debt within the total liabilities section of the balance sheet and the firm size, with the smallest firms having 65 percent of their debt comprising short-term indebtedness as compared to 47 percent for the large business entities. This "compulsory" reliance upon short-term debt, often times by necessity, places the small firm in a greater financial risk posture. This risk is further compounded when we realize that small firms also employ more financial leverage than do their larger counterparts. Thus, when viewed from the total capital structure, the small firm's heavy indul-

TABLE 15-2

Debt Composition Relative to Firm Size

Asset size	First quarter, 1976 current debt / total debt
Less than $1 million	65%
$1 million to $5 million	68%
$5 million to $10 million	65%
$10 million to $25 million	62%
$25 million to $50 million	55%
$50 million to $100 million	51%
$100 million to $250 million	50%
$250 million to $1,000 million	47%
$1,000 million and over	47%

SOURCE: Federal Trade Commission–Securities and Exchange Commission, *Quarterly Financial Report for Manufacturing Corporations, 1st Quarter, 1976*, (Washington, D.C.: U.S. Government Printing Office, 1976), pp. 56–77.

gence in short-term liabilities is quite significant and has a direct impact in increasing the operation's financial risk.

Having the foregoing in mind for finalizing the debt-maturity structure question, attention is now directed toward the possible sources for the small company in acquiring short-term capital.

Sources of Short-Term Credit

Sources of short-term capital may be segmented into three categories: (1) credit available from suppliers in the form of trade credit, (2) debt provided by financial institutions, and (3) capital available through governmental agencies.

Trade credit

Trade credit is characteristically different from other forms of short-term credit in that this source is not associated with a financial institution. However, this fact should not minimize the significance of trade credit as a primary source of financing. Specifically, on the average, approximately one-third of a firm's current liabilities comes from trade credit. These payables are all the more important when viewed from the perspective of the small firm. In perusing Table 15-1, trade credit is observed to represent 50 percent of current liabilities for firms having assets less than $1 million. Even when we view operations with assets between $1 million and $5 million, this proportion falls only slightly to 45 percent. However, for the largest firms, with assets exceeding $1 billion, trade payables comprise 30 percent of current debt, still a significant amount but substantially lower than experienced by small business entities. Stated differently, although trade credit is important for almost all organizations, the firms in the smallest asset size classification finance 2.75 times more assets with trade credit than businesses whose assets exceed $1 billion.

characteristics of trade credit

Trade credit differs from the other types of short-term credit in several significant ways. First, and probably most important, trade credit is granted on an informal basis. That is, there are usually no documents representing the debt; instead, the credit is in the form of an open-book account. As a result, the "borrower" is not required to secure the loan with tangible assets or cosigners, although occasionally firms require a promissory note to be signed by the purchaser. As a general rule, the only evidence that credit has been extended is an entry in the accounts receivable ledger as well as the invoices that describe the items delivered, prices, and credit terms.

A second important characteristic is that there is no *computable cost* associated with trade credit unless a discount is made a part of the credit terms. This is important because, as a general rule, the cost of not taking this discount is quite high when compared to other forms of short-term credit.

A final characteristic of trade credit is that it is used to finance inventories, whereas other kinds of short-term credit may be used to finance fixed assets as well as current assets. As a result, trade credit is relatively more important to firms whose inventories constitute a larger percentage of total assets. Thus, as would be expected, the importance of trade credit as a short-term source of financing varies by industry.

cost of trade credit

As a general rule, businessmen use trade credit for two reasons. First, it is more convenient to purchase goods and services on an open-book account than to pay cash at the time of the purchase. Second, unless the discounts that are often given by firms supplying the credit are not taken, there is no measurable cost for the use of the credit. The first of these arguments is sound and cannot be refuted. However, there is some question with respect to the concept that trade credit is free even when discounts are taken. Let us examine the cost of trade credit.

It is commonly understood by businessmen and students of finance that there is a definite cost of foregoing discounts. For various reasons, many firms offer a discount to their customers if they pay cash within a certain period of time. If payment is not made within the stipulated period, the customer is required to pay the full amount of the bill; in other words, he is paying the amount of the discount for the number of days between the end of the discount period and the end of the net period. An example will illustrate this statement.

Suppose company A places an order for inventory in the amount of $5,000 with company B. Company B's credit terms to their regular customers are 2/10, net 30. This means that if company A pays the full amount of the bill within 10 days after the purchase date, it will receive a 2 percent discount; that is, company A will pay only $4,900 instead of $5,000, saving $100. However, if it fails to pay within the discount period, it will be required to pay the full $5,000 by the end of 30 days. The net effect of this is that company A will pay approximately 2 percent for the use of $5,000 for 20 days. Translated to an annual rate of interest, the cost of not taking the cash discount is roughly 37 percent per year. The size of the annual interest cost is determined by the size of the discount and the length of time between the end of the discount period and net period (see Table 15-3).

We can easily see that it is advisable for financial managers to borrow from financial institutions and take the discount. For example, the finance officer could have saved about $75 if he had borrowed $5,000 for 20 days at 9 percent simple interest and taken the discount.

The cost of not taking a discount is easy to see and measure, but there may be a cost even when discounts are not part of the credit terms. There is no question that when credit terms are given, the supplier is providing the buyer with funds for the period set forth in the credit terms. Unless the supplier is receiving these funds free of charge, which is unlikely, his cost of doing business is greater than it would have been had he not financed the buyer of the goods. It is assumed that the cost of the financing is hidden in the price of the goods. This idea is difficult to prove, since in the majority of cases everyone in a particular industry gives the same terms. That is, one supplier will not be selling for cash while everyone else is giving credit terms;

TABLE 15-3

Variation of Cost with Credit Terms

Credit terms	Annual cost [1] (percent)
1/10, net 30	18.4%
2/10, net 30	37.2
3/10, net 30	56.4
1/10, net 60	7.4
2/10, net 60	14.9
3/10, net 60	22.6

$$[1]\text{Cost} = \frac{\text{discount percent}}{(100 - \text{discount percent})} \times \frac{365}{(\text{final due date} - \text{discount period})}$$

therefore, a comparison of prices is not usually possible. We may conclude that there is a definite cost of trade credit when discounts are available and not taken, and there is a good possibility that a cost exists even when discounts are taken, although these costs may be hidden and impossible to measure.

terms of trade credit

The length of time for which a firm receives trade credit is determined largely by the industry in which it operates; in Chapter 14 we provide a detailed discussion of credit terms. Over the years, standard terms for the various industries have been established. The cash flow cycle of the selling firm also influences the length of time that trade credit can be extended. As cited previously, normally a firm attempts to synchronize the flow of cash into the firm with its outflow; in other words, it gives the same terms that it receives. In addition to these considerations, credit terms are influenced by the buyer's characteristics. If the buyer's purchases are smaller than the average, there will be a tendency for the seller to shorten the terms. The terms will be much shorter, and in some cases nonexistent, for those customers who do not have a good credit rating. Finally, the status of the seller also influences the credit terms. If the seller is weak financially, he will attempt to grant the shortest terms possible, or in lieu of this, he will offer an attractive cash discount.

Needless to say, trade credit is an advantageous and important source of credit. The financial manager should be careful to use it wisely, since the trade credit that he receives will influence the amount of trade credit that he gives.

Financial institutions as suppliers of short-term credit

The volume of short-term credit supplied by financial institutions fluctuates more widely than the volume supplied by trade credit. Although banks are the largest group of financial institutions supplying short-term credit, other financial institutions also play a major role in this type of lending. The purpose of this section is to explore the characteristics of lending habits pertaining to short-term credit supplied by various financial institutions.

commercial banks

Traditionally, banks have been one of the major sources of short- and intermediate-term capital for business firms. In October 1976, total outstanding commercial and industrial loans stood at an all-time high of $556.4 billion, representing 70 percent of the banks' investments (see Table 15-4). Although the bulk of the funds supplied by banks consists of short- and

TABLE 15-4

Loans and Investments, All Commercial Banks
($ billions)

Year[1]	Loans Total	Loans Amount	Loans Percent of total	Securities U.S. govt	Securities Other
1970	$461.2	$313.3	68%	$61.8	$ 86.1
1971	516.5	346.9	67%	64.9	104.7
1972	598.8	414.7	69%	67.0	117.1
1973	683.8	494.9	72%	58.3	130.6
1974	744.1	549.2	74%	54.4	140.5
1975	775.8	546.2	70%	84.1	145.5
1976	796.9	556.4	70%	93.5	147.0

[1]Year-end figures except for 1976, which represents October balances.
SOURCE: *Federal Reserve Bulletin*, Nov. 1976, p. A14.

intermediate-term capital, it is impossible to ascertain to what extent these funds are used to finance working capital, since many firms use both types of capital to finance fixed assets. Financing of fixed assets with short-term capital is accomplished by an arrangement between the owner or finance officer and the banker, whereby a short-term loan is contracted with the understanding that upon maturity partial payment will be made and the balance renewed. In some cases a business firm will rotate loans among banks; that is, it borrows from bank B to repay an outstanding loan at bank A at the end of the first year and then borrows from bank C the following year to repay bank B. This, of course, is necessitated by the so-called clean-up rule that some banks follow; that is, borrowers are required to pay the entire amount of the loan each year. When these loans are used to finance assets that are not self-liquidating within the contract period, the firm must resort to this course of action. This type of borrowing is being replaced by term loans.

Banks have traditionally supplied capital to all kinds and sizes of business firms. For example, although 91 percent of the total number of short-term loans outstanding as of October 1957 were held by firms with assets of $1 million or less, the same group held only 31 percent of the dollar volume outstanding. In other words, firms with assets exceeding $1 million borrowed more than two-thirds of the dollar amount of all business loans made by commercial banks in 1957. We can assume that these ratios have changed somewhat since 1957, but it is doubtful that they have experienced substantial alteration.[2] In fact, on a more timely basis, the importance of

[2]"Member Bank Lending to Small Business," *Federal Reserve Bulletin*, (April 1958), pp. 400–401.

bank capital to the small business relative to large corporations may be witnessed in Table 15-1 in which all forms of bank loans in 1976 accounted for 14.6 percent of the capital structure for small companies with assets not exceeding $5 million. In contrast, for large firms having assets in excess of $1 billion, bank credit represents only 3.15 percent of the corporation's total capital.

As may be expected, the size of the short-term loan varies with the size of the borrower. For example, in 1957 the average size of the loan made to firms with assets of less than $50,000 amounted to $3,000, but the average for firms with assets of $100 million was about $1,363,000. This, of course, is one reason large firms receive a lower interest rate than small firms.

The security behind every business loan is earnings, but the future of any business is fraught with uncertainties; therefore, banks require many businesses to secure loans with various types of collateral. As a matter of fact, many loans are described by their security, for example, inventory loans. Small businesses are called upon to provide specific security more often than large firms. For example, some years ago a survey revealed that 78 percent of the loans made to businesses with assets of less than $50,000 were secured, but only 17.5 percent of the loans made to firms with assets exceeding $100 million were secured.[3] It is not accurate to describe loans as being unsecured, since these so-called loans are backed by the general credit of the firm, and any assets not specifically pledged as security for other liabilities are considered security for so-called unsecured loans.

The cost of short-term credit at banks is determined by several factors, three of which are the state of the economy at the time of the loan, the credit status of the firm, and the cost of processing the loan. Generally speaking, the firm pays a simple rate of interest; for example, a firm that borrows $500 at 9 percent for 12 months pays $45 in interest charges. In some cases banks will discount the loan; that is, they collect the interest in advance. If the 9 percent in the above were discounted, the effective rate of interest would be 9.89 percent ($45 ÷ $455). Smaller firms are often required to repay their loans periodically, for example, monthly. If the interest is paid at maturity and is not based on the declining balance, the effective rate will be about twice the size of the contract interest rate. Generally, interest charged to smaller firms is higher than that charged to larger firms. For example, in August 1976, the interest rate, without respect to risk, for a short-term business loan averaged 9.06 percent for a loan size less than $10,000. The same rate for a loan between $100,000 and $499,000 approximated 7.99 percent, with loans exceeding $1 million normally having an attached interest rate of 7.18 percent.

Many banks follow the practice of requiring that a business firm maintain a minimum balance at all times when a loan is outstanding. This

[3]"Member Bank Lending...", p. 403.

policy affects the firm by (1) increasing the effective rate of interest, (2) causing it to borrow more funds than are actually needed, and (3) lowering the firm's investment turnover, which has the effect of reducing its rate of return on investment. To illustrate, suppose a firm borrows $1 million at 9 percent with the condition that it maintain a compensating balance of 20 percent. In this case the borrower has the use of $800,000 instead of $1 million, and the effective cost of the $1 million is 11.25 percent rather than 9 percent; if the firm actually needs $1 million, it will have to borrow $1.25 million. Finally, the firm's investment turnover is reduced because $250,000 is not gainfully employed.

One of the primary ways in which a firm can lower its investment is to establish a line of credit with its bank. Specifically, a line of credit is an indication that a bank is willing to loan up to a certain amount during a particular period of time provided the firm's financial condition does not undergo a substantial change. During this period the firm can draw against the line of credit. In many cases there is no charge for the line of credit; that is, interest is charged only for the amount of funds that is borrowed. Some banks, however, charge a small fee for the unused portion of the line.

The selection of the firm's banking facilities is one of the financial manager's more important functions, since the ability to obtain funds at a proper cost affects not only the firm's profitability but also its ability to compete effectively with other firms in the industry. Many excellent discussions are available to the student concerning ways and means of selecting the bank; it is recommended that one be read and studied.

The volume of credit made available to business firms by banks indicates that many advantages accrue to users of this source. Following are the advantages normally associated with bank borrowing:

1. Advice and counsel can be obtained from experts in finance.
2. Credit information is available.
3. Banks are a source of information regarding potential mergers and consolidations.
4. Aid with regard to future financing is obtained.
5. Banks provide contact with other sources of capital.
6. Banks are major sources of both short- and intermediate-term capital.

Several disadvantages are also associated with bank borrowing; the most important are the following:

1. Confidential information must be revealed if loans are to be secured.
2. Firms are compelled to maintain compensating balances, and this increases the cost of funds.
3. Periodic reports are usually required by banks.
4. Banks often demand that they be allowed to ratify managerial decisions.

business finance companies

Three principal types of finance companies have developed in this country: consumer finance companies, sales finance companies, and business finance companies. The first type provides funds to consumers in the form of small loans repayable periodically. Sales finance companies purchase installment sales contracts from retailers of consumer durable goods, such as autos, appliances, and house trailers. Whereas the consumer finance company and sales finance company supply capital to consumers, business finance companies supply capital to business firms for working capital purposes. In a few cases, they also supply funds to finance fixed assets.

Generally the business finance company is a specialized company whose primary function is to supply funds to small- and middle-sized companies. In general they provide funds for (1) the purchase of commercial, industrial, and farm equipment; (2) financing commercial accounts receivable; (3) factoring; (4) the purchase of commercial vehicles and auto dealers' vehicle inventories;

TABLE 15-5

Business Receivables of Finance Companies

June 30, 1965

Type of receivable	Amount (in millions)	Percentage distribution
Wholesale loans	$4,242	35.4
Automobiles	2,897	24.2
Other consumer goods	318	2.7
Other, including inventory loans	1,026	8.6
Retail loans	4,034	33.7
Commercial vehicles	1,614	13.5
Business, industrial, and farm equipment	2,419	20.2
Lease paper	843	7.0
Business equipment and motor vehicles	818	6.8
Other	25	.2
Other business credit[1]	2,867	23.9
Commercial accounts receivable[2]	1,036	8.7
Factored accounts receivable[3]	608	5.1
Advances to factored clients	200	1.7
Rediscounted receivables[2]	305	2.5
Other[4]	717	6.0
Total business receivables	$11,986	100.0

[1]Includes export/import credits.
[2]Net of balances withheld.
[3]Less liability to factored clients.
[4]Includes loans on open credit, dealer capital loans, small loans for business or farm purposes, and all other business loans not elsewhere classified.
SOURCE: *Federal Reserve Bulletin,* (Oct. 1968), p. 816.

284

(5) leased equipment; and (6) rediscounting for other finance companies. Table 15-5 depicts the type of business as well as the relative importance of each type of financing done by business finance companies.

Although it is impossible to describe the size characteristics of business finance companies, it is reasonable to conclude that the great majority are relatively small. A survey made in 1965 revealed that of the 571 companies that reported only 12 had assets in excess of $100 million and 133, or 23.3 percent, had less than $100,000 in assets.[4]

With respect to volume of business, wholesale and retail equipment financing is by far the most important function of business finance companies, accounting for 69 percent of all receivables. Loans on commercial accounts receivable, factored accounts receivable, advances to factored clients, rediscounted receivables, and other loans accounted for 33.5 percent of the total credit granted by the 571 companies included in the survey.

Business finance companies trade heavily on their equity in order to increase their return to equity. To illustrate, 83 percent of all capital was from debt sources, and of this total approximately 65 percent was obtained from short-term sources. The usually large amount of short-term capital reflects both the high ratio of short-term loans in their portfolios and the seasonal and cyclical nature of the demand for funds from these companies.

factors

The factor is one of the oldest financial institutions, and yet it is probably one of the least known. Its origin can be traced back for centuries; for example, Shakespeare spoke of the factor in *Richard III, Henry IV, Antony and Cleopatra,* and *The Comedy of Errors.* During the fifteenth and sixteenth centuries, England, France, and Spain were engaged in shipping large quantities of goods to their colonies. Because of the distances and because of inadequate communication and transportation facilities, factors were appointed by manufacturers to arrange for the sale and distribution of their goods. Factors never received title but were responsible for the safekeeping of the goods as well as the proceeds of the sale. They investigated the credit standing of potential customers and advanced funds to their principals. During the nineteenth and twentieth centuries, the functions of the factor changed somewhat in that the manufacturer retained the distribution function but transferred the financing and credit and collection functions to the factor.

The modern factor has experienced unusual growth during the past three decades; moreover, factors have expanded their operations both horizontally and vertically. Whereas the early factor operated at the manufacturing level in the textile industry, the contemporary factor has expanded into such industries as lumber, leather, furniture, plastics, toys, and sportswear.

[4]*Federal Reserve Bulletin,* (Oct. 1968), p. 816.

Furthermore, factors are currently operating at the wholesale and distribution levels as well as at the manufacturing level.

Factors perform three primary functions for their clients: (1) purchasing accounts receivable, (2) selecting credit risks and collecting receivables, and (3) providing advisory services. The purchase of accounts receivable without recourse is the method employed by factors to supply funds to business firms. The procedure is generally as follows: The client, upon receipt of an order, submits it to the factor for credit approval. After approval, the shipment is made and the invoice is sent, along with the shipping documents, to the factor. The amount of the invoice is credited to the account of the client, who may withdraw his credit balances, less a reasonable reserve, at any time. This reserve is held in anticipation of (1) merchandise that may be returned and (2) any claim that may be made against the client by a customer.

Certain advantages accrue to firms that factor their receivables. First, cash is received for the majority of the outstanding receivables immediately after the sale has been made. Second, factoring permits the firm to improve its financial position. A simple example will explain this point. Assume that before factoring a firm's current assets and liabilities consist of the following: cash, $5,000; receivables, $50,000; and inventory, $7,500; accounts payable, $5,000; notes payable, $37,500; and accrued taxes, $6,500. The current ratio under these conditions is 1.3 to 1. Now assume that the firm factors its receivables and receives $45,000 in cash; the remaining $5,000 is held in reserve, appearing on the balance sheet as "due from factor." Accounts payable and notes payable are reduced, and the remaining $2,500 is transferred to the firm's cash account. The current ratio after factoring is 3.07 to 1, and the cash account has been improved. Finally, factoring accounts receivable reduces the amount of working capital required for a particular volume of sales, thus improving investment turnover. If the cost of factoring does not exceed the economies accruing to the firm, then factoring is advantageous. This will be examined later.

The second function mentioned is that of credit and collection. Pursuant to an agreement between a business firm and a factor, the credit and collection function and all expenses associated with the function are assumed by the factor. Among the more important advantages gained by small- and middle-sized firms by transferring this function to a factor are the following: (1) The firm receives a superior service, since the function is placed in the hands of a specialist; (2) the function is accomplished more cheaply, since the factor is able to pass on the cost of maintaining complete credit records to the many different firms; and (3) the firm is able to reduce its credit and collection expense to a fixed percentage of net credit sales.

The third important function that factors perform is to provide advice on marketing, finance, and production. The factor is in position to provide information concerning product design, prices, market conditions, and economic prospects, areas in which many firms are unable to do effective research because they have neither the funds nor the skills. The benefits obtained from such services are difficult to evaluate, but in many cases the economics gained tend to offset the cost of factoring.

Although the primary financing function performed by factors is the purchase of accounts receivable without recourse for credit losses, factors also make secured and unsecured loans to their clients. However, when such financing is performed, the factor is acting in the capacity of the commercial finance company.

The factor's charge includes two major components: first, a fee for performing the credit and collection function and for purchasing the firm's receivables without recourse for credit losses, and, second, an interest charge on funds loaned to the business firm.

The first of these costs, the commission rate, is determined through negotiation; it is influenced by several considerations: (1) type of industry, (2) volume of sales, (3) average size of sale, (4) average annual sales volume per customer, (5) credit standings of the firm's customers, and (6) credit terms offered by the firm.[5] The commission rate is expressed as a percentage of the full net face value of the receivables sold; it generally ranges from 1 to 2 percent.

In addition to the commission or fee, the factor charges an interest rate on the funds advanced. This is usually a simple interest charge and not a discount rate.

In deciding whether to use a factor, the finance officer must compare the cost of shifting the credit and collection function to a specialist with the cost of operating it as a part of the finance function. In some cases, particularly for small- and middle-sized companies, it is cheaper to use the factor, but in other cases this may be an expensive way of raising capital.

Governmental agencies as suppliers of short-term capital

The majority of the governmental agencies offering financial support to small businesses are at the federal level, with a few possibilities being provided by the states and the local governmental bodies. Within the federal government, the Small Business Administration is the primary agency having oversight of the federal government's role in fostering small business. In addition, several other agencies sponsor loans to certain firms in selected industries and/or for specific purposes. Examples of these special-purpose loans include financing in connection with defense contracts, foreign trade, public works, and agriculture. In this regard, the small business executive should make serious inquiry into the various financing alternatives that might be available from the federal government. However, in the present context,

---

[5]Clyde Phelps, *Role of Factoring in Modern Business Financing, Studies in Commercial Financing No. 1*, (Baltimore: Commercial Finance Company, 1952), p. 53.

attention is limited primarily to the Small Business Administration and to brief remarks regarding state and local agencies as financing sources.

the Small Business Administration

The Small Business Administration (SBA) is multifaceted in its functions, including active support in ensuring small businesses a "fair" proportion of governmental contracts, either loaning or acting as the guarantee for credit extended to the small firm, providing management consultants to the owners of the small company, and performing research of interest to the small-business community. These responsibilities of the SBA, as listed, certainly do not represent all activities. However, they do typify the types of support provided by the SBA. Naturally, the interest for the present chapter is the agency's role in actually providing short-term capital or facilitating the acquisition of these funds.

ELIGIBILITY REQUIREMENTS FOR SBA LOANS   In working with small firms, the legislature necessarily had to provide an operational definition of a small business. To be considered a small firm, for the purpose of SBA interest, the following criteria, as appropriate, must be met[6]:

1. Wholesale—annual receipts from $5 million to $15 million, depending on the industry.
2. Retail or service—annual receipts from $1 million to $5 million, depending on the industry.
3. Construction—annual receipts of not more than $5 million, averaged over a three-year period.
4. Manufacturing—from 250 to 1,500 employees, depending on the industry.

These guidelines are not intended to be strictly interpreted but rather to be thought of as representing approximations in identifying eligible loan applicants. Exceptions to these general benchmarks for defining a small entity are also provided, with organizations operating in the following types of operations not having access to SBA loans:

1. Loans to nonprofit businesses.
2. Lending for investment.
3. Loans for withdrawals by principals.
4. Publication of magazines and newspapers loans.
5. Loans which encourage monopolies.
6. TV or radio broadcasting loans.
7. Financing for unwarranted changes in ownership.
8. Loans to businesses selling mainly alcoholic beverages.
9. Businesses involved in gambling.

[6]For a more detailed definition, see Section 121.3-10, Part 121, Chapter I, Title 13, *Code of Federal Regulations*, (Washington, D.C.: U.S. Government Printing Office, 1976).

APPLICATION PROCEDURES The approach to be taken in processing a loan application is somewhat dependent on the status of the company in terms of being an established concern versus a new business. Regardless of the age of the enterprise, the loan request should originally be presented to a bank. Only subsequent to their review of the loan and denial of the credit may the company approach the SBA. In other words, the SBA is a "source of last resort." In fact, if the community population exceeds 200,000, two banks must have rejected the loan. Having completed the process of requesting bank funds, the owner may then inquire as to the banker's interest in working with the SBA in terms of a guarantee or participation in the loan. Typically, if the banker has had satisfactory experience with SBA cooperative efforts and cannot justify accepting the loan singularly, he will initiate the idea of SBA involvement, thereby avoiding an outright rejection of the loan request. For established organizations, the required information in filing for the SBA loan would include the following:

1. Company background.
2. Current balance sheet.
3. Income statements for several recent years.
4. Budget projections for the forthcoming year.
5. Current personal financial statements for the owners, including any individual having at least a 20 percent interest in the firm.
6. A specification of the collateral to be offered as security for the loan, including estimates of the market value for each asset.
7. A specific indication of the amount and purpose of the loan.

If the firm is new, the proprietors should provide any of the foregoing information that is available. In addition, data relating to the following areas are to be provided:

1. A detailed description of the new business.
2. A presentation of management experience.
3. An indication of the total financing required and the amount of other financing sources, including private capital being invested.

TYPES OF LOANS AVAILABLE THROUGH THE SBA When the needed financing is coming entirely from the SBA, the agency is *authorized* to loan up to $100,000 to an individual business. The interest rate for funds received by the SBA is limited to an attractive $5\frac{1}{2}$ percent. Additionally, if the loan involves the participation of a bank, this ceiling is raised to $150,000, with a maximum interest rate on the bank's portion being established by the bank at a "legal and reasonable rate." However, in view of the policy of the agency to avoid direct loans, the typical limitation in size when granted has been between $5,000 and $25,000.

Instead of the direct loans, the SBA has preferred to serve strictly in a support function as a guarantee for bank credit. When approved by the SBA field representative, a bank may obtain a guarantee of the loan repayment from the SBA not to exceed the lesser of 90 percent of the loan or $350,000. The interest rate is generally set by the bank. As to maturity, the purpose of the loan dictates the repayment schedule. The limit as imposed by the SBA is ten years, with a shorter period of six years for working capital requirements.

State and local agencies

The states have become increasingly involved in providing financial assistance to businesses situated or considering locating in areas under the state's jurisdiction. Making an effort to attract new industry, certain local and state governmental institutions have become quite liberal in terms of financial packages. The broad spectrum of financial incentives being offered by the respective states and local authorities naturally precludes an extensive listing. However, the small businessman should make contact with the state and local government personnel associated with industrial development.

Summary

Short-term financing is, without any question, significant for any firm, without regard to the size of the business. However, small firms by necessity have to rely more heavily upon short-term capital. These smaller companies simply do not have the degree of accessibility to as many sources of capital as do large corporations. Consequently, short-term liabilities play a more substantive role in the financing of the small enterprise.

In view of the significance of short-term credit for the small business concern, determining the appropriate level of short-term debt becomes an important issue. The relevant variables to be analyzed in ascertaining the organization's debt-maturity structure are divisible into two frameworks, these being the respective advantages generally favoring either short- or long-term capital and the firm attributes that either suggest or compel a given decision.

As to sources of short-term financing, the owners of a business have three primary avenues for acquiring short-term capital. First, credit extended by suppliers, frequently labeled trade payables or trade credit, represents the single leading source of short-term funds. Second, short-term notes or lines of credit from commercial banks comprise a key source of short-term financing. Although these loans are formally reflected in the balance sheet as short-term, the intent may be closer to long-term in that many small businesses borrow short-term, fully intending to renew the loan upon maturity. For many small businesses, the credit from the bank is secured by using specific assets as collateral or by requiring the chief operating officer to sign the note personally. In addition to banks, other financial institutions are employed by small firms, including business finance companies and factors. Last, the federal and state governmental agencies may afford a viable source of financing for the small organization. These loans typically ensue from the Small Business Administration and/or special-purpose grants. The maturity of the government funding is a function of the purpose of the loan. Yet, these obligations may well extend beyond the immediate short term.

QUESTIONS

1. Compare the importance of short-term financing for small firms with that of large businesses.

2. Explain how the firm's flexibility is increased by financing with short-term debt.

3. What additional risks are incurred by a firm that finances largely with short-term credit rather than by long-term debt?

4. What *should be* the relationship between a company's business risk and the amount of short-term credit used in financing investments?

5. In what way is the debt-maturity mix related to the firm's asset structure?

6. Compare the use of trade credit by small and large businesses.

7. What are the advantages of trade credit as a source of financing?

8. May we conclude unequivocally that trade payables have no cost even when the time discount is taken?

9. Compare the cost of a bank loan for a small and large enterprise. What reason(s) might exist for the difference?

10. How does the small business *implicitly* convert short-term into long-term bank loans?

11. What are the purposes of (a) business finance companies and (b) factors?

12. Explain the application procedure for acquiring an SBA loan.

PROBLEMS

15-1. Your firm is faced with the decision of whether to finance a recent expansion through a short-term bank note or by placing a long-term bond with private investors. The bank, North Bancshares, has indicated that the going interest rate for firms of similar risk is 10.25 percent and that this rate would be applicable for the loan to your enterprise provided that as president you would be agreeable to cosign the note both for the company and personally. The note, having an original balance of $200,000, would be payable in full with interest on or before 180 days from the date of the note. However, Jack Griggs, president of the bank, anticipates no difficulty in renewing the note each six months, provided the principal is reduced by $10,000 each six-month period along with a payment of the accrued interest to date. Additionally, if the loan is to be extended, as president you would be required to take out insurance in the form of decreasing term. The insurance coverage would coincide with the remaining balance of the note and would cost $\frac{1}{2}$ percent annually of the average outstanding loan balance. Griggs also has informed you that a 10 percent compensating balance would be necessary. The company maintains a minimum cash balance of $25,000 presently, and no compensating balance is being required for existing loans. The bond under consideration would mature in ten years. Long-term obligations of similar quality have been selling to yield 9 percent. However, the investment banker would require a 10 percent commission for his services in placing the security.

    a. (1) At the time of this financing, what is the nature of the yield curve?
        (2) Is the yield curve typical? Explain.
    b. With the information given,
        (1) What factors would favor the bank note? Explain.
        (2) What factors favor the bond? Explain.
    c. What additional information would be of help in making your decision?
    d. Based on the limited information given, which choice would you make?

15-2. The Small Supplier Corporation has not consistently taken the discount offered by the firm's suppliers. The terms generally available within the industry are 2/10, net 45. The policy of Small Supplier has been to pay invoices only after the controller and the field manager have had an opportunity to review the statements. Payment is made immediately after this meeting; however, the time lag may be as long as 30 days after the invoices have been received.

    a. Determine the cost of not taking the discount if the payment is made
        (1) 15 days after the statement date.
        (2) 20 days after the statement date.
        (3) 30 days after the statement date.
        (4) 45 days after the statement date.
    b. What policy would you recommend for the company?

15-3. What is the effective cost for the following short-term loans?

    a. A $1,000, 9 percent note that is to be repaid at the end of the year. However, the note is discounted, with the amount received by the company being net after interest.
    b. A $1,200, 9 percent note, with the interest being based on the original $1,200. The note is to be repaid in monthly installments of $100, with the interest payable at year end.

chapter 16

INTERMEDIATE FINANCING

In the preceding chapter we were concerned with short-term financing, that is, credit which is repaid or renewed within one year from the date of the loan. In this chapter we shall deal with intermediate credit, which may be defined as credit extended for periods longer than one year but not long enough to be classified as long-term credit. Although intermediate credit is secured in many different ways and evidenced by various types of credit instruments, its major sources are term loans and leasing. The relative importance of leasing and term loans in small businesses is not available, but it is believed that both are major sources of financing, more so in long-term than in short-term debt, and certainly deserving of consideration by the managers of small businesses.

The Nature of Term Loans

The term loan as we know it today is a relatively new type of credit-granting device, even though it has been employed in principle for many years in the form of extended and renewed short-term loans. Data concerning the total dollar volume of term loans to small businesses are not available, but to show their increasing importance in all firms, the following figures are cited. The dollar volume of term loans made by all member banks in the Federal Reserve System rose from $4.5 billion in 1946 to $15.4 billion in 1957, an increase of 243 percent.[1] Data are not readily available for term loans of banks between 1957 and 1968; however, in 1968, the Federal Reserve Board began to report "Term Commercial and Industrial Loans of Large Banks." These loans amounted to about 90 percent of such loans held by all weekly

[1]Carl T. Arlt, "Term Lending to Business," *Federal Reserve Bulletin*, (April 1959), pp. 357–362.

reporting banks and about 70 percent of those held by all commercial banks. Based on these data, term loans rose from $41.1 billion in November 1968 to $66.6 billion in November 1975, an increase of 62 percent. Since this does not include loans from institutions other than commercial banks, we can conclude that term loans not only grew at a very rapid rate during the past three decades but consistently maintained their importance; e.g., throughout this period they accounted for approximately 40 percent of all commercial and industrial loans.

In seeking out the primary reasons for the importance achieved by term loans, it was observed that the increase originated from users as well as suppliers, although financial literature tends to emphasize the reasons associated with the latter. One important reason was that during the late 1930s and 1940s banks discovered they were holding large free reserves, averaging around $2.25 billion. Since traditional investments provided low yields, banks began seeking new types of loans that would provide higher yields, and term loans seemed to answer this need.

A second reason for the increased importance of term loans was the decision of regulatory agency examiners to delete the "slow" classification for term loans and to evaluate them on their "probable collectability" rather than on maturity. Third, commercial banks were encouraged by favorable experience to participate in term loans with the Reconstruction Finance Corporation and the Federal Reserve. Fourth, commercial banks moved from the discount theory, which in essence required loans to be self-liquidating during short periods, to the anticipated income theory, which promulgates the idea that a loan may be liquidated from future income rather than from existing earnings or assets.

It is obvious that there will be no demand for a particular type of loan unless the user benefits from its use; therefore, it is presumed that all types of businesses benefit from term loans since all types of businessmen use them to some degree. In analyzing the reasons for the demand for term loans, the following seem to be the most important. First, since the mid-1930s the federal income tax has increased considerably, creating at least one reason for management to retain a greater proportion of its earnings. It should be remembered that businesses are required to pay a penalty tax on funds retained in excess of their needs. Financial managers concluded that the periodic repayment of term loans certainly qualified as a legitimate need; therefore, it may logically be concluded that the income tax contributed much to the rapid rise in term loans.

Second, during this period the cash flow of businesses experienced substantial growth, providing an excellent source of funds required to retire term loans. Third, term loans prevent banks from canceling credit to the borrower on short notice, since they are, in effect, "long-term" loans. Fourth, many businesses in their early years cannot finance capital requirements internally or from short-term credit, yet they are not mature enough to go to the public for debt capital. In such cases it is not unusual for them to resort to such sources as commercial banks and insurance companies for intermediate funds in the form of term loans. Undoubtedly businesses employ term loans for other reasons as well, but these appear to be the most important ones.

Characteristics of Term Loans

The characteristics of term loans, like those of other loans, vary with the economy, and any descriptions of loan characteristics should be considered in the light of existing economic conditions. Nevertheless, a brief discussion is given here in order to familiarize the reader with this type of credit.

Maturities of term loans depend to a great degree on the financial institution granting the credit; for example, the greatest majority of the loans made by banks have maturities between 1 and 5 years. The smaller firms receive the shorter maturities, whereas the larger firms receive longer terms. Life insurance and pension funds tend to grant longer terms—5 to 15 years—but they, too, give shorter terms to smaller companies.

As the title implies, the term loan is repayable over the life of the loan. As a general rule, the payments include the interest, and the amount remains constant over the life of the loan. Occasionally, the firm is able to have a balloon payment at the end of the loan's life. Since the repayment schedule is of vital importance to both the lender and the borrower, the manner in which it is formulated will be explained.

Assume that a firm borrows $100,000 on a five-year loan at an interest rate of 10 percent on the declining balance. The payments, including interest and principal, will be made in five equal installments. These payments are calculated through the use of the following formula:

$$P = \frac{A_n}{\text{PVIF}_a}$$

where P = annual payment—including interest and principal,
    A_n = present value of the term loan (annuity),
  PVIF$_a$ = present value interest factor of an annuity—see present value tables.

To determine P (annual payment of interest and principal) we simply divide the amount of the term loan by PVIF$_a$—in this case $100,000 ÷ 3.791. The annual payments of $26,378.26 will retire the loan and yield the lender a return of 10 percent; see Table 16-1. The separation of the payments into interest and principal is necessary for income tax purposes since interest is deductible for the borrower and taxable income to the lender.

TABLE 16-1

Term Payment Schedule

Year	Annual payment	Interest	Debt retirement	Balance
1	$26,378	$10,000	$16,378	$83,622
2	26,378	8,362	18,016	65,606
3	26,378	6,561	19,817	45,789
4	26,378	4,579	21,799	23,990
5	26,378	2,399	23,999	8[1]

[1]Error due to rounding.

Banks generally require some type of collateral from their borrowers, and this is especially true for small companies. The collateral may include personal assets such as stock and bonds as well as real property such as machinery and equipment. Occasionally the firm is required to secure the loan with real estate.

During recent years many lenders have required "sweeteners" in addition to fixed interest payments. The most common "sweetener" is the option to purchase common stock. A word of warning is appropriate at this point. There have been an increasing number of court cases in which the borrower has contended that stock options result in usurious interest being charged. While the majority of these suits have been won by the lender, several have not. Care should be taken when options are required in addition to fixed interest payments.

Lenders usually include several restrictive provisions in term loan agreements. While the exact nature of each restrictive clause varies among firms, it is important for the reader to know their general nature. The more common restrictive clauses pertain to (1) volume of working capital, (2) long-term debt, (3) payment of dividends, (4) changes in key managerial personnel, (5) sale of assets, and (6) additional borrowing. In addition to these general limitations, many lenders impose specific limitations on the use of the funds, investment in nonoperating assets, and amount of executive compensation.

It should be remembered that protective provisions should be designed to protect both the lender and borrower and that care should be taken when agreeing to these provisions. If they are either too strict or too "loose," financial embarrassment may result, causing losses to be incurred by both parties. The following are the covenants that were actually incorporated into a term loan that one of the writers assisted in negotiating:

Covenants

The following covenants are mutually agreed upon and warranted by the Bank, the Borrower, and the Principals. It is mutually agreed and understood that only by the specific written consent of the Bank, the Borrower, and the

Principals may any covenant herein contained be altered or changed in any manner.

1. The Principals will execute a continuing line guaranty in favor of the Bank by which each, _____ and _____, will become jointly and severally liable on the indebtedness herein described.

2. The above loan and any future loans are to be secured by the pledge of all accounts receivable, business equipment, and all vehicles. In addition the Principals shall pledge $_____ from their savings account.

3. The Borrower will assign to the Bank life insurance on the life of _____ having a minimum death benefit of $_____.

4. The Borrower will provide to the Bank on a timely basis (monthly) a balance sheet, a profit and loss statement, a cash flow statement, and a list and aging of accounts receivable. This presentation is to be made monthly and shall provide both past month's data as well as year-to-date data.

5. Relationships with commercial banks other than the _____ National Bank will not exist or be established by the Borrower.

6. Total compensation paid to the Principals shall not exceed $_____ per month without prior approval of Bank.

7. No dividends shall be paid by Borrower to the Principals until the debt/equity ratio reaches 50/50 and then only with approval of the Bank.

8. There shall be no fixed asset purchases made without prior approval of the Bank.

9. The Borrower will not pledge, give away, or hypothecate any of its assets or permit any material change in its asset structure.

10. The Borrower and the Principals will not cause or allow any alteration or change in the ownership of the capital stock of the Borrower.

11. As long as there is any indebtedness outstanding, the Bank shall have a representative on the Board of Directors, and regular monthly meetings shall be held to review the financial conditions of Borrower.

In the majority of cases, the interest rates charged on term loans are higher than those charged on short-term loans to the same borrower. Moreover, the rate can either (1) remain constant over the life of the loan or (2) move directly with the prime rate. In addition to the interest charge the lender may also charge a service charge to cover such items as legal and credit analysis costs.

Interest on term loans may be charged either on the original amount or on the outstanding amount of the loan. If charged on the outstanding amount, the dollar amount of interest declines as the loan is repaid—see Table 16-1. If charged on the original amount, the interest rate is higher. In many cases this method of charging interest is used in computing interest charges for small firms. The writers recommend that small businessmen resist this method of calculating interest since it is discriminatory and detrimental to the firm. Another technique of raising the cost of borrowing is to require the small businessman to maintain a compensating balance with the bank. The practice is of little importance to the borrower unless the required balance exceeds the normal balance needed for precautionary purposes.

Term Loans as a Financing Device

Although term loans are employed for many valid reasons, they may create some operational problems under certain conditions. First, the use of term loans may "disturb" a firm's optimal capital structure, which could adversely affect earnings on equity and cost of capital. To illustrate, assume the following: Company A negotiates a term loan in the amount of $2.5 million, repayable in equal installments over a five-year period. The balance sheet data in Table 16-2 depicts A's capital mix at the time the term loan is made and after the loan is repaid.

Table 16-3 depicts the changes that take place in the firm's capital structure when a term loan is used to raise funds. Note that in the beginning the ratio of debt increases sharply—from 33 percent to 50 percent debt—but as the loan is retired out of current earnings, the ratio declines. The net effect of the increase in debt is to increase the return on equity capital, but in so doing risk is also increased. The reader remembers that the cost of equity

TABLE 16-2

Company A

Balance Sheet Data

	Time loan made	*After loan repaid*
Current liabilities		
Trade credit[1]	$ 400,000	$ 400,000
Notes payable[2](6%)	500,000	500,000
Other	100,000	100,000
Term loan[3]	2,500,000	0
Long-term debt[4](6%)	1,500,000	1,500,000
Common stock[5]	5,000,000	5,000,000
Retained earnings	0	2,500,000

[1]For simplicity, trade credit remains constant and has no cost.
[2]Assume the company maintains a constant short-term balance of $500,000.
[3]Interest at 6%.
[4]Interest on long-term debt is 6%; however, interest rises as additional leverage is employed.
[5]Cost of equity rises as additional debt is added, and vice versa.

TABLE 16-3

Changes in Balance Sheet as Term Loan Is Repaid (in millions)

Year[1]	Debt/Equity ratio	Equity amount	Long-term debt		Notes payable and other		Trade credit		Term loan		Total	
			Amount	Percent	Amount	Percent	Amount	Percent	Amount	Percent	Amount	Percent
0	33/67	$5.0	$1.5	20.0	$.6	8.0	$.4	5.3	$0	0	$ 7.5	100.0
1	45/55	5.5	1.5	15.0	.6	6.0	.4	4.0	2.0	20.0	10.0	100.0
2	40/60	6.0	1.5	15.0	.6	6.0	.4	4.0	1.5	15.0	10.0	100.0
3	35/65	6.5	1.5	15.0	.6	6.0	.4	4.0	1.0	10.0	10.0	100.0
4	30/70	7.0	1.5	15.0	.6	6.0	.4	4.0	.5	5.0	10.0	100.0
5	25/75	7.5	1.5	15.0	.6	6.0	.4	4.0	.0	0	10.0	100.0

[1]End-of-year data.

capital increases as additional risk is incurred, and should the term loan add too much risk, the total cost of capital will rise, causing a decrease in the desirability of all projects.

As the term loan is paid off from earnings, the return to equity as well as risk decrease. The reduction in risk would have a tendency to cause the value of the firm to increase, but this increase in value may be offset by a decline in the return to equity. It should also be noted that after the term loan is repaid (out of equity) the firm's debt/equity ratio is smaller than it was when the loan was undertaken. In the above example, debt constituted 33 percent of the total capital before the loan was made, but after the loan was repaid, it accounted for only 25 percent. In other words, the firm's capital is no longer at its optimum, thus causing a permanent decline in the firm's return of equity and more than likely the value of the firm as well.

A term loan can avoid distorting return to equity and value if it is not very large relative to other debt and if installments are paid with debt rather than equity capital. This is not to suggest that term loans should be avoided; rather, it suggests that *care* should be exercised when term loans are used in the financing process.

The term loan does have certain advantages. First, it permits flexibility in that the terms of the loan can be tailored to fit the needs of the small business. Second, small businesses do not have access to the capital markets, and term loans are a fairly good substitute for long-term securities. Even if there is access to the capital markets, term loans may be obtained much more quickly and possibly more cheaply than publicly issued bonds.

The Nature and Importance of Leasing

Leasing as a method of procuring assets is probably the most significant development that has taken place in the field of finance during the past three decades. Originally the emphasis was on real estate leasing, but during the past several years firms have been able to lease almost any type of fixed asset. Although there are no figures measuring the amount of leased equipment presently in use, we may safely conclude that lease financing is one of the major methods of external financing being used by many industries. Although a firm would probably never lease all its fixed assets, there is a definite trend toward owning less and leasing more. It is difficult to say whether the increased importance of leasing is a result of the financial officer's desire to conserve funds or whether it results from increased effort on the part of the leasing companies.

Prior to discussing the pros and cons of lease financing, we should examine briefly the two principal techniques of leasing, which are (1) leasing rather than purchasing the asset and (2) the sale and lease back of an asset that has been previously acquired and financed out of the firm's own funds. In general there are two types of leases: operating leases and financial leases.

Operating leases are usually cancelable, and the asset is maintained by the lessor. The type of assets covered by this type of lease includes computers, copying machines, and telephone services. Another important characteristic is that the cost of the asset is usually not fully amortized. The financial lease, on the other hand, is a noncancelable lease of a fully amortized asset which the lessee normally maintains and services.

The sale and lease back arrangement involves nothing more than transferring the title of an asset owned by a firm to another party in exchange for a price that reflects the market value of the asset, following which the asset is leased by the original owner. The net effect of the transaction is for the original owner to "trade" a fixed asset for a current asset. The new owner and lessor expects to receive the cost of the asset plus an acceptable return. The rental price is calculated in the same manner as the payments of term loans. That is, the cost of the asset (A_n) is divided by the PVIF_a (present value factor) of the return desired.

Suppose a firm wanted to execute a sale and lease back contract on a piece of equipment with a value of $10,000. The purchaser (lessor) desires a return of 10 percent on the declining balance of the investment during the ten-year lease back arrangement. The annual base payments under these assumptions are $1,627.33, computed as follows:

$$P = \frac{\$10,000}{6.145} = \$1,627.33$$

That is, if the lessee pays ten annual installments of $1,627.33, he would return to the lessor $10,000 plus a 10 percent return on the declining balance of the lessor's investment. Table 16-4 illustrates the division of the principal and interest received by the lessor.

TABLE 16-4

Distribution of the Sale and Lease Back Payments

Year	Lease payments	Interest	Principal	Residual investment
1	$1,627.33	$1,000.00	$ 627.33	$9,372.67
2	1,627.33	937.27	690.06	8,682.61
3	1,627.33	868.26	759.07	7,923.54
4	1,627.33	792.35	834.98	7,088.56
5	1,627.33	708.86	918.47	6,170.09
6	1,627.33	617.01	1,010.32	5,159.77
7	1,627.33	515.98	1,111.35	4,048.42
8	1,627.33	404.84	1,222.49	2,825.93
9	1,627.33	282.60	1,344.73	1,481.20
10	1,627.33	148.12	1,479.21	1.99[1]

[1]Error due to rounding.

As stated above, sale and lease back financing is the sale of an asset previously acquired and financed out of the firm's own funds to another party, from whom it is then leased back on a long-term basis. Although it is difficult to say precisely why this method of financing has increased in importance during the past several years, the change may be attributable to the growth of financial institutions and their effort to find attractive investments. Also, this technique allows firms to convert long-term investments in fixed assets to current assets. For example, firm A could sell its home office building for $100,000 and sign a long-term lease with the purchasing unit. Immediately, its permanent working capital is increased by $100,000 without an increase in debt or equity capital.

The following advantages, which accrue to both financial institutions and business firms, reveal some of the reasons this particular technique has enjoyed such success during the past several years. The advantages for the financial institution are several. First, it is able to obtain a higher yield from such an arrangement than it could by holding high-grade bonds.

Second, it is generally conceded that the lessor is in a relatively safe position since the types of firms that enter into these agreements have relatively small amounts of debt outstanding. In the event of insolvency, the lessor is not in so strong a position as a general creditor since the lessee can obtain legal relief from rental obligations; however, until insolvency occurs, the lessor is in a very strong position since the asset involved is of such character that the lessee cannot operate without it.

Third, in many cases the asset will have a value at the expiration of the lease. This offers the investor several courses of action. First, the lessor may allow the firm to repurchase the property at the amortized value. Since tax problems may result from such a course of action, however, many firms refuse to grant options to repurchase the property. Second, the investor may sell the property and pay a capital gains tax, or, third, the lessee may renew the lease at the going market rate, which means that the investor receives an even higher rate of return.

Two advantages often accrue to the lessee. The first involves the release of capital funds for current use. If a firm can sell its fixed assets and reinvest the funds in current assets, it may improve its return on investment in two ways: First, the funds will be invested in assets that turn over faster; therefore, in the long run their return will be higher than if the funds had been invested in assets with a slow turnover. Second, if the firm raises needed capital from equity sources at a time when the cost of equity capital is high, the earning power of each share will be diluted; therefore, it will benefit the firm more to raise the necessary funds by selling its fixed assets.

The second major advantage of the sale and lease back technique is that, under certain conditions, the firm can experience a definite tax saving. For example, suppose a firm sells the land and building that it has owned for the past 10 years for $60,000. The firm paid $20,000 for the building and $5,000 for the land. The economic life of the building is estimated to be 20 years, and depreciation is computed on a straight-line basis. Under these conditions, the transaction yields a net profit of $45,000. Since the firm pays a capital gains tax on the profit at 30 percent, the amount of tax is $13,500. The firm has increased its current assets by $46,500 and realized a profit on the sale, and it will be allowed to charge off the rental payments as an expense. A sale and lease back arrangement can also result in a tax saving when the value of the property has declined below the original cost.

Operating and Financial Leases

Operating leases are vitally important to small businessmen since this may be the only way in which they can obtain the use of the asset in question. While this is an important subject, we will focus on the financial lease.

First and foremost, the small businessman should be aware of the contents of the financial lease contract. In the majority of cases the contract includes the following: (1) the term of the lease (during which time the lease in noncancelable); (2) periodic rental payments, which include the cost of the equipment plus a return on the lessor's investment; (3) cost of maintenance, taxes, insurance, etc; and (4) a renewable clause.

Advantages and disadvantages of financial leases

An examination of the literature in the field of lease financing reveals there is no unanimity of opinion about the advantages and disadvantages of lease financing. Students of finance should know by this time that authorities never agree completely; therefore, we shall list those advantages that have not been seriously questioned and follow them by those that have been set forth and discredited.

The following advantages of financial leases are currently acknowledged as being valid:

1. Permit a lessee to obtain the use of property that cannot be acquired in any other way.
2. Provide facilities that are needed only temporarily.
3. Avoid the risk of obsolescence.
4. Relieve the user of maintenance, service, and administrative problems.
5. Provide an additional source of financing.
6. Give the lessee flexibility.

Advantages as obvious as these do not require individual explanations. It should be pointed out, however, that under certain conditions it is possible to question one or more of them. In the past, various attempts have been made to establish the beneficiality of four alleged advantages, although recent literature has discredited them. The more important of these are that leasing (1) frees working capital, (2) yields a tax saving, (3) improves the lessee's apparent financial position, and (4) spares management the need to review capital expenditures.

The most frequently mentioned disadvantages of leasing are (1) high cost; (2) loss of residual values; (3) the possibility that a premium will be demanded for vital equipment unless adequate care is taken when the lease is negotiated; (4) inadequate evaluation due to habitual leasing; (5) the lack of accumulation of equity, which could have some adverse effects on future financing; and (6) the possibility that control of the facility may be lost at the end of the lease period.

The validity of each of these disadvantages depends on the alternatives and the care exercised when negotiating the lease agreement. To illustrate, the cost of a lease may or may not exceed the cost of alternative sources. There are several elements that determine whether a lease is more "expensive" than the alternative sources; these include the tax rate, the repayment schedule, the depreciation method used, and the rate of interest charged on the balance of the investment—see pages 306–309 for further discussion of the cost of leases.

Sources of Funds

Funds to finance leases are obtained from several important sources, chiefly the following: independent leasing companies, banks, insurance companies, pension funds, and industrial development agencies. Of these sources, it is believed that independent leasing companies and banks are the most important, especially for small- and middle-sized companies. To a lesser extent insurance companies and industrial development agencies provide funds for small- and middle-sized firms, especially the latter.

It is believed that the independent leasing company is the most important of the sources listed above. Operationally speaking, there are three types of independent leasing companies: the service leasing company, the financing leasing company, and the lease broker. The latter acts as a "go-between" for the supplier of funds and the lessor and deals primarily with large businesses. Because of this, the operations of the lease broker will not be discussed here.

Service leasing companies generally specialize in automobiles, office equipment and computers, and, occasionally, industrial equipment. As mentioned previously, the leases of such equipment are often cancellable and run from two to four years. The leases are rarely amortized; in fact, the profits of many service leasing companies depend on the residual value of the leased equipment. That is, the equipment is re-leased or sold to the same or another firm.

The finance leasing company actually provides funds to a company to secure the use of capital equipment. The process is quite simple in that the leasing company will, upon instruction of the customer, purchase the desired equipment. The equipment is usually delivered directly from the manufacturer to the lessee. While the cost of the equipment is usually fully amortized, some leasing companies issue leases for approximately 10 percent of the value of the equipment. This permits them to realize a profit from the residual value of the assets. This practice is more prevalent among the smaller leasing companies.

Financial institutions, such as banks, are the major source of funds for both service and finance leasing companies. While it is difficult to estimate the amount of equity that each type of firm employs in its capital structure, it is safe to say that both are highly levered. The debt capital of smaller leasing firms is often obtained after the lease has been arranged, and in most cases the equipment serves as the security for the loan. The large, well-capitalized leasing firms are able to raise large blocks of funds at opportune times in order to secure the most advantageous interest rates. During the period 1969–1974 many leasing companies, especially those dealing with small- and middle-sized companies, experienced operational difficulties, and, as a result, many failed. The principal reasons were high cost of funds, high operating cost, and increasing competition from such institutions as banks and pension funds.

Banks have increased their participation in leasing during the past several years. While specific data as to their involvement are not available, it is believed that they have become a major supplier of leases. The increase has been aided and abetted by the 1963 ruling of the Comptroller of the Currency which allows national banks to engage in leasing. Another reason would appear to be that banks decided to cut out the middleman (leasing companies) and in so doing increase their return. The increasing importance of banks in leasing benefits small companies by providing an additional source of intermediate capital.

To a lesser degree insurance companies and pension funds are leasing equipment. For the most part, these institutions are not important sources of funds to small- and middle-sized companies; rather, they concentrate their efforts in the area of rather large businesses. For example, they often act together and provide funds for such equipment as offshore drilling rigs. While these funds are often supplied to closely held companies, they are rarely small. Furthermore, insurance companies are subject to certain restrictions in their lending activity. For example, state laws spell out the nature and quality of investments that they are permitted to make; as a result, most states limit the amount of admitted assets that insurance companies can invest in such activities as leasing.

Industrial development agencies have been active in leasing entire plants to small- and middle-sized firms. This activity is done in order to attract industries in certain underdeveloped areas. Generally this is accomplished by the community's issuing or guaranteeing the agency's low-interest, tax-free bonds which will be used to build the plant for the firm. Since this type of leasing is for entire plants rather than for specific equipment, this type of lease activity will not be discussed further here.

In summary, small- and middle-sized companies should look to leasing companies and banks as their primary sources of lease financing. If negotiated properly, the funds obtained in this manner can be most important to the ultimate success of the firm. The next section, calculating lease costs, will aid the small businessman greatly when making the decision whether or not to lease.

Calculation of Lease Payments

The calculation of lease payments may be determined by two methods. First, they may be determined by solving the equation

$$P = \frac{A_n}{\text{PVIF}_a}$$

which the student recalls was used to determine the term loan payments and lease payments of the sale and lease back problem. Assume the following: cost of leased facilities, $9,000; useful life, three years; term of the lease, three years; scrap value, zero; nominal rate of interest of lease, 10 percent on the declining balance; and income tax rate, 20 percent. The annual lease payment equals $3,618.82 before tax and $2,895.05 after tax. These payments are determined as follows: $9,000/2.487 = $3,618.82 \times (1.00 - .20) = $2,895.05$. The proof of the accuracy of these payments may be seen in Table 16-5.

A much less sophisticated method of determining the annual lease payments is to solve the following formula[2]:

$$\frac{\text{Cost of leased facilities} + \text{Required return}}{\text{Number of years lease is outstanding}}$$

Substituting the lease information into the formula, we find that the before-tax payments equal $3,600 and that the after-tax payments equal $2,880; for example,

$$\$9,000 + 1,800 \div 3 = \$3,600 \times (1 - .20) = \$2,880$$

It was mentioned above that the cost of a lease may or may not exceed the cost of alternative sources. The elements influencing this decision are the repayment schedule, the depreciation method used, and the rate of interest charged on the investment. In the example below, these elements are considered in the determination of whether to lease or own a piece of equipment costing $50,000.

[2]This method ignores the compounding process and is somewhat different from the dollar value derived through the use of the formula

$$P = \frac{A_n}{\text{PVIF}_a}$$

TABLE 16-5

Division of Rental Payments
Between Return and Principal

Year	Gross lease payment[1]	After-tax payments[1]	Return on investment[1]	Return of principal[1]	Residual investment[1]
1	$3,618.82	$2,895.05	$900.00	$2,718.82	$6,281.18
2	3,618.82	2,895.05	628.12	2,990.70	3,290.48
3	3,618.82	2,895.05	329.05	3,289.77	.71[2]
4	0				

[1]End of year.
[2]Error due to rounding.

Assume that a firm has three alternative sources of funds available to finance the machine. The first alternative is to lease the equipment under the following conditions:

1. Cost of leased equipment, $50,000.
2. Level lease payments.
3. Life of equipment, three years.
4. Residual value, zero.
5. Income tax, 20 percent.
6. Lessor's expected return, 10 percent computed on declining balance.

The second alternative is to purchase the equipment directly from the company. The equipment would be paid for in the following manner:

1. Down payment of $12,500.
2. Three equal installments of $12,500.
3. Interest at 8 percent on declining balance.

The third alternative is to borrow the funds from a financial institution. The loan would be repaid in the following manner:

1. Repay principal at end of three years.
2. Interest on outstanding balance of 8 percent is paid annually.

There are two primary ways to evaluate the alternative methods of financing the equipment: (1) calculate the interest cost of each source, and (2) compute the present value of the "payments" made to each source. In the first, the most desirable method would be the one with the lowest cost, provided, of course, that all other things are equal. When using the second technique, the most desirable method would be the one in which the outflow has the lowest present value, provided, of course, all other things are equal. Tables 16-6 and 16-7 depict the "percentage" cost of each method as well as the method of calculating the "cost" of a lease.

TABLE 16-6

Comparison of the "Interest Cost" of
the Three Sources of Funds

Source	Before-tax cost	After-tax cost
Lease	10.0%	8.05%
Installments sale	8.0%	6.40%
Financial institution	8.0%	6.40%

TABLE 16-7

Calculation of the Cost of a Lease

End of year	Lease payments Gross[1]	Lease payments After tax	Depreciation Gross	Depreciation After tax	Actual cost	Present value 7%	Present value 9%
1	$20,105	$16,084	$16,667	$13,334	$19,417[2]	$18,155	$17,805
2	20,105	16,084	16,667	13,334	19,417[2]	16,950	16,349
3	20,105	16,084	16,667	13,334	19,417[2]	15,844	14,989
						$50,950	$49,144

Interpolate: $\dfrac{\$950}{\$1,806} = .526 \times 2\% = 1.05\% + 7.0\% = 8.05\%$

[1]Gross lease payment is computed by solving the following equation: $P = A_n/\text{PVIF}_a$. In this case $50,000/2.487 = \$20,104.54$ (rounded to $20,105).

[2]Actual cost equals after-tax outlay plus loss of tax savings on depreciation, e.g., $16,084 plus $3,333 (column 3 minus column 4).

Using the above information as a basis, we see that the lease is the most expensive when compared to the other two methods of financing; however, the writers do not recommend this technique of valuation since no consideration is given to the time value concept. To do so requires a comparison of the cash flows of each method.

If one is employing the value of the firm's cash outflows, it is necessary to assume a discount rate that approximates the firm's cost of capital. As mentioned many times, the cost of capital of a small firm cannot be measured precisely; however, the average weighted internal rate of return (weight of the firm's IRR_i and IRR_e) may be used. For purposes of this calculation it is assumed that the firm's cost of capital is 18 percent—see Table 16-8 for a comparison of each method of financing.

In the above example the loan from the financial institution has the lowest cost—$30,160 compared to the lease cost of $34,967 and $36,097 for the installment loan. Comparing the actual out-of-pocket cost (before taxes), we find that the installment loan would be the "cheapest" ($56,000 for the installment loan, $60,315 for the lease, and $62,000 for the loan from the financial institution). Comparing the effective out-of-pocket cost (after tax), we find that the lease payment would be the smallest of the three sources, i.e.,

TABLE 16-8

Present Value of Payments Made Under
Available Alternatives

Alternative 1: leasing

$20,105 \times (1 - .20) \times 2.174 =$	$34,967

Alternative 2: installment loan

Down payment: $12,500 \times 1.00 =$	$12,500
Interest payments:	
Year 1: $37,500 \times .08 \times .847 \times (1.00 - .20) =$	2,033
Year 2: $25,000 \times .08 \times .718 \times (1.00 - .20) =$	1,149
Year 3: $12,500 \times .08 \times .609 \times (1.00 - .20) =$	487
Principal payments: $12,500 \times 2.174 =$	27,175
	$43,344
Less: Present value of depreciation:	
Straight-line depreciation $= \$50,000 \div 3 = \$16,667 \times .20 \times 2.174 =$	7,247
Present value of cash outflows (net) $=$	$36,097

Alternative 3: loan from financial institution

Down payment $=$	0
Interest payments:	
Year 1: $50,000 \times .08 \times .847 \times (1.00 - .20) =$	$ 2,710
Year 2: $50,000 \times .08 \times .718 \times (1.00 - .20) =$	2,298
Year 3: $50,000 \times .08 \times .609 \times (1.00 - .20) =$	1,949
Principal payment: $50,000 \times .609 =$	30,450
	$37,407
Less: Present value of depreciation:	
Straight-line depreciation $50,000 \div 3 = \$16,667 \times .20 \times 2.174 =$	7,247
Present value of cash outflows (net) $=$	$30,160

Note: The tax rate assumed to be 20 percent; the discount rate equals 18 percent.

lease, $48,252; installment loan, $54,800; loan from financial institution, $59,600. The student and practitioner should remember that the time value of funds concept requires that the funds be employed at a rate equal to the firm's cost of capital. In summary, the cost of any source of funds depends on several factors, namely: interest rate, tax rate, method of repayment, method of computing depreciation, and the firm's cost of capital.

Summary

Term loans have experienced unusual growth during the past three decades. Some of the more important reasons for this growth are: (1) regulatory agencies' examiners decided to delete the slow classification for term loans and to evaluate them on their probable collectability; (2) commercial banks changed their requirement from the idea that loans should be self-liquidating to the concept that the loan could be liquidated from future income; (3) the cash flows of businesses increased rapidly during this period, which encouraged the use of term loans; and (4) term loans constitute a major source of "long-term" capital for small and middle-sized businesses.

Term loans in a small firm are usually about 5 years in length, and the interest is charged on the declining balances. Generally, the term loan is secured either by cosigners or by the assets of the corporation.

The term loan can create a serious problem if it is repaid from earnings. For example, return to equity decreases and the capital structure of the firm is affected, causing the firm's value to be impaired. If used properly, however, the term loan can be advantageous in that it permits flexibility as well as being reasonably easy to negotiate.

Operating and financial leases are a principal source of capital for small firms. While the operating lease is of importance to the small firm, we paid particular attention to the financial lease. The financial lease provides certain advantages to the lessee, the more important of which are: (1) it permits the lessee to obtain the use of equipment that cannot be acquired in any other manner, (2) it avoids the risk of obsolescence, (3) it provides 10 percent financing, and (4) it provides an additional source of financing.

Financial leases are obtained from the following sources: independent leasing companies, banks, insurance companies, pension funds, and industrial development agencies. It is believed that independent leasing companies and banks are the principal sources for small companies.

Care should be exercised before employing a financial lease since some other source may be more economical. It is recommended that the manager compare the present value of the cash outflows of each potential source of funds before accepting or rejecting leasing as a principal source of funds.

QUESTIONS

1. What are the primary reasons for growth in term loans?

2. List the principal characteristics of term loans.

3. What formula is used to determine the annual payments (including principal and interest) required to liquidate a term loan?

4. Why should care be taken when giving "sweeteners" to lenders of term loans?

5. Criticize term loans as a source of debt to small firms.

6. What are the primary sources of lease financing?

7. Briefly describe two principal techniques of leasing.

8. Describe the process of arriving at the percentage cost of a lease.

9. One method of evaluating the cost of a lease is to compute the "present

value" of the after-tax cash outlay. Compare this method of costing with "percentage cost" of a lease. Which method do you consider to be the more accurate?

10. Contact a bank and an insurance company, and compare their leasing policies.

PROBLEMS

16-1. The NYOB Corporation is attempting to determine the most effective way to finance a machine which will expedite the movement of inventory in its warehouse. The machine will cost $10,000. The following methods of financing are available:

1. Lease the equipment on a five-year contract for $2,637.82 per annum. The lease does not include maintenance or service.
2. One manufacturer will finance the equipment on an installment contract. The terms of the contract are (a) a down payment of $2,000, (b) five annual payments of $1,600, and (c) 12 percent interest on the declining balance.
3. Finance the equipment through a local insurance company. The insurance company would advance $10,000 for five years. Only the interest at 12 percent is required to be paid semiannually.

Requirement:

Which of the three methods would be the most desirable? Assume a tax rate of 20 percent and a hurdle rate of 18 percent.

16-2. Calculate the monthly payments of a five-year, $170,000 term loan which has an interest cost of 10 percent (on the declining balance). What would be the payments if the loan were repaid annually rather than monthly? Calculate the present value of the payments—assume a discount rate of 18 percent. Which method of payment would you prefer? Why?

chapter 17

LONG-TERM FINANCING

Determining the relative importance of the various financial problems faced by a small company would be both difficult and subjective; however, the cost and availability of long-term funds would have to be considered of prime import. Raising permanent capital for the expansion of an enterprise is not accomplished with ease, particularly for the small company. In general, the small firm is thought to incur higher costs for its funds as well as a greater limitation in terms of the diversity of sources. In this chapter we shall review the considerations which must be recognized in determining which financing plan should be accepted by the company. Second, the material highlights the common forms of long-term financing of the small corporation, with particular emphasis being put upon long-term debt and equity capital. Next, the procedures for acquiring capital are examined. Last, the retained earnings, a major source of financing for the small concern, are briefly presented.

Relevant Considerations in Selecting the Financing Package

A number of basic principles should be followed in determining the preferred means for meeting the financing requirements of the firm. For the most part the guidelines are generally applicable to either small or large corporations; however, the level of importance of each concept may be expected to vary depending on the size of the business.

In determining what kind of financing would be most appropriate, the financial manager must first decide the maturity structure of the financing instrument. Stated differently, prior to investigating the type of funds, the key question would be "Should the company finance with long-term or short-term sources?" This issue was addressed in Chapter 15, providing an overview of the key variables. However, in brief, the underlying criterion should be the type of assets being financed, with a distinction between *permanent* and *temporary* assets being necessary. As reflected in Figure 17-1, the demarcation line separating permanent assets from cyclical or temporary assets becomes the relevant determinant of whether the funds should be financed with short-term or long-term funds. Ideally, all permanent assets should be financed with either long-term debt or equity financing, and the remaining current assets should be sponsored by short-term sources. However, such a policy assumes that management is able to predict asset requirements with a great deal of certainty. If such an assumption is unrealistic, the financial executive is compelled to finance a portion of the cyclical current assets with long-term sources in order to allow for contingencies. The foregoing principle, while conceptually not difficult, often represents a serious problem for the manager of a small company. Due to either limited funds or management's naiveté, many small companies place themselves in financial difficulty by violating this principle. Time and time again, the small business manager will attempt to finance permanent growth with short-term financing only to find himself facing serious cash flow problems, particularly in an economical downturn. In this context, the corporate leadership should take care to avoid financial problems resulting from the failure to distinguish between permanent and cyclical needs.

Having determined the need for long-term financing, a number of matters must be recognized in ascertaining which source of funds should be drawn upon. Although a host of specific factors might be cited, the determinants in choosing the financing source is a function of the trade-off between the owner's preference for return, risk, and control. Specifically, as new

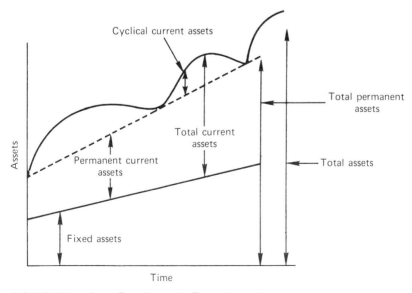

FIGURE 17-1. Asset Requirements, Financing of Assets

common stock is issued, the already existing shareholders must share future income and control, but the total risk of the organization both in terms of variability of earnings to common stockholders and the likelihood of insolvency is reduced. However, as new debt or preferred stock is issued, the current shareholders receive the "residual" income from investments, that being the profits remaining after the payment of fixed financial charges. Furthermore, the shareholders continue to maintain their existing control. However, in contrast to these two benefits, risk is increased. Although such trade-offs are easily recognized on a conceptual basis, the actual decision-making process is quite difficult, with a number of factors being involved. The primary concerns are discussed below.

Trading on the equity

The use of debt capital in the financing process is one way that management may improve its return on equity capital without increasing the return on total investment. This potential opportunity is important in that occasionally management finds itself in a situation where it is impossible to increase the overall return, and yet it is imperative to increase the return on equity. The process of using debt capital to increase the rate of return on equity and earnings per share is called financial leverage, or trading on the equity[1], and may have favorable impact. If the capital secured from debt securities is used in projects that produce a rate of return higher than the cost of debt, the return on equity would be increased. The impact of trading on the equity is best depicted through an EBIT-EPS graph, as was developed in Chapter 9. The results of this type of examination should be a key determinant in management's final decision.

The capital-structure mix

Although the level of sophistication of the analysis may be diverse, management may expect the provider of capital to examine the company's current capital structure relative to an industry norm or some subjectively determined standard. As a brief example of the examination, assume that the Albert Company has a book value of $100,000 with a capital structure mix as indicated in column 2 of Table 17-1. Furthermore, the industry averages for similar firms are shown in column 3 of the table. Assume that management is considering an investment of $20,000 to be financed either by issuing long-term debt for the amount needed or by issuing additional common stock. The results of doing either are reflected in columns 4 and 5 of Table 17-1. As may be observed from the proforma section of the table, additional debt would push the company's level of debt considerably beyond that of the industry

---

[1]No distinction between *trading on equity* and *financial leverage* is made; however, see Pierson Hunt, "A Proposal for Precise Definitions of Trading on the Equity and Leverage," *Journal of Finance*, (Sept. 1961), pp. 377–386.

TABLE 17-1

Capital-Structure Proportions

Source (1)	Percentage of total assets		Proforma[2]	
	Albert Co.[1] (2)	Industry (3)	Debt (4)	Common (5)
Current liabilities	30%	20%	25%	25%
Long-term debt	15	20	29	13
Total	45	40	54	38
Common stock	55	60	46	62
	100	100	100	100

[1]Based on a $100,000 asset base.
[2]Based on a $120,000 asset base.

norm. Even though such a disparity may be justifiable, management may have to defend its position if the debt issue is selected. Two additional comments which have proven to be particularly relevant to the small firm may be made. First, the supplier of financial resources may not look only at the corporate assets but will probably also consider the financial worth of the private owners. The president of the corporation may be required to cosign the note personally with the corporation so that his personal assets are also available to the lender in case of default. In other words, in financing a small corporation, lenders draw heavily upon their faith in the private owner. In this respect, while a review of the capital-structure mix alone may suggest the extension of additional debt as being infeasible, the creditor may in fact lend the money purely based on confidence in the private ownership of the organization. Second, bankers may not specifically review industry norms but may rely upon their personal experience in determining the amount of debt to be provided. Thus, the banker may have a basic rule of thumb, such as the bank not providing any more capital than the owners provide. In summary, the analysis of the present capital mix relative to the industry norm, while continuing to be an important factor, is altered in light of personal relationships between the private owners and the provider of funds.

The ability to cover fixed financing charges

In examining a corporation's ability to absorb financial charges, a number of approaches have been suggested in the literature, varying from a simple ratio to a probability analysis of cash flows. However, in the context of a small business, the techniques have generally involved a basic ratio analysis. The measures generally used to test the capability of assuming fixed obligations have been the *times-interest-earned* relationship and the *times-fixed-charges-earned* ratio. In measuring the times interest earned, the earnings before interest and taxes are divided by the interest charges. For the times fixed charges earned, the income available for meeting all financial fixed charges is divided by total financial fixed charges. Both of these relationships are indicated below:

$$\text{Times interest earned} = \frac{\text{Earnings before interest and taxes}}{\text{Interest}} \qquad (17\text{-}1)$$

$$\begin{bmatrix} \text{Times} \\ \text{fixed} \\ \text{charges} \\ \text{earned} \end{bmatrix} = \frac{\text{Earnings before interest and taxes}}{\text{Interest} + \begin{bmatrix} \text{Before-tax} \\ \text{preferred} \\ \text{dividends} \end{bmatrix} + \begin{bmatrix} \text{Before-tax} \\ \text{debt sinking} \\ \text{fund payments} \end{bmatrix}} \qquad (17\text{-}2)$$

To illustrate, assume a company has earnings before interest and taxes of $100,000 with a 40 percent marginal tax rate. The current debt level is at $125,000 with an interest rate of 8 percent. In addition, $40,000 in preferred stock is outstanding, having a dividend yield of 10 percent. As a part of the debt agreement, a sinking fund payment of $3,000 is made annually. The computations for the two ratios would be as follows:

$$\text{Times interest earned} = \frac{\$100,000}{\$10,000} = 10X$$

$$\text{Times fixed charges earned} = \frac{\$100,000}{\underbrace{\$10,000}_{\substack{\text{Interest}}} + \underbrace{\$6,667}_{\substack{\text{Before-tax} \\ \text{preferred} \\ \text{dividend}}} + \underbrace{\$5,000}_{\substack{\text{Before-tax} \\ \text{sinking} \\ \text{fund}}}} = 4.61X$$

In view of the fact that the preferred dividend and the sinking fund payment are not tax deductible (paid with after-tax dollars), a before-tax amount must be determined. For instance, to have $4,000 after taxes for the payment of preferred dividends, the firm must earn $6,667 before taxes, computed as [dividends/(1 − tax rate)] = [$4,000/(1 − .4)] = $6,667. In like fashion, the sinking fund requirement on a before-tax basis is computed to be $5,000. Having calculated these ratios, the question then becomes, What is adequate? In response to such a question, management must consider the creditors' perspective as well as their own views relating to the trade-off between expected return and risk. In this effort, reliance upon industry norms for comparison with similar operations and an examination of historical earning levels in order to ascertain subjectively the probability of various levels of earnings would be critical factors.

Relative cost

Naturally, as a financial manager within the small firm searches for additional financing, a comparison of cost among the sources is a natural reaction, with a preference for the source having the cheapest cost. Management within a small company no doubt has a stong desire to minimize its cost of financing, and due recognition should be given to these costs. However, two potential problems may develop if the attempt to minimize costs is carried to its extreme. First, the small entity has only limited ability to shop around for cut-rate deals. In fact, in reality what might initially appear to be the "cheapest" route may have hidden costs attached only to be discovered with the passage of time. Second, as a result of practical problems in measuring the "true" costs of capital, misconceptions may arise. More specifically, identifying the *implicit* costs of financing is difficult, but failure to give recognition to these hidden costs may result in invalid decisions. For instance, if the relative amount of debt is increased, the actual cost would include the explicit cost, as quoted by the banker, plus an implicit cost due to the equity shareholders increasing their required rate of return as financial risk is increased.

Nonfinancial influences of the financial mix

Several nonfinancial factors come into play in determining the financial package; the chief ones are the following: (1) Debt may be the only source available to the small firm regardless of cost; (2) debt does not disturb the voting position of existing shareholders; and (3) *financial flexibility* may not be possible when equity securities are employed.

There are times during the life cycle of many firms when additional equity funds are not available at reasonable costs, but the same firms may have assets that would serve as security for either long- or short-term credit. Also, it should be remembered that many financial institutions are severely limited or completely prohibited from providing equity funds. Firms wishing to use these institutions as a source of funds must use debt in their capital structure. Finally, institutions that have been created or sponsored by the government to aid small businesses make available, at least in the beginning, only debt capital. For example, the Small Business Administration provides only debt financing. Although small business investment corporations ultimately take an ownership position, they rarely do so in the beginning, with a preference for convertible debentures.

Many small- and middle-sized firms employ debt capital in order to preserve control. If equity capital is acquired through the sale of common stock, existing shareholders are required to increase their stockholdings proportionally if they wish to preserve their relative position. Although the problem of control is of little consequence to "managers" of firms whose stock is widely distributed, for the small firm, in which ownership of the stock is concentrated, control is of major consequence in that the right to be an officer rests with the amount of stock held. Thus, many smaller firms resort to the use of debt rather than equity securities. Yet, the owner of the small business should not lose sight of the fact that effective control may be lost or at least significantly diminished through restrictive covenants in the loan agreement.

Every firm operates in a constantly changing economy; therefore, management must continually plan for financial flexibility by being able to contract or expand the amount of capital that is invested in current and/or fixed assets as the need arises. Looking first at the need to reduce capital, a problem may arise when cash cannot be reinvested in profitable projects; that is, if these funds are to remain idle, the rate of return on invested capital declines. If the firm is able to return the "excess" capital to the original investors, the rate of return is unaffected. If a certain portion of debt is used in the firm's financial mix, management can reduce the excess by repaying the debt obligations. On the other hand, in striving to maintain flexibility in the expansion of funds, heavy levels of debt may preclude further debt financing, thereby compelling management to seek out new equity funds, regardless of the existing costs. However, if the debt capacity has not been reached and the market for equity securities is weak, management can use short- or intermediate-term debt to finance the firm's asset requirements and replace the debt either with retained earnings or from the proceeds of stock sold when the market rights itself.

The management of the small operation should consider a number of key elements in finally deciding upon the choice between debt and equity. The foregoing factors certainly do not represent every facet of the analysis but do comprise the major considerations.

Sources of Long-Term Financing

As depicted in Figure 17-2, the business firm in the earlier segment of its business life cycle passes through three primary financing stages. Phase 1, the initial investment, consists of the owner's personal capital, the credit provided by the commercial banker, and a host of miscellaneous sources. Examples of miscellaneous sources in this phase would include (1) savings and loan associations, (2) the Small Business Administration, (3) friends and relatives, (4) leasing companies, and (5) commercial finance companies. These five sources are certainly not intended to be all-inclusive but are only indicative of the types of sources employed by the small-business manager.

The second phase of a young corporation's financial existence may be referred to as the *gap*. During this period, the firm has grown to the level beyond which the owners have the capability to finance all investments; however, the company is not large enough to justify a public offering. Hence, the corporation must place securities with private individuals or groups. As set forth in Figure 17-3, a number of sources for private placements exist and may either be directly placed or come through an investment banker. For

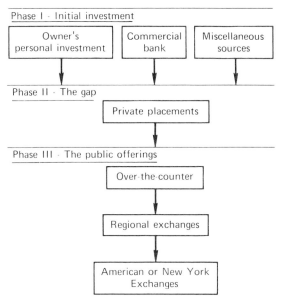

FIGURE 17-2. Business financing stages

instance, financial institutions, private investor groups, and venture capitalists may be approached either directly or through an investment banker acting as a liaison. On the other hand, small business investment companies and large corporations are generally approached directly. Furthermore, the kind of financing available from these respective sources varies, with financial institutions providing primarily debt financing and large corporations offering equity financing. Between these two extremes, a mixture of debt and/or equity capital would be available.

The final stage of development for the small company in terms of long-term financing sources is in the public markets. An in-depth review of this phase is addressed in Chapter 18. Attention is now directed to the primary sources of long-term funds for the small business.

Long-term debt as a source of financing

Assuming the owners have either deleted all available equity funds or have a desire to take advantage of what hopefully will be *favorable financial leverage*, that being a return on assets exceeding the cost of borrowing, the management will no doubt search for debt financing. Potential sources of such financing include (1) commercial banks, (2) life insurance companies, (3) venture capital groups, (4) the Small Business Administration, and (5) miscellaneous debt sources.

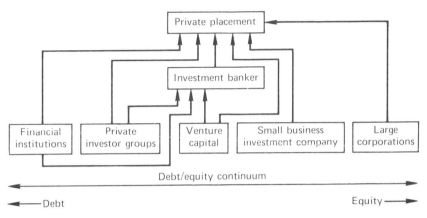

FIGURE 17-3. Sources of Private Placements

commercial banks

Without question, the commercial bank is the leading source of borrowed funds available to the small business. The loans available through the bank are primarily of two types, short-term notes and mortgage loans. However, the short-term instruments, while "formally" being defined as short- to intermediate-term in nature, provide considerable long-term financing for the small business entity. Although statistics indicate that the bank is principally a provider of short-term capital, such figures are misleading. For instance, a loan with a maturity of 90 or 180 days, while being "classified" as short-term, provides long-term financing through regular renewals as the indebtedness approaches the due date. Thus, turning the debt over is a frequent technique by which the owners of a small firm convert short-term financing to an equivalent long-term status. This approach carries with it one distinct disadvantage in that the firm's financing is at the discretion of the banker each time the debt matures, which may produce some anxiety for the small businessman. The second and more formal source of long-term financing is the mortgage loan. These obligations relate to a specific purchase of real estate that is employed in securing the financing arrangement.

In making the decision whether or not to loan the firm any capital, the banker's analysis will naturally vary depending on the bank's philosophy and the levels of sophistication on the part of the investigator. However, a number of basic factors are generally given attention by the banker with varying degrees of emphasis. First, the organization's management, both in terms of quality and structure, represents a cornerstone in the banker's analysis. Second, the corporation's financial position, including the adequacy of the accounting system necessary for accurately measuring the firm's financial status, is also of key import. Third, if the ability of the company to repay the loan is closely tied to the success or failure of the product or services being provided, the marketing phase of the business enterprise becomes of serious interest, particularly in terms of product demand. Finally, the security of the loan is important, with the banker gaining a more secure position by relying upon either the security of specific assets or the personal worth of the ownership of the firm. Thus, while a bank may be unwilling to loan the funds solely on the business prospects, the loan may be made based on the personal signature of the president of the company or through the refinancing of personal assets of such an individual. Furthermore, restrictive provisions may be incorporated into the terms of the loan, such as stipulations for minimal working capital levels, requirements for financial statements and audits, and limitations in the use of the loan proceeds, with possible restrictions in the pledging of assets to other creditors.

In relying upon the bank as a source of funds, the small businessman should develop a relationship with the banker prior to the actual need for funds. Ideally, the interaction should be both on a professional and personal basis. As a part of the relationship, the company owner should be completely open with the banker. Only in this way can the banker be of maximum effectiveness in providing services. The concealment of relevant facts, whether or not such omission would be considered fraudulent, should be avoided. Also, in maintaining an association with the banker, the manager should continue to examine the benefits being received. In so doing, company ownership should be aware of the services being provided by competitive banks as well as the costs related to these services. Nevertheless, the affiliation with a banker is not purely a function of the interest rate being charged but relates to a number of factors. Thus, the mere fact that a bank is charging a slightly higher interest rate does not necessarily justify changing banks. A long-term relationship is important, especially in tight monetary conditions or if the firm temporarily encounters adversity. Finally, an inquiry into the special expertise of the banker and the bank's capabilities in terms of loan size should be examined. The firm's owners should seek out a bank having particular expertise in their type of operation. Stated differently, not only is the accessibility of capital important, but also a source of counseling may be of substantial benefit. Also, the selection of a bank should also be a function of the size of the bank. If large sums of money are to be required, a small bank may not have the capacity to service such loans. On the other hand, if the credit requirements are not so extensive, a small bank in which the corporate executive has access to the key bank officers may be quite beneficial.

insurance companies

The executive of the small corporation may find an insurance company to be a viable source of financing. As a financial intermediary, an insurance firm has large sums of money available for investments. Although only a small portion of such funds are available for the small firm, to the extent such funds may be used, the extension of credit generally comes in the form of a mortgage loan. Hence, the life insurance company may be a potential long-term source of financing for a small firm planning the construction of a real estate investment, such as a plant or office. In examining the request for a loan, the insurance firm looks closely at the type of building being constructed, with a preference for a facility having potential multiple uses. As to the size of loans, most insurance firms are interested in making loans in large amounts; however, loans for as little as $10,000 have been granted. In general, mortgage loans extend over a 10- to 20-year period, with the amount of the mortgage being limited to approximately 70 percent of the appraised value of the property.

In addition to the mortgage loan, the insurance corporation may issue credit on an unsecured long-term basis to the borrower having unquestionable integrity and an excellent credit rating. In such circumstances, the historical and potential financial strength of the debtor would have to be quite evident. Such loans, if granted, generally extend for periods of ten years with an interest rate exceeding that of the bank by 1 to 2 percent.

In applying for a loan with an insurance organization, the borrower should be aware of the relevant regulatory stipulations. Such requirements would include (1) the corporate form of doing business by the company, (2) a minimum number of years that the borrower has conducted business, and (3) demonstrated historical and present earnings records. Also, information may be required relating to projected cash and operating budgets, plans indicating the intended application of the funds being borrowed, sales forecasts by product line or service line, and background information relating to the corporate management.

If an insurance company is utilized as a source of funds, a number of restrictive covenants may be attached to the loan. These requirements would incorporate stipulations for meeting state regulations, maintenance of a specified working capital level, limitations on debt, restrictions limiting the level of cash dividends and salaries, and constraints in the purchasing of fixed assets. Thus, if insurance company funds are to be granted, the small company may have to accept restrictions that at times are burdensome.[2]

venture capital companies

If a financing package comprised of debt financing is presented to a venture capitalist, two concerns exist for the venture capital investors. First, the prospective investors may insist upon covenants in order to protect themselves in the event that the financial condition of the firm either deteriorates or does not materialize as anticipated. These covenants, similar

---

[2]Harry Gross, *Financing for Small- and Medium-Sized Businesses,* (Englewood Cliffs, N. J.: Prentice-Hall, 1969), pp. 151–153.

to the protective restrictions of a bank loan, are particularly common in start-up situations, with effective control of the organization being more easily lost through default on these long-term covenants than through the loss of majority ownership of the equity shares.

A second ingredient involving debt financing with a venture capitalist is the trade-off between the interest rate and the conversion privilege. The utilization of debt by venture capital investors generally involves a convertibility feature or bonds with warrants attached. By attaching either warrants or a conversion privilege, a significant reduction in interest charges usually results. For a small growth corporation this reduction in interest payments is not only desirable but critically essential, since most small businesses may have difficulty in meeting the interest requirements associated with straight debt.

Small Business Administration

Recognizing the importance of small business in the economy, Congress created the Small Business Administration in 1953 with the express purpose to "...aid, counsel, assist, protect in as far as is possible the interest of small business concerns." In attempting to fulfill this stated purpose, the SBA has provided a number of services, among which is assistance in satisfying the needs of small businesses for intermediate- and long-term funds. If a firm is unable to qualify on an independent basis for private commercial financing, the SBA attempts to service the company's financial requirements. The SBA loans may be either "direct" or involve a "participation" with a commercial bank. Five basic categories of loans exist:

1. Direct loans not exceeding $100,000 may be acquired provided certain qualifications are met and adequate collateral is available.
2. Bank participation loans are made in which the SBA supplies up to 75 percent of the loan required, not to exceed $150,000.
3. Displaced business loans represent financing made to firms displaced by federally funded programs.
4. Economy opportunity loans are available for physically handicapped persons or minority groups for establishing a small business under the economic opportunity program.
5. Guaranteed loans are available in which the commercial bank services the loan at standard interest rates, with the SBA providing a 90 percent guarantee.

As an overview of the government's role in the financing of small enterprises, Table 17-2 is provided. As may be witnessed from the table, the role of government in small business finance has increased notably. For example, total government financing and the SBA support has increased in excess of 100 percent since the beginning of the 1970s. Yet, the financial

TABLE 17-2

The Government's Role in Small Business Lending

Fiscal year	Number of loans	Millions of dollars	
		Total amount	SBA share[1]
1960	3,707	$ 173.5	$ 148.9
1961	5,062	261.3	225.1
1962	6,373	380.6	316.7
1963	6,282	337.6	265.8
1964	6,537	342.1	275.6
1965	14,034	472.4	391.1
1966	12,686	444.7	371.9
1967	11,830	504.5	420.0
1968	13,100	624.3	505.7
1969	14,523	699.3	570.1
1970	15,102	709.6	596.0
1971	21,495	1,122.7	963.2
1972	28,025	1,573.8	1,360.8
1973	33,948	2,196.2	1,915.8
1974	27,485	1,947.3	1,698.6
1975[2]	20,280	1,442.3	1,259.8

[1]Includes both direct loans and guarantees.
[2]Estimate.
SOURCE: Cited in "Small Business: The Maddening Struggle to Survive," *Business Week*, June 30, 1975, p. 101.

support afforded by the SBA and other government agencies continues to represent only a small segment of the financial requirements for small businesses. Furthermore, the delay in loan approvals by the SBA has lengthened significantly, with the average processing time now averaging 29 days, which at times causes timing problems for the executive of a small business.

Small Business Investment Companies (SBICs)

A small business investment company, one form of a venture capital organization, does extend long-term loans, usually in excess of $75,000 for periods exceeding five years. Historically, the loans have been in high-technology industries, involving medium-sized operations. In addition, the firm normally must have a "track record" in terms of proven profit capabilities and growth potential. An in-depth explanation of the SBICs is offered in the next section.

Equity financing in the small business

The term *equity* relates to the investment of both preferred and common stockholders in a company. The amount of investment of these two categories of shareholders is reflected in the capital stock, capital surplus, and retained earnings accounts within the balance sheet. Common equity represents the portion of total equity identified with the common stockholders. Thus, the equity segment of the firm may be altered as a result of one of three factors: (1) the sale or purchase of the company's preferred stock, (2) the sale or reacquisition of common stock, or (3) a change in retained earnings, which are increased by profits and reduced by any dividends distributed during the period.

preferred stock

Preferred stock is seldom used as a financing instrument by small businesses. However, if such a security is employed, a conversion feature generally accompanies the issue. Although the use of preferred stock does increase the firm's net worth, which is favorable to the creditors, the dividend payment represents a fixed charge. This problem is further accentuated by the fact that such payments are not deductible for tax purposes. However, while a convertible issue may not be of the company's choosing, such an issue does attract investors having a desire for fixed income with the potential opportunity to participate in any prospective growth of the firm.

common stock

The unique characteristic of common stock relates to the shareholders being the residual claimants of (1) all corporate earnings after the payment of operating expenses, financial charges, and taxes and (2) all assets upon liquidation after prior claims have been satisfied. In addition, several advantages and disadvantages exist in the use of common stock.

ADVANTAGES The use of common shares by the small corporation carries with it two basic advantages. First, the equity capital represented by common stock serves as a "cushion" for the creditors, which in turn increases the credit worthiness of the company. Since owners of common stock are the last group to participate in the assets in the event of dissolution, any losses that may be incurred are first absorbed by the common stockholders. A second benefit of common stock comes from there being no fixed financial charges. Since dividends are not mandatory, the firm does not experience "legal" failure upon failing to generate a profit. Thus, increased latitude is provided. In addition, the refinancing process is avoided since a maturity date is not forthcoming. However, even though there are several sound reasons for using common stock, several disadvantages are incurred by the small firm attempting to employ common stock in the financing process.

DISADVANTAGES   The difficulties in making use of common stock as a source of capital may be classified into two categories, these being the problems associated with issuing common equity, regardless of the size of the business concern, versus disadvantages having a direct relationship to the firm's size. In looking first at the problem areas that are relatively independent of company size, the following items could be cited:

1. The tax deductibility of interest payments places debt financing at a distinct cost advantage.
2. Unless management is careful in establishing the price of a new issue of common stock, existing shareholders may lose a portion of their net worth. Specifically, when new shares are sold for a price less than the book value of the stock outstanding, the old stockholders in effect are transferring part of their net worth to the new shareholders.
3. Since common stock shares equally in the income, management cannot increase the return on equity capital except by increasing the overall return on investment or by trading more heavily on the equity. In the latter instance, the additional financial risk incurred could create potential problems.

In addition to the foregoing problems, difficulties may develop that are of particular relevance to the small firm. These problems tend to surface when the equity requirements of a small growth firm exceed the owner-manager's capabilities to provide such funds. In such circumstances, the need may arise for the existing common stockholders to issue common equity to "outside" investors. In such a setting, several problems may arise:

1. As the result of a lack in marketability of most securities of small firms, particularly common stock, it may be necessary to price the stock so that it will yield a significantly higher return than a similar firm having a ready market for its shares. Naturally, such a practice results in the cost of common capital sharply increasing.
2. The flotation cost of selling a small issue, particularly in the public markets, becomes almost prohibitive for the small firm. For instance, such expenses may approach 25 percent of the issue size.
3. Issuing common securities to external investors permits a potential dilution of control for existing shareholders. Although such a loss may be only psychological, experience indicates that most small owners are quite averse to placing themselves in a position that even slightly compromises their control over the firm.

FORMS OF COMMON STOCK   Common stock may be *classified* in terms of the shareholders claim on income, claim on assets, and voting rights. Typically, Class A stock has a higher claim on dividend income and assets but less extensive voting power, even to the point of voting being nonexistent. In contrast, Class B common stock has a lesser claim on income and assets but greater voting power. This classification mechanism permits the owners to maintain greater control or be able to attract outside investors by providing greater income and protection upon liquidation. In the same context, "founders' shares" have been used by small business. These shares are similar to a Class B stock except that the owners of the shares maintain the sole voting rights but generally have no right to dividends for specified number of years. The objective of founders' shares is to permit the organizers of a company to maintain complete control of the corporation during the early years of the operation, often with a minimal investment being required.

venture capital and the small business

A complete understanding of equity markets in the small business context requires a grasp of the functioning of the venture capital industry.

THE NATURE OF VENTURE CAPITAL INVESTING   No one precise definition may be given for *venture capital investing*. The term simply has different connotations to different individuals. While Webster defines a venture as "an undertaking involving chance, risk, or danger, especially a speculative business enterprise," such a definition is not operational in that someone might interpret such an explanation as being limited to start-up businesses. Venture capital is more inclusive. In fact, a spectrum of definitions exists for venture capital investing, along with some basic characteristics of venture investors which better delineate the nature of venture capital than does a single definition. In this context, a number of definitions could be cited, with four such explanations being as follows:

1. Providing capital for any high-risk financial venture.
2. Providing "seed capital" for a start-up situation.
3. Investing in a firm that is unable to raise capital from conventional sources.
4. Investing in large publicly traded corporations where the risk is significant.[3]

As to which definition might be optimal depends in part on the "eyes of the beholder." For instance, certain venture capitalists consider seed money as being entirely too risky for venture capital. On the other hand, others would contend that such start-up capital is the primary intent of their investments. Thus, generalities become difficult. However, without being able to specify such an objective, three underlying attributes do generally prevail with venture capital investing. First, the investor is usually "locked in" to the firm for some duration of time, without an opportunity to sell stock quickly in response to a change in the company's position, either favorable or unfavorable. Second, the venture capitalist normally represents the first equity financing from an "independent" party, as opposed to a friend or relative. However, additional financing may be required at a later date on the part of

---

[3]See Patrick R. Liles, "Venture Capital: What It Is and How To Raise It," *New Business Ventures and the Entrepreneur*, (Homewood, Ill.: Irwin, Inc., 1974), p. 461.

the venture capitalist. Finally, venture capital investors have divergent interests. Hence, an investment having no appeal to one venture capital group might be of extreme interest to other venture investors. For this reason, the management of a company seeking funds should be aware of the compatibility of interests of the firm and the venture capitalist being approached.

TYPES OF VENTURE CAPITAL SOURCES   Although the "types" of venture capital sources could be expanded almost indefinitely, a number of major sources may be briefly described:

1. *Small business investment corporations (SBICs).* When the SBA was established in 1953, attention was directed to the long-term debt and equity financial requirements of the small business; however, no governmental action was taken at that time. Finally, in 1958 the Federal Reserve completed a study, concluding that the banks and the SBA were satisfactorily meeting the short-term and intermediate debt requirements of the small businessman but that the small firm was encountering an ever-increasing need for longer-term loans and equity financing.[4] After extensive hearings, SBICs were established as private profit-seeking companies to be regulated by the SBA. As a means of encouraging private individuals or institutions to initiate these organizations, government loans were to be granted on favorable terms and tax advantages were offered.[5]

At the present time, slightly more than 300 SBICs exist, down from over 600 such operations, with assets ranging from $300,000 to $20 million. The objectives and the operational philosophies of the various SBICs are extremely dissimilar, making it difficult to describe SBICs in a general context. However, a basic classification does exist in terms of *captive* and *noncaptive* SBICs, in which the management of a captive SBIC is dictated by the objectives of a parent organization, usually a bank. In contrast, the noncaptive SBICs operate independently, with ownership ranging from several private individuals or institutions to a broadly based public. Despite being able to segment SBICs into two categories, large disparities within either group remain, depending on the management.

Regarding the nature of financing, most SBICs are interested in equity participation via convertible debentures. Such securities generally carry a 5- to 20-year maturity date. The interest rates are quite divergent depending on the growth potential of the company; however, if no conversion privilege is attached, an interest rate, if acceptable at all, would approach 15 percent. The size of loans is limited by several factors, including the willingness of the

[4]U. S. Federal Reserve System, *Financing Small Business*, Parts 1 and 2, Report to the U. S. Congress, Committee on Currency and Banking and the Select Committees on Small Business, 85th Congress, 2nd Session, (April 11, 1958), pp. 77–90.

[5]"Providing Risk Capital for Small Business: Experience of the SBIC's," *Quarterly Review of Economics and Business*, (Spring 1975), pp. 77–90.

SBIC management to participate in the financing being requested. In addition to the SBIC's discretion in extending the loan, the SBIC is prevented by regulation from investing more than 20 percent of their capital in a particular venture. Also, the SBIC is not permitted to develop a majority interest in an organization, except as a result of a violation in the terms of the loan. Accordingly, the amount of financing being provided varies with the size of the SBIC, with the smallest SBICs disbursing an average amount of $29,000, while the largest SBICs have provided an average financing of $232,000.[6]

2. *Publicly owned venture capital investment companies.* These organizations are publicly owned by a broad base of investors including companies listed on the New York Stock Exchange. Examples of publicly owned venture capitalists include American Research and Development Corporation, Herizer Corporation, and SMC Investment Corporation. As with other venture capital sources, public companies are quite divergent in their interests and objectives.

3. *Private venture capital investors.* The private venture capital investor is concerned primarily in the development of small enterprises needing long-term capital for growth, companies for sale due to the death or retirement of the owner, or firms requiring professional management. These private companies operate under a high degree of flexibility and therefore may be able to tailor their agreements to meet special situations. These entities are concerned with long-term capital appreciation, in which funds are frequently invested in participation with others to enable the small private venture company to maintain diversity. Thus, private venture capital investors may possibly offer not only another source of venture capital but also an avenue for increased flexibility relative to the publicly owned companies.

4. *Wealthy individuals.* Wealthy persons within the community should be recognized as a viable source of venture capital. If relatively small amounts are required (less than $100,000) and the management of the corporation desiring the funds is well known within the business community, wealthy individuals may be quite receptive to incurring significant risk for the purpose of achieving high expected returns. The attraction becomes even greater if the returns are tax sheltered. The advantage in developing such arrangements relates to the informality and the often negligible formal reporting requirements. Typically, the investors are relying upon their "faith" in the chief executive and not upon long and detailed accounting reports. Yet, management should proceed with caution in the selection of local investors in that such individuals occasionally develop a strong propensity for participating in the management of the firm.

5. *Large corporations.* Approximately 30 corporations have developed formal venture capital operations, with an aggregate amount of capital exceeding $160 million. As to the impetus for large companies entering the

---

[6]"Providing Risk Capital…", pp. 77–90.

venture capital field, two possible reasons might be cited. First, the hopes of striking a capital gains bonanza, such as Scientific Data Systems, no doubt has appeal. However, a second and more probable reason for their entrance is the search for technology, with a potential acquisition in mind. Prime examples of corporate involvement include General Electric, Hercules, Inc., Du Pont, and more recently Sun Oil Company and Johnson and Johnson. However, Du Pont, among others, has withdrawn from the venture capital area. Yet, the large corporate entity should be considered as a potential source of funding, especially when the financial markets have deteriorated.

6. *Other sources.* In addition to the foregoing sources of venture capital financing, an entrepreneur may look to other sources, including (1) community development corporations, (2) local development corporations, (3) the Economic Development Administration, and (4) various state and local agencies. Each of these sources has limitations as to the types of financing to be provided.

ARRANGING VENTURE CAPITAL FINANCING   In arranging for financing with a venture capital group, the corporate management seeking funds should be cognizant of the general perspective of a venture capitalist. For instance, if the public equity market has been encountering losses, such that the new-issues market is inactive, most venture capitalists would prefer a convertible debt issue. In so doing, if no opportunity materializes to sell the common stock when the firm should be ready to make a public offering, the venture capitalist at least has a "senior" security which offers some fixed income with greater protection if liquidation becomes necessary. Another illustration of the venture capital investor's preferences relates to the type of firm being supported both in terms of product and the maturity stage of the organization. In the latter 1960s, highly technical companies were the "favorite sons," as opposed to medical services or leisure companies in more recent times. Furthermore, the emphasis several years ago in start-ups has shifted considerably toward the corporation having at least a limited track record. In summary, the individual searching for venture money has to remain sensitive not only to plans and events indigenous to the company but also to the changing external financial environment.

After the foregoing general considerations have been recognized, attention needs to be given to the particular aspects of interest to the prospective investor that are unique to the firm in question. In other words, when a venture capitalist is considering an investment, what is deemed to be of importance? This question relates directly to the nature and content of the written presentation to be made to the venture capitalist, which has come to be termed the *business plan.*

Formulating a thoughtful, carefully prepared plan of the corporate objectives and strategies, supported by ample documentation, is essential in satisfying the company's financial requirements. By developing such a document, the small business increases its accessibility to financing while minimiz-

TABLE 17-3

The Business Plan

I. The miniproposal
  A. The terms of the issue
  B. The market to be served and the uniqueness of the product/service within this market
  C. The firm's history
  D. The qualifications of management
II. The formal business plan
  A. Introduction
  B. Table of contents
  C. The management
  D. The board of directors
  E. Supporting professional services
  F. Marketing
    1. The market to be served
    2. The products and/or services
    3. The marketing strategy
  G. Research and development
  H. Facilities
  I. Concept in capsule form
III. The Appendix
  A. Sales forecast
  B. Historical and proforma financial statements
  C. Current and projected staff requirements
  D. Current and projected plant requirements
  E. Legal form of business
  F. Founders' resumes
  G. Blanket references
  H. Key publications of founders
  I. Founders' personal financial statements
  J. Founders' compensation

ing the personal efforts of management and economizing the corporate financial resources. These efficiencies are the result of the proposal being a valuable promotional tool as well as an in-depth analysis of the firm's strengths and weaknesses. In fact, a well-prepared business plan offers the firm a certain degree of uniqueness in that too often managements approach prospective investors with ill-conceived ideas or possibly sound but poorly presented thoughts, either of which may be detrimental to the attempt to raise funds.

In constructing the business plan, a number of sources may be of assistance. For instance, attorneys and accountants having had experience with other clients in this regard could be quite helpful. Also business consultants and public relations firms could possibly offer valuable insight. Finally, one should peruse prospectuses for public offerings, business plans of other companies, and public references identifying financial relationships for business organizations of like size and business purposes. Primary sources for relevant financial data would include *Statement Studies* (Robert Morris Associates), *Dun's Review and Modern Industry* (Dun and Bradstreet, Inc.), *Barometer of Small Business* (Accounting Corporation of America), and *Standard and Poor's Industry Surveys*.

As to the structure and content of the proposal, no single approach can be recommended as superior; however, three basic ingredients are generally considered to be necessary, these being the miniproposal, the formal section of the plan, and an appendix offering support to the plan. An outline of a business plan might appear as shown in Table 17-3. In developing the plan, a portion of the proposal in the table may or may not be of significance. Only management's knowledge of its own organization and of the prospective investors can adequately dictate the inclusion or exclusion of a specific item. Thus, Table 17-3 is a possible departure point to be revised in accordance with the situation. In other words, generalities concerning the significance of any section of the plan are difficult to make.

Upon receipt of the proposal, the venture capital investor typically performs a relatively cursory review of the material with the objective being to determine whether or not an in-depth examination is thought to be justified. A complete examination of the plan seldomly occurs. Hence, after investing extensive time and effort in the plan, the small businessman has to be disappointed and even frustrated when finding someone to read the business plan proves difficult. Thus, the question facing the entrepreneur is what procedures may be taken to enhance the probability of finding a readership? Regretfully, the significance of this question may not become apparent to the small business manager until the "damage has been done." In addressing the question, two issues are of prime materiality: (1) the method of distribution of the plan and (2) an awareness on the part of the preparer of the proposal as to the specific components of the presentation that determine the "first impression." The first concern, the distribution process, is best resolved by the plan being delivered personally by an individual having credibility with the venture investor. Mass mailings or delivery of the program by a person unknown to a potential investor is not effective. Also, the actual delivery of the plan should be anticipated by the investor, a result of "preselling" efforts. If the prospective investor is made aware of a viable company six months before the plan is presented, followed by frequent updates of operational developments, the chances of a receptive audience are substantially increased.

In addressing the second interest, the readability of the plan during a preliminary screening, the management of the small firm would need to know the examination process. Such information is generally not available. However, some commonalities exist between most venture capitalists in their review process that should be recognized in constructing the content and format of the plan.[7] In a relatively quick manner, the venture capital investor is interested in ascertaining the characteristics of the company and the related industry, noting the terms of the financing proposal, identifying the basic financial condition of the firm as reflected in the balance sheet, determining the quality of the corporate leadership, and discovering what, if any, characteristics differentiate this business from the remaining companies within the industry. Having this information along with possible other data of interest, a decision is made whether or not to continue the investigation.

If interest remains after the first pass at the business plan, a scrutinizing examination is then undertaken. As with the initial screening, speculation as to the relative importance of the respective portions of the plan is hazardous. Yet, experience does offer limited insight into the general framework of most investors considering a commitment of funds. First and foremost are the *qualifications* and *breadth* of the management team. Second, and of approximately equivalent interest, are the financial aspects of the operations. Last, the venture capitalist analyzes closely the marketing sector of the firm. Beyond these criteria, attention is directed to a host of other relevant considerations as perceived by the investigator. Yet, the foregoing underlying issues (management, finance, and marketing) may be expected to be instrumental in the majority of accept-reject decisions.

retention of earnings as a source of financing

The last source of long-term financing, while not having the glamour of a stock offering or the excitement of negotiating with a venture capitalist, is of primary importance to the small company. Unquestionably, the retention of earnings is a major source of equity financing for any organization, regardless of size. As shown in Table 17-4, even for the largest corporations, with assets exceeding $1 billion, approximately 55 percent of company earnings were retained. Additionally, 40.8 percent of the book value of these giants' financial mix is comprised of accumulated retained earnings. This significant contribution results from the fact that even the large firms seldom issue new common stock but rather rely heavily upon the retention of profits as a means of building an equity base for company growth. Thus, large corporations do rely heavily upon internally generated funds. Yet, in comparison, the small business entity draws even more heavily upon profits in financing its growth. Specifically, an inverse relationship between size and the percentage of profits being retained for reinvestment is clearly evident in Table 17-4. Although accumulated earned surplus does not represent so large a proportion of the small companies' capital structure, this lower percentage

---

[7]For a more thorough explanation of the screening procedures of venture capitalists, see Joseph R. Mancuso, "How a Business Plan Is Read," *Business Horizons*, (Aug. 1974), pp. 33–42.

TABLE 17-4

Profit Retention Relative to Asset Sizes

Total Assets

	Under $1 Million	$1–$5 Million	$5–$10 Million	$10–$25 Million	$25–$50 Million	$50–$100 Million	$100–$250 Million	$250–$1,000 Million	Over $1,000 Million	All asset sizes
Cumulative retained earnings relative to total assets[1]	30.65%	35.15%	38.23%	36.08%	34.13%	36.15%	33.98%	35.00%	40.80%	37.95%
Percentage of earnings retained in the firm[2]	80.07%	81.59%	81.18%	83.40%	78.03%	70.22%	67.78%	60.02%	54.80%	62.42%

[1]The period ends March 31, 1976.
[2]The time period includes April 1, 1975 through March 31, 1976.
SOURCE: Federal Trade Commission, *Quarterly Financial Report*, (Washington, D. C.: U. S. Government Printing Office, June 16, 1976).

has to be due, at least in part, to the fewer years of existence of most smaller businesses. In brief, the data support the relatively well-known fact that small firms do rely more extensively upon retained earnings as a source of equity financing.

The relative retention rates hold implications regarding the dividend policies of the different-sized companies. Granting the assumption that perfect markets do not exist in the financial community, the firm's dividend policy is believed to be a function of two factors. First, the corporation's investment opportunities should be a key input into the dividend decision. If the expected returns from prospective investments exceed the organization's cost of capital, an incentive exists to retain greater amounts and therefore pay less dividends. Reciprocally, poor investments suggest higher dividend payments. Second, the common stockholders' preference for dividends versus capital gains is given as an important variable in ascertaining the appropriate dividend strategy. Inducements frequently noted for the distribution of profits include the favorable informational content associated with an investor receiving a dividend, the resolution of uncertainty, and the preference for current income.

The foregoing incentives for the payment of dividends for a large company having a broad base of stockholders may not be so relevant for the small business. For instance, the informational content from dividends might be of importance to a "distant" investor in a large enterprise but is meaningless to the stockholders in the small firm, who are also actively involved in the management of the operations. Also, the small businessman would not appear to be so concerned about the resolution of uncertainty as might be the individual who is strictly an investor seeking a given return. The small-company owner-manager continues to have the opportunity to act as a decision maker with respect to the risk-return relationship without having to receive the monies in the form of dividends. Thus, on a purely intuitive basis, this potential lack of a preference for dividends, complemented by a strong incentive to minimize taxes, would appear to explain the larger retention of earnings by the smaller companies.

Summary

In making the financial mix decision, the first issue to be resolved is the appropriate maturity structure. The criterion by which this issue should be examined frequently plagues the small businessman, either due to the prevailing environment or as a consequence of the manager's failure to be cognizant of a relatively simple but often overlooked principle. Subsequent to determining the maturity structure, the relevant factors may then be examined for ascertaining the desired debt/equity mix. With these standards in mind, the small-business management may approach a variety of potential financing sources. In attempting to attract prospective investors, the executive should have made an effort to determine the interests and evaluation procedures of the investment group being approached. Finally, the particular importance and necessity of retained earnings to the small firm as a means for building an equity base should be recognized.

QUESTIONS

1. Explain the criterion for determining whether a proposed financing should be long-term or short-term with respect to the structure.

2. Define *trading on the equity*.

3. What consideration must be recognized in using the relative costs as a determinant for choosing between debt and equity financing?

4. Explain the types of financing that might be available from
   a. Banks.
   b. Insurance companies.
   c. Venture capitalists.
   d. Small business investment companies.

5. What disadvantages exist with common stock as a source of financing? Which of these disadvantages are particularly relevant for the small firm?

6. Explain the different forms of common stock.

7. Describe the nature of the venture capital industry.

8. Designate the process in arranging for venture capital financing.

9. Why is the retention of earnings greater in small companies?

PROBLEMS

17-1. Scott Corporation currently has $200,000 in total assets and has been able to maintain a before-tax return on investment of 12 percent. Currently, the firm has no debt outstanding and pays taxes at a 50 percent rate.

   a. What would be the impact upon the stockholders' rate of return if $50,000 of common stock is retired and long-term debt (8 percent) is issued?
   b. Assuming an additional $60,000 in common stock is repurchased, with a corresponding $60,000 in debt being issued (12 percent), what would the return on equity be? (Debt now totals $110,000, with $50,000 costing 8 percent and $60,000 having a 12 percent rate.)
   c. Assume a downturn in the economy occurs, resulting in a 4 percent return on assets. Compare the return on equity with all equity and if $50,000 debt is issued.
   d. Comment on the implications of the foregoing results.

17-2. Compute the times fixed charges for Griggs, Inc. The company has $500,000 in total assets and earnings before interest and taxes of $50,000. The appropriate tax rate is 48 percent. The company has a 25 percent debt-to-total-asset ratio, with its debt having an 8 percent rate. Also, 10 percent preferred stock is outstanding in the amount of $30,000. The debt has an annual sinking fund requirement of $5,000.

chapter 18

GOING PUBLIC

Public sources of financing, generally available to large corporations, may also be accessible to smaller firms provided certain conditions exist, including a large amount of creativity on the part of corporate personnel. While the sources of funds cited earlier in the text represent the principal avenues for financing, the small, closely held growth firm may eventually have to rely upon the general public for additional funds. Such a decision to *go public* should be approached both cautiously and with adequate knowledge regarding the potential benefits and pitfalls. All too often a firm has attempted to enter the public market only to be faced with insurmountable barriers, resulting in an unpleasant experience even to the point of hindering future growth.

In analyzing the process of *going public*, a natural departure point is a definition, or, more precisely, a clarification of the term itself. What is going public? This terminology, in a legal context, is defined with difficulty due to the numerous peripheral technical questions. However, in general going public simply relates to the procedures involved in selling the securities of a privately owned firm. The securities sold may be shares belonging to the owners of the company, that being a *secondary distribution*, or the company itself may sell additional shares to raise new capital.[1] The latter acquisition of public owners is of prime concern to the financial manager as a source of funds to finance growth.

In this chapter we shall first review the historical trends for going public. Next, an evaluation of the merits and demerits of the public offering is given, followed by the desired characteristics of the corporation seeking public funds. Third, securities regulations are briefly described. Last, the public-offering procedures are highlighted, with a particular emphasis upon the investment banker's role in the process.

---

[1]Louis H. Rappaport, *SEC Accounting Practice and Procedure*, 3rd ed. (New York: Ronald, 1972), p. 6-1.

Going Public: Recent Trends

Going public, particularly for the smaller enterprise, is an extremely cyclical phenomenon. As noted in Table 18-1, the number of effective registrations peaked in 1969, fell back in 1970 and 1971, coming back to reach an all-time high in 1972 only to begin a downward slide of 25 percent during the following three years. Reflecting back upon the 1970–1975 period, several items are of interest. During 1970, the market made a recovery, with the average price of new issues showing a strong comeback in the ensuing year. For example, as of February 1971, the average price of the 417 newest public issues had increased from a July 1970 low of $4.91 to $8.64, a 75 percent increase in only an eight-month time period. Accordingly, the investment banker's interest in new issues naturally increased. As the partner of an underwriting firm commented, "All the boys are back again. How quickly it changes. Stock salesmen who not long ago were ready to jump off the World Trade Center now are out again with their smiles and shovels."[2] Accordingly, a number of companies were thought to be reviving their plans for a new issue. However, despite the 1971 enthusiasm, the new-issues market did not

TABLE 18-1

Effective Registrations
(dollars in millions)

Fiscal year ended June 30	Total Number	Total Value	Common stock	Cash sale for account of issuers Bonds, debentures, and notes	Preferred stock	Total
1965	1,266	$19,437	$10,638	$ 3,710	$ 307	$14,656
1966	1,523	30,109	18,218	7,061	444	25,723
1967	1,649	34,218	15,083	12,309	558	27,950
1968	2,417	54,076	22,092	14,036	1,140	37,269
1969	3,645	86,810	39,614	11,674	751	52,039
1970	3,389	59,137	28,939	18,436	823	48,198
1971	2,989	69,562	27,455	27,637	3,360	58,452
1972	3,712	62,487	26,518	20,127	3,237	49,882
1973	3,285	59,310	26,615	14,841	2,578	44,034
1974	2,890	56,924	19,811	20,997	2,274	43,082
1975	2,780	77,457	30,502	37,557	2,201	70,250

SOURCE: *Securities and Exchange Commission Annual Report*, (Washington, D.C.: Superintendent of Documents, U.S. Government Printing Office, 1974), p. 167.

[2]Charles N. Stablers, staff ed., "Going Public," *Wall Street Journal*, (Feb. 26, 1971), p. 1.

TABLE 18-2

Offerings Under Regulation A

	Fiscal year			
Size	*1975*	*1974*	*1973*	*1972*
$100,000 or less	28	40	69	52
$100,000 to $200,000	42	79	107	46
$200,000 to $300,000	39	66	96	118
$300,000 to $400,000	24	39	86	182
$400,000 to $500,000	132	214	459	689
Total	265	438	817	1,087

SOURCE: *Securities and Exchange Commission Annual Report*, (Washington, D. C.: Superintendent of Documents, U.S. Government Printing Office, 1974), p. 167.

revitalize until 1972. Following 1972, the optimism turned to disinterest, shifted to pessimism, and finally encountered a broad-base deterioration that has continued to exist through 1976. Consequently, for all practical purposes, the public market has been closed to the small firm.

In addition to the general cyclical pattern in new offerings, an even more accentuated variation in public issues occurs for the small company. As evidenced in Table 18-1, the number of registrations fell more sharply than did the dollar value, signifying a larger reduction in small equity registrations. In fact, practically all of the decline in the number of 1974 and 1975 filings was accounted for in the reduction of first-time registrants. Finally, in viewing Table 18-2, the number of offerings under Regulation A for *small issues* diminished by 75 percent during the 1972–1975 period, a rate threefold that of the reduction in the overall number of issues. In summary, the public issues of smaller companies are acutely sensitive to the general market conditions.

Inherent Problems in Going Public

In examining the question of whether or not to go public, the owner of a small business should give considerable thought to such a decision. While the prestige accompanying a public security is a strong inducement to the owner of a closely held corporation, disillusionment may well set in during the offering process and/or the ensuing years of the "public life." Caveats to be given to the individual appraising the desirability of going public with a corporation would be as follows.

Time and cost requirements

The registration process carries with it a substantial commitment on the part of management both in terms of time and expense. In terms of time, management has to be prepared to allocate a significant portion of its efforts to the task for some six months preceding the actual sale. This estimate would not include the preliminary work and thought required for at least two years prior to the first offering.

With respect to the issuing costs (legal, accounting, underwriting, filing fees, and printing), management will expend a significant sum of money in completing the public offering. Such costs would include

1. *Legal fees*, representing the costs associated with the legal preparation of the registration statement, finalizing the underwriter agreement, and a host of administrative details such as a recapitalization of the firm's financial mix and modifying the corporate bylaws. These expenses for a first offering generally vary between $25,000 and $40,000.
2. *Accounting expenses*, primarily related to the certified audits of a company preparing a public issue. As would be expected, these expenses vary, depending on the nature of the business and whether or not the examination in question is a first audit. Assuming no prior audits and the engagement of new accountants, fees begin at a $25,000 to $40,000 price range.
3. *Printing costs*, with the amount depending on the length and the number of copies of the prospectus being prepared for distribution, the complexity of the financial statements, the amendments to the registration statement, the relative location of the printer, and the time constraints imposed upon the printer. Printing expenses range from $15,000 to $30,000, with the majority of cases being closer to the upper $30,000 figure.[3]
4. *Underwriting fees*, usually measured in terms of the spread between the price the underwriter pays the issuer and the price expected to be received from the public. This spread allows for compensation to the selling group, a management fee for the managing underwriter, an allowance for miscellaneous expenses, and a fee for the risk assumed by the underwriter. The cost is a function of the quality and size of the issue, the nature of the industry, the reputation of the issuer, and the general market conditions, especially as related to new issues. A typical discount associated with a first offering might be as low as 7 to 9 percent for a $3 million issue and 15 percent for a "small' $500,000 public offering.[4]
5. *Other expenses* associated with a public offering, including (a) a registration filing fee approximating .02 percent of the offering price, (b) issue and transfer taxes, (c) Blue Sky filing fees of between $1,500 and $2,500, (d)

[3]Carl W. Schneider and Joseph M. Manko, "Going Public," *Villanova Law Review*, Vol. 15 (Winter 1970), pp. 283–312, as revised in Sept. 1977 by the original authors in collaboration with Robert S. Kant.

[4]Brian Sullivan, "An Introduction to Going Public," *Journal of Accountancy*, Vol. 120 (Nov. 1965), pp. 48–53.

registrar and transfer-agent fees of at least $1,000, (e) the National Associa-
tion of Securities Dealers, Inc. (NASD) filing fee costing as much as $5,000,
(f) an expense allowance for the underwriter, and (g) indemnity insurance
with premiums being about 1 percent of the amount of coverage.[5]

As a result of the foregoing expenses, the feasibility of a small issue may
become questionable. For example, as shown in Table 18-3, the total costs
incurred in going public for a $500,000 offering could easily reach $146,100,
representing 29 percent of the funds being sought. Although these individual
amounts may not prove to be accurate in a single instance, this variation does
not take away from the fact that substantial costs are encountered in the
going-public process, especially in underwriting, legal, accounting, and printing expenses.

TABLE 18-3

Potential Public-Offering Expenses
(for a $500,000 issue)

Underwriting expenses:	
Commissions	$ 50,000
Legal fees	8,000
Advertising	5,000
Miscellaneous	4,000
Printing costs	15,000
Legal fees	30,000
Accounting fees	25,000
Blue Sky expenses	2,000
Registration	100
Issue taxes and sundry	6,000
Transfer Agent's fees	1,000
Total expenses	$146,100

Disclosure

As an aftermath of the public offering, the principal owner-manager is
not in a position to administer the operations in the personal manner typical
of the small closely held enterprise. Publication of many facets of the
concern's activities is required by the regulatory authorities, not only at the
outset of the issue but also on an annual basis. Such disclosure of "inside"
transactions are not only bothersome at times to the life style of the small
owner but generally represent a significant cost of reporting for the firm, both

[5]See Richard W. Jennings and Harold Marsh, *Securities Regulations: Cases and
Materials*, (New York: The Foundation Press, Inc., 1972), pp. 147–148.

in effort and money. Illustrations of recent SEC disclosure requirements could range from efforts to compel bank-holding companies to reveal information relating to weak loans to requisites for detailing the sources of revenues within a corporate entity.[6] Furthermore, the registration statement necessitates information regarding the income of officers and directors and "insider" transactions in the company's securities. In short, management has to be willing to increase substantially the level of information being provided the public, including information previously thought to be confidential for competitive reasons.

Reduction in flexibility in major decisions

While most executives of small growth firms have become accustomed to making decisions quickly and decisively with little thought having to be given to the opinion of others, going public can modify significantly the decision-making process. The acquisition of stockholder approval is required for a public firm in such matters as stock option plans, acquisitions, and major modifications of the company's capital structure. The new formality does delay the timeliness of management's decisions, which may be a "thorn in the flesh" to the aggressive decision maker. Additional inflexibility may develop through a potential misplaced emphasis upon the short-term effects of decisions, especially as these decisions have an immediate impact upon the company's stock price. Thus, a temptation may exist to forgo long-term investments in favor of shorter-lived projects.

Formal dividend policy

Prior to the involvement of the public in a corporation, the concern's dividend decisions may be largely a function of investment opportunities and tax considerations. For these reasons, the payments may occur irregularly. However, the aftereffect of the public issue would include the requirement for maintaining a more stable dividend policy. For the public firm, the omission of a dividend can have a devastating impact upon the market price of the company's stock, a result ill afforded by any operation, much less a growth business.

Liability of directors and officers

The liability for directors and officers is significantly increased when a corporation becomes a public entity. The strong tendency for individuals or groups to sue corporations places the senior personnel and directors of public firms in a precarious situation. Although insurance may be purchased to cover this increased liability, the premiums are expensive.

[6]Kenneth H. Bacon, staff ed., "Telling All, Full-Disclosure Push by SEC on Companies Worries Some Critics," *Wall Street Journal*, (May 15, 1975), pp. 1, 23.

An unpredictable source of financing

As a last item associated with going public, the public market has to be recognized as being a relatively unreliable source of funds. While the larger organizations must be sensitive to the conditions of the general stock market, the smaller issuers face an extra dimension, that being the status of "hot issues." The market may be relatively bullish but may not be receptive to the issue of a new and/or smaller business. As already noted, experience indicates the interest of the public market in smaller firms to be highly volatile.

In summary, no easy path is available for a small firm desiring to go public. This fact is emphasized in a study in which individuals having recently been through the process were questioned as to the problems faced on their part.[7] As reflected in Table 18-4, the disadvantage identified almost unanimously by management is the sizable amount of time taken from the manager's schedule. Also, in excess of one-half of the executives being sampled complained of the costs of floating the issue, the difficulty in the determination of an appropriate price for the offering, and the substantive disclosure requirements being imposed upon the firm. As a further indication of the significance of the unanticipated difficulties encountered by small corporations in "bearding the lion's den" to the public market, business leaders of corporations having gone public during the ten-year time span ending in 1971 were asked if the opportunity to go public were at their discretion again, would they do so? Sixty percent of the company managements responded negatively. Thus, a serious and thorough examination of whether or not to go public cannot be emphasized too much.

TABLE 18-4

Difficulties of the Public Offering

Problem area	Percentage response
Amount of key management time consumed in underwriting	91%
Unanticipated costs of the underwriting	58%
Pricing of the issue	52%
Amount of disclosure in prospectus	51%

SOURCE: Gramme K. Howard, Jr., "Going Public When It Makes Sense," *Guide to Venture Capital Sources*, 3rd ed., ed. by Stanley M. Rubel (Chicago: Capital Publishing Corporation, 1974), p. 76.

[7]Gramme K. Howard, Jr., "Going Public When It Makes Sense," *Guide to Venture Capital Sources*, 3rd ed., ed. by Stanley M. Rubel (Chicago: Capital Publishing Corporation, 1974), p. 76.

Reasons for Going Public

While the number of public offerings has been reduced significantly in the recent past, this source of financing continues to be a major ingredient for a limited number of corporations. Why would a company go public, or, in other words, what benefits are deemed to result from such offerings? In this context, numerous reasons are typically cited. However, before directing attention to the advantages of a public offering to the firm, an important fact should be recognized. For the advantages to materialize, one key reason must be noted for entrance into the public market, that being the *evident justification* for needed funds combined with an apparent shortage of other sources of capital. Typically, the management/owners rely upon the retention of earnings or the investment of private funds for additional equity funds. Only subsequent to the depletion of these two equity sources would the corporation normally turn to the public for additional equity capital. In other words, the public market is typically an *avenue of last resort* from the corporate perspective. With this thought in mind, the corporate motivations for a public offering are given below.

An established market for future financing

In addition to the primary impetus for issuing public securities, that being the acquisition of needed funds, several indirect benefits relating to future financing accrue to the business organization. First, when the securities in question become recognized by the investment public, later issues should face a more receptive market. Stated differently, the firm subsequently has increased accessibility to a source of financing. Second, creditors are typically more interested in lending money to firms having a proven market for their common stock. Naturally, the lending institutions view this improved marketability as increasing the options available to the corporation for building a larger equity base. Third, when a corporate entity is attempting to finalize a merger or acquisition, a security having a tested value in the market place becomes an invaluable instrument of negotiation. Most shareholders of an enterprise being merged or acquired are simply not interested in trading their private stock for other private securities.

Encouragement for key personnel

The employment of a stock option plan as an encouragement to key personnel has received considerable attention in the business literature. However, the actual merit of such programs has to be considered somewhat tenuous when a market for the security is nonexistent. Thus, for the concern utilizing stock option plans, going public should provide a more effective employee incentive plan.

Public relations

The broad distribution of a company's stock among the public is thought to afford favorable *publicity*. Such positive exposure is particularly beneficial if the general public comprises not only the shareholders but also the consumer of the firm's products and/or services.

Diversification

Often the owner of a closely held operation has invested his life, both emotionally and materially, in the company. However, if and when the company becomes sufficiently large to justify external equity financing, the owner may wish to diversify, thereby affording an opportunity to broaden the financial base. Yet, such spreading of wealth is typically constrained by the desire to maintain unquestioned control of the business.

Collateral for personal credit

In borrowing on a personal basis, the owner of a firm is in a more favorable position by offering a public security as collateral as opposed to a stock having no public market activity.

Estate planning

Briefly stated, the public ownership of a security significantly minimizes the difficulty of establishing the value of the firm for estate tax purposes.

In summary, an entire host of reasons could be given for the need and/or desire for going public. By no means could the justifications stated above be considered as all-inclusive. However, as a synopsis of the reasons which might be given, as well as their perceived importance, Table 18-5 is provided. While the information comprising the table is somewhat dated, going back to the early 1960s, the results still provide some indication as to the impetus for a firm going public. In examining the exhibit, *financial needs* are seen as being the fundamental reason for a corporation going external for common stock. In this regard, over 50 percent of the chief executives responding to the questionnaire gave financial needs as the rationale for issuing equity securities in the public market. Within this category, working capital requirements appear to be of paramount concern. However, interpretation of the data must be made with caution. So often a business concern will commit all available working capital to a capital expenditure such that the level of working capital becomes deficient. As the corporate leadership then instigates a search for funds, the expressed justification is the need for additional working capital, although the reduced working capital is a symptom and not the underlying cause.

TABLE 18-5

Reasons for Small Company Public Offerings

	Percent of total
To meet company objectives:	
Financial needs	
Working capital	36.0%
Fixed capital	9.5
Research and development funds	5.7
Investment activity	
Establish market for later offering by shareholders	9.5
Probable purchase of another firm	3.8
Contemplated merger	2.4
To meet owners' personal considerations:	
Minimize estate taxes	13.4
Resolve personal conflicts	2.4
Provide "nest egg"	4.8
Diversify investments	4.8
Take advantage of a bull market	3.8
Other reasons	3.8

SOURCE: Cited in Solomon J. Flink, *Equity Financing for Small Business*, (New York: Simmons-Boardman Publishing Corp., 1962), p. 87.

What may be said about the key factors in the 1970s in determining the need for small corporations going public? Without being aware of any formal study from which to draw conclusions, experience does suggest that small businesses are facing increased difficulties in raising needed capital, with the implications being that financial needs would be an even more critical factor in the management of the small business. Therefore, if the markets are conducive, going public may become more significant for the smaller organization in the future.

Prerequisites for Going Public

If after having reviewed the advantages and disadvantages of going public management still believes that a public issue would be of merit for their firm, the question then becomes whether the firm is a viable candidate for a public offering. In identifying the prerequisites for going public, the comments of two investment bankers epitomize the basic criteria involved. In their words, "When we originate an underwriting, we want it to be a company of exceptional potential, above all, and secondly of large enough size so that it might be bought by some of the more enterprising institutional investors....

We are looking for good small companies with a solid record of earnings, good management, and better than average growth prospects [for the firm's product or services]."[8] Thus, the key words become size, marketability, earnings record, management, growth potential, and the products or services. With these six variables providing the structure, the following prerequisites for a public offering are explained.

Size constraint

As would be expected, management of the small enterprise has to be concerned with the question, "Is the firm large enough to go public?" The size criterion generally comes in two aspects: (1) the level of earnings and (2) the size of the issue. With the earnings capacity being addressed in a later section, attention may be given to the size of the offering. Not only may a small issue in terms of dollars be infeasible due to high costs, but a related factor, that being the number of shares, also has to be considered. In this respect, a general guideline comes with difficulty, with the minimal size depending on the philosophy of the investment banker. Regardless of the number of shares being quoted by an individual banker, an important standard is the potential for developing an active market. Specifically, without a reasonable number of shares outstanding for active trading, the investment banker has difficulty in justifying involvement in the financing. As an illustration of a minimum-size offering, one New York investment banking institution is not interested in managing an issue of less than 250,000 shares. Although this number may be somewhat on the high side for many investment bankers, the point is that most bankers do have some predetermined standard for the minimum size of an offering. The issue has to be large enough to support their involvement. Regardless of the limit, the underwriter has to believe that in return for his commitment of time and energy, a relatively attractive payoff may be expected.

Marketability

A second item of concern to investment underwriters is the creation of a substantial market. All else being constant, they prefer to develop a market sufficiently large to provide the investor additional liquidity in terms of the ability to buy and sell securities as needed. In brief, the investment banker has as his primary concern the depth and liquidity of the market. Without the possibility of developing such a market, investment bankers are usually not interested.[9]

---

[8]Elmer L. Winter, *A Complete Guide to Making a Public Stock Offering*, (Englewood Cliffs, N.J.: Prentice-Hall, 1962), p. 28.

[9]Henry W. Enber II, staff ed. *How To Go Public*, (New York: Practising Law Institute, 1971), pp. 16–17.

Established earnings record

Management of a firm entertaining the thought of going public must be aware that the size, the quality, and the trend of earnings are of utmost importance in public financing. A firm must reach a certain size in terms of net income. Again, no one number can be expressed as the optimal amount. Although some investment bankers indicate that a firm with less than $300,000 annual net income would not be of interest to them, examples may be cited where successful issues were accomplished with net income substantially below $300,000. The *quality* of earnings is of primary importance, with the quality being a function of the stability and the source of earnings. Finally, the *trend* of earnings is related to the likelihood that a long-term upward trend from the *current source* of income will continue to exist. The earnings trend must be "significant," must have grown at a steady rate for the most recent years, and must be expected to continue into the future.

The management team

The investigation into a company preparing for public financing includes an analysis of the basic *quality* and *philosophy* of top management. In examining the quality of management, the factors to consider include experience, integrity, and the depth of the corporate leadership. While not one of these three factors can be emphasized at the expense of the others, the depth of management is often a difficult problem to resolve for the small concern. For instance, a family-owned company typically relies upon the capabilities of the second generation. Thus, the second generation has to have the ability and interest to continue the operation, or management personnel external to the family must be available within the organization. With regard to the philosophy of top management, the underwriter is sensitive to management's attitude toward accepting the responsibility to satisfy queries of inquisitive investors, brokers, and analysts. In essence, can management not only conduct a sound business but also conduct sound public relations in what frequently is an annoying situation?

Growth potential

Although "growth" and public markets are not necessarily mutually exclusive, the owners of an enterprise interested in making a public offering should be aware of the uphill battle to be fought if growth is not evident. When competing for funds, an organization having negligible growth potential can anticipate serious difficulties in attracting the public investor. Hence, steady growth patterns expected to continue into the future are a strong factor in one's favor when entering the public market. In addition, the public disclosure requirements may be incompatible with the continued growth of some operations. For instance, if the information being submitted to the public affects the company's competitive position, going public is certainly a questionable avenue for funds. Although such an event rarely develops for most firms, the concern may be a definite psychological factor that would need to be recognized.

Products and services

The major concern in this instance becomes the *reputation* and *image* of an entity's products or services. Concisely stated, the sound reputation of an organization's products or services is an essential ingredient for a successful public offering. In a related sense, the image of the product is of key importance. Although the latter factor is generally a psychological barrier, it may well prevent a public issue from being a feasible alternative for a firm. In other words, a "glamourous" or "romantic" firm has a distinct advantage over the more commonplace type of operation.

If after serious thought and critical self-analysis, the executives of an organization still consider the public market as an advantageous route, the follow-up question has to be, "How is it done?" Thus, the attention of management must then be directed to the procedural aspects of consummating a public issue. In so doing, the personnel involved are well advised to proceed with extreme caution, employing experienced professionals. Two important reasons, among others, necessitate management's diligence. First, despite the manager's best intentions not to defraud or even misrepresent facts to the investment public, the slightest miscue which might be "interpreted" as being misleading or in violation of existing securities legislation may impose upon the principal owners and/or management a liability for damages "incurred" by an investor. Second, a haphazard execution of the details encompassing the public issue significantly decreases the probability of a successful offering, which will undoubtedly be detrimental to the company and the investors. In undertaking a public offering, the corporate representatives, in addition to working with their attorneys and accountants, will be heavily involved with the governmental regulatory authorities and an investment banker.

Federal Regulations[10]

A corporation issuing a public security has to be responsive to the relevant federal securities regulations being enforced by the Securities and Exchange Commission. The initial federal statute relating to securities (the Securities Act of 1933) had two principal objectives:

[10]This material is primarily taken from Louis H. Rappaport, *SEC Accounting Practice and Procedure*, 3rd ed., (New York: The Ronald Press, 1972), and Henry W. Enber II, staff ed., *How To Go Public* (New York: Practising Law Institute, 1971).

1. To provide full and fair disclosure to prospective investors of the character of new securities or new offerings.
2. To prevent fraud and misrepresentation in the sale of securities, old and new.[11]

This piece of legislation was in turn followed one year later by the 1934 Securities and Exchange Act. This second act has a broader frontage in terms of its intended objectives. In addition to adding additional protection for the investor from misrepresentative or fraudulent actions on the part of the company, the latter regulation also attempts to give greater strength to the securities exchanges and markets. However, restricting interest only to those items of primary concern to a manager attempting a public offering, the relevant objectives of this act are to compel corporations and certain security buyers to furnish adequate information for publicly traded securities and to minimize unfair use of information by corporate insiders.

The implications and consequences of the legislation and its subsequent amendments may best be highlighted by noting the procedures arising from these laws. As a result of the 1933 act, the issuer is required to file a registration statement with the Securities and Exchange Commission, incorporating sufficient information about the company to permit the investor an opportunity to make an informed evaluation of the security. The content, although fixed by law, may vary in accordance with the type of operation, the firm's length of existence, the type of security to be issued, and the purpose of the issue. An indication of the reporting requirements for most firms is provided in Table 18-6. As shown in the table, the commission makes a distinction between the data required and not required for the "prospectus." The prospectus is intended for use by the investment public in their evaluation and must be included with the registration statement.[12]

Upon completion of the registration statement, the documents are to be filed with the Division of Corporation Finance of the SEC in Washington. The material is generally reviewed by a divisional office, including an attorney, an accountant, and an analyst. This group performs a thorough examination of the disclosure, relying not only upon the personnel within the SEC but also upon parties outside of the commission who might have relevant information related to the case. The nature and extent of the examination is dependent on the circumstances of the particular registration. For example, large publicly owned firms will require little independent investigation on the part of the SEC, while a firm not having a broad-based reputation will be subject to more extensive examination. When the investigation is completed, the company is notified as to the deficiencies in the

[11]*Securities Regulation*, (Englewood Cliffs, N.J.: Pressor, Inc., 1976), paragraph 1422.

[12]Louis H. Rappaport, *SEC Accounting Practices and Procedures*, 3rd ed. (New York: Ronald, 1972).

TABLE 18-6

Information Needed for Registration

Part I. Information required in the prospectus:

1. Offering price information and distribution spread.
2. Plan of distribution, names of underwriters and their participations, and nature of the underwriters' obligation.
3. Use of proceeds to registrant.
4. Sales of securities other than for cash.
5. Capital structure.
6. Summary of earnings.
7. State and date of incorporation and type of organization of the registrant.
8. Parents of the registrant and basis of control.
9. Description of the business and its development during the past five years. This item requires disclosure in certain cases of information with respect to principal lines of business.
10. Description and location of principal physical properties.
11. If organized within the past five years, names of and transactions with promoters.
12. Pending legal proceedings other than routine litigation.
13. Information as to capital stock, funded debt, or other securities being registered.
14. Names of directors and executive officers and the principal occupations of the latter during the past five years.
15. Remuneration paid by the affiliated group during latest fiscal year to (a) each director, and each of the three highest paid officers of the registrant who received more than $30,000, and (b) all directors and officers as a group.
16. Outstanding options to purchase securities from the registrant or subsidiaries.
17. Principal holders of registrant's securities.
18. Interest of directors, officers, and certain other persons in certain material transactions during last three years or in any proposed transaction.
19. Financial statements.

Part II. Information not required in the prospectus:

20. Arrangements limiting, restricting, or stabilizing the market for securities being offered.
21. Expenses of the issue.
22. Relationship of registrant with experts named in the registration statement.
23. Sales of securities to special parties.
24. Recent sales of unregistered securities.
25. List of subsidiaries of the registrant.
26. Franchises or concessions held by the registrant and subsidiaries.
27. Indemnification arrangements for officers and directors.
28. Accounting for proceeds from sale of capital stock being registered.
29. List of financial statements and exhibits.

SOURCE: Cited in Louis H. Rappaport, *SEC Accounting Practice and Procedure*, 3rd ed., (New York: Ronald, 1972), pp. 8-3 and 8-4.

registration statement. In response to the deficiency statement, the company files an ammended registration statement, which may involve either a unilateral reconsideration of the facts or a request for a conference with the investigator. Upon the settlement of any differences and the submission of the revised instrument, the SEC then enters an order declaring the registration statement to be effective. At this point in time, the securities may be sold. However, a final copy of the prospectus must be delivered to any individual purchasing the security. If the distribution of the issue continues for an extended period, the prospectus may ultimately be considered as being obsolete and subject to a requirement for an update.

The 1933 Securities Act contains a number of exemptions to full registration, both in terms of certain securities and selected types of transactions. For example, the issuance of government and bank securities, short-term notes, drafts, and bills of exchange is not contingent upon the registration statement. Furthermore, exempted transactions would include, among others, statutory mergers or consolidations or reclassification of securities, dealers' transactions, or treasury stock. Although an extensive coverage of the exemptions would be prohibitive within the scope of this chapter, a brief explanation of several basic types of exemptions is in order.

Regulation A offerings

The commission is authorized by the 1933 Securities Act to exempt any securities from being subject to file a complete registration statement if the size of issue is such that the protection of the investor is not of a material concern. To qualify for the relief from the registration statement, the issue size may not exceed $500,000, with an additional constraint of $100,000 maximum for each investor. In addition to these two restrictions, the regulation contains a number of other provisions which limit exemption status of certain types of securities or certain issuers.

If a business does qualify for Regulation A exemption, the filing requirements and procedures are less complex, and a reduced lag time between submission and approval of the issue should exist. As to the filing procedures, a firm must file a Form 1-A with the SEC regional office. The informational content of the form is reflected in Table 18-7. The reduction in requested data by being able to file a Regulation A offering becomes quite apparent by comparing Table 18-6, a listing of the needed information for a large offering, with Table 18-7. While the objective of the Regulation A legislation by Congress is to reduce the registration requirements for the small issue, such intent has not proven to be the case at all times. For instance, a shortened ten-day waiting period from the time the information is filed with the SEC to the actual date of use of the material is stipulated in the regulations; however, small companies filing Regulation A offerings in the New York regional office have at times encountered as long a time in

TABLE 18-7

Information Requirements for Regulation A Offerings

1. Information regarding the issuer, including the name, date, and site of the corporation.
2. Predecessor affiliates and principal security holders of the issuer.
3. Directors, officers, and promoters.
4. Counsel for the issuer and underwriters.
5. Legal actions against the issuer or against affiliated issuers.
6. Legal actions against directors, officers, and others.
7. Connection of underwriters with other offerings.
8. Jurisdiction in which securities are to be offered.
9. Unregistered securities issued or sold within one year prior to the filing of the current notification.
10. Other proposed offerings.
11. Exhibits:
    a. Instruments defining the rights of the holders of the securities.
    b. Underwriting contracts.
    c. Underwriter consent and certification form.
    d. A statement by the issuer indicating no conflicts of interest between the issuer and a personnel stockholder.
    e. The offering circular including basic financial information.

completing the registration as larger issues submitted to the national office in Washington.

As to advantages and disadvantages of the Regulation A offering, the potential savings in direct costs and time commitment have to be considered the primary benefits. To illustrate, a Regulation A filing might result in a cost approximating $20,000, a significantly smaller sum than that occurring in a full-fledged offering. Yet, such an advantage does not come without some negative effects. First, the investigation by the regional office typically is not so thorough as that conducted by the Washington office. In other words, an extensive review by the SEC can be more than just a formality and may prove to be quite beneficial to the issuer. Second, the Regulation A offering may have negative connotations for some investors. They simply question the quality of an issue being filed under this exemption.

Private offerings

A second means by which a business organization may circumvent the registration requirements is through a *private offering*. In distinguishing between a public offering and a private offering, the line of demarcation is not always clear in that the legislation offers little information in separating the two types of placement. Hence, the difference must be established by examining SEC reports and court decisions. In this regard, several criteria have been developed, including the type of investor, the investors' access to information, an absence of any planned distribution, and the number of offerings. In determining whether or not an issue is private, the principal factor becomes the "sophistication" of the offeree. However, this determinant is not independent of the accessibility to relevant information and the type of business in question. In essence, the prospective investor must be able to fend for himself and not need the protection of the Securities Act. The extent of the sophistication is a function of the type of business being investigated. Although an individual may have the competence to examine a retail operation, he may not have the capabilities to understand and properly evaluate an electronics firm. Indicative of the person's ability to examine and independently determine whether or not an investment is appropriate are the opportunity and ability of the investor to execute a personal investigation, although in certain circumstances the potential investor may employ an agent in the examination process without the offering being considered to be public. Another factor that might imply a lack of sophistication is the determination of the terms of the offer prior to the offeree's inspection. The interested party should be able to negotiate with the firm as to the terms of the issue. In brief, management is well advised to select prospective investors with considerable care, seeking out individuals of substantial means and giving them access to the information by which they may determine the worth of the issue.

In addition to the level of investor sophistication and the accessibility of material information, the intent of the purchaser is of essence. To maintain the private placement exemption, the investor must indicate that the purchase is being made as a personal investment and not with the intent for further distribution to the public. For control purposes, an investor needs to express this intent through an *investment letter*. In addition, the issuer should include a statement on the certificate specifying that the security is not for resale without a subsequent registration statement becoming effective or without an opinion of the firm's legal counsel stating that this security may be resold. Also, a stop-transfer order is placed on the transfer books of the company, thereby precluding any transfer of ownership. Such a restriction is not intended to inhibit the sale of the securities if a change of circumstances develops for an investor; however, such a change must indeed be material, with the real test being based on the *original* intent of the investor. The need for the change to be significant is humorously related in the story of an individual who had signed an investment letter but now had a desire to sell the stock:

> [An investor] wanted to sell his stock, and he had perfectly normal, legitimate reasons for doing it, like paying bills, sending children to college, contributing to charity. His lawyer said, "You can't do that because that would violate the securities laws." In desperation, the client said, "Somewhere I went wrong." The lawyer said, "Probably because you came to me because I know all about these exemptions. If you had gone to a lawyer who didn't know anything about this, you could sell the private placement but you would have to take a discount in that." The client's response is, "Over my dead body." The lawyer paused at that

point and answered, "If that were to happen, probably your estate would be free to sell the stock, since your death was an unanticipated change of circumstances." Whereupon the lawyer walks out of the room, the client jumps out of the window and everybody else lives happily ever after. [However, death] was not a legitimate change of circumstances because that was self-induced.[13]

The last primary standard which has to be met for a private offering is the *number-of-offerees* requirement. As the number of offerees increases, the probability that the offering will be deemed to be public also is increased. Historically, the SEC has considered any number beyond 25 as being a public offering unless evidence proves otherwise. More recently, the commission has used the criteria of 35 *purchasers* rather than offerees. Regardless of the number, however, the point to be made is that the private placement generally must be restricted to a relatively small number of purchasers or possibly even offerees. Yet, it should be remembered that these numbers are simply test figures and not final determinants. The ultimate question still remains, "How knowledgeable are the prospective investors?"

In summary, the management of a firm contemplating a private offering has to proceed with extreme caution, remembering that if even one individual fails to satisfy the sophistication criterion, whether or not the investment is actually made, the private offering exemption may be lost.

Intrastate offerings

A securities issue being offered only to investors living within the state in which the corporation does business may be exempt from federal registration, thereby only needing to comply with the appropriate state authorities. However, meeting the qualifications for the intrastate exemption may prove difficult simply due to a lack of clarity in the section authorizing the exemption. Yet, as a result of a recent ruling by the SEC, additional guidance is being provided to prospective issuers attempting to benefit from the exemption. This recent proclamation, in an attempt to decrease current ambiguities, sets forth the following standards:

1. The issuer must be a resident of and doing business within the state in which the securities are offered and sold.
2. All offerees and purchasers of the securities must be residents within such state.
3. Resales of the securities to non-residents may not be made until nine months after the sale to a resident within the state pursuant to the original offerings.
4. The issuer must take certain precautions to assure compliance with the exemption, including stock-record quotations, stock-transfer instructions, appropriate legends on the stock certificates, written representations from all

---

[13]Henry W. Enberg II, staff ed., *How To Go Public*, (New York: Practising Law Institute, 1971), pp. 63–64.

purchasers that they are residents of the state, and disclosure in writing of the limitation imposed by the rule on transfers and resales.[14]

Thus, four essential ingredients are required for an intrastate exemption, with two key characteristics of the issuer and the purchaser predating the offering. First, the site of residence and the area in which the firm conducts business must be satisfied. To be considered a resident of a state, the issuer must be organized under the state laws and have its principal office in the state. To be considered as "doing business" within the state, at least 80 percent of a company's operating gross revenues must be generated within the state, with the issuer planning to employ at least 80 percent of these revenues within the same jurisdiction. In addition, at least 80 percent of the consolidated assets must be located within the state. As an illustration of the strictness of the exemption, the same developer operating separate companies within separate states and doing the same kind of business is not permitted to draw upon the intrastate exemption.

The second prerequisite of an intrastate offering relates to the residence of the offeree. Again, extreme care must be taken to avoid any attempt by individuals to circumvent this qualification. The offeree or purchaser must have his principal place of abode within the state in question. Furthermore, the use of a corporation or partnership organized for the intent of acquiring intrastate offering status will be disallowed. In such an instance, all of the beneficial owners must be residents of the state in order to satisfy the requirements. In summary, the SEC has a twofold purpose: (1) minimize the uncertainty surrounding the intrastate offering exemption and (2) minimize the extent of abuses occurring under the exemption. The end result has been to tighten this particular exemption, making its use more difficult and requiring the potential issuers in most cases to turn to other types of exemptions.

As becomes quite obvious, going public is not intended for the novice. Assistance to the executive of the small firm is important. Such assistance may come in many forms, but none are more critical than the relationship with the investment banker.

Investment Banking and the Small Business

In 1933, Congress finalized the Glass-Steagall Act, with its primary objective being to provide enhanced stability and security in the banking community. As a result of the act, the operational duties of the commercial banker and the investment banker became distinctly separate. While the investment banking community provides a number of services, the primary

[14]*SEC Regulations*, Vol. I, (Englewood Cliffs, N.J.: Prentice-Hall), p. 1200.25.

concern of these institutions relates to providing long-term capital requirements for business. In this respect, the investment banker operates as a liaison between the business firm desiring permanent funds and the prospective investor.[15] More specifically, the basic function of providing long-term capital for the firm may be segmented into the two categories of wholesale and retail investment banking. Within these two classifications, an entire range of activities prevails. At one end of the continuum is the wholesale investment banking firm involved in the underwriting of public offerings, arranging private placements, and assisting in mergers. At the other end of the spectrum is the retail investment firm, which is primarily involved in the selling of secondary securities. In addition to this single-dimensional scaling, investment bankers may be further categorized with respect to their interest in various sizes of offerings and in different industries. In this vein, some firms are nationally orientated as opposed to others that are strictly regional in nature. Also, certain investment bankers are interested only in large corporations, as opposed to others maintaining an interest in the small-business entity. Finally, some investment firms restrict themselves to given industries in which they maintain a special expertise. With these comments, attention is directed to the functions of the investment banker, the chronological activities of the banker in the offering process, and the final pricing decision.

Functions of the investment banker

Investment banking organizations have four primary responsibilities: (1) underwriting the issue, (2) marketing the new securities, (3) making a secondary market for the securities, and (4) general advice and counseling. The first type of operation of the underwriters involves a personal arrangement between the investment banker and the issuer. The issuer may desire the securities to be sold on a "best-efforts" basis, in which case the investment banker is responsible only for the shares that are actually sold. Any remaining securities are returned to the company. In contrast, the investment banker may be requested to underwrite the "risk" involved with the issue. This risk comes in two forms. First, the potential risk from price fluctuations is borne by the underwriter by guaranteeing the issuer a fixed amount of money at the time of the issuance. The investment banker must in turn go to the marketplace with the securities, facing the possibility that the price of the security may fall while the banker still holds an inventory. For example, if an issue is selling for $25, the underwriter might pay $23, with the $2 spread being the underwriter's fee for services and tax-assuming risk. However, if the price subsequently declines to $20, the investment banker is faced with potential loss. The second risk might be referred to as an "absorption risk." Essentially,

---

[15]Donald M. Dible, *Up Your Own Organization*, (Santa Clara, Calif.: The Entrepreneur Press, 1971), pp. 234–235.

when a large number of shares are being placed on the market at one time, the market may simply not be willing to absorb such a large number of shares at a given point in time. In this instance, the banker may be forced to maintain an investment in the securities for an undesirable length of time.

The second service performed by the investment banker is in the marketing of the new security. Stated briefly, most firms, either large or small, are not in the security business. The banker has a permanent dealer staff with the expertise for distributing new securities. An investment firm is generally more efficient and economical in the actual distribution of the securities. Unless the issuing company can place the securities privately, corporate management is well advised to seek the counsel and assistance of the investment banker for distribution purposes.

Although the investment banker's legal accountability terminates upon the "closing of the books," a traditional service performed by the banker is the making of a market. Even though this activity may not be considered so critical in the short run as the successful initial marketing of the securities, its significance should not be minimized. A sound after-issue market is essential in maintaining favorable stockholder relations and future financing. Hence, the investment banker provides an invaluable service by continually affording the financial community and the investment public information relating to the company's financial condition and plans, while actively soliciting buyers and sellers.

The last general area in which the investment banker has an active role is in the general advice and financial counseling offered the management of the issuing corporation. These efforts should not be restricted to a time period preceding the issue. As indicated by one banker,

> We are frequently asked to help new issuers with general problems of a company going public for a first time such as advising them on the basis of our experience on handling stockholder relations, stockholder reports, meetings with the investment community and analysts.... Related to [this point], we are available as a sounding board as to how the financial community and the public generally might react to proposed corporate actions.... We advise the company on a broad range of their financial problems including such matters as the need for new financing, the methods of obtaining new financing either publicly or privately, dividend policy, and the desirability of mergers, acquisitions.[16]

All in all, the relationship between the issuing firm and the investment banker may be said to be acutely important. Few relationships have more far-reaching effects upon the firm's future financing.

---

[16]*Securities and Exchange Commission Report of the Special Study of the Securities Markets*, Superintendent of Documents, 88th Congress, Session I, House Document 95, (Washington, D.C.: U.S. Government Printing Office, 1963).

Proper selection of the underwriter

In underwriting a stock issue, the selection of an underwriter is an important element in a public offering.[17] In this regard, several factors are of consequence.[18] First, the *timing* has an impact. Even though investment bankers tend to constrain their interest in terms of the size of the issue, these institutions alter their range of interest as the level of the general market shifts. Thus, the accessibility of a small firm to a large underwriter is relatively limited during a bear market. Second, the underwriter should provide evidence of a strong *interest* in the issue. As cited earlier, the small business is especially susceptible to market reversals, to the extent that a change in the environment in a two-month period can completely eliminate the feasibility of a public issue. In this event, the investment banker, provided a strong commitment exists, can work to place the issue privately rather than publicly. Finally, the *after-market support* of the underwriter is of prime import to the smaller business. With almost 10,000 companies competing for attention in the public markets, a definite plan of action is essential in developing a market for the security. Failure to build a relatively active market for the security can have a significant impact upon future financing. In this context, Seibert suggests a number of basic questions to be resolved in the selection process of the investment banker:

1. Does the underwriter understand the business? Since the underwriter must tell your story to his customers, if he does not have the ability to understand your company, he will not be able to communicate effectively.

2. Does the underwriter have SEC problems? This is a major concern for a number of the small underwriting firms that have been under investigation by the SEC as a result of activities during the 1968 and 1969 market period. Do not associate with a small underwriter that is having SEC problems because his reputation could well rub off on your company.

3. Does the underwriter help maintain an after-market? It is important that an active market be maintained after the company goes public if the stock price is to be maintained. The underwriter should trade the shares himself and interest other market makers if there is to be a liquid market after the public offering.

4. Have the underwriter's other deals been of comparable quality to your situation? A major area of homework in selecting an underwriter is to

[17]The use of underwriters for Regulation A offerings has been materially reduced. Although 54 percent of such issues were accomplished through underwriters in 1972, this number fell to 26 percent by 1974—a 48 percent reduction. No doubt, the increased costs of issuing securities and the depressed market have encouraged business executives to attempt offerings without an underwriter in an effort to minimize costs.

[18]Charles Symington, "Key Aspects of Public Financing," *Guide to Venture Capital Sources*, 3rd ed., ed. by Stanley M. Rubel, (Chicago: Capital Publishing Corporation, 1974), p. 73.

actively review the types of companies the firm has financed. It is important to interview some managers of companies the firm has underwritten to learn about their experiences and impressions after the deal was closed.

5. Does the underwriter have a history of being unable to complete deals? When the market runs down precipitously, almost all underwriters have problems handling offerings. But if the market merely dips from time to time or if it is not particularly exuberant, a good underwriter who makes a commitment should be able to complete the financing. It is important to review the issues that the underwriter has put into registration to see how many of them have subsequently gone public and to determine the reasons why such firms might not have been able to obtain public financing.

6. Can the underwriter ensure that there will be enough shareholders after the public offering so that the company can be traded on NASDAQ, the American Stock Exchange, or the national over-the-counter market?[19]

Hence, the selection of an investment consultant should be made with care. Having made such a choice, the company's management, in conjunction with the banker, initiates the distribution process.

The distribution process

The underwriting process is initiated when the investment banker gains the right to underwrite the issue either through negotiation or through competitive bidding. The latter method is conducted by investment bankers submitting sealed bids to the company at a designated time, with the highest bidder receiving the issue. Negotiated underwriting results from direct negotiations between the underwriter and the issuer. As a general rule, the buying or underwriting department performs the function of acquiring the securities. In addition, this department is charged with developing new business, recommending effective financial plans, and assisting the issuer both in selecting the provisions to be included in the contract and in the actual writing of the prospectus or indenture.

Since securing the right to distribute securities through negotiation is more involved than competitive bidding, it becomes necessary to set forth briefly the various steps involved in the negotiation process. The process usually includes (1) the investigation of the merits of the proposed issue by the buying department; (2) the negotiation of an informal agreement with the issuing firm; (3) the formation of an underwriting group, if warranted due to the size or risk of the issue; (4) registration with the SEC or a state securities board if required; (5) the creation of a formal agreement between the participating members of the underwriting group and the manager; (6) the

---

[19]Donald Seibert, "How To Select and Work with the Small Underwriter," *Guide to Venture Capital Sources*, 3rd ed., ed. by Stanley M. Rubel, (Chicago: Capital Publishing Corporation, 1974), p. 77.

creation of a selling group, if the issue is so large that more than one seller is required; (7) negotiation with the issuer with respect to price and spread; (8) signing of the purchase contract with the issuer, subject to clearance by the SEC or the appropriate state agency; and (9) the sale of securities to the public, subject to delivery after the closing.

A brief description of these steps should be helpful. First, the buying department of the originating house analyzes the general nature of the firm's business; that is, it determines the firm's relative position in the total market, assesses the potential of the firm's future demand, and ascertains the ability of the management. Second, an investigation is made of the firm's past and future potential. This normally includes past financial data and a forecast. Third, the firm's facilities are carefully examined by the investment banker, and, if necessary, an outside engineering firm or other professional group may be called upon to assist in evaluating the firm's assets and requirements. The buying department then makes its recommendations as to the desirability of the proposed financing and the amount and type of new securities to be issued. If the proposal is acceptable to both the company and the investment banker, an informal agreement is drawn up, stating the amount and type of securities to be offered and when the offering is to be made. For the small business, the originating house generally manages the account alone; however, if for some reason assistance is needed, an underwriting group may be formed.

The registration statement is drawn up by the following individuals and groups: the officers of the issuing firm, the underwriting firm, lawyers of both the issuing company and the underwriting organization, accountants for both groups, and any additional specialists whose services are necessary. After completion, the registration statement is filed with the SEC—or with the state securities commissioner if the issue is to be sold intrastate.

Two agreements are necessary at this point in the negotiation, one between the participating members of the underwriting group and the manager of the originating house, if such relationships have been established, and the other between the issuing corporation and the underwriter. The latter agreement is commonly referred to as the purchase contract and includes the price of the securities to be issued to the public and the price the underwriter is to pay. Once the purchase contract has been signed, the underwriter is obligated to buy the entire issue from the company. (Included in each purchase contract, however, is an "out" clause, setting forth the conditions under which the underwriter is not required to fulfill the agreement.)

The final step is the actual sale of the securities. After the completion of the above steps, the sales department of each member of the underwriting group assumes the responsibility of selling a proportionate share of securities to the investing public. If the securities have not been sold during the period agreed upon by the underwriters, either of two courses is open. The period may be extended in the hope that the securities will be sold. Or if failure is acknowledged, the agreements may be dissolved, with each firm taking its proportionate share of unsold securities either to hold until the stock can be moved at the offering price or to sell at any price that can be obtained.

A second method of distribution involves the process generally referred to as *standby* underwriting. This method entails an agreement by the investment banker (or group) to sell securities that, for one reason or another, are offered for sale by the issuer. For example, suppose a firm makes available 50,000 shares of common stock to its stockholders through its preemptive agreement. To assure itself that the entire issue will be sold, the issuer signs a standby agreement with an investment banker to take up the securities that are not sold by the business firm through the preemptive right process. In some cases, the underwriter charges a small fee for this service; for example, $.25 per share for all shares of the issue plus an additional $1.00 per share on all shares the investment banker is called upon to sell. Occasionally, investment bankers charge a fee for the actual amount they are required to sell.

A third approach employed by investment bankers in disseminating the securities is *best-efforts* selling. As noted earlier, under this technique, investment bankers serve as agents for the issuing company, but unlike underwriters, they do not own the shares; they exercise their best efforts to sell the security and are compensated in direct relation to the number of units sold. Again unlike underwriters, investment bankers assume no risk, since they do not take a position in the issue. Generally a best-efforts distribution is employed in highly speculative issues and in the case of securities that are new and untried.

Pricing the issue

For most managers of a corporation attempting to effect a public offering, the most tense point in the negotiation process comes in the actual finalizing of a price. Management, while being desirous of a high price for their security, is naturally aware that the underwriter's fee for services comes through a low price. In this framework, management becomes quite cognizant of a potential conflict. However, the executives of the offering company should be aware of other dimensions of the problem. First, the underwriter, similar to any retailing concern, is sensitive to the market demand and supply and therefore must be competitive in order to survive. This is not to say that the issuing firm should blindly follow the recommendation of the investment banker. Continued analysis on the part of the firm's leadership is essential in all facets of the operation. Second, the owners and the underwriter have a common goal, that being a sustained market price for the security after the issue has been completed. This commonality is difficult to perceive from the perspective of the corporate proprietorship. However, the fact that maintaining the security price subsequent to the original issue is vital for future financing should not be minimized. In essence, generating interest in a security for which the market value has significantly declined since the last public offering is next to impossible. Thus, without any question, the corporate interests are the best achieved in the long run by not overpricing an issue, even though that price could have been received in the short run.

Summary

Going public is particularly difficult for the small firm, with the availability of public funds being extremely susceptible to general economic conditions. The potential problems for the small concern in attempting to effect a public offering are numerous. The discouragements faced encompass sizable commitments of time and effort, increased disclosure requirements, the need for a more stable dividend policy, inflexibility in major decisions, and the volatility of the "hot-issues" market, which causes the public market to be quite unpredictable as a source of capital. For these reasons, a public issue, from the small corporation's perspective, should be an avenue of last resort. However, if such a need exists or for personal reasons the owners elect to go public, several possible benefits, in addition to the acquisition of funds, may result. When the hurdles of a first public offering have been surpassed, several financing options become more accessible to a company. The feasibility of future growth through acquisitions or mergers is increased. Also, public securities afford an opportunity to enhance the public image and goodwill of the company both with employees and the general public. Last, the owners may have a personal incentive for a public offering such as the occasion to diversify their investment position or as a means of assigning value for estate tax purposes.

The prerequisites to be met by a firm desiring to issue a public security may be set forth only in general terms, due to divergent attitudes and preferences of the participating institutional personnel. Yet, general criteria include the size of the company and the issue itself, the marketability of the security, the track record of the corporation, the quality and breath of management, the growth prospects of the firm, and the nature of the products and/or services of the organization.

In making the public offering, the financial executive of the small firm is required to become familiar with an almost bewildering world of investment bankers, attorneys, accountants, and regulatory authorities. Compliance with complex governmental edicts and with the negotiation process in a financial community unfamiliar to the small business owner is difficult at best. In achieving a successful offering, the investment banker is usually an important link between the company and the investment public, with the banker providing services in the preparation and the distribution of the securities and counseling in developing a secondary market for the stock.

QUESTIONS

1. Briefly explain the following basic problems involved in going public:
   a. Time and cost requirements.
   b. Disclosure.
   c. Increased time in major decisions.
   d. Formal dividend policy.
   e. An unpredictable source of financing.

2. When a firm decides to go public, what is the main basis on which the decision should be made?

3. What are the principal benefits of going public?

4. Certain prerequisites should be met before a firm attempts to make a public offering. Explain these requirements.

5. What are the procedures required by federal law in making a public offering?

6. Explain (a) the Regulation A offering and (b) the intrastate offering.

7. What criteria are considered in determining whether an offering is public or private?

8. What are four responsibilities of an investment banker? Explain.

9. Explain the types of arrangements that may be made with an investment banker in selling an issue.

10. What is the difference between an underwriter and an investment banker?

PROBLEM

18-1. Ralph Baker and William Britan are the sole stockholders in Southeastern Steel, Inc., an Atlanta, Georgia firm which furnishes custom structural steel framework for construction of shopping centers, warehouses, office buildings, and manufacturing plants. These jobs are done throughout the southeast; however, approximately 75 percent of the company's business is done in Georgia. The firm began as a partnership in 1960 and then incorporated in 1965, with Baker and Britan each receiving 175,000 shares. The firm has grown from 4 employees and sales of $700,000 in 1960 to 80 employees and sales of $8 million in 1975.

Baker and Britan have been the only managers of the business since its beginning in 1960. Baker is 45 years of age and is in charge of the sales, marketing, and administrative affairs of the company, and Britan, age 54, manages the production phase of the operations. They both are in excellent physical condition. The top-level managers below them have been with the firm for over 10 years and are considered highly qualified to run the business in Baker and Britan's absence. Baker has a son Jack, age 20, who has entered a college of business at a local university, with the expectations of working for Southeastern Steel upon graduation. Britan has two sons, Steve, age 24, and Richard, age 22, both of whom have B.B.A. degrees, and Steve is currently working toward the M.B.A. degree. Richard is a manager in the production area of the firm. Both owners feel they have a conservative attitude toward business, attempting to maintain an excellent credit rating and produce quality products. As a result of these efforts, the reputations of Baker and Britan among contractors within the industry and among businessmen within the community are excellent. Although the corporation has developed a sound reputation, the investment community lacks information about the company due to the company being a subcontractor and having only private investors. However, while no similar business in the area has publicly issued securities, firms of similar operation, but in different segments of the country, do have shares traded publicly. These firms' shares are actively traded over the counter with price earnings multiples generally between 6 and 10. Southeastern Steel has received some negative public relations due to problems on a major shopping center being built in another city. Some of the steel failed to comply with the contract specifications, having to be reworked or returned, thereby causing delays for the contractor.

At the present time, Southeastern Steel, Inc. is needing to replace old machinery as well as acquire equipment for expanding the firm's production capabilities. The total costs of the production machinery should approximate $450,000, with an additional $150,000 being necessary for expanding the plant floor space in order to facilitate the new equipment. Also, another large expansion, probably requiring the attraction of public investors, is expected in three to five years.

The earnings of the company were on an upward trend until 1976 when construction activities dropped. However, in the opinion of most security analysts, the industry as a whole has excellent growth prospects of 6 to 8 percent per year for the next ten years, with Southeastern Steel, Inc. generally having grown faster in both sales and earnings than the industry in the past. Historically, the firm has paid only nominal dividends, these being either when a surplus of funds occurred in excess of investment requirements or when Baker and Britan needed personal funds.

In financing the investments, the company generally relies upon retained earnings, short-term credit from the bank, and/or private placements of long-term notes. However, due to the reduction in profits in 1976, only a small portion of the investments may be financed through the retention of earnings. Active bidding for jobs increased substantially during the last half of 1976, thereby indicating the probable rebound in sales and earnings during 1977 to be equal to or greater than 1975. The bank is hesitant to accept Southeastern Steel's loan request, with the reluctance ensuing from the recent recessionary period in the construction industry. When other lenders were approached, they contended that Southeastern Steel needs a larger equity base to serve as a buffer if further downturn in the economy should ever occur. However, Baker and Britan are not in the position to invest funds themselves.

With the usual sources of financing temporarily closed to Southeastern Steel, management has begun a search for new sources of capital. As a part of this search, they have investigated the feasibility of either a public issue of $750,000 in stock or a smaller $600,000 stock offering, obtaining a loan for the remaining $150,000. As a result of their efforts, an investment banker, Smith, Brownlee and Co., has expressed a tentative interest in assisting the firm with a public equity offering. The personnel of Smith, Brownlee and Co. has had extensive experience with similar companies, both in terms of size and industry. They have excellent accomplishments in underwriting issues, marketing the new securities, making secondary markets for securities, and giving general advice and counseling to their clients. If Smith, Brownlee and Co. underwrites the issue, they will require an underwriting spread of 15 percent for an issue amount under $500,000, 12 percent if $500,000 to $749,999, and 10 percent of $750,000 to $1 million. They prefer the issue size to be approximately 150,000 shares or more, so as to provide for an active secondary market. They generally require a firm to have between $200,000 and $250,000 minimum in earnings before accepting an issue.

Southeastern Steel currently uses an attorney having his own practice for handling their general legal requirements, with a local independent CPA performing basic auditing needs. If they do go public, new attorneys specializing in equity offerings and an in-depth audit of the firm by a national accounting firm will be required. Southeastern Steel's latest balance sheet and income statement are reflected in Exhibit 1 and Exhibit 2, respectively.

Questions

a. Evaluate Southeastern Steel, Inc. in terms of qualifying to go public.
b. What would be the approximate net proceeds that might be available to them if a decision is made to sell stock publicly? (Note: Consider underwriting fees, legal fees, accounting expenses, printing costs, and other expenses, approximated from the figures mentioned in the chapter.)
c. Generally, by what other available means might Southeastern Steel raise equity capital?
d. What are the advantages and disadvantages of going public?

EXHIBIT 1

Balance Sheet

		1976			1965			1954
Assets								
Current assets:								
Cash		$ 70,000		$	70,000		$	50,210
Accounts receivable		330,000			310,000			210,890
Inventory		1,000,000			1,000,000			700,550
Total current assets		1,400,000			1,380,000			961,650
Fixed assets:								
Land & building		$ 730,000		$	895,000		$	762,000
Machinery & equipment	$570,000		$560,000		290,000	$450,000		200,000
Less: Depreciation	300,000	270,000	270,000		150,000	250,000		90,350
Leasehold improvement		360,000						
Total fixed assets		1,360,000			1,335,000			1,052,350
Total assets		$2,760,000			$2,715,000			$2,014,000
Liabilities and Net Worth								
Current liabilities:								
Accounts payable		$ 300,000		$	300,000		$	250,000
Short-term notes payable (7%)		270,000			250,000			300,000
Long-term notes payable (8.5%, due 1986)		1,100,000			1,100,000			800,000
Total liabilities		1,670,000			1,650,000			1,350,000
Capital stock:								
Common—par value $.50;		$ 175,000		$	175,000		$	175,000
Authorized, 1 million								
Issued, 350,000								
Retained earnings		915,000			890,000			689,000
Total net worth		1,090,000			1,065,000			864,000
Total liabilities and net worth		$2,760,000			$2,715,000			$2,014,000

EXHIBIT 2

Income Statements

Sales	$5,000,000	$8,000,000	$7,000,000
Less cost of goods sold	3,500,000	5,500,000	4,800,000
Gross profit	1,500,000	2,500,000	2,200,000
Selling & adminstration expenses	1,275,000	1,900,000	1,700,000
Earnings before interest & taxes	225,000	600,000	500,000
Interest	112,400	111,000	89,000
Net income before taxes	112,600	489,000	411,000
Taxes (50%)	56,300	244,500	205,500
Earnings available to common	$ 56,300	$244,500	$205,500

PART VIII SELECTED REFERENCES

ALEXANDER, D. H., "Dilemma of the Small Businessman, Or How to Get That Loan," *Credit and Financial Management*, January 1977, pp. 8–9, 36.

American Institute of Certified Public Accountants, *Financing the Small Business*, New York: American Institute of Certified Public Accountants, 1971.

BACON, KENNETH H., "Telling All: Full Disclosure Push by SEC on Companies Worries Some Critics," *Wall Street Journal*, May 15, 1975, p. 1.

BATY, GORDON B., *Entrepreneurship: Playing to Win*, Reston, Va.: Reston Publishing Company, Inc., 1974.

BEECHY, T. H., "Quasi-Debt Analysis of Financial Leases," *Accounting Review*, April 1969, pp. 375–381.

BERMAN, DANIEL S., *Going Public: A Practical Handbook of Procedures and Forms*, Englewood Cliffs, N.J.: Prentice-Hall, 1974.

BOWER, R. S., F. C. HERRINGER, and J. P. WILLIAMSON, "Lease Evaluation," *Accounting Review*, April 1966, pp. 257–265.

BOWER, RICHARD S., "Issues in Lease Financing," *Financial Management*, Winter 1973, pp. 25–34.

CHAMBERLAIN, DOUGLAS C., "Capitalization of Lease Obligations," *Management Accounting*, December 1975, pp. 37–38, 42.

CLARK, DAVID C., "Leases as Loan Security," *Journal of Commercial Bank Lending*, April 1972, pp. 25–30.

COFFMAN, ROBERT M., "Problems of Displacement in Public Offering," *Journal of Accountancy*, October 1974, pp. 65–71.

DIBLE, DONALD M., *Up Your Own Organization*, Santa Clara, California: The Entrepreneur Press, 1971.

ELLIOTT, GROVER S., "Leasing of Capital Equipment," *Management Accounting*, December 1975, pp. 39–42.

ENBER, HENRY W. II, staff editor, *How to Go Public*, New York: Practising Law Institute, 1961.

FERRERA, W. L., "Lease vs. Purchase: A Quasi-Financing Approach," *Management Accounting*, January 1974, pp. 21–26.

GORDON, M. J., "General Solution to Buy or Lease Decision: A Pedagogical Note," *Journal of Finance*, March 1974, pp. 245–250.

GROSS, HARRY, *Financing for Small and Medium-Sized Businesses*, Englewood Cliffs, N.J.: Prentice-Hall, 1970.

HENERY, J. B., "Leasing: Cost Measurement and Disclosure," *Management Accounting*, May 1974, pp. 37–41.

HOUGET, GEORGE R., "Techniques of Term Loan Analysis," *Journal of Commercial Bank Lending*, March 1975, pp. 30–36.

HUNT, PEARSON, "A Proposal for Precise Definitions of Trading on the Equity and Leverage," *Journal of Finance*, September 1961, pp. 377–386.

HUTCHISON, GEORGE SCOTT, *Why, When and How to Go Public*, New York: President's Publishing House, Inc., 1970.

JAMES, JOHN ROBERT, "Before You Make That Lease Deal, Do Your Risk Management Homework," *Banking*, American Bankers Association, New York: April 1975, p. 74.

JENNINGS, RICHARD W., *Selected Statutes, Rules and Forms Under the Federal Securities Laws*, New York: The Foundation Press, Inc., 1975.

JENNINGS, RICHARD W., and HAROLD MARSH, *Securities Regulation Case and Materials*, New York: The Foundation Press, Inc., 1972.

JOHNSON, R. W., and W. G. LEWELLEN, "Analysis of the Lease or Buy Decision," *Journal of Finance*, September 1972, pp. 815–823.

KELLEY, DEAN, "Raising Capital for Small Businesses," *Business Week*, November 3, 1973.

LAZERE, MONROE K., *Commercial Financing*, New York: Ronald Press Co., 1968.

LILES, PATRICK R., "Venture Capital: What It Is and How To Raise It," *New Business Ventures and the Entrepreneur*, Homewood, Ill.: Irwin, Inc., 1974, p. 461.

MANCRESO, JOSEPH R., "How a Business Plan is Read," *Business Horizons*, August 1974, pp. 33–42.

METHVIN, D. G., "Monolithic to Go Public," *Electronic News*, April 30, 1972, p. 58.

MIDDLETON, J. WILLIAM, "Term Lending—Practical and Profitable," *Journal of Commercial Bank Lending*, August 1968, pp. 31–43.

MITCHELL, G. B., "After-Tax Cost of Leasing," *Accounting Review*, April 1970, pp. 308–314.

MUCH, MARILYN, "New Issues Still Slump," *Commercial and Financial Chronicle*, March 25, 1974, p. 2.

PHELPS, CLYDE WILLIAM, *Accounts Receivable Financing as a Method of Business Finance*, Baltimore: Commercial Credit Co., 1957.

PHELPS, CLYDE WILLIAM, *Role of Factoring in Modern Business Finance*, Baltimore: Commercial Credit Co., 1956.

PRECOURT, H. W., "What's Happened to Term Lending," *Journal of Commercial Banking*, August 1973, pp. 2–7.

RAPPAPORT, LOUIS H., *SEC Accounting Practice and Procedure*, 3rd ed., New York: The Ronald Press Co., 1972.

REED, ALEC, "Public Issue—Private View," *Director*, Vol. 24, June 1972, p. 103.

ROBINSON, GERALD J., *Going Public*, New York: Clark Boardman Company, Ltd., 1962.

ROENFELDT, RODNEY L., and JEROME S. OSTERYOUNG, "Analysis of Financial Leases," *Financial Management*, Spring 1973, pp. 74–87.

ROGERS, DEAN E., "An Approach to Analyzing Cash Flow for Term Loan Purposes," *Bulletin of the Robert Morris Associates*, October 1965, pp. 79–85.

RUBEL, STANLEY M., ed., *Guide to Venture Capital Sources*, 3rd ed., Chicago, Ill.: Capital Publishing Corporation, 1974.

Securities and Exchange Commission Annual Report, Superintendent of Documents, Washington, D.C.: U.S. Government Printing Office, 1974.

Securities and Exchange Commission Report of the Special Study of the Securities Market, Superintendent of Documents, 88th Congress, Session I, House Document 95, Washington, D.C.: U.S. Government Printing Office, 1963.

SMITH, PIERCE R., "A Straightforward Approach to Leveraged Leasing," *Journal of Commercial Bank Lending*, July 1973.

STERN, JOEL M., "Private Firms Going Public," *The Commercial and Financial Chronicle*, Vol. 217, No. 7290, March 15, 1973, p. 7.

SULLIVAN, BRIAN, "Introduction to Going Public," *Journal of Accountancy*, 1965, pp. 48–53.

VAN HORNE, JAMES C., *Financial Management and Policy*, Englewood Cliffs, N.J.: Prentice-Hall, Inc., 1974.

WESTON, J. FRED, and EUGENE F. BRIGHAM, *Managerial Finance*, 5th ed., Hinsdale, Ill.: Dryden Press, 1975.

WINTER, ELMER T., *A Complete Guide to Making a Public Stock Offering*, Englewood Cliffs, N.J.: Prentice-Hall, Inc., 1962.

WYMAN, H. E., "Financial Lease Evaluation Under Conditions of Uncertainty," *Accounting Review*, July 1973, pp. 489–493.

APPENDIX: PRESENT VALUE TABLES

TABLE A-1

Present Value of $1 (PVIF)

Period	1%	2%	3%	4%	5%	6%	7%	8%	9%	10%	12%	14%	15%
1	.990	.980	.971	.962	.952	.943	.935	.926	.917	.909	.893	.877	.870
2	.980	.961	.943	.925	.907	.890	.873	.857	.842	.826	.797	.769	.756
3	.971	.942	.915	.889	.864	.840	.816	.794	.772	.751	.712	.675	.658
4	.961	.924	.889	.855	.823	.792	.763	.735	.708	.683	.636	.592	.572
5	.951	.906	.863	.822	.784	.747	.713	.681	.650	.621	.567	.519	.497
6	.942	.888	.838	.790	.746	.705	.666	.630	.596	.564	.507	.456	.432
7	.933	.871	.813	.760	.711	.665	.623	.583	.547	.513	.452	.400	.376
8	.923	.853	.789	.731	.677	.627	.582	.540	.502	.467	.404	.351	.327
9	.914	.837	.766	.703	.645	.592	.544	.500	.460	.424	.361	.308	.284
10	.905	.820	.744	.676	.614	.558	.508	.463	.422	.386	.322	.270	.247
11	.896	.804	.722	.650	.585	.527	.475	.429	.388	.350	.287	.237	.215
12	.887	.788	.701	.625	.557	.497	.444	.397	.356	.319	.257	.208	.187
13	.879	.773	.681	.601	.530	.469	.415	.368	.326	.290	.229	.182	.163
14	.870	.758	.661	.577	.505	.442	.388	.340	.299	.263	.205	.160	.141
15	.861	.743	.642	.555	.481	.417	.362	.315	.275	.239	.183	.140	.123
16	.853	.728	.623	.534	.458	.394	.339	.292	.252	.218	.163	.123	.107
17	.844	.714	.605	.513	.436	.371	.317	.270	.231	.198	.146	.108	.093
18	.836	.700	.587	.494	.416	.350	.296	.250	.212	.180	.130	.095	.081
19	.828	.686	.570	.475	.396	.331	.276	.232	.194	.164	.116	.083	.070
20	.820	.673	.554	.456	.377	.312	.258	.215	.178	.149	.104	.073	.061
25	.780	.610	.478	.375	.295	.233	.184	.146	.116	.092	.059	.038	.030
30	.742	.552	.412	.308	.231	.174	.131	.099	.075	.057	.033	.020	.015

Period	16%	18%	20%	24%	28%	32%	36%	40%	50%	60%	70%	80%	90%
1	.862	.847	.833	.806	.781	.758	.735	.714	.667	.625	.588	.556	.526
2	.743	.718	.694	.650	.610	.574	.541	.510	.444	.391	.346	.309	.277
3	.641	.609	.579	.524	.477	.435	.398	.364	.296	.244	.204	.171	.146
4	.552	.516	.482	.423	.373	.329	.292	.260	.198	.153	.120	.095	.077
5	.476	.437	.402	.341	.291	.250	.215	.186	.132	.095	.070	.053	.040
6	.410	.370	.335	.275	.227	.189	.158	.133	.088	.060	.041	.029	.021
7	.354	.314	.279	.222	.178	.143	.116	.095	.059	.037	.024	.016	.011
8	.305	.266	.233	.179	.139	.108	.085	.068	.039	.023	.014	.009	.006
9	.263	.226	.194	.144	.108	.082	.063	.048	.026	.015	.008	.005	.003
10	.227	.191	.162	.116	.085	.062	.046	.035	.017	.009	.005	.003	.002
11	.195	.162	.135	.094	.066	.047	.034	.025	.012	.006	.003	.002	.001
12	.168	.137	.112	.076	.052	.036	.025	.018	.008	.004	.002	.001	.001
13	.145	.116	.093	.061	.040	.027	.018	.013	.005	.002	.001	.001	.000
14	.125	.099	.078	.049	.032	.021	.014	.009	.003	.001	.001	.000	.000

Period	16%	18%	20%	24%	28%	32%	36%	40%	50%	60%	70%	80%	90%
15	.108	.084	.065	.040	.025	.016	.010	.006	.002	.001	.000	.000	.000
16	.093	.071	.054	.032	.019	.012	.007	.005	.002	.001	.000	.000	
17	.080	.060	.045	.026	.015	.009	.005	.003	.001	.000	.000		
18	.089	.051	.038	.021	.012	.007	.004	.002	.001	.000	.000		
19	.060	.043	.031	.017	.009	.005	.003	.002	.000	.000			
20	.051	.037	.026	.014	.007	.004	.002	.001	.000	.000			
25	.024	.016	.010	.005	.002	.001	.000	.000					
30	.012	.007	.004	.002	.001	.000	.000						

TABLE A-2

Present Value of an Annuity of $1 (PVIF$_a$)

Period	1%	2%	3%	4%	5%	6%	7%	8%	9%	10%
1	0.990	0.980	0.971	0.962	0.952	0.943	0.935	0.926	0.917	0.909
2	1.970	1.942	1.913	1.886	1.859	1.833	1.808	1.783	1.759	1.736
3	2.941	2.884	2.829	2.775	2.723	2.673	2.624	2.577	2.531	2.487
4	3.902	3.808	3.717	3.630	3.546	3.465	3.387	3.312	3.240	3.170
5	4.853	4.713	4.580	4.452	4.329	4.212	4.100	3.993	3.890	3.791
6	5.795	5.601	5.417	5.242	5.076	4.917	4.766	4.623	4.486	4.355
7	6.728	6.472	6.230	6.002	5.786	5.582	5.389	5.206	5.033	4.868
8	7.652	7.325	7.020	6.733	6.463	6.210	5.971	5.747	5.535	5.335
9	8.566	8.162	7.786	7.435	7.108	6.802	6.515	6.247	5.995	5.759
10	9.471	8.983	8.530	8.111	7.722	7.360	7.024	6.710	6.418	6.145
11	10.368	9.787	9.253	8.760	8.306	7.887	7.499	7.139	6.805	6.495
12	11.255	10.575	9.954	9.385	8.863	8.384	7.943	7.536	7.161	6.814
13	12.134	11.348	10.635	9.986	9.394	8.853	8.358	7.904	7.487	7.103
14	13.004	12.106	11.296	10.563	9.899	9.295	8.745	8.244	7.786	7.367
15	13.865	12.849	11.938	11.118	10.380	9.712	9.108	8.559	8.060	7.606
16	14.718	13.578	12.561	11.652	10.838	10.106	9.447	8.851	8.312	7.824
17	15.562	14.292	13.166	12.166	11.274	10.477	9.763	9.122	8.544	8.022
18	16.398	14.992	13.754	12.659	11.690	10.828	10.059	9.372	8.756	8.201
19	17.226	15.678	14.324	13.134	12.085	11.158	10.336	9.604	8.950	8.365
20	18.046	16.351	14.877	13.590	12.462	11.470	10.594	9.818	9.128	8.514
25	22.023	19.523	17.413	15.622	14.094	12.783	11.654	10.675	9.823	9.077
30	25.808	22.397	19.600	17.292	15.373	13.765	12.409	11.258	10.274	9.427

TABLE A-2

Continued

Period	12%	14%	16%	18%	20%	24%	28%	32%	36%
1	0.893	0.877	0.862	0.847	0.833	0.806	0.781	0.758	0.735
2	1.690	1.647	1.605	1.566	1.528	1.457	1.392	1.332	1.276
3	2.402	2.322	2.246	2.174	2.106	1.981	1.868	1.766	1.674
4	3.037	2.914	2.798	2.690	2.589	2.404	2.241	2.096	1.966
5	3.605	3.433	3.274	3.127	2.991	2.745	2.532	2.345	2.181
6	4.111	3.889	3.685	3.498	3.326	3.020	2.759	2.534	2.339
7	4.564	4.288	4.039	3.812	3.605	3.242	2.937	2.678	2.455
8	4.968	4.639	4.344	4.078	3.837	3.421	3.076	2.786	2.540
9	5.328	4.946	4.607	4.303	4.031	3.566	3.184	2.868	2.603
10	5.650	5.216	4.833	4.494	4.193	3.682	3.269	2.930	2.650
11	5.938	5.453	5.029	4.656	4.327	3.776	3.335	2.978	2.683
12	6.194	5.660	5.197	4.793	4.439	3.851	3.387	3.013	2.708
13	6.424	5.842	5.342	4.910	4.533	3.912	3.427	3.040	2.727
14	6.628	6.002	5.468	5.008	4.611	3.962	3.459	3.061	2.740
15	6.811	6.142	5.575	5.092	4.675	4.001	3.483	3.076	2.750
16	6.974	6.265	5.669	5.162	4.730	4.033	3.503	3.088	2.758
17	7.120	5.373	5.749	4.222	4.775	4.059	3.518	3.097	2.763
18	7.250	6.467	5.818	5.273	4.812	4.080	3.529	3.104	2.767
19	7.366	6.550	5.877	5.316	4.844	4.097	3.539	3.109	2.770
20	7.469	6.623	5.929	5.353	4.870	4.110	3.546	3.113	2.772
25	7.843	6.873	6.097	5.467	4.948	4.147	3.564	3.122	2.776
30	8.055	7.003	6.177	5.517	4.979	4.160	3.569	3.124	2.778

INDEX